THE SIERRAS OF THE SOUTH

By the same author

SABBATICAL YEAR (a novel)
THE ROAD FROM RONDA
THE COMPANION GUIDE TO MADRID AND CENTRAL SPAIN
THE ESSENCE OF CATALONIA

THE SIERRAS
OF THE SOUTH

*Travels in the
Mountains of Andalusia*

◆

ALASTAIR BOYD

Illustrated by Philip Amis

HarperCollins
An Imprint of HarperCollinsPublishers

For Hilly and Jaime . . .
y para Ana, Mateo y familia

First published in Great Britain in 1992
by HarperCollins Publishers,
77/85 Fulham Palace Road,
Hammersmith, London W6 8JB

9 8 7 6 5 4 3 2 1

Copyright © Alastair Boyd 1992

A CIP catalogue record for this book
is available from the British Library

ISBN 0 00 215488 9

Map by Leslie Robinson

Typeset in Trump Medieval by
Intype, London

Printed and bound in Great Britain by
HarperCollins Manufacturing, Glasgow

CONTENTS

ILLUSTRATIONS

APOLOGY AND ACKNOWLEDGEMENTS

It might appear from this book that I and my immediate family were, over the past thirty years or so, almost the only foreigners on the 'scrap of planet' which is my subject. That is not so. There were and are others just as immersed in its life and ways as I and mine, and just as well qualified to comment. I trust they will forgive me for not including them in these pages, and sometimes even for editing them out of incidents in which we shared. This is not a symptom of megalomania but rather the result of a strict rule I have imposed on myself: that is to concentrate – within the space allowed by the publisher, which I have stretched to its limits – on the people of the region themselves and their reaction to the changes that have swept the world around them and stretched fingers up their valleys in the quarter of a century since I last wrote about them in *The Road from Ronda*.

Also, it must be a rule of thumb for any writer, whether of fiction or of travels, to avoid bringing on stage characters who are simply paraded but not given a part of their own. To leave a tantalising reference in the air is to do no service to the person concerned and to leave the reader with the irritating question: whatever became of that glamorous American friend . . . or that engaging cad? Nor have I wanted to use this book as a vehicle for dropping names of talented authors and artists who have crossed our doorstep from time to time. That is a perfectly legitimate literary exercise but is not the one attempted here.

None of this is to say that I have no acknowledgements to make. On the contrary, I am much indebted to Martin Shuttleworth for his subtle guidance through the maze of the *Morisco* rebellion; to José Antonio Castillo Rodríguez for sharing his knowledge of the history of the Berber villages of the Genal; and to John and Marie Corbin for their dry but never inhuman or unhumorous social anthropology of the region. I also owe a great deal to Ana Mari Segura and the dozen or more people active in local affairs who were unfailingly helpful and patient in answering my many questions: I do not instance them all here because I have tried to give their personalities and views some prominence in the text. Finally, I must thank all those whom I did not formally interview but whose pungent opinions, whether on chance encounter or through more frequent contact, brought me as close as I shall ever get to the essence of the mountain pueblos and the spirit of their inhabitants.

1
THE SPELL OF RONDA

Those unscheduled meetings with my father on the Underground were an embarrassment to both of us. If I saw him board the same train at Sloane Square, I would bolt into another carriage. I was supposed to be at my desk by nine. As chairman, ten was his usual time. If we coincided, it meant I was seriously late.

The test of character came when we both alighted at the Monument. One side of me wanted to outflank him and get in first, or to slink in behind him. The other side wanted confrontation. Confrontation usually won; it was a point of honour then to wait for him at the ticket barrier. A flicker of annoyance would cross his face and he would glance at his watch. We would walk up Gracechurch Street together. He cut a fine figure in his well-made suit and bowler hat. One year he was named by the *Evening Standard* as one of the ten best-dressed men in London. I wore no hat and frequently sported a bow-tie and suede shoes in deliberate defiance of City taste. This was intended to annoy, and it did. We would part on the office doorstep: he to his mock-Chippendale suite on the first floor and I to a booth near the top of the building. Each of us had made his point in polite silence.

On such days I would think about Mombeltrán. It must have been in 1948. The post-war travel allowance of foreign currency was twenty-five pounds. The trip would have been impossible without the connivance of business connections in Spain, who lent us a car and gave us pesetas in return for sterling in London. With two friends I drove south across the aching distances of Old and New Castile. I was not, I confess, much concerned with the effects of Spanish destitution after the Civil War, famine and isolation during the World War and subsequent ostracism by the victorious Allied powers. What seized my imagination were the dramatically sited old cities that had hardly changed since the seventeenth century; the grand and solemn architecture; the sense of boundless space and light. As we drove with a feeling of light-headedness across the high plain, rimmed by distant mountains, the towns, with their barn-like churches, shimmering mirages from a distance, turned out on arrival to have a crumbling but real substance, fissured and frayed by long decay. Around them the rhythm of life and agricultural tasks seemed to descend directly from pre-Christian times.

Then we came to the hillier country of the province of Avila, desolate moors littered with gigantic boulders, giving the landscape an immensely primitive air. Climbing higher, we spent the night at the Parador de Gredos, a state-run hotel and hunting lodge whose walls were covered with an assertive display of antlers and other trophies of the chase. Man the hunter was still very much alive up here. As we came down from the Gredos mountains, I was overwhelmed by the view over the castle and village of Mombeltrán, with fold upon fold of hills billowing down to the valleys of the Jerte, the Tiétar and the Tagus. For someone brought up between London and the Home Counties with the odd holiday in Scotland and no greater grandeur than the Cairngorms, it was a revelation.

Later, there was Bilbao. The firm had a branch there, to which I managed to get myself posted with the ostensible object of learning commercial Spanish. I was a perfect nuisance in the office, where there was really nothing for me to do, so to my delight I was encouraged to spend the afternoons with my Spanish teacher, Felipe de Zubizarreta, a mildly bibulous and cultivated man who instilled into me, largely in cafés and bars, the principles and nuances of the language I love next to, if not more than, my own. Total immersion in a foreign tongue is highly therapeutic. There are some Britons who find it desperately hard to achieve self-expression, and thus lead a satisfying life, in their own land; perhaps this is particularly true of those endowed with an introspective and romantic nature. But in a new clime, equipped with another language, their personalities undergo a sea-change. They sprout their new tongue like a beard and strut more confidently on their new stage. French or Spanish words and ways assume extraordinary, almost magical significance because they are the instruments of release. The convert becomes more popish than the Pope, frequently annoying his host country by his pedantic passion for its history and ostentatious familiarity with its way of life. Something of the sort happened to me, and the magician who mediated the process was my mentor, Felipe de Zubizarreta of happy memory.

Bilbao, nonetheless, through the iron-ore and shipping industries, had strong British connections. 'Babcock and Wilcox' was a powerful name. There was a 'Gibraltar Room' in the main club. There were tennis parties. There was a thriving British Institute and a small British colony. It was a stolid place dominated by a few commercial dynasties and given to enormous six- or seven-course Sunday meals. Situated in a bowl of hills, on the banks of the dark and sluggish Nervión, it would have been oppressive but for the rounded green slopes of steep pastures which could be glimpsed at the end of every major street. Its eighteenth-century seaside charms, so daintily depicted by Luis Paret (a disciple of Boucher), had all flown – though the fishing ports of Bermeo, Lequeitio and Zarauz still preserved, in their coastal *fjords*, a picturesque tug-and-trawler vitality of their own. Bilbao itself, with its lugubrious park and museum devoted largely to the Basque painter Ignacio de Zuloaga, was thrilling to me compared to Newcastle,

3

Middlesbrough and Preston, where I had previously been sent on uncongenial assignments connected with our business; and it was the gateway to the whole of that majestic peninsula of whose extent and mysteries I had received intimations at Mombeltrán.

The telephone in London rang, a standard black receiver on my standard wooden office desk, jerking me back to reality. 'Mr Boyd? This is Major General Rahli Dahl. How are you? What an exquisite pleasure as always to talk to you! I think we have it in the bag. I talked to the Chief only this morning. He and I, as you know, are like brothers. He said to me, "Rahli, you have convinced me. I will talk to our procurement people immediately." I thought I would let you know first, my dear friend, as you have been so intimately involved. I must say to you in confidence that had it not been for the intervention of superior minds such as yours and mine, we should not have brought this off. Mr O'Donovan is a fine businessman but he is a bit, shall we say, heavy-handed. He lacks a certain lightness of touch. Now there is one other thing . . .'

It would be nice, he went on to suggest, if we – that is my firm – gave a little dinner at the Savoy for the Chief, his entourage and their ladies. It so happened that the great man had one night free before proceeding to other capitals. He would leave the arrangements in my hands. With further expressions of esteem he rang off.

Our firm was an odd agglomerate. Founded in such traditional activities as maritime insurance, chartering and coastal shipping, it had branched out after the war into the headier atmosphere of international trade, including arms deals. My immediate superior, O'Donovan, had prised his way into the latter. The 'Chief' to whom Rahli Dahl had referred was the Chief of Staff of the Indian Army.

At eleven I went along to my morning 'O Group' with O'Donovan, who had left the army as a lieutenant-colonel and was given to military parlance. He stroked his bristly

4

moustache and chain-smoked while I reported my conversation with Rahli Dahl.

'Of course friend Rahli's a con man,' he said. 'But sometimes con men deliver the goods. They have to, otherwise they've no stock in trade. If he can deliver the Chief to the Savoy, I take my hat off to him and we'll pay for the dinner. But make sure he bloody well does, otherwise it's a waste of money and I'll have to dock it from your bonus.' He grinned and gave me a flash from his most charming feature, his periwinkle blue eyes. 'Though I'm sure that won't be necessary. This is ADC's business, the sort of thing you do very well.'

He switched off the charm as quickly as he had switched it on and picked up the telephone to speak to Stockholm. I returned to my desk, and made a booking at the Savoy for twelve. Then I rang Rahli Dahl and conveyed as delicately as I could that I hoped there would be no hitches.

'Hitches, my dear friend?' answered Rahli smoothly. 'Do not think of hitches. Did I not tell you that the Chief and I are like brothers?'

After I had discharged my duties, I reverted in my mind to Bilbao. I had tried to restrict my reading as far as possible to Spanish. But the bookshops there were not well stocked with modern Spanish literature in the continuing crackdown after the Civil War and I found myself subsisting on a strange diet of translations from Kafka, Thomas Mann, Pierre Benoît, Maurice Baring and Osbert Sitwell. When I tired of these I would turn to the authors who had first excited my interest in Spain. The British view of the Peninsula has always been the romantic one. Spain formed no part of the eighteenth-century Grand Tour; it was too unsafe and too uncomfortable. It was only after the Napoleonic Wars, with the rise of the Romantic movement, that travellers began to venture across the Pyrénées. As the smokestacks of the Industrial Revolution rose in England, enthusiasm increased for rugged scenery and pastoral simplicities, both of which Spain possessed in abundance. The threat of bandits and the certainty of discomfort were added incentives to ardent travellers.

This new mood was roused and fed above all by George Borrow and Richard Ford, Washington Irving and Théophile Gautier. Aided by David Roberts and J. F. Lewis and later by Gustave Doré, they were enormously influential in creating and popularising the legend of picturesque and primitive Spain. Between the 1830s and the 1870s the number of British travellers in the Peninsula increased to an extent that caused concern to the editor of *Spanish Pictures drawn with Pen and Pencil* (c. 1870), who took issue with Richard Ford's claim that 'the beef-steak and the tea-kettle which infallibly mark the progress of John Bull, and have been introduced into Greece and the Holy Land, are as yet unknown in the ventas and posados of the Peninsula'. On the contrary, said the editor, 'this statement is becoming, year by year, less true. Old residents and tourists in Spain are beginning to complain of the invasion of Northern hordes. Numerous English and American travellers may now be met with not only in such places as Granada and Seville but in Segovia or Ronda, or Avila. And books on Spain have multiplied in proportion.'

By the time I reached Bilbao that movement – as a result of the Civil War, the World War and subsequent currency restrictions – seemed to have been reversed. Neither John Bull nor 'Northern hordes' were much in evidence in the Spain of the early 1950s. So I had some hope that the situation as it had been in Ford's day had been almost restored – with the difference, naturally, of old trains and buses in lieu of mules and diligences. An opportunity to find out arose when my father, on whose bounty I still very much depended, despite our differences, appeared with friends in Bilbao and took me off to Madrid and then to Seville for Holy Week. It must have been 1953.

Fascinated though I was by the famous *Semana Santa*, I was itching to get away to remoter places. So I forsook my party before the week was out and took the yellow bus to Ronda, for which my appetite had been whetted by a friend who knew the Andalusian hinterland well. The road came up to expectations, shaking bones and stomachs as the gallant vehicle ground over its pitted surface and lurched round its many curves. A landslide near Algodonales obliged us to change buses. Shepherds appeared off the hillside, in the best Ford tradition, and humped our luggage across the rubble to an identical yellow peril on the other side. As we topped the Montejaque pass, the road at last revealed what seemed to me, through half-closed eyes and the filter of much romantic reading, a mighty Arab fortress roseate in the evening sun.

I could not then know that I was looking at the place which was to become my home, inspire two books and give rise to many other important events in my life besides. I had four more London years ahead during which my discomfort with myself in what used to be called 'the rat-race' increased for reasons that I found hard to define but nonetheless weighed heavily on me. The dinner party with 'the Chief' took place and was accounted a success, but ultimately the deal set up by Rahli Dahl collapsed. Despite this, O'Donovan became more and more reliant on me; he seemed to feel that I had social skills which he lacked. He took me off to Hamburg on business and told me in the lounge of a luxurious hotel, looking out over the Aussenalsters, that he would report favourably on me and secure a substantial rise in my salary, if I would pledge myself to stick with him. I had a great future, he said, if only I would seize it.

But the discomfort of having to live with a deception demanded a mask of conformity that I constantly wanted to tear off, and sometimes did. That many of my age and class released into civilian life from the Forces were on the same treadmill was not much consolation. I was also under the influence of my strong-minded, anti-establishment mother, who was always at odds with her plutocratic background (though not above using it imperiously on occasions); and I had conceived a genuine aversion to the 'braying classes', especially as personified in the upper-class English female, whose piercing tones continue to fill me with horror to this day. I did not entirely manage to avoid the 'season', debutante balls and the country-house circuit. But I sought refuge from it in a number of ways. I married Diana, a beautiful model, who did not belong to that world and was dismissed by my father as 'middle class', almost his greatest term of condemnation. I managed to publish a novel, which I had written at my desk in intervals between doing O'Donovan's bidding, and which received a few friendly reviews. I quarrelled with my lunch-time cronies in the City over Suez. But, perversely, I was still favoured by O'Donovan. This precipitated a personal crisis in me: from a certain glibness and adaptability I was becoming more and more adept in the service of a master with whose aims and values I was completely out of tune. But, even worse, I found myself speaking derisively and satirically of him behind his back, which was dishonourable. With the loyal support of Diana, I resigned, to the incomprehension of most of my family for whom, not before time, I was 'doing rather well'.

In late 1957 Diana and I took ship on the lowest deck of a P. & O. liner via Lisbon for Algeciras. We were in a romantic, defiant and somewhat exalted mood, which saw us through a rough and unpleasant passage. Eventually, our old trunks were heaved onto the train at the Estación Marítima and we took first-class seats (for the last time, we told ourselves correctly) in the *Exprés*, a huge slow train bound for Madrid and packed with Moroccan passengers, which was drawn by two locomotives up the picturesque defile of the Guadiaro to Ronda; there we delivered ourselves willingly to the porters and were conveyed with our possessions in a horsecab to the Hotel Reina Victoria.

In those days fires were still kindled in the hotel bedroom

grates. I asked for a proper writing table and settled down to my second novel, on which all our hopes were rashly pinned. I had decided to call it *The ADC* and it included characters not a million miles removed from O'Donovan, Rahli Dahl, my father, Diana and myself. I thought it was coming on rather well, and Cape's reader in London, William Plomer, had been encouraging.

In the afternoons, with the assistance of the cabbie and the town's only guide, a mournful individual who haunted the hotel lobby, we went house-hunting. I had arranged from London that we would take one floor of the Casa del Rey Moro, a large pseudo-Moorish town house restored in the nineteenth century by an arts-and-crafts minded duchess, with hanging gardens over the gorge. But the tiled patio with potted palms that had seemed so delightful one summer holiday afternoon turned out to be dark and dismal in winter, so we extricated ourselves from the agreement and came to rest in Villa Paz, an apartment walled off from its parent body, the Casa de Mondragón, for the purpose of letting to summer visitors.*

With our lease came a secret garden, surrounded on three sides by buildings or walls and containing a palm, a medlar, a cypress and clumps of tough old irises, intermingled with a colourful weed called *dompedro*; there was also a lemon tree which struggled against the winds to produce a few fruits. The open side of the garden ended in a clifftop railing, beyond which a *mirador* or observation post with stone benches and brick parapet protruded on an outcrop of rock and provided sweeping views over the countryside and mountains.

A kilometre or two from the *mirador*, across the valley floor, was a ridge dotted with umbrella pines, culminating

---

*To avoid confusion, the appropriately named 'Casa', a perfectly adequate description of a rambling and incommodious town mansion has since been pretentiously upgraded by the tourist authority to 'Palacio'; they are one and the same place.

in an old shrine called the Virgen de la Cabeza. To the left was the Barrio de San Francisco, an extramural village which had grown up after the Reconquest and still possessed a distinct life of its own, like a mountain *pueblo* magically set down right under the city walls. Immediately below us was a track which wound down, through the vestiges of Arab fortifications, to the ruined mills put out of business by electricity, and the market gardens, still meticulously cultivated. We could not quite see the mouth of the gorge, of which Ford had written, 'like Wilson at the Falls of Terni, we can only exclaim, "Well done, rock and water, by Heavens!" ' But most days, crossing the great bridge, we peered down and shared his sentiments. A fitting backdrop was provided by the Sierra de Grazalema, behind whose jagged silhouette the sinking sun would sometimes create extraordinary effects, as if incandescent piles of rock were about to fall into a molten sea.

Life indoors was very simple. Although the place was let regularly every summer to a prosperous family from Jerez (for whom we should have to evacuate), there was no cooker. Everything had to be heated on a round charcoal grill, several of which were let into a tiled slab in the kitchen. The slow-burning fuel had to be coaxed to life with the aid of kindling and a *soplillo*, a fan made of cane leaves or esparto; then it would settle into a bluish-pink glow and remain in as long as required, if regularly fanned and replenished. Baths were a major operation: the log-fired stove fed a cistern which produced fitful spouts of scalding hot interspersed with much longer spells of tepid or cold. But the main room was grand with its carved *Mudéjar* ceiling and fireplace set in old tiles, which drew well. We had a maid, Dolores, who was thin and pale and rather scatty; she invariably wore a long brown dress under her apron, which made her look like a dishevelled nun. Frasquito, the woodcutter and charcoal burner, brought our fuel, which he would tip unceremoniously off his donkey's back onto the cracked flagstones outside the front door. Dolores would then shriek at him to bring the wood in and clean up the mess, because that was not her job. I would then run down and pacify them, because I wanted another instalment of Frasquito's story.

In his sixties now, with only one tooth, Frasquito still had a humorous eye. He would grin at Dolores and chide her for her shouting; then he would recall his past. As a young man he worked twelve years with his father making charcoal, always on the same large estate. They were only working men themselves with the concession to 'clean' a rich man's forest, but they were able to give some sort of life to others, employing anything between two or three and twenty men at a time at a maximum of eight *reales* (two pesetas) a day. That was a time of great hunger, and men would implore his father to take them on. The *finca*, which belonged to a Ronda landowner, had forty-four small houses or huts scattered over it, in one of which they would make their headquarters each season. Wherever they settled for a few months, his parents made a kitchen garden and grew tomatoes and potatoes and other vegetables for themselves and their workers. They seldom came back to Ronda, their home town, except for *ferias* and feast days. Frasquito married and had children without ever having a real house of his own. But they lived well in comparison to many. Butane gas had not yet arrived. Every household in the south of Spain depended on wood charcoal for its braziers and its cooking. They sold their fuel far and wide, to Algámitas and Cañete la Real and Cuevas del Becerro and Alcalá del Valle and even to Olvera . . .

I asked how it was transported over these distances. In those days there were presumably few lorries. How else, he asked, but by the *arrieros*? I recalled at once that famous fraternity of muleteers who formed, according to Ford, 'a class of themselves . . . honest, trustworthy, and hard-working; full of songs, yarns, lies, and incorrect local information'. Frasquito told me the names of some of the *arrieros* of his day, amongst them Farándula, a low comedian;

Acebuche, the wild olive; Pelayo, legendary hero of the battle of Covadonga; El Melón, the melon; and Primito, the little cousin. The whole thing, he said, came to an end with the Civil War and never really revived. Now that he was old he simply bought a few trunks of oak or olive, split them in his back yard, and worked the town with his single donkey . . .

'And a more ill-natured beast never was seen,' protested Dolores, 'shitting right in the front door! And anyway, the load you have just tipped here is green through and through and I don't know how you have the face to bring it to this house . . .'

Frasquito grinned at her. Despite his lack of teeth, he had plenty of face.

So we were installed in our outpost on the shrinking frontiers of the old world, in dignified and uncomfortable quarters, with a servant, £600 a year and a view, made possible by a residue of earnings from the modern world we had fled. I had determined that if I failed to escape from the City by thirty, I never would. That birthday was now some months past but, saving that small lapse, I had done it. Conventional wisdom then laid down forty as the minimum age by which you could accumulate enough to take such a risk, and indeed my resources were very slender. But I had a secret weapon, I thought, in my writing. My wife was with me and behind me. She had sacrificed a career in fashion on my behalf. But that world, I told myself, was notoriously treacherous and fickle; whoever was in one year was out the next. Somehow, miraculously, we had escaped our respective bondages. There was nothing raucous or dissonant to trouble us. In the mornings we were woken not by traffic or the alarm clock but by the ring of hoofs on cobbles, as the mules and mares brought up the produce of the valley to be piled up on the market stalls. Or, during the novena of the patron saint, we might be woken by the pure voices of her women devotees rising under our windows, as they

12

Diana . . . had sacrificed a career in fashion

processed to the church of Nuestra Señora de la Paz, Our
Lady of Peace.

Although we had come to rest in Ronda, we did not
intend to be entirely static. We wanted to carry on the great
tradition of British travellers in Spain, which had produced
such superb narratives as those of Borrow and Ford – whom
we hoped to emulate. The Romantic movement and the
rise of *costumbrismo* (the interest in regional differences
and customs which became fashionable among cultivated
Spaniards; the forerunner of today's self-conscious folklore)
inevitably directed the nineteenth-century traveller's attention to local dress and dances, to *fiestas* and fairs, to *arrieros*,
smugglers and bandits, to the bullfight, and (with an almost

masochistic relish) to the vileness of the inns. Even when they wintered in the country for several years, like the Fords, or had diplomatic status like Washington Irving, their inspiration remained much the same: they delighted in architecture, archaeology, history and cultural events; in legends, processions and pageants. Social anthropology had not yet been invented.

Following the old model, we first borrowed, and later acquired, horses in order to visit in the most authentic manner possible the surrounding mountain villages, some still without motor roads. We rode to the Pileta caves and to Roman Ronda, properly Acinipo but Ronda la Vieja to the locals; I developed a taste for the three-hour ride to Alcalá del Valle, where I would stay the night and wrestle with some passage in my book, when I got stuck with it; I also made a much longer trip across country to Osuna. Then a friend in the Household Cavalry, Johnnie Watson, came out bringing two splendid army saddles and we spent nearly a fortnight on a wet and windswept November journey from Ronda via Grazalema and Arcos de la Frontera to Jerez, returning via Medina Sidonia, Alcalá de los Gazules, Jimena de la Frontera and Cortes. Johnnie had also equipped us with voluminous Metropolitan Police macintoshes, which we were obliged to wear much of the time, giving us a distinctly British air. Indeed, a photograph which appeared with an article by Johnnie in the *Household Brigade Magazine*, describing this ride, shows us together as the perfect pattern of British officers on a riding tour in a foreign land.

I had excluded Diana both from the Osuna and the Jerez expeditions on the grounds that they would be too gruelling: her health was not good and had not been improved by our exchange of modern amenities for a more antique mode of life. But when it came to the longest journey of all, she flatly refused to be left behind. This was a ride of several hundred kilometres, lasting more than a month, which we undertook with a Spanish friend, Diego Martín Narváez, in 1966. This time we were much more ambitious. We struck

out across the very wild country of the mountains of Antequera and of Málaga as far as the Alpujarras (the southern
slopes of the Sierra Nevada) and thus down to distant, dusty
Almería on the coast, returning in a north-westerly sweep
over the arid Sierra de los Filabres to Baza and Granada,
where saddle sores and other setbacks finally forced us with
our mounts onto the train home. It was an unforgettable
trip, on which Diana – despite frequent bouts of pain – was
well out ahead of us for most of the way on her black mare.
Her reward and ours was that we must have been among
the very last to enjoy the flavour of Old Spain, as it had
appealed to our nineteenth-century predecessors. For almost
as we rode, the giant studded wooden doors of the *posadas*,
the famous inns accommodating man and beast – the latter
usually better than the former – were closing behind us for
good.*

Yet this was not the whole story. For as our Ronda years
unfolded, we had to adjust to the change in our own status
from travellers to settlers. Our forerunners, whom we so
much admired, remained very much a race apart from the
natives, a band of quizzical observers, returning eventually
to their homelands, armed with astute notes and often with
exquisite sketchbooks as evidence of a successful tour.
Though they would all have shrunk from any association
with the word tourism in its current connotation, they were
in fact the first tourists.

Now, tourists have never caused Spaniards any serious
problems. Their aims, whether cultural or hedonistic, are
easily understood, if not always shared; in any case they are
birds of passage. Or, with the development of mass tourism,
they might perhaps be likened to a sort of perpetual crop,
which can be reaped like lucerne throughout the year; for
los turistas today, apart from the odd attractive girl exciting
lascivious thoughts, are as indistinguishable to the average

*I gave an account of this journey in *The Road from Ronda*,
Collins, 1969.

Spaniard as blades of grass, leaves of clover or ears of corn. Settlers, as we were to discover, are very different. Their motives are more difficult to fathom. Retired people along the coastal corridor are one thing, but a foreigner who establishes himself in or near a pueblo of the interior is quite another. There will always be something suspicious about those who have forsaken their own pueblo and *tierra* in favour of one with which they have no organic connection. The normal relationship of the tourist to the native is reversed. The observer becomes the observed, the scrutineer is scrutinised. This in turn leads to self-scrutiny: what am I really doing here? By uprooting and replanting myself in another soil, am I flourishing or withering? Am I justifying the upheaval? Have I really 'escaped'?

The settler is also quite differently affected by the climate and diet than is the native, or indeed the tourist. The heat may mock efforts to create; the wine may first stimulate then blunt the imagination. The spectacular silhouettes of buildings and the impressive mountain massifs are easily snapped up and pinned down in albums by the camera in a ready-reference sort of way, but present a tremendous structural challenge to the artist. Painters find it hard to maintain self-respect and a sense of purpose when their responses on canvas seem to them inadequate. Writers, who have pinned their hopes on hard-won leisure in a promised land, suddenly dry up. Even simpler souls, aiming at a measure of self-sufficiency on a Mediterranean plot, find that amateur peasants are no match for the professionals. Jokes from back home about lotos-eating in the sun seem cruelly inapposite when that same sun beats down like a fist on the shimmering, pulverised contours of the hills and nothing but the great grey heat prevails. The elusiveness of the landscape to the painter; the sheer power of the sun enforcing the siesta over and above other aims; the whispers, rumours, comment and speculation that rustle in the background of the settler's life; all these pressures building one on another can become too much. One artist we knew barricaded himself in his cottage: he was lucky to be extricated with some shreds of his sanity.

Then there are particular hazards for women. When Diana and I reached Ronda, she had had four or five miscarriages. She still longed to have a child. This was well known to the people we mingled with, but there was no lack of Spanish women who would press her, 'Diana, don't you like children? Wouldn't you like to have a child?' Obviously insensitive, this might be thought intentionally wounding, but it was not in fact malicious. It simply reflected the Spaniard's overriding preoccupation with reproduction and the family. One of Diana's tormentors, a genteel middle-class lady, was herself barren but neither sought nor gave pity, for, as she sighed, it was God's will. Diana did not share this Catholic fatalism and her own equilibrium was quite severely shaken by the devastating Spanish frankness on topics which we preferred to shroud in privacy and reticence.

Those are some of the tests to which settlers are exposed. Yet there is another, deeper source of friction, which only becomes fully apparent over time. Expatriates are drawn to a pre-industrial mode of living with its combination of husbandry, pastoralism and simplicity. But all these entail poverty by modern standards. The local response to the prospect of poverty is to vest priority in certain instruments of survival, notably the family, kinship, offspring, land, animals. If some form of patronage can be secured, so much the better: leisurely jobs in local government, the agricultural savings bank or on the railways are much sought after and prized as a step up from rural toil. But these are available only to a few, so the family remains the fundamental support mechanism; almost all the stock of Spanish sentiment attaches to it, and especially to children. Disconcertingly to the northern romantic, the land and animals are viewed from a purely utilitarian standpoint; there is no beauty in them which is not functional; they have no appeal as the obverse of industrialism or the essential furniture of Arcadia.

Liberal bourgeois sensibilities are of course fudged, relying heavily on industrialism but despising it and escaping from it on every possible occasion. Spanish rural realism is not fudged; it would willingly sell out to an urbanisation scheme but, failing that, it will get on with the job and make the best of it. If there is a subsidy to grub up olives, it will grub up olives, however time-honoured a feature of the landscape they may be. Thus the romantic northerner finds himself in a thoroughly unromantic southern climate. If he has friends and some standing locally, his foibles will be looked on indulgently, but he should be under no illusion that his views are shared by his neighbours.

Some foreign residents find this upsetting. One cultured lady took her own life and it was rumoured that this was due, at least in part, to the complete failure of a campaign she had passionately waged against certain unsightly developments in Ronda. Then again, some friends carried out a faultless conversion of an attractive old mill set in several acres of olive grove. Not long after, a retired Civil Guard captain built a modern chalet two or three hundred metres below them, surrounded it with a barrack-like wall with turrets and placed industrial strength loudspeakers at the four corners, from which he blared out military marches, or his children hard rock, throughout the summer evenings. Our friends could at least grow trees to screen off the national and other flags he hoisted on tall poles around his compound, but from the music there was no escape.

'Noise pollution' is an unknown concept in the south of Spain, and indeed noise is a hazard generalised across the Peninsula. On the other hand, nowhere else in Europe is such deep and absolute silence found as in that magic interval after the ceasing of the frogs and crickets and before the farm dogs' chorus starts.

Among such complexities some flourish, others decline. Sadly, Diana was one who gradually declined. But the rift that opened between us was not only of local origin. My great hope in the early days, my novel *The ADC*, was first accepted, then turned down on grounds that it was libellous; the rewrite took the guts out of it and it died. City funds dried up. I resorted to the last refuge of all destitute Britons abroad and started teaching English; the classes were popular but the gains were small. Were it not for a modest allowance from a disappointed but long-suffering father to a son approaching forty, we should not have survived. In the mid-sixties we had something of a renaissance with a series of summer courses we put on for English and other foreign students wanting to improve their Spanish; some of the young were brilliant and Diana, recovering in part her earlier dazzling form, became a deserved focus for their admiration and affection. But her health continued to worsen; I could offer no prospect of leaving Ronda and ultimately she left me.

The next two years of my life were enveloped in low-level swirling cloud. I aspired to a café-society Spanish lady who fortunately rejected me. I formed a doomed relationship with a Spanish girl half my age. My teaching business almost collapsed but was temporarily rescued by a link with Seville. Then out of the blue Hilly, my present wife, walked across the threshold one day, lured by her daughter's insistence that I harboured Arabian princelings under my roof. And a whole new cycle began. It was not only a question of a new and strong and durable attachment, the need for which happened to coincide in us both at the right time. That might have happened elsewhere. It was also for me a renewal of Ronda, which I was able to see fresh again through Hilly's eyes: the mountains seemed as sharp, the air as pure, the light as brilliant and the atmosphere as thrilling as they had ever been. When we went to Seville, it was more intoxicating than ever. By the time we joined the famous Whitsun pilgrimage to El Rocío, our son Jaime had been conceived and survived Hilly's midnight canters on a black horse through the thronged and torchlit celebrations which lasted three whole days and nights. A second child, Romulus, was born and died within hours and is buried in the communal grave among the dark cypresses, whitewashed burial niches and urns of artificial flowers in Ronda's San Lorenzo cemetery. We rejoiced in one son, mourned another: both in life and in death Ronda continued to exert its spell.

2

A TAVERN IN THE TOWN

Despite its undoubted antiquity and claims to gentility, Ronda has for long been a commercial town, the shopping centre for nearly thirty surrounding pueblos. This function continues and has contributed to the preservation of its character. During the late sixties and early seventies the impact of mass tourism began to make itself felt, but to a much lesser extent than in smaller and previously more primitive places on the coast – such as Torremolinos, Marbella and Estepona – which speedily lost any resemblance to what they had been before the boom. All the same, change – if at a slower rate – was also in the Ronda air. By the time of General Franco's death in 1975, it was gathering pace, albeit with an uncertain stride.

One of the most alert and percipient observers and beneficiaries of changing times was Hamid the Moor, who had the profitable concession of the carpark on the empty lot beside the town hall, overlooking the gorge. A veteran of the Moorish cavalry which had retaken Ronda from the temporary commune established just before the outbreak of the Civil War in 1936, he had stayed on and settled when it was over. Much of the time he sat on a folding chair with his hands clasped over his monumental belly and his whole great frame wrapped in a dark blue Berber cloak and cowl, for it was fiendishly draughty on the brink of the horrid abyss about which so many romantic artists had enthused. This was the place said by some to have provided Hemingway with the setting for the gruesome scene in *For Whom the Bell Tolls*, in which the Fascists are forced to run the gauntlet between two rows of countrymen with flails and then pushed over the edge if still alive. Did Hamid's mind ever dwell on some such scene? If so, he was not telling; but certainly, when cloaked against winter winds, he sometimes seemed to me the sombre guardian of a sinister place.

In fine weather, however, Hamid blossomed out, wearing one day a tarbush, the next a station porter's cap, the third an Austrian sailor's from the time of the empire, the fourth a skullcap, the fifth a monstrous, tasselled Mexican sombrero . . . and so on. On such days serious money crossed his ever-ready palm. He also had a little shanty stall from which he sold djellabahs, Moroccan slippers and raffia shopping bags – though he pressed none of these wares very strongly, for his best line of business by far was to sit and hold out his hand to motorists. There was one charge for strangers and another for locals, and he would invariably heave a deep insincere sigh as he took the money from someone like myself, as if it were a most regrettable necessity. But once the money had slipped into his little wicker cashbox, he would thank one handsomely with the time-honoured formula: 'May God repay you!'

Once, as we drove from our house in the old city into the centre to go to the market, we were met by the sight of a couple of hundred people, crammed shoulder to shoulder, peering over the parapet of the bridge.

'What's up?' I asked Hamid, when we had parked.

'Nothing,' he said. 'A man has thrown himself over. And everyone is gawping. They have no shame.'

'I'm afraid I want to see,' said Hilly.

We went to one of the balconies, which was packed with boys whose faces were pressed against the iron grille. One of them wriggled sideways to make room for us.

'Where is the body?' I asked.

'There is nothing to be seen. Do you see the electricity

pylon? He fell into those bushes right underneath it.'

When we passed Hamid again, he beckoned.

'They say he was a man from the Barrio . . . and his wife saw him do it . . . he had been in hospital . . . possibly he had *una cosa mala* . . . who knows?'

He imperiously beckoned a hesitant car that did not know its way around the town. *Una cosa mala* in Ronda meant one thing, cancer.

We next ran into Rafael the builder.

'Hamid says it was a man from the Barrio,' I reported.

'Not at all,' Rafael said, grinning. 'It is not the man they thought it was. He has just been seen having a coffee in the Bar Gonzalo. He is alive and well.'

'So they haven't identified him?'

'The municipal police have just gone down to go through his pockets. But it's a bad place on that shelf. And there are a lot of brambles. And the *municipales* are not very agile. Why, they can't even control the traffic in the town, which is only a matter of waving their arms.'

We went on about our business. When we returned to the Plaza de España, Paco, the waiter at Anselmo's bar, was standing in the doorway. His tables were very thinly populated considering the time of day. There was still the same tight scrum of backsides belonging to people who were clinging like barnacles to the parapet.

'They are bringing him up now,' Paco said. 'They have his papers already.'

'Who was it, then?'

'A man of sixty-six who used to work at Puya's.'

Puya was the main builders' merchant.

'Any known motive?'

'Look,' said Paco, 'from this bridge one person a year, on average, takes his life. No one knows their motives but themselves. It is a secret that dies with them.'

Anselmo's bar was on the side of the bridge from which you looked down on the infernal rock faces etched by Gustave Doré.

**'... from this bridge one person a year, on average,
takes his life.'**

'Do they mostly jump from this side or the other?' I asked
suddenly.

Paco pondered.

'From the other,' he said.

'From Hamid's side?'

'Yes, from Hamid's side.'

We carried our shopping back to the carpark, which

24

afforded a superb view over the sierras to the south and west, crowned by the majestic triple peak of San Cristóbal: if you jumped from this side, your last vision would be of a wide-open panorama, not at all lugubrious like Doré's depths. I wondered if this distinction was ever taken into account by those contemplating their final act.

Hamid also had the latest news. He was not in the least perturbed that his first version had been wrong.

'The man was well off,' he said. 'He had his retirement pension and he owned two or three flats.'

'Do you think it was a terminal illness then?'

Hamid rolled his eyes up to Heaven.

'The Lord knows. But what is certain is that his father threw himself out of a train window. And his sister cut her throat at an early age.'

A foreign-registered car was circling the plaza in an undecided way. On its second circuit Hamid jumped up and advanced, flapping his arms with surprising vigour for a man who seemed to have been expressly designed for sloth.

'Parrk,' he shouted, flagging the car down, 'parrk . . .'

At that time we were regulars of Hamid's and he kept a special place for us. This was because we were then running a bar in the cavernous garage and stable area of our house. The car was therefore required most days for shopping and I often went to the market with Hilly to help her with the supplies for the light meals she served. Our barman was called Jerónimo. He had come to me at fourteen on the insistence of his mother, who had died shortly after. Now he was in his late twenties. The bar was intended to provide us with an income and him with work; I had no other job for him to replace the odd-job role he had fulfilled while I was still running a school. It was not entirely to Jerónimo's liking, because there was an element of the frustrated intellectual in him, but he did his best. During the week he could usually cope on his own, but at weekends we all set to, including Jaime's ex-nurse Ana, and worked almost round the clock, as the place had become suddenly popular – not as we had expected with tourists, but with Rondeños, who flocked across the bridge on Saturdays and Sundays and consumed large quantities of Hilly's *sangría*. They also appreciated her *tapas*, delicious hot and cold appetisers advertised on an old school blackboard, which she sent down in little oval saucers from the kitchen above. In its heyday our bar was quite an institution in the town.

Knowing all this – for he knew everything – Hamid plucked at my sleeve one morning. It was one of his tarbush days.

'I hear you are doing rather well with that bar of yours.'

'Not half as well as you do, just sitting here with your hand out.'

'Ah, but I heard that you are also looking for a little place in the country,' he added slyly. 'How well the rich live!'

It was true that we had been searching for a country retreat, however small, away from the increasingly brash and vibrant town, but nothing to our taste or within our means had yet turned up.

'Everything is too expensive,' I said. 'People ask sky-high for everything.'

'They will come down, if you have real money in your pocket. Now, I have a house in the city,' he said, tightening his grip on me. 'If you can find a purchaser among your compatriots, there will be a good commission for you.'

He described the house.

'But that's where you live, isn't it?'

'Bah, that is nothing. I can move further out or into a *piso*. Foreigners like the *Ciudad*.'

'And will your wife agree?'

His expression became pained.

'How many wives have you had, *chico*?'

'Two.'

'And children?'

'One.'

He regarded me with disdain.

26

'I have had four wives and I have eight living children and fifteen grandchildren. Do I not know how to handle a wife? What has a wife to do with any of this anyway?'

A white Volvo estate had just nosed over the bridge. Hamid released me and advanced into the plaza.

'Parrk,' he yelled, waving his arms and indicating his entrance, 'parrk . . .'

The way into the market was by an arcade with stalls along one side. The first stall belonged to the cross-eyed spice and birdseed seller, who very slowly and carefully wrapped minute quantities of cinnamon or herbal teas or peppercorns into neat envelopes of coarse brown paper. Then came the widowed egg-and-chicken lady with the sweet, worn smile, who was obliged to ask her customers to convert the weights of the dismembered birds into the correct money – a function performed by her husband until his recent death. After her came the banana stall run by a large florid man who also sold Mexican hats to tourists. At the end of the arcade was a small, heavily-laden stall, piled high with attractively coloured and expensive fruit, the sort you took to people in hospital: this was the stage of a cadaverous old mountebank with a red carnation always in his buttonhole, whose capable little wife did all the donkey work or weighing and despatching and taking the money and giving the change, while he cried out the wares and totted up the dues on a small schoolboy's slate.

'*Venga!*' he would cry. 'Come along, roll up, come and get it, cheap and good, good and cheap! What tomatoes! What peaches! What grapes! *Venga, Señores!*'

Venga, as we called him, had been doing the same thing for fifty years. When he slipped his wife's grasp, he was said to enjoy brandy and politics.

From the arcade you emerged into the market proper, an iron and glass structure like a railway terminus with rows of counters instead of platforms and the fish section running across the whole width of the building where the buffers would have been. One of the stalls on the right was a stand-up bar which did a steady trade between 8 a.m. when the *plaza de abastos* (the market's official name) opened and 2 p.m. when it closed. Among the regular customers were Moro the fish-porter who gave a military salute to anyone who would buy him a drink; Frasco the nightwatchman who needed several drams of anis to end his long night's journey into day; Eusebio the blind lottery-seller who enjoyed a beer and a chat with anyone who was around; and even the great Hamid himself. For when Hamid wanted to show off his influential friendships, he would propel Don Torcuato, the mayor's secretary (a small man made nervous by the influence he was wrongly supposed to possess), or some other local bureaucrat round to the market bar, where they could be observed together by all and sundry.

Many people said it was impossible for the *plaza*, as it was universally called, to survive much longer. The stall rentals were becoming too expensive. The local *hortelanos*, the market gardeners, were being put out of business by early fruit and vegetables brought up by lorry from the coast and sold in supermarkets. Then, the government's sanitary inspector made life even more difficult by insisting that all market personnel must wear white – white caps and medical jackets for the men and white bonnets and smocks for the women. Was the place a hospital? Were they all nuns or orderlies? Furthermore, the inspector had ruled that no customer must handle any of the produce, which was absurd: how could you possibly be expected to buy a melon or a peach or a nectarine without having felt it for ripeness? Finally, the town council was proposing to pull the whole *plaza* down and sell the site to developers for a luxury hotel.

As a result of these rumours and the rising rents and the sanitary harassment, some stalls had become vacant and served to store Venga's boxes and crates or were hired on Saturdays only by vendors of trinkets and cheap clothing. Venga alone looked as if he enjoyed his white jacket, perhaps because it set off his red carnation so becomingly and gave him a faint look of Jack Buchanan or Fred Astaire; otherwise little of the white raiment survived after the first few months with the exception of some caps and bonnets, usually tilted at an angle disrespectful to authority. Whatever the town hall's plans, the development capital did not materialise, so there was a stay of execution: the doomed market went on.

Ironically enough, it was in its stubborn decline that it became a tourist attraction. Twenty or thirty full coaches a day now reached the town in summer, bearing perhaps a thousand souls or more. These were off-loaded near the bullring, marshalled into companies by their militaristic official guides and then conducted in their outlandish apparel, like aliens protected by their guards, through the alleys of the old city to the 'Cathedral Square' – to which dignity the Plaza de la Ciudad with its parish church had been upgraded. Having dealt with culture, they were firmly led to the souvenir shops, in the hope that they would buy something from which their guides would derive a commission. Possibly the least wearying of these stations of the cross was a rapid dive into the *plaza* to observe real natives buying watermelons and haggling over fish. At least it was out of the fierce sun. Occasionally a tourist, greatly daring, would make a sortie from the group to buy an orange or some olives. But this was frowned on. No commission.

The mayor and council, not unnaturally, saw these foreigners as brightly coloured, incongruously dressed birds of passage, who made a contribution, if a rather disappointing one, to the commerce of the town. But they did at least eat, drink and buy postcards and film and the odd souvenir; then they went back to the coast in the afternoon and left the town in peace.

On the other hand, those who came for longer periods tended to belong to the *wrong sort*. The wrong sort came for a month, a whole summer, or even to settle. Often they were writers or painters, or claimed to be such. They rented houses or apartments mainly in the old quarter, and some allowed their children to go about barefoot despite their pretensions to superior culture. They shopped in the *plaza*, bought the cheapest wine which they consumed in large quantities, did not patronise the guides or the souvenir shops and were, in short, of little use to commerce or industry. A small percentage of them would buy a property, in which they would continue their Bohemian ways, bringing no renown to the region and little profit to its inhabitants.

My suspicion that this was the official view was confirmed to me one day by Don Torcuato, who was tippling gently with Hamid at the market bar. He opened up and described an occasion when the mayor happened to notice from his window a couple, laden with uncouth bags, crossing the square towards Anselmo's where they sat down for a drink. He rang for Torcuato, from whose account I have reconstructed the following conversation.

'Haven't I seen those people before?' asked the mayor. 'That pair with the shopping bag full of spinach or beetroot or some such stuff?'

Torcuato squinted out of the window and replied in his rapid stammer, 'Yes, I think they have been here about a fortnight. I believe he is a painter . . . and they are looking for a place in the country.'

'More of that sort!' sighed the mayor. 'Just as I thought. Why can't we attract proper people who build proper chalets in proper urbanisations and play bingo . . . or bridge . . . or *golf*?'

'We have no golf course,' said Torcuato.

It was his function, as the mayor's foil, to make idiotic remarks which his master could pounce on.

'I know that,' snapped the mayor. 'But it would make a great deal of difference if we had. I was saying so only the other day to His Excellency the Civil Governor and he fully agreed.'

'I believe they need a lot of water,' Torcuato ventured.

'Precisely,' said the mayor. 'And it could easily be provided if we took over the water rights of the *hortelanos* down in Los Molinos. What could be more charming than an undulating area covered with lawns and those little pits of sand, which we could all look out on and enjoy from the Alameda or the bridge?'

'But what would become of the *hortelanos*?' Torcuato gasped, almost overcome by this daring vision.

'Few of them are still in business seriously and they would be properly paid for their properties. Also, of course, new jobs would be created by the demand for those who cut the grass and carry the clubs. There is a development company that is distinctly interested and they would build the luxury hotel on the site of the *plaza*, which would lead to yet more employment. His Excellency the Civil Governor is most impressed with the idea. And we should certainly get a more desirable class of foreign visitors . . . and residents.'

The mayor looked down on the square again and watched the couple gathering up their untidy shopping after paying their bill at one of Anselmo's tables.

'Find out,' he said abruptly, 'if they do buy some old ruin in the country, because they will almost certainly start tinkering with it without getting a municipal licence.'

Though Ronda had aspirations, there were many aspects of its life which did not change much. The *Ciudad*, as the old quarter was called, soldiered on much as before. It could not be pulled down, because it was what the tourists came to see. True, it had lost population to the newer quarters, but there were some who would never abandon its tortuous streets until called to their maker, and perhaps not then if they had heirs or successors. These included certain families of landed gentry, a number of artisans with small workshops, three convents of nuns, *las carabineras* (the four gossiping daughters of a deceased Civil Guard) and – as I then thought – ourselves.

Our bar had by now become quite celebrated. There was no competition on our side of the bridge apart from a couple of Zolaesque dramshops, patronised in the main by the casualties of modern life. Sometimes an adventurous tourist or two would peer into one of these and then hastily withdraw, sensing correctly that it was not for the likes of them: this was no bodega full of merry peasants but a last refuge for the down and out. Retreating from such stark encounters, such people would sometimes end up with us. But the average day-tripper had very little hope of slipping the leash on which his group was held. Those who did sometimes seemed to be in considerable discomfort, as it was often too hot or too cold or too wet for the clothing they were wearing; the tour operators on the coast had obviously not bothered to brief them on what conditions to expect up in the hills. A few of them would spill over into our bar for hot soups in winter or iced drinks in summer, but they were not a significant part of our trade; their warders had reduced them to such subservience that they were in constant fear of getting lost or missing the coach. Every day I would chalk up on the blackboard outside the bar a list of delicacies and prices which I hoped would tempt at least a few. From time to time an intrepid splinter group would rush in and down a quick coffee and brandy or gin and tonic according to season, then dash out again like truant children. I must say I felt for them. They had paid good money for their excursion, only to be treated like a group of delinquents. There is no more tyrannous profession than that of the tourist guide.

Not all our contacts were secular. The Iglesia Mayor stood only a couple of hundred yards from our house. The tourist authorities might promote it to 'cathedral' in their propaganda but in fact it was just the parish church of the *Ciudad*. Jaime loved being taken by Ana round its Churrigueresque and Rococo altars – the brighter and bigger the better. They would pause too in wonder beneath the *Cristobalón*, an enormous fresco of Saint Cristopher with a whole tree as his staff, carrying a child over a river on his shoulder; this was so placed that no one could leave the church without seeing it willy-nilly and thus acquiring its protection for a safe journey. Hilly, too, would slip in alone sometimes for a quick prayer. We were therefore all quite familiar figures to Don Antonio Gamboa, the saintly parish priest, who would give Jaime his blessing as he glided on his way from the sacristy towards some sick-bed or returned to take up his post in the confessional. His soutane – which he had refused to abandon in favour of more up-to-date clerical rig – aided the impression that he was not really propelled by his own feet but moved, like a hovercraft, on a cushion of air.

There were also three convents of nuns in the *Ciudad*. The Poor Clares and the Carmelites were enclosed orders, but the Hermanitas de la Cruz, the Little Sisters of the Cross, went out to beg for alms. Habitually they went in pairs, and our local pair was formed by the venerable Sor María José and the younger, eager Sor Angela de la Cruz. Their regular route used to include all the more imposing old houses, where they would receive a donation from the lady of the house or a superior servant. Now some of these mansions had been converted into flats for foreign visitors, who had not the habit of charitable giving, believing for the most part that the poor were the responsibility of the state. But Doña Mercedes, the wife of Don Iñigo, the largest land-owner, still gave; so did Doña Paca, the wife of Don Miguel the Marquis, despite her husband's deplorable financial mess; and the *beatas* still gave, while constantly stressing their limited means.

The *beatas* were unmarried ladies of good family and mature years who spent much of their time in church and were active in the preparation of the Virgin's robes and adornments for the Easter and Corpus Christi and other processions. They came in for much ridicule and mimicry by the working class for their demure air of self-sacrifice – after all, did they not belong to the property-owning class, which provided them with the leisure and the funds for their good works? But there were some humble folk who still welcomed both the *beatas* and the nuns: amongst them the spinster seamstresses and widowed sewing ladies, who took in and housed the collecting boxes for the various saints' days. These were wooden aedicules about eighteen inches high, containing the image of the Virgin or Saint in question, with a compartment for money underneath. This portable moneybox-cum-shrine would be set up for several days on the table or dresser of each devotee, who would collect a few coins from her friends and neighbours before passing it on to someone else in the street.

Though such customs and observances still continued, the climate in which the Hermanitas pursued their rounds was undoubtedly becoming less propitious. Even in the *Ciudad*, which was home ground, they were not accorded the same respect as before. For example, every youth of fifteen or sixteen now seemed to have a 50cc motorbike, which made much more noise than the larger sort. Their riders would tear through the labyrinth of ancient alleys, destroying the calm, threatening small children and their mothers and barely missing the mendicant sisters as they hugged the walls, dressed in the brown and black garb they had worn since their foundation – they would have no truck with the new nurse-like uniforms other female orders were adopting. One day the two sisters were grazed and very nearly knocked down by a flying squad of the motorbike brigade erupting from the alley to the right of our bar. Sor María José's robe was ripped and Sor Angela suffered a cut hand. They sought refuge for a few minutes in our profane establishment, where Hilly administered first aid.

'*Ay, Dios mío!*' sighed the older nun. 'I think our trials resemble Our Lord's Stations of the Cross more and more every day.'

'Though our travails are but a pale imitation of His,' breathed Sor Angela ecstatically.

'I shall report this to the Mother Superior,' Sor María José went on. 'She and Don Antonio must make representations to the mayor to have these terrible little machines banned from these narrow streets.'

Sor Angela looked dubious.

'They are only young,' she said. 'They know not what they do. I don't think Don Antonio would want to ban them; perhaps a speed limit would be sufficient. Don Antonio is a true saint and he loves the young.'

'That's all very well,' said her companion quite sharply, 'but we are none of us perfect . . . not even Don Antonio. Why, he has certainly had money from the Countess of Fuentes for an embroidered altarcloth, which has never been seen yet. And the American lady gave him a *tocadiscos* for himself . . .'

'But I have heard he only plays sacred music on it in the priests' residence!' replied Sor Angela triumphantly.

'Be that as it may,' said Sor María José, 'we must be moving on. Mother Superior will be wondering what has happened to us.'

I knew indirectly, from a reliable source, that the Mother Superior was less perturbed than might have been expected by the daily discomfiture of her mendicants. What a mercy it was, she was reported to have said, that the order was still left properties by good widows, which could be sold for redevelopment. Otherwise, what would become of them? Was not the hand of God visible in this as in all things?

The motorbike brigade had slightly older brothers who loitered on the bridge, which was the best place for observing the arrival of newcomers and for offering their services as unauthorised guides and, if the occasion arose, as gigolos. In warm weather they wore their shirts open or hitched up with a knot above their navels, preening themselves on the seductiveness of their flat, sunburnt bellies. Hilly christened them 'the Bridge Boys', and had good reason to be wary of them.

Not long before, two of them had followed her home from the *plaza*; she had gone on foot instead of by car, as her requirements were fewer than usual. Just over the bridge one of them tripped her up, so that the contents of her shopping bag – vegetables, oranges, fish for the cat, lights for the dog – rolled all over the road. The second member of the team then rushed forward in the role of gallant knight, helped her recover her purchases and then insisted on accompanying her to her door, ignoring her protests that she was perfectly all right. His mate, the tripper, followed at a discreet distance. They converged on her as she entered the porch and she had to fight them off tooth, fist and nail. Had it not been for Ana appearing providentially with some laundry and a basin of gazpacho for our lunch, they would certainly have prevailed over her resistance and inflicted on her God knows what indignity.

We went of course to the police, where Hilly made a statement. But I knew perfectly well that they would shelve it in a mental category of their own labelled 'Provocation of our lads by blonde foreign women' and that the matter would not be pursued with any vigour, let alone lead to a charge or conviction. To be blonde was in itself almost a confession of guilt. It was the notorious Swedish and Danish sex symbols on the coast who had started the corruption of innocent Spanish youth.

To add insult to injury, the Bridge Boys used our bar with some frequency, and we had no legal grounds for keeping them out. They patronised it insolently, consuming little and sprawling around as if they owned the place. Understandably, Jerónimo didn't like to refuse to serve them in case he was beaten up. The daughter of a friend, a busty girl of sixteen, who was staying with us while learning Spanish, fell heavily for the Bridge Boys and went out with them regularly despite my warnings; once she was picked up drunk on the bridge and brought back about one in the morning by the municipal police. The next day I was asked to go and see the Comisario de Policia.

Don Eduardo, the comisario, was a small, neat man with jet-black hair sleeked back, aquiline features and elegant

Ana

hands and feet. He was a zealot who believed that his duties extended well beyond the sphere of public order; he had made himself the town's prefect in matters of morality too.

'I never liked that bar of yours,' he said. 'I would never have given the necessary police approval for it if you hadn't assured me you wanted to provide a job for one of your employees . . . Gregorio?'

'Jerónimo.'

'Jerónimo, then. However, there is no doubt in my mind that the foreigners you have there attract the worst elements in the town. Trouble is bound to ensue. I must tell you that whatever goes on down on the coast in Marbella or Torremolinos, it is not going to spread up here as long as I am in this office. Ronda is different. Please ponder what I say. I shall not warn you again.'

It was a strange year in Spain. Franco's death was universally expected within a short time. Everyone was jumpy.

One morning Communist slogans were found scrawled on the snow-white walls of the Monte de Piedad y Caja de Ahorros de Ronda, that powerful banking institution which liked to proclaim its good works with large inscriptions in blue and yellow tiles on the tower blocks and other social projects it financed. To smear slogans on the sacred walls of its head office was the sort of sacrilege that would have been unthinkable a year or two before.

Yet not all such signs of the times were attributable to social or political tension. There is no doubt that most people in our region were enjoying a sense of liberation from past miseries and drudgeries. The Spanish economic miracle was under way. Admittedly, the interior of Andalusia was classified as one of the poorest areas, but this did not stop parties of boys and girls trekking down to the river, singing all the way, freed of the old taboos against the mingling of the sexes except under the severest vigilance. With the rapid increase in car ownership the bourgeoisie were beginning to rediscover the countryside, long rejected as brutish and brutalising. And many citizens who did not leave town at the weekends came to our bar with plenty of money in their pockets to sample Hilly's famous *tapas*. These new patterns of behaviour may not have pleased the comisario, but they were part of a strong tide, rising and rippling into many creeks well before Franco's death. The comisario's attempt to encircle Ronda in a *cordon sanitaire* was doomed to failure.

General Franco finally died in December 1975. At first an uncanny hush fell over the whole nation. There was no outburst of rejoicing, nor of wild lamentation. Everyone who was anyone in Ronda, and many who were not, went to sign the book of condolence in the town hall; most people, myself included, felt this was a fitting mark of respect on the passing of a head of state. Then we all waited with bated breath.

The majority had known no other government; they simply didn't know whether to fear or welcome political

change. This mood of uncertainty had its social repercussions. Behaviour was often volatile and unpredictable.
Slogans proliferated on walls, not only the Monte's. Pilgrim-
ages were made to the graves or birthplaces of Republican
poets. The army was lampooned in a play which led to the
trial and imprisonment by a military court of its author and
actors. Joan Miró, the grand old man óf Catalan art, had
designed the sets and costumes for a grotesque mimed satire
of the late regime, which travelled to England and the
United States; this was not repressed, because it was wordless. In the south the authorities, studying these portents,
clamped down on public meetings, cultural events and any
kind of assembly likely to generate unrest. The comisario
continued to keep a beady eye on our bar. Unfortunately
for us, he was looking for a scapegoat.

I got in latish one evening after an expedition to see a place
in the country. It was about ten o'clock. As soon as I entered
the bar I was met by an atmosphere that was distinctly
tense. Hilly and Ana were in charge. Jerónimo was off duty.
A small group had taken possession of the inner room; I
had never seen any of them before, which was in itself
unusual, as mostly our evening customers were local. This
was a raffish, mischievous-looking lot. I thought at first
they might be gypsies, but they lacked the heavy, brooding
melancholy and the tribal solidarity one associates with the
People of Egypt; their companionship looked of a fragile,
fortuitous sort. One of their number had a cockerel a few
weeks old, which he would produce from his jacket, tease
on the tabletop and then stuff back into his clothing. This
led me to think they could be circus folk or entertainers of
some sort come to town for the fair. Whatever their origin,
the one with the cockerel went on repeating his little routine until it became tedious; the bird escaped more than
once and had to be recaptured, inconveniencing other customers. Its owner and his friends were fairly drunk – not
incapably so, but well on the way. I did not clean their table

or offer them any more drinks. Eventually, the cockerel man came to the bar and asked for a round of *cuba libres* – gin and coke. I told him he must first remove the bird from the premises. He simply grinned and started playing with it on the counter.

One of our regulars, Antonio, was a sensitive young man who had a hot temper when roused. He had no regular employment, working most frequently as a labourer on the restoration of the old city walls. But government funds for this were always running out, and then he would turn his hand to any old job; at this time he was working in an ice-cream factory. Whatever his fortunes, he was a great reader and addicted, like me, to modern Spanish poetry; so we swapped books. He lent me Rafael Alberti, Miguel Hernández and Vicente Aleixandre; I countered with Dionisio Ridruejo, Carlos Bousoño and others. Antonio was discussing a new poet with me across the counter when the cockerel was released upon it.

'Take that fowl off the bar!' Antonio said at once.

The other just continued toying with it. I could see what was coming but felt powerless to prevent it. Antonio wore thick-lensed glasses but he was broad-shouldered, burly and very strong. I never knew who hit who first. At one moment they were vertical, the next they were rolling together on the tiled floor. Immediately the brawl spread, as if this was what the whole evening with its menacing atmosphere had been building up to and waiting for. A pregnant woman came out of the inner room; she appeared to belong to the cockerel fellow and threw herself onto Antonio's back; others joined in the fray on both sides. I was torn between the urge to throw a pail of water over them as if they were dogs, and the barman's golden rule, which is never to leave his side of the counter in a fight. The decision was taken from me. The bar was a flimsy affair with a wooden frame, chipboard counter and bamboo covering, anchored to the wall on only one side. One of the contestants grabbed it for support and it crashed over. My barricade gone, I entered the mêlée, with the object of pulling the writhing bodies apart. I heard tables, bottles and glasses falling and splintering around me. I got hold of the great strong pregnant woman by the hair and hauled her off Antonio, who had by now lost his glasses; she at once wrenched herself free and threw herself back into the tangle of heads and limbs. At this point I stood back panting to take stock of the situation.

Suddenly I was caught in a harsh glare. A car with a flashing blue light on its roof had jerked to a halt, with its headlights punching mercilessly into our pandemonium. The woman had finally hauled her man back up from the floor. Antonio had recovered his glasses and looked as if he was squaring up for another round. Then men in uniform appeared in the doorway and everyone froze into positions of studied innocence. Someone in the square must have rung the police. Our gramophone was still playing a scratched record of Dionne Warwick singing 'I'll Never Fall in Love Again' . . .

The next morning I was called in to see the comisario, who was in his element. This time a breach of law and order had undoubtedly taken place, just as he had warned me it would. Antonio and the cockerel man had summonses. The bar would have to close. It was of no avail for me to point out that there had been no provocation of Spaniards by foreigners; that it had been a purely Spanish bout of fisticuffs, which might have happened in any establishment; or that it had been caused by total strangers. Don Eduardo would not accept that it could have happened anywhere else; in no other café or bar in the town centre would the owners have allowed the matter to go so far. He agreed we were innocent of an offence – there were no grounds for prosecuting me – but he held us guilty in the wider sense of creating a setting, an atmosphere that was conducive to this sort of thing. He had no alternative but to recommend to Málaga that our permit be withdrawn.

When I got back, the women were up in arms. It was no

fault of ours, Hilly said, it was not fair. The troublemakers were Spanish vagrants, Ana confirmed; they were not Ronda people, what had it to do with us? And we would lose money, Hilly added. We were having a good season. What were we going to do for a living? How was I going to provide for Jeronimo? And what was this nonsense about creating an atmosphere? Like a scent, did he mean? Making quarrelsome Spanish veins pulse faster? Like an aphrodisiac? How absurd! Surely I had some strings I could pull? At any rate, they were in favour of carrying on regardless, at least until the formal notice came.

In the event, I did not put out the blackboard next morning. Though the women fumed and accused me of pusillanimity, I had little appetite for snatching a few days' trading while waiting for the inevitable. I knew the comisario's thumbs-down meant certain closure within a fortnight, and there was no appeal against an administrative decision of this nature. Our gloom did not persist for long, as we simply had to put our minds to the next step. This was not the first of my crises with the Spanish system, nor was it to be the last. But with Jaime flourishing mightily on Spanish soil there could be no question of uprooting him and separating him from Ana and his friends. Besides, we had no 'home' to go back to in our own country. Within a day or two the new plan had emerged: in truth it had been lurking in our minds for some time. Instead of just getting a little bourgeois retreat in the country, which had been our original intention, we would do it properly: we would have a go at the land. All Hilly's long-suppressed small-farm instincts found glorious release in this idea, and we set about our search for the right place with fresh enthusiasm.

3

UNSKILLED PEASANTS

'Look,' said Juan. 'If you squat down like this you can see the whole *huerta* from one boundary to the other.'

It was a hot, late autumn afternoon. I did as he suggested, but he was the shorter man and had the advantage of having grown up on the place. I peered under the low branches of the closely planted old fruit trees but, even where there was a clearing, tall grasses and thistles impeded any coherent view. I glimpsed what looked like a curtain of bamboo canes through the dense foliage and undergrowth. We continued our inspection. Eventually we emerged from the trees onto a rough track which followed the canes. A breach in these showed a crescent of stony ground bordering the river, on which nothing grew but fennel, low scrub, oleanders and a fringe of willows. This was called the *chirrascal*, a sort of no-man's-land belonging really to the river bed and subject to floods. The canes formed the boundary of the property on that side; the main body of the land ran down to a plantation of tall poplars, round which the river described a tight curve before continuing its hundred-kilometre journey to the sea.

We started back towards the house. In that direction everything was very clear and unequivocal. Beyond the gate a big field of sunflowers stretched as far as the railway line and then, across the tracks, the ample folds of the big arable farm, the Cortijo Grande, rose to the cliff-like base of the table mountain that formed one of the valley's walls. With Juan, his brother Sebastian and Mateo, Ana's husband, still at my shoulders I finished my tour and found Hilly standing on the threshold waiting for me. She was wearing a sleeveless white blouse, a denim skirt and sandals, and had grown her sun-bleached hair just long enough to be able to put it up, freeing her neck from skeins and tangles in the heat. She had already investigated the inside of the house. I signalled to Mateo that they should wait for us outside. Indoors it was luminously dark and much cooler than on the unsheltered terrace. Gradually my eyes adjusted. The cowl of the fireplace ran across the whole width of the main room. The floor was covered with large cracked terracotta tiles, except for a cobbled strip a metre or so wide, leading from the double wooden doors into a cavernous dark chamber with an earthen floor.

'Look, mangers!' Hilly said.

There were indeed, I now saw, two mangers of the oblong sort used for horses and mules, and two more with round troughs for cows or bullocks.

'Everyone under the same roof,' I said, 'family and animals.'

But the stable had not been used as such in recent times. An old paraffin stove and wooden plate-rack showed that it had done duty as a kitchen. Strips of brown paper from fertiliser sacks were nailed to the beams, presumably to prevent dust and grit falling into the food from the loft above. We went back into the main room and Hilly led me up the stairs, which were steep with tall treads, so you felt you were scaling a ladder. The whole upper floor was one large loft, ten or eleven metres long and seven or eight wide. It was subdivided by breast-high partitions into several compartments; one of these still contained some dark vetch straw, dusty and prickly to the touch; in another were some maize cobs; in a third a few walnuts. Overhead, the hefty roof-tree ran from the gabled end of the house to a thick pillar from which two auxiliary trusses carried the stress

Mateo

down to the corners of the other end wall. The building exposed all the dynamics of its structure, concealing nothing.

Where the roof met the walls it was only just possible to stand upright – except at the gabled end, which contained the great chimney flue. The windows were small and low and set in deep embrasures with a large sill or window-seat. We sat in one of these after forcing the swollen shutters open. Our hands touched and gripped as we gazed out over the unkempt expanse of ancient fruit trees, above which rose more than a dozen great walnuts, the pride and glory

45

of the place according to Sebastian, the most recent occupant, who had told me that every year one could expect a thousand kilos of them, which at sixty pesetas . . .

We heard voices down below, then steps on the stairs. The men were getting impatient. Mateo's head rose above the balustrade.

'Good big loft,' he said, without advancing any further.

'Yes,' I agreed, 'but it needs a lot of repair. The whole roof needs to come off. And the floor is a death trap. I advise you to stay where you are.'

'Well,' he said, 'it's all a question of price if you are interested.'

When we left, Juan drew the old double doors together and padlocked them. The lower part of the woodwork had so weathered away that sheets of tinplate had been nailed over the boards, giving the doors a patched-up air. But they still swung sweetly on their hinges and you could have driven a heavily loaded mule through them; they could be secured on the inside with a stout pole that slotted into two cavities in the wall, making you impregnable.

We stood in an awkward group. Hilly's eyes and mine roamed from poplars to quinces to walnuts to pigsty and back to the house, as if we sought a sign from Heaven. The gazes of the others were blank and remote, as if they were contemplating something far superior to our pitiful doubts and trepidations. I knew what was on their minds. They had come to do a deal. When a deal is under way, or even in the offing, everyone's blood quickens in Andalusia. The seller or sellers repeat *ad nauseam* that nothing is of so little value as money. The buyer wonders what the asking price is designed to get. Does two mean one and a half or one and three quarters? Where should he pitch his offer, so that it is on the low side but not derisory? If he pitches it too high and the difference is then split between the offering and the asking price, he may be paying too much. If he pitches it too low, the usual form is for the seller to turn his back and walk away in disgust. Then it is the role of the broker or brokers to step in and haul the parties together again, by physical manhandling if necessary, so that the negotiation can be resumed. All the while these intermediaries – here there was only one, our friend Mateo, but frequently there are more – are calculating their margins of commission and balancing the aim of effecting a quick sale against their reputations for securing a good price. Suddenly, life acquires a sharper edge, because an animal, an object or some fixed property is about to move from the fascinating limbo of speculation into the reality of the marketplace. I could tell from the set of the men's shoulders that, as I had made no move, they felt they had been wasting their time.

'Why don't you ask them to quote you a price?' asked Mateo, by now visibly irked with me. 'It can't do any harm.'

'All right,' I said, turning to Juan. 'How much are you asking?'

His brother Sebastian had a naturally sombre expression, but Juan had a bright bird-like face which immediately lit up.

'Well, look,' he started off. 'You have seen our *huerta* . . .' He then entered on a long panegyric of it, after which he paused and said, 'We have done our arithmetic and we want to get 300,000 pesetas.'

Hilly looked at me enquiringly; she was still not at home with large Spanish numbers. Mateo's craggy profile jerked up and he looked hard at me, as if I would be a lunatic not to jump at this.

'We'll think about it,' I said.

Juan continued smiling.

'As you wish,' he said, 'but remember my *huerta* has many suitors.'

That evening, back in Ronda, we decided that we loved it and rang Mateo to make an offer. Both he and Juan would be working next day, so there was no way he could deliver the message till the evening. We possessed our souls in patience as far as we could. My anxiety must have been contagious, for it affected Hilly. 'Perhaps you should have

47

offered what they asked,' she said. We were in the patio when Ana came round with Jaime. She had been looking after him all day: as a baby in arms one of his hands had been constantly plunged between her ample breasts; now he was a sturdy little chap but the bond was still there.

'Mateo is on his way to talk to you,' she said.

I could not tell from her expression, which was always composed, whether the news was good or bad. And she was not letting on. These things were *cosas de hombres*.

We were drinking beer when Mateo appeared. I poured him one and he drank gratefully.

'The Lord knows the work it cost me,' he started, passing his handkerchief over his brow.

'That's right,' Ana chimed in, now her husband was present. 'They wouldn't . . . and they wouldn't . . . and they wouldn't . . .'

'You said two fifty and go to two seventy-five,' Mateo went on. 'They were most reluctant to drop anything even for prompt payment . . . but I insisted . . . and insisted . . . and insisted . . . and they did!'

He banged his glass on the table triumphantly. He was usually a sombre and judicious man, and I had never seen him so jubilant. It was grounds for particular satisfaction that there was an exact symmetry between the amounts that we had gone up and they had come down. This was the correct way to do business. It was the proper price.

'The *huerta* is yours, Señora,' Ana exclaimed to Hilly. 'Yours and the Señor's and Jaime's.'

Hilly embraced her and then Jaime and then Mateo and then me.

'I can't believe it,' she said. 'All that land and all those trees. Won't it be marvellous for Jaime. Think of the swings. And the house is a duck. Has it got a name?'

'Some call it the "Huerta de los Membrillos", others the "Huerta del Moral" and yet others the "Huerta del Rincón",' Mateo said.

'Quince Orchard, Mulberry Orchard or Corner Orchard,'

48

. . . the age-old lure of the simple life . . .

I translated. 'You can take your pick.'

'Those are not names,' Ana said scornfully, 'just descriptions. Listen, let's call it "Villa Jaime". I tell you what, I'll order and pay for the letters in blue and white tiles over the door . . . no, Mateo?'

Mateo was not a drinking man, but he was well into his second beer.

'Call it what you like,' he said. 'Yes, that's fine. Why not "Villa Jaime"?'

I could think of a number of reasons why not, but this wasn't the time to quibble. Mateo raised his glass and proposed a toast, in which we all joined, Jaime not least.

The place did not in fact acquire any of these names. It just became the '*campo*' or, for Jaime, '*mi campo*'. We put in hand a programme of works, which included taking the roof off and replacing most of the old beams and rafters with new timber; but we did not depart in any way from the constructional principles or materials of the original framework. In the spring we moved in, having sold up in town. After the closure of the bar we had no steady means of sustenance there; besides we wanted to try something quite different. It might seem a far cry from south Wales but in the campo we should at least be able to realise some elements of Hilly's childhood dream of a Welsh hill farm. And there was the age-old lure of the simple life and self-sufficiency.

On a typical summer's afternoon some months later the mare was very sensibly sheltering under one of the walnut trees, while the useless donkey we had bought for Jaime was standing immobile as a statue in the glaring sun: almost its only redeeming feature was the engaging picture it presented when the young female kid – white with black and orange markings – jumped perkily onto its back, as had just happened. On such occasions, if we had visitors, they always dived for their cameras. We felt less sentimental and were more interested in the prospect of milk once the kid had been mated and given birth.

Jaime and his friend José came hurtling round the side of the house.

'Hey, Cadbury, get down you fool!' Jaime yelled. 'Cadbury' had been his earliest approximation to the Spanish *cabra* and thus had he christened the kid, though his command of the colloquial tongue equalled that of his classmates in the rural school.

Dropping their battered bikes in the dust, the two boys ran to the donkey. Cadbury skipped down; Jaime jumped up. José belaboured the animal's rear; Hasso, our handsome Spanish-bred Alsatian, danced around it; the donkey lurched forward a couple of steps and resumed its immobility. Hilly now emerged onto the terrace, stretching after her siesta in the delicious indoor coolness, which was ensured by the old rubble and limewash walls nearly a metre thick. Calling the boys, she went into the kitchen, which was a separate building at right angles to the main house. There she gave each of them a great wedge of crusty bread with a slab of black chocolate. Then she set off on her regular round to feed her hens and collect the eggs. The silly things preferred all sorts of places to the boxes provided for them in their shady run. But Florrie the lame duck (Jaime had launched her from an upper window too early in her life) was extremely predictable. She always delivered in a convenient place near the house. Today it was under the fig tree. Hilly came back caressing a great white egg.

As the boys munched, I asked José what he wanted to be when he grew up. His father worked on Miguel's pig farm, known as 'La Granja'.

'Me? A legionnaire.'

He imitated, rather accurately, a burst of sten-gun fire.

'And you, Jaime?'

'Me . . . a legionnaire too.' He frowned as he spoke and glanced awkwardly at his slightly older friend before correcting himself. 'Well, I would rather be a helicopter pilot.'

'But supposing there weren't enough helicopters . . . or there were too many pilots . . . so you couldn't be one . . . would you like to be a farmer?'

Jaime made one of those ultra-mobile how-should-I-know faces that can only be registered by features which have not yet set in a mould. It was like a huge facial shrug.

'I wouldn't *mind*,' he said, 'if I could have the mare. I like galloping the mare.'

'She might be dead by then, I'm afraid. She's pretty old. But you could get another . . . if you were a farmer.'

'Oh, all *right* then,' he said considerately; he already knew that parents needed to be humoured.

They dashed off again to perform more feats on their old bikes with Hasso, who combined the roles of watchdog and Jaime's principal playmate, leaping and prancing around them.

He strode down the rough bit of drive onto the loose gravel space for turning cars, from which he surveyed the *huerta*. We were working on the patch called the *huerto* or kitchen garden. I straightened up.

'*Quien vive?*' (Who's alive here?) he called.

We walked back to the house to find a man in his forties with a handkerchief round his forehead, pirate-style, open shirt tied at the midriff, shorts and rubber boots.

'Arturo Román Santiago,' he said, grasping our hands and shaking them vigorously, 'to serve you and God. Have you a scythe?'

Clearly he was our new neighbour, who had just bought the *huerta* two along from ours. If his garb was unusual, so was his physical appearance. Springing from a strong torso, his head and features reminded me of a warrior or hunter on some ancient Iberian vase: small ears tight to the skull, aquiline profile, narrow piercing eyes. His hair under his sweatband was curled tight and close like a bullock's round his glistening brow. He was accompanied by a fierce-looking black hound, whom he addressed as 'Infierno' and whom Hasso regarded with deep distrust.

We had no scythe, but expressions of goodwill were exchanged and he departed.

Over the next few days and nights we were treated to an amazing scene, clearly visible to us across the small intervening property. Arturo of the resounding name (incorporating the patron saint of Spain) and the Iberian countenance had apparently decided to take out all the trees on his *huerta*, not only the dead ones as we had done, but the lot, and render it as flat and smooth as a billiard table. A machine on caterpillar tracks did the uprooting by day. Some of the fruit trees, particularly the ancient pears and cherries, were six or seven metres tall. Arturo took their trunks by mule and cart back to a huge bonfire he had erected at a prudent distance from the house and which he fed without cease for two whole nights. Each time he replenished the blaze his naked torso was silhouetted, armed with a pitchfork, against the flames, and to us he looked then like nothing so much as some kind of demon at the heart of the fire. All the while he sang strange melan-

choly songs we had never heard before. A full moon contributed to the eeriness of the effect. Each time he cast yet
another whole tree-trunk onto the great pyre, he sent a
spray of hot sparks up into the pure, cool, silvery radiance
of the night sky.

After the great clearance and the great purification by fire,
he began to build a long dry-stone wall.

'He is terribly strong,' said Jaime. 'He takes his mule and
cart up onto the mountain and loads it single-handed with
big stones and rocks. Sometimes he has to move them with
an iron bar. Then he brings them down the hill and puts
them onto that enormous wall he is building . . .'

This, we understood, was to enclose the byre which he
was preparing for proper cattle – none of your sunken-
flanked African-looking Andalusian specimens – he was
proposing to bring down from 'mi tierra'. For Arturo was
no southerner. His family had land near Benavente up in
the old kingdom of León, the cradle of the Castilian monarchy. He inherited some of this, sold it, moved to Bilbao,
married a cultured lady (a teacher), had three daughters by
her, quarrelled with her and separated from her, worked for
some years abroad, returned with some money, put it into
the Monte, bought a flat on the coast and let it, lived like
a señorito in Ronda on his rents and dividends, got bored
(having failed to persuade any young Ronda lady to share
his fortune, owing to his undissolved marriage), sold the
flat, took his money out of the Monte and bought his huerta
– with which went the lease of a large arable field belonging
to the railway company.

These things emerged only gradually as our intimacy deepened. It did so because Arturo was almost as much of a
foreigner and hence a figure of mystery to the locals as we
were, and came to be known among them as 'El Zamorano',
the Man from Zamora, that being the province in which his
home town was situated. Our common condition as self-
imposed exiles forged a bond between us, and almost every
evening he would drop by, very often staying for supper. If

I was away on a trip, he would keep a sharp eye on Hilly and Jaime. Thus our sense of mutual obligation deepened.

One night, fairly early on in this relationship, we went out to dinner with English friends further up the valley. On our way back, as we approached our gate, a confused yelping and shouting came to our ears.

'It's Hasso,' said Jaime. 'But there's another dog there too. Drive faster, Papa. It sounds like a fight.'

As soon as I drove into the yard it was apparent that Hasso had slipped his collar. Jaime saw a light further down the land and ran ahead with his torch. Following him to the place of the commotion, we found a little group consisting of Cadbury the kid, now almost fully-grown, lying limp on her side and being sniffed by Hasso and Arturo's evil-looking Infierno. With his hissing lantern on the ground Arturo was on his knees, his lips applied to the young goat's salivating muzzle in an attempt to revive her with the kiss of life. But the animal's eyes were already glazing; she was on the point of expiry, and Arturo soon straightened up, allowing her head to drop back onto the coarse grass and swearing at the over-excited dogs with their inquisitive snouts to keep their distance.

'What on earth happened?' I asked. 'Was it Hasso?'

I thought at first that one of the dogs had attacked her. But there was no blood.

'No,' he said. 'I heard Hasso barking. I thought it was thieves or gypsies, so I came over quickly. Hasso was jumping about like the devil, so I released him and then heard the bleating, and found this creature almost strangled to death. She had got her leash entangled in that quince tree. The slipknot was badly made. I cut her free and did what I could, but as you can see, it was too late.'

'I thought you had put her in the stable,' I said to Hilly.

'It's such a fine night I thought she would be better outside.'

'Oh, Mum, how *could* you?' asked Jaime, putting his cheek to the warm breast of the dead animal. 'Just think of the fun she used to have jumping up on the donkey's back and down again.'

Hilly's lips were compressed; capability was in her blood; she hated making this sort of mistake.

'I'm terribly sorry, darling,' she said. 'It was entirely my fault. And I was so much looking forward to her milk. We'll have to get another.'

'We'll have to bury Cadbury first!' Jaime said.

When Arturo heard this, he laughed boisterously.

'But, *chiquillo*, are you out of your mind? You can't bury sound meat like that. And there's a pretty pelt there too.'

'Jaime darling,' Hilly said, 'Arturo's right. We have to be practical.' She turned to Arturo. 'How long can she hang?'

'Just tonight. I'm not a butcher, but Vallejo at La Granja will do it well. I'll take her first thing, before the insects get to her.'

Hearing this, Jaime rushed into the house. Arturo picked up the dead goat and slung her over his shoulder. I carried the lantern, which flared on his sharp warrior's profile: again I thought of Iberian hunters on Numantine vases. Infierno leapt at the carcass and was kicked by his master back to heel.

One day I walked out of the house in the morning to rinse my face in the irrigation channel, only to find it empty. A perturbed-looking turtle was going bandy-legged across the path, obviously preoccupied by the same problem. A little later Arturo came round to tell me that a sector of the bank had given way. I went up the ditch to see for myself. The breach, about two hundred metres above our house, was not very large, but an abundant waterfall was frothing through the gap and pouring back into the river several metres below. A number of men were standing on the narrow brambly footpath discussing the remedy.

Carrasco, the *cabero*, arrived shortly. He was the overseer of the whole system for our section of the river, a post traditionally held by the farmer lowest down on the irrigation loop, who was naturally the most at risk from a leaky channel or his neighbours' abuse of their water rights. Everything depended, in the first place, on the dam which checked the river's flow a kilometre or so upstream from me, capturing enough water to fill the ditch which carried the lifeblood of the dozen or so small farms on the loop. The dam, of sand and rubble, was rebuilt every year, usually in May, and each *huerta* was bound to send a number of men determined by the amount of its irrigable land: ours was due to send two men a day; Arturo's, which was larger, two men on the first day, three on the second, and so on alternately as long as the work lasted. In practice bodies (the word in this context is *peón*) could no longer be found in such numbers, so you paid in cash for the missing *peones*; this money went to pay for the bulldozer which now did most of the heavy work; where twenty or thirty men used to assemble, a bare dozen went these days with the machine.

As regards distribution of the water, each *huerta* has its own days and times, usually twice a week. Between the allotted hours it can open its sluice and divert most of the water to its own purposes. The ration belonging to each *huerta* is not embodied in any document, but is firmly embedded in the memory and practice of the valley. There is no regular surveillance, but if you fail to switch the water downstream when you should, your neighbour may come up and do it for you. And if you persistently take more than your fair share, the *cabero* will come and call you to account.

In this emergency Carrasco sent Arturo and me off to find some poles. When we returned with these on my roof rack – mostly walnut branches and willow trunks – more neighbours had answered the call. Two, Vallejo and another, had been sent from La Granja. Rafael Alarcón dropped by a little later; though a hill farmer, he was also affected, as he rented some of the fertile land in the valley.

We were never more than half a dozen in the repair team, but that was about the maximum on so narrow and treacherous a site. To enable us to work, the head of water in the ditch had been diverted into an overflow higher up. The trunks and branches were first laid like girders across the breach and tied into the broken wall; then smaller uprights were laid against them, forming a kind of palisade to hold the earth and rubble we threw up by spade from the ditch's bed. Also, we hacked away at the overhanging bramble-clad slope above us, causing little landslides whose debris we shovelled into the gap. Stakes and poles revetted with earth, roots, brambles and small stones – when cooked by the sun – make a surprisingly strong mix.

'Better than *hormigón* (cement and rubble),' said Carrasco with satisfaction.

As we worked, I saw that my companions knew every inch of the ditch and exactly how to repair it with the minimum of material. These were skills that Christians coming south in the wake of the Reconquest had acquired from the Moors remaining in Al-Andalus. After the final expulsion of the *Moriscos* in 1610–14 (of which more later), there must have been hundreds, if not thousands, of Moorish irrigation systems in place, which the Catholic colonists took over, calling them *riberas* from the Castilian word for river bank. The rest of the vocabulary remained and remains unequivocally Arabic: *acequia* for the main ditch, *alberca* for the irrigation tank, *aljibe* for the cistern or well, *noria* for the great wheel with little buckets bringing water directly out of the river, *alcantarilla* for the duct under or alongside a road, and many more besides. Some of the older *riberas* around Ronda were no doubt laid out by the Moors themselves: this applied to Los Molinos in the mouth of the Ronda gorge and Sancho Jaén on the tributary river, the Guadalcobacín. Our *ribera*, though following the same principles, seemed more recent: 'Huertas Nuevas' presumably meant what it said. But how new? Did anybody know when the land had been ceded or expropriated for a new colonisation?

'Well, it must have been before the railway was built,'

said Vallejo, 'because they had to allow all these unguarded crossings to get to the *huertas*, which must have been already there.'

The railway was about a century old. But none of them would hazard a guess further back than that. Could the *ribera* be Moorish after all? There were uncomfortable shrugs all round. The attitude to the Moors was always ambivalent, despite all the words inherited from their language. Yes, they were clever and cunning and had invented all sorts of useful techniques, but were they not also the enemies of Spain since time immemorial?

'The Moors are *gentuza*,' said Arturo. 'Do they not fill up the express from Algeciras on their way to France, so that we cannot get on it, and do they not smuggle drugs to corrupt our youth? *Quita, quita!*'

The latter phrase on Arturo's lips was the ultimate dismissal. He would have no truck with the idea of a Moorish origin for our properties. Though this was an instinctive and emotional response, he was almost certainly right. Our solid but rudimentary houses could not be dated easily, as rural architecture had varied little over the centuries. When we first arrived I was inclined to attribute our place to the wave of rural settlements under Charles III in the 1760s and 1770s, but I fear this was a typical piece of British 'Georgian' snobbery. On reflection it seemed unlikely that Huertas Nuevas came into being before the Peninsular War. The mid-nineteenth-century sequestration of first the monastic then the municipal lands would much more probably have spawned this type of agricultural resettlement. When I suggested this, the others shrugged again, but the notion appeared more acceptable to them.

'Whatever you say, Ali,' they said cheerfully.

'When I was a lad,' Rafael Alarcón reminisced, 'the *acequia* collapsed right down from the dam to the Casa de Ali. Not just a bit, like this, but the whole stretch. There was no machinery in those days and anyway it wouldn't have been suitable here. A good twenty-five *peones* came every day for at least two weeks. I worked alongside my father; I was thirteen or fourteen at the time and earning half a man's wage . . .'

Now the population of the valley was probably a third of what it was then . . . and we were seven on the job . . . eight if you counted Rafael Valiente from La Mimbre who had climbed down from his tractor on the track above to watch. And it was not only the human population: the draught animals had diminished even more drastically.

'How many *yuntas* (yokes of mules) were there on the Cortijo Grande in those days?' I asked Alarcón.

He paused, leaning on his spade and pushing his straw hat up on his forehead.

'Eight or ten working pairs, I should say. Altogether there must have been thirty or forty mules and horses including foals in the corral.'

I could almost hear the ploughmen dealing out their honeyed curses to their animals and singing to themselves or calling out to one another as they passed in contrary directions on the undulating hillside.

Now with one tractor you could do it all . . . but that meant one man immured in the sound of his engine, shaken in his bones and probably doing little good to his kidneys or liver by such a juddering, sedentary method of work. And if he overturned or some other accident befell, who would come to his rescue?

I called these thoughts up to Valiente, sitting on the bank above us.

'*Que va, hombre!*' he called back in derision. 'Do you want us to go back to the slavery of ten hours a day toiling behind those beasts in the blazing sun?'

But Arturo was loyal to the mule.

'What an efficient and economical animal, working like the devil day in, day out on a few handfuls of straw and a few gleanings! No gas-oil, no breakdowns, no accidents! What about when you dropped your levelling bar on your foot, Valiente, and had to go to the doctor, so you couldn't

plough my land as you had promised and I had to go to Juan
Carretero, who was too busy to come and I lost three weeks?
So much for your precious tractor! *Quita, quita*! The mule
is the most marvellous creature invented by God!'

We had almost finished the repair work. The channel
wall was pronounced watertight. While we were putting the
finishing touches to it, Carrasco went off to give the water
its head and soon it came nosing around our feet. We hauled
ourselves and our tools back onto the track. Valiente took
the contingent from La Mimbre up onto his tractor. When
I reached my gate, the water was again flowing strongly in
the ditch and I spotted the turtle waddling back to its cool
subaqueous lair under the mulberry tree.

Not to be outdone, I went for a towel and stripped off.
Where the ditch changed direction by our gate, it was deep
and wide enough for me to float, with the water from the
dam coming down fast over my body. After a minute or so
of its rough massage, I stood up and scrubbed, hidden by a
curtain of brambles and willow fronds; then I stretched
myself out again, splashing my feet against the cold onrush
of the current. No Ritz or palace bathroom has ever given
me the pleasure of those dips in the dark water running
between stone and mud walls – with the limestone cliff of
the table mountain, visible through the foliage, rising above
the dazzling white buildings of the two big hill farms, the
Cortijo Grande and the Cortijo de la Mimbre.

Despite the primitive clothing he wore in the country,
Arturo was no yokel. He dressed sharply when he went to
town; disapproved of my going about my business in Ronda
in beret, jersey and Wellingtons or straw hat and open-
necked shirt according to season; disliked unwashed cars;
could hold his own in French; signed his name with a rubric
worthy of a notary; and was prodigal with refined attentions
('*Oh . . . la . . . la . . . Madama*!') towards any female visitor
who came our way.

Why then had he opted for a life of toil? Especially among

Andalusians, whom he seemed to despise and upon whom he sometimes heaped fierce condemnation, ranging from 'gypsies' and 'thieves' to 'traitors', if he was particularly incensed. The answer seemed to lie in his past. His separation from his wife would have debarred him from the companionship of another woman in his austere homeland. Perhaps also his sharp-edged temperament had led him at one time or another into some violent incident or unfortunate indiscretion which made it difficult for him to return and live at ease, with honour, among those grave and upright worthies who were his kith and kin. Whatever the cause, he had plunged south as far as he could reach, seeking to obliterate his family's knowledge even of his whereabouts. But there was more to it than mere escape. For he was also an idealist. The historian Jaime Viçens Vives has pointed to the contrast between Castilian idealism and Mediterranean realism. Arturo was, for me, a living embodiment of the former. There was something in his make-up which required him to pit himself against a society that fell short of his ideal.

A vivid instance of this was provided by a place called La Peluza. This was an enclosure of about an acre between the railway track and the river. A low stone wall surrounded buildings that had once served as a drovers', muleteers' and smugglers' inn. The house was now a ruin and the only assets were twenty or thirty well-grown poplars. La Peluza had been bought several years before by a Canadian couple who had spent a summer in it with their four children and, by dint of much effort and some ingenuity, made it just habitable. They had never been back since. Much of the upper storey had collapsed, dragging with it their so-called 'minstrels' gallery', which they had proudly made out of the balustrade of an old veranda. All the doors hung open; one of the best poplars had been felled by someone who wanted a roof-tree; a largely symbolic wire fence had long since been pulled up; the pebble-and-gravel driveway made by the Canadians in good suburban style, now overgrown with

61

weeds, was used as a shady parking place by townees who came down to cast their fishing lines not too seriously in the murky river and to picnic with their folding furniture on the bank.

The decay of La Peluza would probably have continued without giving rise to much interest, had it not been for a flash-flood occasioned by a torrential summer storm. The low-lying 'bridge of tubes', which was barely more than a ford, was covered. All of us affected went down to survey the scene. Miguel, the entrepreneurial owner of La Granja, was fuming that he could not get his car across to do his business in the town; he appeared to be afraid of losing some contract.

'We shall have to remake this section of the track at a higher level,' he said. 'We could take it through La Peluza.'

'But for that it would be necessary to get the owner's permission,' Arturo objected. 'And he is not here.' He looked at me. 'Do you have an address for him?'

I said I did not.

'No one has been near the place for years,' said Miguel. 'And there is the whole neighbourhood to consider. Besides, strictly speaking, the land belongs to the *cañada real*.'

The *cañadas* used to form a network that criss-crossed Spain from Castile to Estremadura and from the Pyrenees to Andalusia. They served as drovers' roads for transhumant flocks, had a statutory width of seventy metres, were often bounded by low stone walls and were – in the late Middle Ages and Renaissance times – protected by their own police force. Essentially they were and remain common land, and have in some cases been turned into modern roads. But landless labourers and others who could not afford to buy property would often encroach on them, building cottages and surrounding them with cane fences, and planting figs or prickly pears in the dusty soil. It was on such a stretch that La Peluza stood. There was a strong tendency to respect the acquired rights of such buildings, though they did not figure in the registry of property. When they changed hands it was usually by some very rudimentary piece of paper, with no state taxes. Whatever title existed to La Peluza was probably in that category.

'This man . . . this Canadian family or whatever they are . . . have not been back for four or five years,' said Rafael Alarcón, baring his fine gold tooth. 'Do I not pass the place twice a day every day of my life when I take the milk up to town in the Land-Rover? Do not people walk in and take whatever they want to take? I do not say that is right. Let us respect the house, what is left of it. But the *chopos* are certainly planted in the *cañada*. And if we cannot get through any other way in time of flood, it seems to me that we, the neighbours, have a right of passage.'

Vallejo assented vigorously. He was Miguel's man. 'That is well said. There are more than thirty of us down the valley, if you count women and children. And we have no other way out to school, to the doctor or for our produce.'

'I mean to say, where is this man?' Rafael added. 'Why doesn't he come? What is the point of buying something and leaving it to fall down?'

'Every man makes his own calculations,' Arturo said fiercely. 'If I want to leave my land fallow for four years and let my roof fall in, is it not my right? Who is to stop me? Who is to say it is not mine any more? And then, what about the trees here? To cut them down the owner must apply to the forestry department, and if the owner is not present, who would make the application?'

'I think Miguel Macías, who is the forestry guard, would not refuse permission for a mere twenty or thirty *chopos* . . . on public land,' said Rafael with a wink. 'After all, we all know him . . . and in the circumstances of public interest as Vallejo has said . . .'

Arturo cut him off sharply.

'As well as being wrong, making a bypass through La Peluza would mean going out onto the road over that blind level crossing. The remedy is worse than the disease, especially for Miguel's feed lorries. The only solution is to build a proper bridge here where we are. Neighbours should contribute per hectare of their property, but the bulk of the money must come from the government, which is always making great promises for the countryside. We should therefore make a proper project for the track and bridge and go with it to the town council . . . and if necessary to Madrid.'

Miguel was watching Arturo warily through narrowed eyes; he didn't know what to make of him.

'And who is going to organise all this?'

'I can't give money,' Arturo said, 'but I will give my labour . . . twenty . . . thirty days . . . or whatever is necessary. And my time, if it is needed, to visit offices. But there is one condition.'

'What is that?' Vallejo asked.

'That it is done properly as I have said. You will take it through La Peluza over my dead body. What is mine I defend with my balls, and people know that and they will touch nothing of mine! But of course the Canadian is different; he is a foreigner and he is not here, and you would treat him as if he did not exist. Well, I say again with my balls that I will not stand for that!'

'Are you threatening us?' Vallejo asked, advancing.

'Not unless you are imprudent,' Arturo answered. 'In which case, here I am.'

Vallejo came no further. Arturo turned on his heel, and I went with him. The others remained in an uneasy huddle, discussing his *démarche*.

'I wonder if that was wise,' I said. 'They may gang up on you.'

'Let them,' he shrugged. 'I have no fear. I have never had any fear. If there is some challenge . . . or I see a shape I don't recognise . . . something happens to me at the base of the neck . . . my blood runs faster and my hair prickles and I go *towards* it. Of course, it may turn out to be only a sheep or a tree in the dusk. But if, for example, there was a war and people said you can't cross that land because there is a war on, I would immediately down tools just for that reason and go towards that land in order to cross it. And if they killed me, so what? That is no reason for fear. They will kill you just the same if you are afraid as if you are not. It makes no difference to *them*. But it makes a great deal of difference to oneself to live without fear. I am not boasting. That is simply the way it is. I have no fear.'

As he spoke, it occurred to me that my first impression of him as a Celtiberian warrior had not been so far-fetched after all. It was perfectly possible to imagine him as one of the defenders of Numantia who resisted the Romans to the death in 135 B.C. Spain has always thriven on great enterprises and collapsed into *ennui* and self-doubt without them. It seemed to me Arturo might have played a part in any of them: the Reconquest from Islam, the Counter-Reformation, the discovery and exploitation of the New World. I think the natives of the valley sensed this too, though they would not have put it in those terms. They might laugh at Arturo's extravagances behind his back, or say that he was touched but, curiously, I have no doubt that he also blew upon the embers of their collective consciousness and lifted up their spirits.

Eventually, it was none other than Arturo himself who secured the desired improvements to the access to the valley. The locals' tradition of loose collaboration over harvesting, pig-killing and annually remaking the dam did not extend to disciplined communal effort in the face of bureaucracy. It was Arturo who bullied and cajoled them into it, on the grounds that it would improve the value of their properties; it was almost entirely due to him that the bridge was built and La Peluza was left untouched. That the trees were later the subject of a dawn raid with chainsaws, which removed the lot, was not his affair: his honour was intact.

'*Canalla!*' he said contemptuously when he heard of this. 'You see what I mean? You can't trust these Andalusians. They're all the same. Thieves and gypsies.'

But they trusted him. They knew energy and integrity when they saw them and were happy to harness these elemental forces to theirs. They elected Arturo 'Presidente de la Ribera', within a year or so of which shrewd move he was to bring them the benefits of electric light, which they would never have had otherwise. When in due course he left us, they never stopped talking about the feats of 'El Zamorano'.

Arturo was never short of projects, and he hated empty land. We had an acre or so down by the river which had not been sown for years. He proposed to me that we should sow it jointly with melons on the raised strips, alternating with sunflowers in the furrows.

'All that water belongs here today,' he announced one morning shortly after the ploughing; he then proceeded to block the concrete tube through which it continued down to the *huertas* below us. To make his dam complete he used plastic sacks filled with sand, broken flagstones and bricks and an esparto mat – all held in place by a wheelless pram body he had found in the stable. I recognised it with a start as Jaime's first – and only – baby carriage. Then he pulled our wooden sluice out of its socket and a truly impressive head of water rushed down and spread over the freshly turned field. At this stage we adjourned for lunch.

When we had eaten, we went out to sow melons. Arturo showed us how. The land was now sodden. He struck with his *azada* (which resembles an entrenching tool) and opened a pocket of squelching soil, into which I quickly cast ten or a dozen seeds, which he covered with a deft movement of the tool before the water could flow in again and flush them out. After a while he went off to guide the water lower down, leaving me to delve and Hilly to cast. It was slippery work and required some skill: she had to extract her feet from the caressing mud and take another step in time to cast the next fistful into the oozing orifice I had opened, which would close within a trice. It all had to be done within a few seconds. All of a sudden, the greedy soil completely sucked off one of Hilly's boots. She lost her balance and fell towards me; dropping my tool I was just able to catch her and hold her half-upright against me.

'This reminds me irresistibly,' I said, 'of that extraordinary poem by Miguel Hernández, called *Barro*, which begins, "Mud is my name . . ." '

At this moment she slipped through my arms into the slime.

'What about a bit less poetry and a bit more support?' she protested.

I hauled her up. Her face and hair were spattered and her clothing caked. But Arturo was adamant. This was no time to knock off and clean up. No sooner were we finished with the melons than we turned to the sunflowers. He took the bucket and strode up and down the furrows, casting with a loose flick of the wrist, while we followed covering each cluster with a layer of the light sandy soil. Finally, the last of the sunflower seeds was buried and we walked back to the house, aching and begrimed. I shed most of my clothes and made for the ditch. Hilly followed me with a towel and a glass of wine. When I tried to entice her into the dark swirling water with me, she resisted; she preferred the hose on the terrace. But she lowered her feet into the ditch with mine and we drank the wine together. A spider's web traversed the narrow watercourse, spun between the tentacles of overhanging brambles; a frog plopped in from the bank; there were no wasps or mosquitoes yet to plague us; willow fronds stirred in the evening breeze; we joined hands in the murmurous dusk.

After supper I dug out the translation I'd done of the Hernández poem and read her the opening lines:

> Mud is my name, although I am called Miguel.
> Mud is my profession and my fate.
> Sated with submission to the turning
> Dagger of the hoof and wheel,
> Beware lest Mud should bear a brood
> Of beasts with rasping skins and vengeful claws.

'Mud is my name . . .'

Beware lest Mud should in an instant grow,
Beware lest it should grow and rise and spread
Gently, gently, zealously over
Your rush-stemmed heel, its torment.
Beware lest it should rise above your lily legs
And higher and higher rise up to your forehead.
Beware lest it should arise, a hurricane
From Winter's bland terrain
And burst and thunder and fall in spate
Upon your blood with unrelenting tenderness . . .

'I don't know about my rush-stemmed heel or lily legs,' Hilly smiled when I had got this far, 'but it certainly reached my forehead. You should have seen the struggle I had washing my hair.'

Although Hilly was kind about my attempt with this poem, she still preferred my translations from Antonio Machado's *Campos de Castilla*. As well as Machado and Hernández, I had tried my hand at Lorca, Alberti, Neruda and Vicente Aleixandre. Why? Well, I like to read translations, preferably with the original on the facing page, as in the old-fashioned cribs. That is how I read Dante, and I should never have come within hailing distance of Rilke without the Spender-Leishman renderings. Furthermore, there is a whole treasury of poets who wrote in Spanish between 1900 and 1975 whose names, other than Lorca's are known to few Britons; they have become the property of academics, who have a tendency to hoard them like misers with their gold.

Rafael Alberti, sly poet of the bay of Cádiz, is one of the few to have escaped this conspiracy. He is something of a showman. I met him once when he was giving a series of recitals with Nuria Espert at the Riverside Theatre, Hammersmith. In Spain itself, in those immediately post-Franco years, the two of them were able to fill amphitheatres with crowds of thousands. Even so, an audience of a few hundred in London was quite an achievement. Alberti had long near-white locks curling up a little at the ends; his bronzed face was still sensuous. He was very conscious of his status back home as a legendary survivor from pre-Franco days. When he heard I had made some translations from Machado, he told me two delightful anecdotes about Don Antonio.

'Machado,' he said, 'was not a *literato*. I went two or three times to the Café Varela, where he presided over a *tertulia* ... but to my great disappointment there were no literary figures present. Don Antonio's favourite companions were a chemist, a small landowner, a minor official, people like that. He enjoyed conversation about the weather, the crops, the government. His dress was slovenly; there were ashtrays on the café tables but his ash fell into the folds of his clothing. I had just bought a volume of Rimbaud. I laid it carefully on the table in the hope of attracting his attention but he simply put his cigarette down on it and burned a hole in the cover without noticing . . .'

Alberti went on to recall that as a very young man he had received the national prize for poetry.

'Machado,' he said, 'was undoubtedly responsible for my getting the *premio nacional*. He was much the most distinguished member of the jury. One day, soon after the award, I saw him out walking; at least I was practically certain it was him . . . in a Homburg hat and heavy coat.

'I caught up with him and asked, "Are you Don Antonio?"

'He went on without answering for some paces, as if the question had to wait for permission to enter his consciousness. Then he stopped.

' "Yes," he said, "I am."

' "I am Rafael Alberti," I told him. "I want to thank you for the *premio nacional*."

' "Yours was simply much the best entry," he said.

'He did not appear to think that any further conversation on the matter was necessary or desirable, and went on with his walk.'

Machado constitutes, in my view, the purest gold in the treasure chest I have mentioned. If any two lines prove it, they are:

> *Caminante, no hay camino*
> *sino estelas en la mar.*

For two or three years we came very close to our ideal way of life. Hilly had her hens, her goat and the mare, and we grew much of the produce we needed. Arturo was close at hand and ate with us most evenings. Jaime had several friends in the valley, loved cantering with his mother on the mare and soon graduated to galloping her alone – even taking off on her to stay the night at other farms where his mates lived. But our connection with the town was not severed. We arranged for Jaime to board with Ana during the week and attend Santa Teresa's in the *Ciudad*, a hundred metres from her house. The rigours of a school of four hundred boys and the rough and ready justice of the playground were cushioned by her warm family atmosphere, the good economical but nourishing cooking, the company of her grandchildren – and not least by television, which we were unable (and unwilling) to receive down in the valley. Also, it was like going home: his street life with his familiars took place in the self-same cobbled alleys that were the scene of his very first squabbles, injuries and escapades.

Yet, as we drew towards the end of the seventies it became increasingly apparent that real self-sufficiency was impossible to achieve without more land, livestock and capital. As one friend tartly put it, we had become 'unskilled peasants'. Without any business activity in the town, I found myself spending more and more time away. I was absent for weeks at a time, either on field work for guidebooks or escorting small groups of culture vultures round the Castiles, Andalusia and Portugal. These were not disagreeable occupations, but they were not particularly lucrative and they did not balance the books. While I was away, Hilly coped magnificently. Arturo's support was crucial, as indeed were her ministrations to him by way of meals and company. But clouds were gathering on our horizon.

Our Hasso had developed into a wanderer. He was a charming and affectionate dog without a hint of evil; he killed no sheep on his travels. Nevertheless, he was a philanderer. Sometimes he would be absent for two or three days at a time, begetting pups, and the fame of his loins spread up and down the valley. Once he went missing for longer than usual. After nearly a week I put out an announcement over the local radio station, offering a reward for news of him. There was no response to this, but the next day Arturo came round and said he had sighted him up on the threshing floor of the uninhabited Cortijo de Villar, which was further down the valley on the other side of the river. Apparently there were two bitches up there, and the owners, who still farmed the land and had some grain and other things stored in the sheds, brought food down from Ronda for them every other day. Hasso seemed to have moved in with the bitches and was presumably sharing their rations.

Jaime and I set off to bring him home. Jaime rode the mare and I went on foot. As we approached the ruinous cluster of buildings, we saw him, ears pricked on the ridge above us; then he came bounding down to greet us and welcome us to his adopted home. His mistress – I could only see one bitch; the other had run off at our approach – was black, flop-eared, short-legged, only half his size and not very prepossessing. But he was obviously attached to her. Thinking that he might be reluctant to come with us, we secured him with a rope.

From the radially-cobbled threshing floor there was a view that swept over much of the valley. On the opposite flank the blue-tiled spire of La Estacada was just visible above tall eucalyptuses. Ah, La Estacada! Perched in a superb position commanding both our valley and a subsidiary running south, it was an enchanting place. Its steeply falling land was profusely covered with domestic and wild olives, cork trees and lichened oaks. Its extensive buildings were not, as one might have supposed, those of a monastery, but belonged to a derelict olive mill, where no animal had turned the presses in many a year. No one lived there, though a bee-keeping family inhabited a small house near by. We had ridden up several times over the years, picnicking once or twice under the swaying eucalyptus grove which stood by the empty barns and the abandoned tower.

Then came, full of vim, an ex-Conservative MP who determined to have it, and did, very cheap with all its land, for his American wife, who was a film producer, and their glamorous family. Central heating, a library and a study for every bedroom were planned. They hired our horses for their first forays. But local government and other assurances (naively accepted) about speedy improvements to the neighbourhood track failed to materialise. Their Porsche and kindred motor cars could not take the surface or the gradients. Having honoured the area with their patronage, they felt they deserved better. The *affaire* turned sour. They sold. But no new owner had ever been seen. It was rumoured that the property was one of a number acquired by an exiled South American politician in order to salt away some of his ill-gotten gains on Spanish soil. The only certain thing was that you could still ride up to La Estacada and picnic in the shade. The place continued to fall into ruin, a monument to British post-colonial fantasy and Spanish dilatory intransigence.

At the time we had derided the pretensions and arrogance of our compatriots during their short and losing battle with the enchantress, and condemned their impatience when Shangri-la refused to emerge overnight. But in a sense there was not much difference, except in scale and ambition, between their endeavour and our quest for Arcadia. In both cases we had fallen for the Andalusian legend of a land flowing with milk and honey, propagated by Spanish writers from the Ancients through the Arabs to the Renaissance. By this account the natural riches of the soil and climate enabled man, in return for a minimum of effort, to live at ease in happy harmony with his surroundings. This belief buoyed up those who repopulated the lands recovered during the Reconquest, animated the eighteenth-century rural resettlements patronised by Charles III, underpinned all the movements for agrarian reform in the nineteenth century, inspired the southern Anarchist movement and even provided the rationale for Franco's programme of rural colonisations. The harsh reality was otherwise, consisting (except in the super-fertile *vega* of Granada) of rock and stone and dusty soil yearning for water, of poor pastures and low-grade ores, requiring toil, skill, endurance and cunning to coax a living out of it.

Of course, like our compatriots, you could try to beat the system with money, but this would not win you much respect or assistance. Or, like us, you could attempt to enter the game, which meant you would be welcomed with amused tolerance. But we were not, and never would be, in the same league as the other folk on the *ribera*: we were not tough enough, and they all knew it. Also, our aims and ends were very different from theirs. Their pay-off after all their labours would be retirement with honour to the town, leaving the land to the next generation, if they had the stomach for it, and if they didn't, then to the property developer or agro-business. Our reward was harder to measure, and more precarious. We were there for the skies and the landscape, the freedom to roam, and the vestiges of the Homeric world that still remained; we were there because of something in the Spanish soul which seemed to have survived the Industrial Revolution, but was constantly threatened by the modern world. This bred in us sensations of impermanence and anxiety, for which we compensated with daily draughts of the natural grandeur around us. Yet these were not always sufficient to steady the nerves and lift the spirit. Whether you aimed to live the Mediterranean life in the grand manner at La Estacada or more modestly like us, you constantly came up against the divergence of your aspirations from those of the natives. You and they were pulling in opposite directions, and there could not be much doubt who would win in the long run. Suddenly, I felt discouraged. 'Come on,' I said to Jaime, 'let's get going!'

We slithered down a steep *barranco* to the river's brink. Jaime splashed across on the mare. I waded with Hasso. When we got back, Hilly made a fuss of him and gave him a chicken carcass which he crunched up in a trice. He grumbled a bit when we chained him up, but then he seemed to settle contentedly enough. By morning, though, he had slipped his new collar, which lay still attached to the shiny new chain I had bought for him. It was Jaime who discovered this.

'Hasso's escaped again,' he came to report, with a brave face that looked not far from tears.

We comforted him. There was no cause for alarm; he must have returned to his mistress on the threshing floor. But Hasso's *wanderlust* undoubtedly contributed to a growing atmosphere of instability.

A hot evening wind was blowing, as it often did in late August. The maize cobs were filling out their tasselled wrappings; the melon leaves were yellowing at the rim; the tomatoes were in glut. The September Fair, the high point of Ronda's year, would shortly be swinging into action and spilling its sound effects down into the bowl of Los Molinos and along the river valley. The odd leaf had fallen from the vine and the October crops – quinces and walnuts – were hanging heavier on their boughs. Autumn could not be far away: one felt it was marking time over the hill, waiting for August's rearguard to march on and September's forces to move in. Hilly came out with a broom to sweep the terrace tiles and a watering can to lay the dust. I took up the *azada* and went to water a panel of maize; I was determined to harvest enough of the grain to keep her hens through the winter months, when I would be away on a series of cultural tours.

The weather broke soon after I had left. Hilly wrote:

'. . . just done the pump (fourth go), my wellies look as if they've got adobe huts attached to their soles . . . There is heavy snow up in Ronda and on all the peaks, but none so far in the valley, just freezing and damp and sleet. Cadbury and moke in the shed, hens shrivelled on the branch like me. Roads icy, heavy sleet blocking window wipers. Car started just, but it was so dark and I hate the lights being wonky and the bridges are all icy and very dangerous-looking, the river swollen again. Sky very yellow . . . just been down to the goat strip – flooded. Huge gravy-coloured waves . . .'

Hilly in August

Jaime was her great consolation. Santa Teresa's in town had been closed owing to a massive school reorganisation, so he was back at the rural school, where Don Antonio the maestro tweaked his pupils' ears and they chanted their multiplication tables aloud just like in the Machado poem:

mil veces ciento, cien mil,
mil veces mil, un millón

'J and I had a hilarious time doing homework,' she wrote next. 'I love trying to do the back-to-front sums. He tells me the numbers. I get it wrong, then he does it and we do a sort of mixture, cracking our sides with laughter. Oh Lord, Don Antonio will *faint* but I have a lot of confidence in Hymie's ability and in the end our answers seem to tally, me doing it the English and he the Spanish way. I had a nap and he woke me with a lovely hot cup of tea, then we played cards and did some funny paintings and drawings . . . sups, bed and stories. He's such a dear little companion, so cheerful, polite and affectionate . . . he cooked the sups (sossies, eggs and tomatoes, fried bread) and an amazing-looking concoction arrived on my plate! Very good too, although everything had merged together and there was an amazing amount of washing up, as though we had had ten guests at least.'

Jaime's friendship with José, Vallejo's ten-year-old son, seemed to be flourishing:

'It's cold but bright today . . . still very damp and muddy. Took Hymie and Hozay to school . . . Cleaned up a bit and lit huge fire to dry off clothes and intend keeping it going now day and night until this patch is over. Am just waiting for Hymie to come home and eat some roast chicken . . . I've got a cock in the coop for emergency – here he comes! Later: Hozay came round for Hym to help him with the cows – good! Freezing now, am wearing the old tweed coat we got from Oxfam in Salisbury – lovely. Now the animals, then wrap up cochie [the car], homework and bath-night in front of the fire.'

I could well envisage this. It would be much too cold for a shower in the washroom, which was barely functional at the best of times, so she would heat up some pans of water on the stove and fill the zinc tub in which she did the laundry, and Jaime would splash and lounge in it and ask for it to be topped up, and she would go for the reserve pan, and so it would go on for nearly an hour, after which he would be towelled, rubbed, brushed and dressed by his mother. When the whole operation was over she would warm up a little more water on the logs and rinse her own feet in it.

Finally, the rural school succumbed to the weather:

'No *colegio* because of awful weather. Hymie went round and checked with Hozay, then rolled up his sleeves, washed up very well, swept the kitchen floor, then held Cadbury's leg while I milked her in the shed, then forked fresh straw for her to eat, *then* tried about twenty times to start the pump but hadn't quite got the strength of arm to pull the toggle hard enough. I finally managed to but he certainly had the know-how if he had been a bit bigger and stronger, and he was so cheerful and pleasant all the time, not one grizzle and it's certainly grizzle weather. The next hurdle will be his birthday . . .'

When she wrote to me about his eighth birthday, it was almost a relief to hear he wasn't growing up too fast:

'Another quite funny incident was Hymie, behind my back and I suspect Ana's (except she was probably nagged to death over it) spending his birthday money (about two mil) on a terrible cochie thing with an awful little man in it *stuck* to the seat that runs on *eight* big batteries which last about two hours and they cost 200 pesetas a go. The cochie itself reverses, jumps and goes round very fast indeed and so do the batteries run out very fast indeed, so the whole miracle is moribound [sic] now for lack of batteries and it's become a subject *not* to be discussed at all. He obviously feels he's made a huge mistake and goes red with horror about it. The best bit was when he had all the money and kept counting it and speculating as to what he could get with it, showing it off to his friends and then, oh dear, the shame of what he's got with it and they all sneered – only rich towny *señoritos* would fall for that kind of toy. Now a big fishing-rod or a big airgun would have been what *they* would have bought, or a smart jacket – *anything* but *that*. Good campo sense really. He had a rather awful couple of days getting over it but has recovered in his inimitable way and is as cheery as the day is long and the dreaded cochie is back in its box and *hidden* in the back room.'

It was not a time of year that encouraged visits, and almost Hilly's only caller was Arturo:

'Arturo turned up for a swig. He is working on his Berlin wall with a brolly stuck on his back like a sort of rucksack.'

The mind boggled as to how Arturo could possibly do

Hilly in winter

heavy manual labour with an umbrella somehow strapped to his shoulders. But Spanish males have a built-in resistance to waterproof clothing, which they consider effeminate, while curiously an umbrella is all right. Arturo was very ingenious, so it was perhaps not wholly surprising that he had managed to turn himself into a weird sort of soft-backed crustacean, something out of Bosch, in order to go on working in the rain. But even he was ultimately defeated:

'Arturo came round for another swig. I gave him a bottle to take back for his bed and some soup, poor soul. He helped me turn the cochie round, which had stuck in the mud. He looked very shrivelled, like me – I think he might be ill, though maybe it's just the cold. My hands looked like skinned rabbits' heads.'

Up till then it seemed that Hilly had been holding the fort in much the same intrepid way as she had the previous year, when I had also been away for several weeks. But a slightly desperate note now began to make itself heard in her letters. The rain continued unabated. As a precaution against getting stranded she took to leaving the car on the other side of the river when she came back from shopping expeditions or collecting Jaime from school, but this meant she had to face almost a mile on foot. She still had the old mare as a lifeline, but we had ploughed most of the land after the autumn crops and sown it with a mixture of grass and clover which would form a permanent pasture in due course; in the meantime there was none of the rough winter grazing that had abounded the previous year. Hilly did the rounds of the tiny estate:

'There is some grass round the river bank and in the quince wood. What I'd really like is to fence the whole of the goatstrip and quince wood and let all the grazing animals free in there – no halters, nothing – so they wouldn't get tangled in any of those witchy trees, and build a good shelter above the usual flooding point and have a couple of black piggies to root around and eat the rotting quinces.'

But the river continued to rise, and the sparse grass went under too. Hilly decided to take emergency measures. She rode the mare up to La Mimbre and asked them to take her in for a couple of months; she would bring up a sack of bran every week, so the old girl could have her morning and evening bran mash. The good folk agreed, and Hilly returned on foot to sort out her other problems. The first of these was that she was out of butane gas, so she determined to lay in two or three of the heavy orange cylinders or *bombonas* in case she got completely cut off.

'The next hurdle will be getting the *bombonas* to the cochie by wheelbarrow and then back again. Will treat myself to *two* nips of anis during this operation.'

She loaded two of the empty cylinders, still by no means light, onto the wheelbarrow and pushed them up the track, but when she got to the bridge she could not cross it; in less than an hour it had become impassable. So she dumped the cylinders at La Peluza:

'There was no way of getting them over the *rio* and no way of getting up to town to bring Hymie down and no way of having an anis! Still pelting down, very cold, mountains beautiful with snow caps. The *rio* looks like black treacle and rather evil and very rapid. Goatstrip right under water now and half the quinces but not as yet in the kitchen garden. I've got one or two bottles of plonk left and plenty of food and a packet of fags and tons of damp wood.'

The next day she woke to bright sunshine. The river had subsided a bit, so she was emboldened to try again:

'You know how amazing the weather is here, so I walked to the cochie and brought it down to the wooden bridge, which looks like a very awful barge, water just lapping over it, and pushed the *bombonas* over and into the car and got new ones from the *tienda*. Decided suddenly to drive to Ronda and get Hymie, who's been staying with Ana, and had a flat, which a man who was driving to Seville stopped and mended free, so I did get him but had huge hot flashes on the road back – roads still icy . . . nearly skidded off the wooden bridge . . . a huge black cloud has just come up and is hovering over the *casa* and a huge thunderclap has just exploded . . . stories and bed now with three hotties . . . nice to have the monkey back . . .'

Even so, she was clearly at the end of her tether:

'I don't feel quite as strong as I did this time last year. I'm cutting down on booze so that I don't lose my bottle. Cocoa instead. Very easy to go bats otherwise!'

In the end it was the loss of the mare that did most to undermine Hilly's spirit. The old creature had been a vital element in the supply line and indeed in Jaime's life; we had planned to buy a filly to train up as her successor and breed from. Now we had not even the wherewithal to feed the old lady, much less another. There had been a heroic pioneering edge to the previous winter, but this had now been blunted by the struggle for survival. Now Hilly could only cling to Jaime – mother and child on a raft:

'It is only Hymie's and Hozays's squeaks of pleasure upon almost anything that keep me going.'

When I got back, the momentousness of the decision we had to make was rather shattering, especially as it could only go one way. After so long in pursuit of the ideal, and much happiness in so doing, there was no option but to pull out – at any rate for the time being. Hilly could not be left to cope with these gruelling winters alone. And now that Santa Teresa's had closed its doors in order to feed a vast new *Instituto* for two thousand children, which we did not like, there were no good alternatives for Jaime's education. But we were determined to keep the *campo* at all costs, even if it meant relegating it for the most part to the kingdom of the mind (which is where we mostly dwell) with occasional sorties to it when we could.

To make this financially possible my sister Juliet and her husband Alan came to the rescue by agreeing to buy a half share: we would split the costs and usage. We also counted heavily on Arturo. If the land was abandoned, it would be invaded by herdsmen desperate for grazing and none too scrupulous about how or where they obtained it. If the house was left uninhabited and unpoliced, it would be broken into. But if it was known that Arturo's writ extended over our place and that it was under his protection, no one would lay a finger on it. It was well-established in the consciousness of the valley and beyond that he was a dangerous man if crossed.

Thus, we agreed with Arturo that he would farm the land to his own best advantage. The house would be empty and locked and he would keep an eye on it, and woe betide anyone, he swore, who tried to break in. In addition, Ana and Mateo and their family would come down from time to time and air it and whitewash it and prepare it for our visits. With these arrangements in place, it was with rather lighter hearts than would otherwise have been the case that we headed for England. Our sense of pointing in the wrong direction was relieved by the knowledge that we could, in theory, return whenever we wished.

This regime worked well enough for some time. Jaime went to a village school and had to stop doing his sums back to front. We got out to the *campo* for short spells in the holidays. The land was in use and our reunions were warm: we picked up the old relationships at once, and Arturo came round to supper just like before.

All the same it became clearer each trip that he was not flourishing. Despite his energy, his ventures did not prosper. The six splendid beige cows he had brought down from León – the whole length of Spain – in his first year had had to be sold because scorched southern pastures were simply not suitable for a breed that would have been more at home in the lush fields of Normandy. He had never really recovered from this stylish error of judgement. He went downmarket into Andalusian cattle, then fell in love with goats, then switched to sheep. Six of the latter escaped and were killed on the railway line. Eventually he was reduced to rabbits and hens. But his canine tribe did not diminish with the harshness of the times; rather it increased. Infierno was joined by Morina, Terrible, Percherón and 'Fox-Terry-Air', a smooth-haired black mongrel without the slightest relationship to that breed. This motley crew provided him with companionship now that we were gone.

Occasionally he would talk of going home. 'I don't know, *chico*,' he would muse. 'My brothers say I should go back to my *tierra* . . . that this is no place for me, among this *gentuza*. But I would find no woman there either. If I were younger, I would go abroad again.'

I never took Arturo's talk of a return to his own folk very seriously. Somehow I imagined that with the addition of our own land he would, in his strange way, get by. When the bombshell came I was totally unprepared for it. Ana rang to say he had sold his *huerta* and was going back up north; she had only found out by accident when she ran into him in the street and he told her he was leaving the next day on the express. On reflection, I realised that his whole way of life must have deteriorated sharply with the withdrawal of Hilly's heartwarming support: man of iron though we took him to be, our flight had triggered his. I could well imagine him on the platform in his khaki double-breasted suit, white shirt and striped tie, two or three pens in his breast pocket, gold-rimmed sunglasses and attaché case . . . 'El Zamorano' going home, keeping up appearances even in straitened circumstances, no doubt as prolific as ever with advice to others how to run their own affairs . . . ever the idealist. Along with this vision I experienced a real sense of loss – tinged, I have to admit, with a certain indignation that someone we had shared so much with had simply walked out of our lives as abruptly as he had walked into them, without so much as leaving an address.

The practical repercussions were also great. His departure struck at the heart of our absenteeism, which had been built on the foundation of a dependable neighbour and friend. I could not get out there immediately, but the place could not be left for long without inviting squatters and other kinds of depredation. Ana and Mateo sought diligently and came up with one Paco, from whom they got their country eggs, who was prepared to take on the land, which would at least demonstrate a presence there. It was the best solution that could be devised from a distance.

The new dispensation did not match up to Arturo's. Paco had some engaging qualities; he had never travelled beyond Madrid and enjoyed hearing tales of foreign parts over a drink. But he lived on the other side of the river and – though assisted by his youngest son, Antonio – had as much land as he could manage properly already. The result was that he was hardly ever on our *huerta*. The house was broken into more than once. On one occasion several people evidently lived in the place for several days, scattering the contents of trunks in the loft, defecating on the tiled floors, burning up the wood supply. It was raining hard at the time and Paco had no cause to cross the river, which was in any case in spate and would have presented a difficult passage to his mules, so he knew nothing of what had happened. It fell to Ana and Mateo to discover it when they went down on a routine check once the weather had improved and the invaders had moved out.

There were other difficulties. A running battle developed between Paco and me over his habits of irrigation. I must have asked him a dozen times not to irrigate more than eight hours consecutively, which was our ration twice a week. If he did, the water table inevitably rose and contaminated river water poured into our domestic well. But with the increasing switch to dry crops some of our neighbours did not claim their share, and Paco could not resist taking advantage of this. Returning from Ronda one evening, I found the land awash like a paddy-field and the well flooded: it would take several hours to pump out, and probably days before the water in the taps was usable. When I went round to complain, Paco listened to me gravely. Naturally, he said, he lamented what had happened. He had told his Antonio to shut the sluice and the boy must have forgotten. He would send him round in the morning to clean up. I had little doubt that Antonio's forgetfulness had been intentional and would happen again. There was no need, I suddenly told myself, to put up with repeated aggravations at the hands of Paco – whatever the good humour with which he inflicted them. There were other valleys where the grass might be greener, the view no less striking and the inconveniences fewer. There were mountain villages which still looked, at any rate from a distance, exactly as I remembered them thirty years before under the lustrous tiles of their church domes or spires . . .

At the next family council we examined our options. I thought it might look as if we were at the end of the Spanish road. Having recently written a book about Catalonia, I tentatively floated as a compromise the idea of the coastal plain dotted with ancient settlements between Gerona and the Costa Brava; it was much closer and cheaper to get to from England. There were no takers. Hilly was much against it: on all our journeys north she had felt we were entering progressively less sympathetic territory. For Jaime the same was true in reverse: whenever we had driven south from Bilbao he had asked plaintively when we would get to 'real Spain', and it was not until well south of Córdoba that his nose wrinkled to the smell of what was, for him, the real thing. Besides, how could he break his links with Ana? That was unthinkable; it would be the death of her, he added cockily. My sister Juliet, who is a passionate naturalist, murmured that plant and wild life was much more interesting in the Serranía de Ronda.

These preliminary soundings greatly reduced the area of our quest. It was clear that any move would have to be within a radius of say a hundred kilometres from Ronda, otherwise the 'real Spain' and wildlife criteria would not be met. The idea of a smaller pueblo than Ronda had some appeal. Even if the remoter villages had changed in character, they would still have their narrow-fronted houses with cavernous depths and rear corrals, conferring coolness and privacy behind their blinding blue-white walls; and there would be neighbours to hold keys and perform other services. Or we might be enticed towards the Atlantic beaches, whose undulating hinterland was graced by a number of small, decrepit cities inhabited by a subtle people, descendants of the Phoenicians and Tartessians, given to song and ritual and bulls and horses and, where possible, a life of ease. Suddenly there seemed to be a host of possibilities and the imagination kindled again.

The trouble was that after a longish period based in England I was out of touch with the scrap of planet I had once known so well. I had no informed view whether a more secure retreat could still be found that satisfied Juliet and Alan's wildlife interests, Jaime's requirements of proximity

Besides, how could he break his links with Ana?

to Ana and the sea, and Hilly's continuing yearnings for at least enough space for such amusing creatures as hens and bantams – her childhood dream of a Welsh hill farm, though scaled down a bit by time, age and circumstance, was still very much alive in its Andalusian mutation.

Eventually it was agreed that I should investigate. I would go out for several weeks at first, and thereafter take such time as I could away from my other concerns to re-explore the land from which I had derived so much sustenance, both emotional and physical, over so long a period. I must say I was pleased with the assignment. While Jaime tussled with his sixth-form college and Hilly with her London job, I would once again become a traveller. It is true that roads and maps and guidebooks and brochures and hotels have removed most of the physical challenge from journeys in

Europe, and for that matter in much of the world. But they do not remove all the mystery. There is a very real sense in which the most rewarding modern travel remains an exploration, because the focus shifts onto the most difficult terrain of all: the character and temper of the inhabitants, grappling with their present while still inhaling the heady vapours of their history. For the romantic traveller of the past, the people were figures in a landscape, picturesque adjuncts to a watercolour. This balance has changed today; the landscape recedes into the background; the figures advance, demanding of the modern traveller a less superficial account of them. For the would-be settler in particular, the finest views, the balmiest airs, the best bargains are empty shells without some link with and sympathy for the life force of the people.

4

THE DIVINE SHEPHERDESS

Seeking an alternative to Ronda and its immediate surroundings, Grazalema, some twenty kilometres to the west as the crow flies, seemed tailor-made. The little town is quite celebrated in its way. It was written up by Richard Ford from the nineteenth-century romantic viewpoint and dissected by Julian Pitt-Rivers in his well-known work of social anthropology *The People of the Sierra*. More recently it has become one of the prize exhibits in the Junta de Andalucía's campaign to promote the *Ruta de los Pueblos Blancos*, the 'white towns' of the interior. Visually it is remarkable for its impeccable pueblo roofscape punctuated by three church belfries (it was once a prosperous wool town); for its situation 'plastered like a martlet's nest' (Ford) under the Pico de San Cristóbal; and for its fine views over Olvera and other pueblos. It also boasts a number of domestic architectural grace-notes deriving from its wool-trade days, among them tall bow windows with old wrought-iron grilles, door-knockers in the form of bejewelled female hands, round or elliptical occulus windows in the lofts under the eaves, a fine plain stone doorway with scalloped lintel and jambs, and finally – a special feature of the place – a steep broken pediment enclosing a little grilled window over the entrances to many of the grander façades.

More modern attractions include a three-star hotel, a municipal swimming pool cantilevered over the cliff and a campsite on the higher edge of the town, from which people make excursions into the *Parque Natural de Grazalema*. In this large 50,000-hectare nature reserve, straddling a mountain massif with deep fissures, the *pinsapo* (a millenarian pine found nowhere else in Europe), the *quejigo* (gall-oak), the *acebuche* (wild olive) and a whole range of flora and fauna are strictly protected – so much so that though Grazalema's name is attached as capital to this well-policed wilderness, one has to go to the administrative office in El Bosque on the road to Arcos de la Frontera to obtain a permit to enter the *pinsapares*, which are fenced in by wire.

Recalling earlier times when I had ridden freely through these mountains, I lamented some of these restrictions to a dark, portly man with a booming voice, who immediately took me to task. He was from Málaga but his wife came from Grazalema, which was his favourite pueblo in the whole world. He delivered a sonorous lecture on its unique micro-climate, said that nature had poured everything into the region and that it was perfectly right to protect it fiercely: access had to be limited and controlled as a precaution against the horrendous forest fires that afflicted these parts. Did I not know that there were two helicopters on permanent standby in the airport of Jerez whose *only* duty was to deal with fires in the Sierra de Grazalema? War might break out, but their first duty was to save those trees, for was not this one of the most grandiose and impressive landscapes in the whole of Spain? In fact, in his view, it was the grandest and most impressive of all!

When a Spanish bourgeois waxes both lyrical and self-righteous over his natural patrimony (to which he paid precious little attention until it became fashionable to do so), the effect is impressive, if only for the suddenness and fierceness of the conversion. Chastened, I bowed to his enthusiasm. There was much in what he said. The micro-climate is indeed unusual. Grazalema is ideal as a summer hill station because the soaring mountain casts it into shadow two hours before the merciful shades creep over

the baking townships nearby; but this blessing becomes
something of a blight from autumn onwards. Furthermore,
Grazalema has the highest rainfall in Spain. Can that really
be so? Surely not in sunblest Andalusia. Alas, yes, the brutal
statistics are there. Of course, it comes in heavy downpours
and is not constant like the Scotch mist of Bilbao. Even so,
I find it a deterrent. There are other aspects of the place
with which I am not quite in tune, for instance the large
painted signs at the entrance to the pueblo proclaiming
official plans in the usual inflated jargon, namely: *Junta de
Andalucía, Plan de Actuacíon de la Sierra de Grazalema*,
or *Sociedad de Fomento de Grazalema*. How do you 'actu-
ate' or 'set in motion' a forest, or 'foment' a small town?
One of the ways appears to be by installing plants in the
main square that are distinctly wrong for it, such as a
totemistic *pinsapo* brought down from the mountain, looking like a junior monkey-puzzle, surrounded by tall silver-
bearded ornamental grasses more appropriate to Dorking or
Haslemere.

At this point I may be accused of ungracious carping.
What else should I expect of the capital of that rural tourism, respectful of nature, which the Junta wants to encourage? That it should remain an isolated, tight-knit and
socially conservative community, suspicious of strangers,
with a wholly rural economy as in Pitt-Rivers's day? I have
no good answer to that. Also, I have to confess that my
reservations are not shared by my son Jaime or by his charming girlfriend or by the young in general, for whom Grazalema is popular for its access to beautiful countryside, for
the neatness of its houses and streets, for its swimming
pool and so forth. Jaime wants to buy a house there when
he marries and then, obviously, I shall visit it with pleasure
and sing the place's praises. In the meantime, whatever
the charms of Grazalema, they are not those I seek in my
Arcadia.

I took the road to Zahara, fourteen kilometres off, on the
other side of one of the most spectacular mountain passes

in southern Spain, the Puerto de las Palomas. It is ill-named after doves and pigeons – this is the haunt of vultures. Driving over it many years before, when there was only an unsurfaced track, we almost had to nose the great unwieldy birds aside with the car radiator; after several clumsy hops and skips they became airborne and landed angrily on a pinnacle of rock. Now there is a metalled road carrying more traffic, but two of the Egyptian variety were planing and wheeling above me as I reached the top. From here the road coils down in tight loops, passing about halfway down some iron gates and a track winding into a sinister ravine, which we used to pretend led to the hideout of a major Nazi war criminal. The village is clustered under a crag, which is crowned by a Moorish keep of some renown – for it was the recapture of this strongpoint by Muley Abul Hassan one night in 1482, by assault with ladders, which is said to have unleashed the Christian war machine, culminating nine years later in the capitulation of Granada. The time was ripe for this at all events, but there is always an immediate *casus belli*, and this affront was it; for Zahara had been taken from the Moors by Ferdinand of Antequera, Ferdinand the Catholic's grandfather.

Zahara, with equally fine views from its plaza, is smaller and more sun-drenched than Grazalema. Its architectural features are less genteel: one or two principal houses have tiled fronts and window grilles down to the pavement level in the style of Cádiz, indicating that the pueblo is over the watershed towards the sea, and its lower houses are built on outcrops of naked rock, which are as lovingly white-washed as the housefronts themselves; the odd palm tree adorns a farm or two under the walls. Once I came with Diana and a group of friends to see a bullfight here: the bulls escaped while being driven in by horsemen across the summer stubble. We saw no *novillada* but were rewarded by a different spectacle as the riders rounded up the errant beasts against a glorious sunset.

The plaza on this occasion was almost completely covered by an awning sheltering a long bar, trestle tables and a dance floor, on which the citizens were gracefully circling to the music of a modern band occupying a platform on the church steps. It was lunchtime on the second day of the fair. An old man plucked my sleeve and asked if I had been reaping. He was alluding presumably to my straw hat, not a gentleman's Panama but the rough country type still associated with those who reap the corn by hand. I said no, my headgear was simply to keep the sun off my pink British face. His friends, quick to avert any suggestion of discourtesy on the part of the pueblo, hastened to assure me he was slightly 'touched'.

The main topic of conversation in Zahara was the dam. Spain is a country whose chronic droughts have stimulated governments of every persuasion into ambitious hydraulic schemes. The view from a plane reveals the great artificial lakes swelling the slender arteries of the Tagus and Guadiana, and the mighty waterworks of the Guadalhorce above Málaga. Now the official finger had pointed at the headwaters of the Guadalete, rising above Grazalema, meandering through saltpans and oleanders under Zahara, and descending past Bornos and Arcos de la Frontera towards the estuary on which the fate of Spain was sealed for centuries when the Moors under Tarik defeated Rodrigo's divided Visigoths.

The unfinished dam, a huge causeway with gravel flanks, stretched grimly across the wide river bed: previously threaded by idling streams fringed with willows, this was now a raw sandpit or quarry criss-crossed by innumerable tracks of earth-moving machinery and lorries. Adequate compensation had presumably been paid to those whose farmsteads and smallholdings were to be inundated, and no doubt some marginal farmers were glad of this largesse, but the whole embryonic lake, a kilometre or more wide and nine or ten long, looked like a battlefield, pending the influx of the water to heal its scars.

The Venta Pancho, on the lower edge of the pueblo, with

a ringside view of these developments, was still quiet at two o'clock in the afternoon; the dancing had not finished in the plaza. I had a light lunch on the terrace.

'It all looks nearly finished,' I said. 'When do you expect the lake to fill?'

'It'll be a while yet,' said Pancho.

'Presumably it'll give a great boost to local life,' I suggested. 'At Arcos, lower down, they have aquatic sports and a paddle steamer.'

Pancho seemed unmoved by this prospect. He shrugged.

'We'll see. It may bring a little more *vida* . . . *una poquilla*. Or not . . .'

He certainly wasn't going to admit that he was sitting on a goldmine. Like most Spaniards his expectations were healthily circumscribed by scepticism. He reminded me of the Montejaque dam, built in the twenties to capture the waters of the Campobuche; this had failed completely, all the water running down to the Guadiaro by an underground river. Pancho bustled off to attend to his dining room, which was now filling up fast with large family parties, twelve or fourteen to a table. Dam or no dam, Spanish feast days (which are not infrequent) gave him as much trade as he could cope with, if not more.

From the next table a jolly woman with red hair, nice eyes heavily ringed with black mascara, big lips and an infectious laugh, asked if I was from Gibraltar. I replied emphatically that I was not. She, it turned out, was from La Linea, and lived in a block of flats looking out over the airport and the Rock. Her family were Zahara people and she had brought her two sons up to the hills for a couple of weeks: they, perhaps fourteen and nine, were in an advanced state of chronic boredom; the municipal swimming pool had cracked and would hold no water; the *feria* was 'crap'; their only solace was a dreadful miniaturised music box, fitting in the palm of the hand, which emitted a variety of hideous computer-selected sounds according to which button you pressed. Mum, initially indulgent, eventually told them to shut up or get lost and then ordered herself a large gin and tonic.

'I can't see why this Gibraltar thing can't be settled amicably,' she said. 'Our royal families get on very well; your Carlos has been with Juan Carlos in Mallorca; I have English friends with whom I am very close. It is just our governments and politicians who keep the whole stupid quarrel going for their own ends.'

'Our Foreign Office would be perfectly happy to hand back Gibraltar,' I said. 'The problem lies with the people of the Rock. They don't want it. They still distrust Spain.'

'Ah, the Gibraltarians, "*los Llanitos*" as we call them!' she sighed, throwing up her hands. 'They are a thick-headed lot. And no sooner does a girl from our side of the frontier marry one of them than she becomes as thick-headed as the rest of them.'

'Main Street would certainly be much pleasanter if it were properly Spanish,' I mused, 'without those awful Wimpy-style cafeterias. They all speak Spanish among themselves anyway. But the shopkeepers fear for their low taxes and the local government wants to hang on to British subsidies. They won't so much as share the airport, even though it would be good for business.'

'Ridiculous!' said the red-haired lady, taking a swig of her gin and tonic, every inch a woman of the world. 'They would lose absolutely nothing. If the Spanish flag was allowed to fly alongside the British, with perhaps the European stars or whatever they are to add respectability, the Gibraltarians could have a permanent tax-free *feria* forever. But they are too thick to see it.'

Calling her children, she rose to go. We clinked glasses in favour of this happy outcome. Perhaps by the year 2000? More probably not. There was no accounting for people's stupidity, was there? Well, it was nice talking. '*Adiós, mucho gusto, buenas tardes . . .*'

The new road to Zahara would run across the great dam

when it was finished. In the meantime one had to drive down into the glaring pit under the grim grey barrier to emerge on the old road not far from where the Roman bridge had once stood. Numbered stone by stone, this had been conscientiously removed and preserved for posterity on some protected site. But it would never again perform one of its most important functions, which was to shelter herdsmen with their goats and pigs or travellers with their picnics from the heat of the day.

I could not help wondering how these changes would have affected Anita Richmond. She was an English girl, enamoured of Spain, learned in the history of the Reconquest, steeped in Prescott and Ford and adept with horses. In the late 1950s she set up in the *posada* of Zahara, organised treks on horseback for foreigners, and gave full rein to her romanticism about the area, but was unlucky both in health and in love: one day she rode onto the bridge of El Chorro, the great gorge of the Guadalhorce in the mountains above Málaga, and cast first her dog and then herself into its depths. These old places, innocently and indifferently wrapped in their history and associations, can have a powerful effect on an eager foreigner's imagination; when coupled with love betrayed, as in Anita's case, the effect can be devastating.

Her imagination had dwelt on Moors and Christians, the campaigns of the Reconquest, skirmishes and ambushes, heroic events from Zahara's past; mine on the other hand had been entranced by the neighbouring pueblo of El Gastor, which had seemed to me to qualify as the capital of Arcadia. Winding up out of the tortured river bed of the Guadalete, I now headed in its direction.

My first acquaintance with Arcadia was made as I returned from my journey to Osuna in the province of Seville back in the mid-sixties. After a long cross-country ride, passing through nothing larger than the hamlet of El Puerto de la Encina, I came to another tiny settlement, La Romera; there I got good directions to Coripe, where I

96

intended to spend the night. I only had two hours of daylight in hand, but the track was marvellous, a real *cañada* with a surface of hard beaten earth winding from farm to farm through gentle holm-oak-studded hills. The contours were soft and rounded; in many places corn was sown under the widely-spaced trees. In front of every farm a little girl tended a flock of turkey chicks. The sheep had recently lambed and the goats given birth to their kids. The whole valley was alive with the cries of young animals and the bells of bell-wethers. Mixed flocks of sheep and goats came browsing along the verges, herded by boys or youths in cloth caps and corduroys, equipped with staffs and slings, usually sided by a small curly-haired dog resembling an unkempt poodle, known as a *turco* hereabouts. This may well have been no closer to the Arcadia of the Elizabethan poets than to the original model in the harsh hinterland of the Peloponnese; but it was Arcadia enough for me.

Beyond hills and trees I glimpsed what appeared to be a great tower or castle on a crag, some twelve or fifteen kilometres away I guessed, with the sun sinking behind it. My expectations had been so heightened by the spell of the area that I assumed it was Coripe. Soon I had to slow from a jogtrot to a walk, and then dismount. There would be no moon for some hours and it was too dark to ride. I led my horse, Chico, with a small torch held downwards, forming a pool of light round his front legs, while I kept my eyes on the prickly but remote brilliance of the stars. Proceeding in this way, I lost all sense of time and place. The universe reduced itself to the stars, the feeble patch of torchlight, the crunch of my boots and Chico's hoof-beats. There was nothing else. Once, this trance-like state was disturbed by a meteor fizzing its brief course across a few degrees of firmament. It had no sooner come than gone, but I knew it was no illusion because the faintly luminous darkness into which it had erupted closed firmly again behind it, as if to demonstrate that it was unimpaired.

Coripe took me by surprise, and I stopped, bewildered, at

the beginning of the first ill-lit street. I found myself in a flat, neat, white, geometrical village. I wondered if the craggy keep had been a fantastic vision, the product of an over-stimulated imagination. When I got out the map later in the *posada*, I saw that it existed all right, but was called Olvera.

Riding next day over the southern slopes of the Sierra de Líjar, I reached a corral where a *capaor* was gelding pigs. I paused to watch him at it – not out of any morbid interest in castration, but because a few days before I had been asked whether this was *my* trade by a countryman unable to imagine why else I should be travelling by horse from farm to farm. I soon moved on, having seen enough of the little bleeding slits in the underbellies of the piglets, who were yelling fire, rape and murder into the unheeding stillness of the afternoon. I continued through Algodonales into a strange land of porphyry-hued earth, scarred everywhere by small landslides, through which snaked, accompanied by reeds and oleanders, the headwaters of the Guadalete.

Thus I came to El Gastor, which I immediately dubbed the capital of my Arcadia. It was the most rustic, the earthiest, the milkiest village of them all. Every house had a stable within a few paces of its low front doorway; every house stirred and breathed and clucked and snorted with animal life. In the house which took me in there were, right under the tiny room allotted me, two huge ruminating cows; I gathered they had been sold and would be collected next day. I was given armfuls of fresh-cut green barley, a great luxury for Chico, who misbehaved by stamping all night, keeping me awake almost till dawn. When I apologised the goodman of the house and his wife showed complete equanimity.

'We are used to it,' they smiled. 'It is nothing.'

Later the neighbours came by to complain, half in earnest, half in jest, about the sale of the cows that had hitherto provided their milk. This was no way to treat regular customers; Frasquita's cow had just dried up too; where would they get their milk from now, and how would they nourish their children? A great big cheerful raucous woman kept this up for nearly an hour. The wife of the house occasionally sighed and wondered gently what indeed they would now do for milk, but the husband, secure in the satisfaction of having effected a good sale, sat silent and inscrutable, allowing the women to chatter on.

As I paid them, I could see there was something on their minds. The man plucked up his courage.

'Are you a novelist, if it is not too much to ask?'

Having been taken for a *capaor*, and earlier for a pilgrim, I ought perhaps to have acknowledged this closer approximation to the truth. However, I discovered in myself a curious reluctance to admit to anything so artificial in this world innocent of artifice, and I denied being any such thing.

Now, after all these years it was to El Gastor that I returned. At first sight it looked very much the same. There were no discordant buildings. The place boasted a new swimming pool, a discotheque, an *alameda* with benches and a lawn overlooked by a not unpleasant housing estate; but these were all standard improvements for any self-respecting pueblo. The real difference was that the patios and yards that had previously housed so much animal life were all spotlessly sterile and clean, without a sign of their original occupants. In one of them, under a wide-spreading vine, a large, cheerful young man was preparing to open his new and expensively equipped restaurant, all lined with ornamental tiles, the next day. It was to be called 'El Gordo La Parra' in allusion to his own girth and the vine overhead. He was keen to show me round.

'Who are you aiming at?' I asked.

'Well, first at the local people. There are more than two thousand souls in El Gastor and there is nowhere to eat.'

'But surely you won't survive just on local trade?'

'No,' he admitted. 'This is a bit of a gamble. There is no tourism here at present. But the new road over the Zahara dam is going to pass just five kilometres from here, and with all the propaganda for 1992 . . . well, we'll see.'

When I had explained my interest in local history and customs, he sent a small girl to accompany me to the door of Don Manuel Nogales, a retired vet, who was the most studious person in the pueblo.

'He does go on a bit,' he warned me, 'but if that's what you want . . .'

Don Manuel was rather different from the reticent *ancianos* who were the repositories of information in most tiny villages. He was a perfect example of the provincial intellectual, as typified by Antonio Machado in *Poema de un Día*. He loved to talk, and took me out to coffee.

'I write a poem almost every day,' he said, thrusting one into my hand signed 'Veterín de la Sierra'.

I expressed admiration and astonishment.

'Oh, it is nothing. It just comes naturally.'

Don Manuel had also had some journalistic success with an article on flying saucers in the *ABC*. But above all, he assured me, he admired modesty, as represented by an auto-didact who was a knife-grinder in Málaga, whom he often consulted as the wisest man he knew. And he had a correspondingly strong dislike of the Spanish Nobel laureate for literature, Camilo José Cela, whose commercialism and greed he deeply deplored.

'He is just an *autobombo* (his own big drum) and he has created a commercial company which is just a publicity machine for himself. Even his son gets into print with a book called *Life With My Father*. It's all part of the same machine, like blaring "Coca-Cola. . . . Coca-Cola" indefinitely. It has the same effect.'

Don Miguel much preferred Miguel Delibes, who was more authentic and more 'Azoriniano' (after Azorín, the dry Castilian prose master of the generation of '98). Azorín, he said, had been asked by an aspiring author, who lived in a pueblo without museum or library or culture, how to begin. 'Have you a kitchen?' asked the maestro. 'Yes.' 'Does it contain an oil lamp and a mortar?' 'Yes.' 'Then go away and write about them.'

Don Manuel had a tendency to take off on enthusiastic mental voyages of his own, one of which concerned the peaceful co-existence of Christian, Moor and Jew in Albarracín up in Aragón during the eleventh century; it was quite hard to bring him back to El Gastor, but once on home ground again he was a mine of information and speculation. The region had been rich in classical times because of its tin mines. The name El Gastor might come from Castor and Pollux, the twin sons of Leda by Zeus, or simply from the Latin 'castro', a fort. The mistress of the famous Ronda bandit José María 'Tempranillo' had been a girl called Rosa from El Gastor. But Mérimée gave her the name Carmen for the story that was the basis of Bizet's opera, and then they made a film called *Carmen, la de Ronda*, which was a travesty . . .

All this misinformation, Don Manuel went on robustly, was the fault of foreign writers like Borrow and Ford, Gautier, Dumas and Mérimée, who had only been interested in '*La España de charanga y pandereta, cerrado y sacristía*' (Spain of the guitar and tambourine, the cloister and the sacristy), to borrow from Machado . . .

'They belonged to the Romantic movement,' I said. 'That is what they wanted from Spain.'

'Precisely. And it still persists. Worse than ever. All the guidebooks pander to it. And most of it is rubbish.'

Despite the sins of the foreigners in this respect, Don Manuel was enthusiastic about the idea of *turismo rural*, which went back to Franco's time but had never been developed as in Italy, France and Britain. The coasts were dens of vice and the package-tour visitors were increasingly fleeced, so there was bound to be a wave of reaction in favour of the interior. That could only be good for the economic life of the pueblos, provided vice and drugs were resisted. Recently, nineteen pueblos had got together to form an association of *pueblos blancos* with the object of getting assistance from central and regional government to expand their network of roads and lodgings. And, hey presto, here was his poem on that subject! It was cast in the loftiest of terms: first naming the 'most grave and principal' of the participating pueblos, including Ronda, then apostrophising the inhabitants as 'heirs of the imperial eagle' and telling them that *un hada*, their fate or destiny, had moulded them all into a great Christian family, or 'a fine white cloth for a great communion'. Finally, he harangued them with a dire threat: the white villages of Cádiz province at last had a solution for their human problems; if they failed to seize it, then let their fate come with its wand of office and pluck out their hearts!

Don Manuel wrote two other poems out for me in his copybook hand. The first was, I think, his poem of the day, though I am sure he had used the charming conceit with which it ended many times before: an angel, lighting on a place so white and clean, wanted to settle; but God would not permit this and the angel, winging his way tearfully back to Heaven, left the gentle breeze of his flight to play permanently on El Gastor's mountainside 'balcony'.

The second poem, which he had no doubt written out many times before, was called '*Esto es El Gastor*'. It was a simple list of attributes: rock, pines, sun, water, mineral waters, fresh mountain airs, the local pastries, black sausages, simple men, lovely women, a thousand balconies with a thousand carnations, old haunts of Moor and of Iberian man, hidden treasures, red-tinged sierras, bandits, ancient legends. This undifferentiated inventory or catalogue expressed pretty well every pueblo's idealised version of itself. It ended on the note that the Irippo of the Romans, now poor, was once rich. The 'riches to rags' ingredient in the mix is important to many places in decline, giving them some kind of residual tribal strength.

While we were still discussing these things over another coffee, El Gordo la Parra strode in.

'Your car started to roll down the hill,' he announced. 'You must have left the handbrake off.'

'Good God,' I cried, leaping to my feet. 'Where is it?' The street outside El Gordo's restaurant was steep.

'Have no fear,' he said, soothingly. 'Some men stopped it.'

I found the car had been manhandled into a side street and a stone wedged under one wheel. Several men were standing around, gesticulating.

'Just as well,' said one, 'that you left the window open so we could swing it into this dead end.'

'It might easily have hit someone, particularly a child,' said another. 'But between us we managed . . .'

I thanked them profusely, and with reason. When I got back to Don Manuel, he seemed quietly pleased.

'You see, they are not bad folk,' he said, as if he had been confirmed in something he had been telling me, though this had not been the subject of his discourse at all.

He took me out on the ground to prove to me that El Gastor was no miserable place without history or culture. First we went to the broad-fronted low-browed house of Rosa, the mistress of 'El Tempranillo', whose blank façade had a single stoutly-grilled window right up under the eaves. Then we went to the Casa de la Cultura, where the library was full of schoolchildren doing their homework under the keen eye of a lady teacher.

'They could do it elsewhere,' said Don Manuel, 'but it gives them a feeling for books just to be in here, surrounded by them. According to a recent survey only seven out of every thousand Spanish adults ever read a book. The hope is that these pupils will not follow that example. There are also adult literacy classes here every evening.'

At the end of the corridor we came to a room in which six or seven young ladies were gravely practising *sevillanas* to music from a tape. Their poise was somehow enhanced by their ordinary skirts or jeans, without the garish, swirling titillation of gypsy dress.

El Gastor these days has perfectly legitimate, even admirable, aspirations. But it was farewell to Arcadia.

◆

I was drawn next to Olvera, which I had visited several times since its first semi-magical appearance on my horizon, but had always left feeling I had failed to get to grips with its character. It had a reputation for religiosity, and as the next day was the feast of the Assumption of the Virgin, Olvera's most famous celebration, I had hopes that this time it would bare its soul. As the town would be crowded, I thought it would be wise to arrive early in order to get a room. Rather than weaving along the more agreeable and countrified route via Villalones, Setenil and Torre Aljáquime, I therefore took the short link from El Gastor to the main road and drove fast towards the spectacular silhouette which vies with any in Andalusia as a temptation to the camera seeking easy prey.

I was indeed only just in time to secure a bed in the new *hostal* on the outskirts; the forecourt was already packed with cars and families arriving from far and wide for the Virgin's day. I went first to the main street, which climbs steeply towards the keep. On the left is an esplanade, above which rises a natural outcrop of rock crowned by a monument to the Sacred Heart of Jesus, who stands aloft on his plinth with outstretched arms. Rustic paths and steps lead up, past a children's aviary of canaries and budgerigars, to the top. The statue, a standard religious image of the interwar years, is of no merit. The inscriptions are of the type whereby people make practical deals with God. One reads: 'All those who take communion on nine successive first Fridays in the month will be granted the grace of perseverance.' This seemed more a matter for one's diary than an invocation to any kind of fervour. But it was well known that the true goddess of the place was Nuestra Señora de los Remedios. It was in her honour that so many people were assembling. Accordingly, I lost no more time deciphering the arid messages around the base of the Christ figure and set off for her shrine, a couple of kilometres outside town on the road to Setenil.

The atmosphere of the sanctuary is very different from

Sanctuary of Nuestra Señora de los Remedios

the tightlipped Christianity implicit in the statue of the Sacred Heart. There is a roadside *venta* and restaurant across the way from the chapel, with good *tapas* and meals and provocative girlie posters. It plays loud music much of the time, but never in competition with the novenas, masses and other rites of the Church. During the public novena of the Virgin (the nine days leading up to the feast of a saint), the chapel doors are open from dawn to dusk and people drift in and out all day. Most of them buy one or more red candles from the shop in the cloister before going in to pray. Though middle-aged people, the majority of them women, predominate, the young are by no means absent. I watched a solitary girl in a T-shirt and cut-off jeans lighting and placing fat candles in front of one of the images; next a very handsome young couple hovered uncertainly in the wide-

105

open doorway, apparently in mild disagreement about whether to enter or not; they went in.

I settled in a pew near the back. The shrine of the Virgin of Remedies is attributed to the year 1400 or thereabouts. Originally she was seated, with the child on her lap, but now she is upright, standing within the upturned horns of a silver moon. In her right hand she bears a trident and with her left she rather awkwardly clasps the fully robed and crowned Jesus to her hip. This change in her posture may have been effected to bring her more into line with the popular imagery of an ascending or floating rather than a sedentary Virgin, which spread in the seventeenth century. Her whole figure with its richly embroidered robe and cloak is surrounded by a 'penumbra' of formalised rays or flames. There is a piquant contrast between her homely face and this aureole of almost barbaric splendour.

The chapel itself dates from about 1600. The walls are frescoed from dado to vault. Recently restored, they include scenes of the Virgin as 'Divine Shepherdess', supported by other worthies, some universal like Mary Magdalen, others of more local interest. These paintings are accompanied by inscriptions: we are told the name of the painter from Ronda who carried out their restoration in 1983; of the Pope and of the Bishop of Jerez of the time; and of the Chaplain of the Sanctuary, Don Juan Manuel de Caballero de las Olivas y Buzón (of whom more hereafter). On one side of the opening into the cloister, the Divine Shepherdess, with a country hat and crook, tells of the flock she adores and of her zest to embrace the whole human race, which can take refuge in her shadow from the infernal tyrant. But perhaps the most charming of the verses painted on the chapel walls is on the other side of this exit. It runs:

> He who seeks a good harvest
> Finds it in the grain.
> He who yearns for fine gold
> Delves in the mine.

> He who searches for Jesus
> Finds him in Mary.

My glance continued to stray over the walls and ceiling for more mural messages. Perhaps the most remarkable was wordless: an all-seeing eye in a triangle, surrounded by ears of corn, over a dove with spread wings.

Pondering this symbolism, I went into the cloister, which is simply a rather over-decorated patio, rebuilt during the early part of this century. The centre is filled with potted plants and ferns round a fountain. All the walls are covered with verses. I was so intrigued by these that I spent most of the afternoon copying them down. Much of one wall is taken up by the tale of the miraculous release of a Christian prisoner of Barbary pirates after eleven years in captivity, stressing one of the prime roles of the Virgin of Remedies, which was to rescue the hostages of those days. On the same wall is the miracle of the rain which finally fell after much supplication 'on the day of Quasimodo 1715' after a long and disastrous drought, through the intercession of the Virgin.

But the most persistent theme of all is the dogma of the Immaculate Conception of the Virgin, promoted here in popular terms. One set of verses runs: 'Being the Mother of God is so far from sin, Virgin, that either sin is good or you had it not; because it would hardly be decent if God, your beloved son, was conceived by you in innocence, but you were in sin begot. ' This is matched by another panel whose texts is: 'At your pure conception, grace struggled with sin, for both of them planned to occupy your dwelling place; so they set off on a race, but the fleetest of foot was grace; arriving first she opened the door and then locked it in sin's face.' These effusions may sound quaint, but the importance attached to the Immaculate Conception throughout Andalusia cannot be overestimated, and if disregarded can have frustrating results. For example, in seeking entrance to an enclosed convent, whether famous for its works of art or its cakes, the traveller will hear the nun inside intone, *'Ava María Purísima'*. If he fails to respond with the countersign, *'Sin Pecado Concebida'* (conceived without sin), he may well not secure admission.

With these things coursing through my mind, and with the aid of some books I had brought with me, I strove to familiarise myself that night with the two linked dogmas concerning the Virgin to which Olvera is so devoted: the Immaculate Conception and the Assumption. But first, why the cult of the Virgin at all, why the attachment to Mariolatry, a word pronounced with a shudder by Protestants and with pride by Spanish Catholics?

According to Américo Castro's interpretation of Spanish history, the cult of Santiago (Saint James the Great) and the famous pilgrimage to his shrine at Compostela in Galicia were vital adjuncts of the Reconquest. The early kingdom of León, and later the more vigorous and expansionist Castile, were equipped with a patron saint who (at least in his Iberian avatar) was Boanerges, son of thunder, riding into battle on his white charger in the sky above the Christian armies on the ground, guaranteeing victory over the Moors. From the battle of Clavijo in 822 till the fall of Granada in 1492 this belief persisted and was expressed in innumerable images of Santiago *Matamoros*, or Moorslayer, with the infidel writhing under the hoofs of his horse – as familiar a figure in Castilian iconography as Saint George and the Dragon in England and Catalonia.

However, well before the completion of the Reconquest, the mood was changing. King Alfonso the Learned (1253–1284) never even went to Compostela; he was more interested in the Virgin whom he exalted in his *Cantigas*. Then came the tender humanism of the fourteenth century, lovingly illustrated in so many Gothic statues of the Virgin and Child. With the retreat of the Moors civil society developed, allowing more space to the feminine principle. A new sensibility was abroad. During the Renaissance this grew apace. The Reformed Carmelites succeeded in persuading Philip III and the Pope to promote Saint Teresa of Avila as co-patron of Spain in 1618. She rose out of the dying embers of the belief in Santiago. In 1629 her co-patronage was declared an optional matter, but the longing for a female share in the religious pantheon prevailed: the Virgin of Guadalupe and the Virgin of the Column in Zaragoza became potent symbols, though they too (this being Spain) had their military honours, the former inspiring the Conquistadors and becoming patron of the Hispanic world, the latter spurring Aragonese resistance to Napoleon. Nor should one forget the Catalan Virgin of Montserrat, on whose altar Saint Ignatius Loyola laid his sword in the course of a long night's vigil before founding the Jesuits.

By now the Virgin was in Santiago's saddle. But what about the theology? The doctrine of the Immaculate Conception postulates that not only Christ himself, but his mother too was divinely conceived, without sexual intercourse: this view received a huge boost when it became a gesture of defiance against the rationalism of the Reformation, a true believer's blow for faith against empiricism and reason. The Reformed Church totally rejected any such superhuman exaltation of Mary as Counter-Reformation propaganda, which of course to some extent it was.

Yet the origins of the cult were much older. In the second-century apocryphal book of James, the conception and birth of the Virgin Mary were considered a special miracle of God: the electric impulse of life miraculously passed between her parents, Saints Joaquim and Anne, when they ran to meet one another; Mary was in effect a miraculous child born to parents in old age. The Greek Church accepted the immaculate birth, but with the *caveat* that Mary should only be venerated as mother of the Redeemer (Mariolatry must not get out of hand). The great Aquinas ruled that no one, not even Mary, could have been redeemed *before* the Redemption, for this would be tantamount to nullifying the sacrifice of the Cross: Mary had been conceived normally but sanctified in her mother's womb. The Dominicans, founded in the thirteenth century, followed Aquinas, but the Franciscans, whose less intellectual brand of piety kept them more in touch with popular feeling, pioneered the Immaculate Conception against the more learned and disputatious Black Friars. The cult was spread by the female wing of the Franciscans, the Poor Clares, throughout France, Savoy, Germany and Flanders; then it caught on in southern Europe, Sicily and Spain, where Mary tramples the serpent's head in a multitude of images: she is no party to the fall of Eve. From their foundation in 1534 the Jesuits also took up the cause.

Things came to a head in the early seventeenth century, and there were frequent and sometimes bloody clashes between Dominicans and Jesuits on the streets of Seville. In 1616 Pope Paul V forbade any discussion of the subject from the pulpit, and this was repeated by Gregory XV in 1622. Silence on the matter was imposed on all parties, with the exception of the sceptical Dominicans, who were permitted to pursue the truth, but strictly within their own four walls. None of this prevented the imagery of the Immaculate Conception from taking off in the hands of painters such as Pacheco, Zurbarán, Velázquez and above all Murillo. The Inquisition was therefore obliged to lay down rules for the depiction of this mystery: Mary had to be shown as a young girl, neither child nor woman, eyes rolling upwards, arms crossed over her breasts, treading either a crescent moon or the serpent or both; the horns of the moon were supposed to be turned downwards in deference to scientific knowledge that it was a solid, though painters usually disregarded this and turned the horns upwards for artistic effect. The most striking feature of these pictures is that the Virgin has lost the Child. Mary does not appear as primarily the *theotokos*, the god-bearer. She has become instead a goddess in her own right, floating among clouds and attended by trains of pages in the forms of *putti* or cherubim and seraphim gambolling around her.

It is not hard to see why the Papacy resisted all this as

long as possible. The official Trinity of Father, Son and Holy Ghost was threatened by a rival Trinity consisting of Saint Anne, the Virgin and Jesus, in which the female principle predominated and poor Saint Joaquim was dropped; Leonardo painted this holy triad three times, and other Renaissance painters followed suit. The cult would not die. Curiously, underlying the hierarchical structure of the Catholic Church, there runs a subterranean stream of democracy which in the long run gets its way. After centuries of resistance Pope Pius IX finally proclaimed the dogma of the Immaculate Conception in 1854. It received further popular confirmation when the Virgin, appearing to Bernadette of Lourdes, told her, 'I am the Immaculate Conception.' Bernadette did not understand this and wrote to the Pope about it. The Holy Father must have been much relieved to receive this simple endorsement of something that had caused so much learned wrangling and controversy, to say nothing of loss of life.

Some Catholic authors, notably Marina Warner, recoil from the dogma on the grounds that it denies the common bond of humanity between Mary and the rest of us, which is one of the springs of her great attraction. Warner writes: 'As the icon of the ideal, the Virgin conceived without sin underscores rather than alleviates the feeling of sinfulness. Any symbol that exacerbates that pain runs counter to the central Christian doctrine that man was made and redeemed by God . . . and is a continuing enemy of hope and happiness.' That was evidently not the view of the poets who composed those verses on the walls of the sanctuary of Olvera.

Non-Catholics who look askance at these things have criticised them for a different reason: they have sought to show that the cult of the Virgin is of pagan origin, and to link the worship of Mary with that of Diana of Ephesus, the Moon Goddess. Richard Ford in particular dwells at some length and with relish on the similarities between the Spanish Holy Week processions and those of the Phoenicians in honour of Astarte. Likewise, parallels are sometimes drawn between the Virgin mourning over the dead Christ and the sorrow of Venus over the death of Adonis. These connections, especially when traced by a British High Tory antiquarian like Ford, suggest a primitive streak in Spanish Catholicism which – it is implied – has long been rejected by the civilised world. But, looked at more objectively, they seem equally to demonstrate a certain genius in the early Church for the assimilation and transformation of pagan rites, a kind of syncretism that provided Christianity with a broader and more powerful base than any other religion.

The other, one might almost say the twin, dogma is the Assumption of the Virgin, which was to be celebrated in Olvera the following day. Known all over Andalusia as the day of 'the Virgin of August', it is the focal point of innumerable village fairs. Again, it has very early origins, probably going back to pre-Christian times. Within the Christian era the manner of the Virgin's passing became a matter of absorbing interest from the second century onwards. The feast day of 15 August to commemorate it was first proclaimed by the Emperor Maurice about the year 600. The medieval tradition of her 'assumption' draws on a number of eastern stories. Significantly there is never any mention of her *death* in any of these; she is *translated* to Heaven and the moment of her *transitus* is attended by the four men of the Bible who also transcended death, namely Enoch, Moses, Elijah and Jesus. Here a link with the Immaculate Conception is immediately apparent, in that she who was not corrupt at conception should not logically suffer corruption in the grave. But as with the other doctrine, it was many centuries before Mary's dramatic assumption into Heaven gained even guarded official acceptance. During the twelfth and thirteenth centuries she does not rise like a pillar of smoke, but expires on her bed and reappears in glory in a separate scene above; this is known as the *dormition*.

Aquinas, as usual, was chary of anything that threatened

the scholastic link between faith and reason, between Christian theology and Greek philosophy. He argued that the spirit could not exist without matter; it was the body and soul *together* that formed the unique individual. From this it followed that the reunion with the body at the resurrection was crucial to Christian belief – which could admit of no outlandish ideas about the migration of souls or reincarnation. Thus arose the great Christian *angst* about failing to be reunited with the body when the last trump sounded. In the light of this teaching it is clear that anything allowing Mary to bypass this process and this anxiety made her more of a deity, and reduced her humanity.

All the same, as the Renaissance advanced, so did hunger for a glorious and heroic Virgin. In this the classical tradition of the apotheosis of the hero played its part: even after embracing Christianity the Emperor Constantine continued to identify himself with the sun, and had coins struck which showed him grandly driving up to Heaven in a triumphal chariot. This theme of apotheosis was seized on by the great Renaissance painters: for example Lippo Lippi's 'La Madonna della Cintola' and Titian's 'Assumption', shortly to be followed by the popular 'Coronations of the Virgin' by Counter-Reformation artists such as El Greco and Velázquez. The Reformed Churches not unnaturally disputed the whole idea of an assumption, because they hated paying equal homage to mother and son.

As with the Immaculate Conception, so with the Assumption, it was popular pressure that finally forced the proclamation of the dogma. Nineteenth- and twentieth-century Mariolatry played a large part in this. Between 1849 and 1940 over three thousand cardinals, patriarchs and bishops petitioned on behalf of their flocks for the upgrading of the Assumption from an optional extra to the status of dogma; the same movement gave rise to dozens of international Marian conferences. When Pius XII finally made the announcement from the balcony of Saint Peter's on 1 November 1950, nearly a million people received the news with rapturous applause and tears of joy.

For anyone bred outside the Marian tendency of the Catholic Church the overwhelming impression, when contemplating these long cycles of opinion and belief culminating in populist concessions by the High Priest, can only be one of awe at the continuing vitality and evolutionary power of Catholicism in general, and its Hispanic branch in particular. Materialism, corruption, sin, forgiveness, relapses, mediation, redemption, spirituality, ecstasy are all somehow accommodated in this capacious cosmos. The deepest springs of the human psyche have been adroitly tapped by those who irrigate the pastures of the faithful. This is not the same as saying that religion is the opiate of the masses, with the pastors as pushers; for the masses too have played their part in fashioning the faith.

Early in the morning of the feast of the Assumption tremendously loud voices pierced my slumber in the *hostal*. Rising and throwing open the window (closed not in breach of the British fresh-air ethic but against mosquitoes) I saw that they came from the Bar Baena across the road, where countrymen, stopping for a coffee or *aguardiente* on their way out to the fields on their 50cc motorcycles, declaimed or disputed in tones that might have woken the dead. By way of contrast the symmetry and purity of church and fort rising against a pearl-coloured sky seemed a perfect symbol of Saint Augustine's City of God.

I dressed and went down to Baena's. Despite the ear-splitting racket made by his early morning customers, he himself was a soft-spoken man of measured utterance.

'This is a good pueblo . . . you can still leave your door open here. Yes, life is much better than it was. There can be no doubt of that. The *miseria*, the terrible poverty, has gone. The municipal council? Socialist – they haven't done a bad job, but the authorities can't do everything. It has to be through all our efforts . . . Yes,' he repeated solemnly as he polished a glass, 'through all our efforts.'

Did religion play an important part? He shrugged – the inimitable Spanish shrug. With some yes, with others no. You didn't need to be religious to be a good neighbour, which was the important thing.

I lunched in the *venta* opposite the sanctuary. The juke-box music had given way to the sanctuary's loudspeaker which broadcast the pure, monotonous voice of a nun reciting over and over again throughout the afternoon the attributes of the Virgin: *'Bendita eres entre todas las mujeres . . . Madre y Virgen . . . Bendita eres . . .'* and so on, without cease. Gradually the numbers swelled to fill the little church and then the forecourt; the parked cars stretched in lengthening file back towards Olvera and on towards Torre Aljáquime. When I joined the throng, it was impossible to see through to the altar and the liturgical acts. But the priest's voice came over strong and clear and gravelly. I imagined an older man than he turned out to be when I was finally able to glimpse him above the heads of the crowd, as he washed his utensils after the communion service. In his address he claimed that this was the oldest feast of the Christians in honour of the Virgin, who was received *immaculate* into Heaven. Having thus linked the two great Andalusian tenets, he went on to say that the belief was not confined to Spain but extended to the rest of Europe, Africa, the Americas and indeed to the whole universal Catholic Church. He said that the image of the Virgen de los Remedios had been in the community for six centuries and had gone through many vicissitudes, but the pueblo had always treasured and defended it; Olvera was thus held in special esteem by Mary as a 'beloved pueblo'.

To the hundreds of people listening to him, the preacher was clearly an authoritative and charismatic figure. He reminded them towards the end of his sermon that in two years' time it would be the twenty-fifth anniversary of the Coronation of the Virgin of Olvera by special decree of the Pope, and they must start preparing for this now; they must celebrate the anniversary not just with a single feast day, but with an entire jubilee year. Then he took them into his confidence: people sometimes said that he was very 'egotistical and individualist' and wanted to direct everything himself. He valued these criticisms from the pueblo; he learned from them and took them to heart; in proof whereof he summoned all interested persons to a general meeting to put in hand the necessary arrangements, and he earnestly hoped for widespread participation in a programme of Christian action that would be worthy of Olvera. This frankness about himself went down well, and there was a buzz of approval; he had them eating out of his hand. From these remarks I gathered that he was not, as I had first guessed, a visiting dignitary but the chaplain of the place, Don Manuel de Caballero de las Olivas y Buzón, whose name was so conveniently recorded along with those of the Pope and the Bishop of Jerez on the walls of his church. Intrigued by his personality and his approach to his flock, I decided there and then to seek an interview with him as soon as possible.

After the service the Virgin was at home to her devotees. She is displayed in a raised *camarín* like the famous Virgins of Montserrat and Guadalupe. This is a little chamber with a revolving platform; normally she is facing the congregation, but when her robes need to be changed she can be swivelled back into her dressing room before returning once again to shed her radiance on her worshippers. On feast days like this the faithful, or the merely curious, can climb a flight of steps and file past her. Some pause in front of her and cross themselves, others sink to their knees. Occasionally a man strolls by the glittering image, self-consciously aloof, in the tow of his wife. The women tend to linger and touch the Virgin's hem or finger her embroidery or, if accompanied by a child, to lift it up to touch the Christ Child's robe. Having paid their respects in this way, families gather and gossip in the forecourt or cross the road to the *venta*, which is so packed that it is hard to get a drink.

◆

By telephone from the *hostal* I was lucky enough to be able to arrange a meeting with Don Juan Manuel for the following day. He welcomed me in the cloister and took me into his panelled study, furnished with chintz chairs and a good big work table rather than a formal desk; it had the air of a schoolmaster's study. No, it was a good time; I was not disturbing him. During term he taught in the mornings at the *Instituto*, but now it was the holidays.

Olvera's population? Fairly steady: it had increased from nine thousand to eleven thousand over twenty-five years. The most significant factor was the steady decline in emigration.

'Really?' I said. 'I thought the economy of the pueblos still depended very largely on the remittances of the people working abroad . . . or perhaps in Barcelona.'

'That used to be the case. Half the active male population, say two thousand men, worked abroad when I first came here. That has all been changed by the co-operative movement. There are twenty-two co-operatives here, and Olvera has the highest proportion of co-operators of any pueblo in Andalusia. Mostly they employ from ten to twenty people, but some are bigger. The strongest are in agriculture and *piensos*, animal feedstock. But there are other producer co-ops in bricks, canning, clothing (four of these), cheese and honey.'

I told him that in Britain the co-operative movement had been a failure. So how had its success come about out here? Through government stimulus? Tax advantages?

'There has been some government help,' he acknowledged, 'especially for agriculture. But really it all springs from the co-operators. The first years are tough; there is little to distribute and there are bank loans to pay off. But there has always been a tradition of saving here, and the work ethic is still very much alive.'

'That is normally associated more with northern and Protestant Europe than with Andalusia.'

'Ah,' said Don Juan Manuel, 'but there's another thing to

117

note about Olvera. There are no big landowners up here, no idle *señoritos*. Instead we have *pelentrines*, small proprietors; down on the coast they call them *mayetos*, here *pelentrines*; and no one can say they are not hard-working – by whatever name they call them. Nor do they like debt.' He paused. 'After them, there are some *braceros*, landless labourers who go down to the plains for the harvests, but they are now very few.'

'What about the younger generation?'

'Most of the co-operatives' members *are* young. Some of our youth goes to Ibiza for the tourist season to work in the hotels and so forth for five or six months a year. There is a tradition of that. But they come back and invest in the pueblo.'

'It sounds too good to be true,' I said. 'What about their morals?'

He smiled in a worldly-wise but slightly deprecating way.

'One has to admit that the sexual ethic has changed. But that of course is general . . . the sixth commandment is not the best observed in Christendom.'

'Drugs?'

'Yes, there is a problem in Ronda, I know. But less here. There may be thirty to thirty-five addicts in Olvera, mostly *porreros*, users of cannabis.'

'What do they have for entertainment? Discos? A swimming pool? Those things seem to be the minimum required to hold the young.'

'Yes, those certainly, and *pubs*, six of them I think.'

I knew these were really in the disco category, with cocktails and dance-floors and usually no food: the traveller should not expect pub 'fayre' or ploughman's lunches.

'I'm afraid,' I went on, 'I've only asked you economic and social questions. What about religion? Olvera has a religious reputation, doesn't it? Is that due principally to this sanctuary . . . and to the monument to the Sacred Heart in the town?'

'Yes, they call that "El Santo de la Alameda". It was put

up in 1929 by Jesuits promoting the cult of the Sacred Heart, taken down in 1933 under the Republic and re-erected in 1939 after Franco's victory. It has been rather subject to political fashion.'

'And it's no rival to the Virgen de los Remedios?'

'Well,' he answered diplomatically, 'she has been here since the fourteenth century. She was in the town for a hundred years and then she was brought out to this place by the Padres Trinitarios.'

'How much of her is original?'

'Her face and hands, which have close affinities with the Virgen de los Reyes in Seville. They too restored their image recently – against a great deal of local opposition, but it had to be done.'

'And is the cult as strong as ever here? Are the young interested?'

'Well, I am biased,' he grinned, 'but I would say yes. Most of the ex-votos you see by the shrine are forage caps of young soldiers, not the offerings of the elderly.'

'But don't people increasingly use the Church just as a service industry for births, marriages and deaths?'

'They do that, certainly. But confirmation is also taken seriously. Some are coming forward now at seventeen and eighteen.'

'As late as that? I always think of children of ten or eleven, the little boys in sailor suits and the little girls dressed up as brides.'

'The recommended minimum these days is fourteen. And then of course you get young mothers-to-be joining pre-baptismal classes.'

'Perhaps they just come for your charisma.'

He deflected this deftly.

'I'll tell you one thing. The Jehovah's Witnesses don't get very far here. They are too keen on people's pockets, asking first for 10 per cent of their earnings and then raising their demand to 50 or 60 per cent. That doesn't go down well here at all. It touches where it hurts, in the pocket. And I can tell you something else. There isn't a single house in Olvera without a Virgin, whether a figure or a picture, and that includes the atheists. I know them all, and they say, "I don't believe in God, but the Virgin is different." They see her as something belonging to the pueblo, like the castle. And even those who go for the civil marriage ceremony still come straight here to be photographed with the Virgin. So you see, it's her they all come for, not me!'

I expressed surprise that the Virgin should be so universally popular in a region which had been famous for its Anarchism and church-burning.

'You have to be very careful about anarchism in Andalusia,' he said after some thought. 'For example, the Anarchists didn't burn a single one of the forty-three churches in my home town, Sanlúcar de Barrameda. And the same was true in Trebujena and even in Jerez, where the concentration of capital was a tremendous problem and still is: Jerez is the breeding ground of the classical *señorito andaluz*. But many anarchists were cultured people, respectful of others, very puritanical – which leads to fanaticism of course. Yet the churches were spared. And up here in Olvera there was very little of it anyway.'

'I have heard that Communism is still firmly entrenched in some pueblos such as Alcalá de Valle,' I said. 'And that is not very far off.'

'Yes, and in Pruna. But they have a mentality still anchored in '36.'

'Stalinists?'

'Leninists, I would say. Completely closed mentalities.'

'And there is none of this in Olvera? You mentioned the atheists.'

'They are not political. Olvera is not very political. It is a nest of ants, very industrious. Even the beggars have savings accounts: we have three or four professional beggars.'

'Do people suffer them gladly?'

'They know they are genuinely unfortunate and, yes, they give.'

'What about consumerism?'

'It hasn't taken off . . . it is very limited. They don't want debt.'

'You seem to be painting a picture of a rather noble, co-operative, self-disciplined people, preserving moral and spiritual values.'

'Yes, I am. And that has its drawbacks too. They are more closed in and less folkloric . . . I mean they do not live their folklore as people do in Huelva and Cádiz, where every child can dance a *fandango* or a *sevillana* from the age of three . . . and they are on the whole more outgoing. In some ways people are more authentic up here. But this has its limitations. Ronda is the same.'

'Ronda is a larger Olvera?'

'Well, obviously it is more commercial. But, yes, you could say that. The *serranos*, the people of the sierras, *are* different from those on the coast.'

I found this comforting. I sensed that I should not stretch his patience much further, but there was one other query I wanted to press.

'Finally,' I said, 'tell me about the cloister and its verses.'

'Well, the cloister was originally of the same period as the church and it was covered with paintings of the apocalypse. By the beginning of this century it had fallen into ruin, and the then chaplain, who people still remember affectionately as "Pa' José" [Papa Joseph], had it pulled down and replaced with the patio we now have, which was finished in 1917.'

'But the verses must be much older.'

'Yes, *El Cautivo* [The Captive] is old; it stems from a mission of the Trinitarians to redeem hostages from Islam.'

'Some of the others have a fifteenth-century feel about them . . . like rustic versions of the work of Jorge Manrique or your namesake, the Prince Juan Manuel . . .'

'No, you are being too literary. They are popular local *coplas* collected by Pa' José. They could not be as early as you say because they are notably *concepcionistas* in inspiration.'

'You mean they celebrate the Immaculate Conception?'

'Exactly. And that did not become a dogma till 1854.'

I recalled my reading on the matter.

'But surely the movement for it had existed centuries before that.'

'That is true, but I think you are showing excessive anti-quarian zeal. Undoubtedly the verses are based on popular tradition, but I doubt if they were collected together and written down in this way until Pa' José came along.'

Our talk was coming to its close.

'All in all, is Olvera's reputation for religiosity justified?'

'Are you asking me for statistics? Well, for instance, I can tell you we have only 2 per cent of separations or divorces locally against 6 per cent for all Spain and many more in your country.'

'I was wondering more about the general texture and style of life.'

'Look,' he said, with his first sign of impatience, 'this place has been Christian *longer* than many parts of Andalusia. Andalusian Christianity is different from that of Castile, because it arrived much later. But it came here to Olvera over 150 years *before* it came to Ronda and Setenil, which are our near neighbours. They were not recaptured till the 1480s by the Catholic Monarchs, but *we* had been liberated by Alfonso XI in 1327 . . . as I have said, a century and a half earlier. From then on Olvera remained on the Christian side of the frontier while pueblos only a few leagues off were still Moorish. All this counts, you know, in the psyche of a people.'

I thanked him for giving me so much time and for talking to me so frankly; it was a quality I had noted in him from the moment I heard him preach and I said as much.

On the way out we paused by a commemorative plaque to Pa' José which read:

José Maria Campos Gil
Padre Campos

Sacerdote de Jesucristo
Que sembró la semilla
de Dios en nuestra
Comunidad de Olvera
Amor y nada mas!
Olvera 1980

'You know,' said Don Juan Manuel as he bade me fare-well, 'there is more good than bad in the world, and much more love than one supposes. The headlines are grabbed by the things that go wrong, not by the very many that go right.'

Coming from a man of God who seemed to me refresh-ingly hard-headed and no sentimentalist, I was cheered by this opinion.

In the afternoon I went to the bulls. There is no permanent ring at Olvera, so a portable one resembling a circus arena without the big top is set up on the outskirts. The shady side was crowded when I arrived, but I managed to squeeze myself in; the seats in the sun were more thinly populated. We were to see a *festival taurino*, a bullfight without moun-ted picadors, whose performers wear *traje corto* or country dress instead of the fancy 'suit of lights'. Though the bulls are *novillos*, less than four years old, or rejects from a formal *corrida*, fully-fledged matadors may and do take part, some-times for practice, sometimes for charity, sometimes, as on this occasion, for money. But novices are also admitted. Gone are the days when Belmonte and other aspirant bull-fighters could acquire their skills only by practising illicitly by moonlight with cows and bulls on the ranches. Now there are a number of *escuelas taurinas* which young enthusiasts attend in their spare time from school or work. Today the school of Jerez was presenting one of its prodigies.

After the procession and the sounding of the trumpet the senior matador, Currillo, arrogantly tossed his flat-crowned *cordobés* hat onto the sand where he intended to kill the bull, but it fell brim down, which was bad luck. Touching

Provoking the bull

his eye to ward off evil, he flipped it over deftly with his foot, but the damage was done. He had drawn a big, strong, animal, which knocked him down and trampled him, drawing from him an outraged response in the shape of some showy passes, but he took several thrusts to kill. The indulgence of the public during pueblo fights is such that he was awarded two quite undeserved ears. The next matador, Lozano, got three good *naturales* out of his bull (natural passes are those with the *muleta* held in the left hand, the area of lure no longer extended by the sword, which is held in the right) but that was about all, because his opponent was *flojo de remos*, as they say of bulls that are weak in the quarters, and was constantly collapsing on the ground. Despite five *descabellos* (attempts to sever the spinal cord with a special weapon when the bull refuses to die from the main *estocadas* or sword thrusts) he received an ear for his labours. The third bull was for Pepe Luis Vázquez, bearer of a famous name with a gentlemanly style but not much mastery over the animal. He cut his own hand on his blade going in to kill and had to be bandaged up with a handker-

A natural pass

chief. He followed up this feat with several *pinchazos* (thrusts which do not enter deeply or hit bone). Mercifully, he despatched the beast with his first *descabello* and was then hurried off to the mobile medical unit. These Jerezanos are not exactly famous killers, I thought.

The afternoon picked up with the performance of Pepe Luis Martín, the latest sensation from Ronda. His bull was not the best, but he got plenty out of it. His capework was close and classical, neatly wound up by the obligatory curlicue, the *media verónica*. He placed his own *banderillas* (left to their assistants by the others). In the final act with the *muleta* he managed good right-handed passes, *derechazos*, and extracted several linked *naturales* from an animal none too keen to co-operate. He then embroidered his *faena* (as the whole work with the *muleta* prior to the kill is called) with a variety of decorative passes, including the eye-catching *manoletina*. The crowd showed its approval by chanting: '*toreró . . . toreró . . . toreró*' with the stress of the word deliberately misplaced onto the final syllable, a mark of high approval. He killed with one *pinchazo*

125

which hit bone, one *estocada* up to the hilt and one *descabello*. In this rural setting and in a climate of hitherto disappointed expectations it was good enough to get him an ovation, both ears and the tail.

The fifth and last bull was for the fifteen-year-old wonder, Rafael Osorio, whose juvenile exaggeration of the matador's traditional *sang-froid* and *hauteur* had an undeniable charm. Having saluted the crowd, he dropped his hat on the sand as Currillo had done, but this time it fell the right way up and the public cheered. It also cheered his *larga cambiada*, the spectacular knee-pass with which he received the bull, as well as his attempts at long, slow *derechazos*, though he lost the *muleta* more than once. Turning to the natural pass, he was less than fortunate: like many of his elders and betters running into difficulties with this touchstone of the classical repertoire, he tended to switch to a hasty *pase de pecho* or chest-pass to sweeten his failures. But the great thing in a pueblo fight is to show willing, and this young Rafael certainly did; he was awarded both ears despite an unholy number of *descabellos* in the gloaming. The only actors to have performed impeccably were the two handsome yoked mules who dragged each bull out of the ring in a fine dusty stampede, urged on by their proud and cheerful owner cracking his whip expertly over their glossy rumps.

The last bull was killed in failing light. When we emerged, I judged it finally cool enough to make the ascent to the top of the town. The fort is one of those fangs of masonry more memorable from a distance than at close quarters. The basilica is a fine Baroque pile of standard design whose twin towers soar above the steep white streets with their biscuit-coloured tiles. Looking down on this roofscape, I was suddenly struck by the abruptness of the edge of the town, the lowest streets forming a clear-cut frontier with the *campo*, which was enhanced now by the fairground lights strung out along them. Beyond there was nothing but billowing darkness stretching away unimpeded to the distant clusters of light marking Zahara, Grazalema and Setenil, where the ocean of night washed up against other equally well-defined perimeters. There were no islands of illumination in between. In the whole area bounded by Málaga, Algeciras, Cádiz and Seville there were fewer inhabitants than in the London borough of Southwark – and everyone who could, landowners and labourers alike, withdrew from the countryside every night into one of the old fortified settlements (of which Olvera was the largest hereabouts) just as they had in medieval times. If anything, with the arrival of the electric light and the car, the town was more of a magnet than ever before.

Did this mean that the Spaniards enjoyed a special sense of community? Or was it merely the primitive urge of a scattered people in a large landmass to huddle together for mutual strength and security behind or beneath ancient walls? There might be something in that, but it had always seemed to me that there was more as well: there was the Spanish love of crowds, as instanced in the *paseo*, the evening promenade, in which the individual and the collective both found expression – couples and their children striving to shine while enjoying at the same time the sensation of a larger whole, which might be the *barrio* or *quartier*, the pueblo, the town or the city. Without a certain pooling of consciousness it is impossible for any so-called 'community' to flourish. But there is an obverse side to this, and those who lament the loss of community in Britain and elsewhere should reflect on it: it is not only a question of co-operating and belonging, because implicit in the community idea are strong urges to criticise, comment and compare. Once the gossips get under way, all privacy flies out of the window.

Olvera's main street is neat and stern and there were few people about, most having been drawn towards the fair. As I walked back down the hill, I remarked on the householders' curious habit of hanging their refuse-bags and buckets from their window grilles, which must have been anathema to the local tourist board. Indeed, the handsome façades, some

127

with grand porticoes, made few concessions to the floral trimmings beloved of the brochures. The place was not tipping its hat to the tourist, and I respected it for that. The refuse policy was almost certainly designed – and well-designed – to defeat scavenging dogs. Olvera was clearly a place with a collective mind of its own. But conformity, I was pretty sure, would be paramount, deviations frowned on and the all-seeing eye of the sanctuary reproduced even more powerfully in the pueblo: both the virtues and vices of 'community' would be strongly in evidence.

By now I was down at fairground level. As if to reinforce the message that it is a serious pueblo, Olvera has a serious fair: five nights till dawn of stalls, bars, swings and round-abouts, sideshows and spectacles of song and dance. This is all strung out along two wide streets at the foot of the town, stretching for nearly a kilometre in one direction and almost as far along another branch. When I reached the scene, the *paseo* was beginning to get into its stride: for the fairground with its dippers and the dodgems, the mountebanks with their patter and their wares, are barely more than a theatri-cal backdrop for the human throng that swells and sways and stops to converse and saunters on well into the small hours.

On either side of the main promenade, dispersed among the various attractions, are the *casetas* or private tents put up by a sporting club, a political party, a group of friends or workmates, indeed any association able to pay for the privi-lege of a stand of its own. From them the members watch the world go by and, just as importantly, are observed sitting at their ease, a little apart from the hurly-burly, with their half-bottles of iced sherry and their *tapas* and their daugh-ters clad in flounced flamenco dresses and their little boys in the *traje corto* of the *toreros*. Thus they watch and are watched. This may seem the community at its most relaxed; on the contrary, it is at its most alert and self-conscious. This is when it becomes clear who is up and who is down, who is in and who is out. Five days of new dresses, pressed trousers, clean white shirts are not within the reach of all, to say nothing of the flashing of well-filled wallets in the bars and clubs. But five days and nights of well-regulated orgy was what the citizens of Olvera had decided they could and should afford; the size and category of the pueblo demanded no less; so they went about it with customary confidence and determination. I limited my participation to the night of the bullfight: as an outsider I did not have to demonstrate the same staying power or the length of my purse.

Next morning, before leaving, I tried to collect my impressions. The visual clarity of the place was certainly important: it fulfilled a longing for simple definition, absence of sprawl, clarity of purpose, precision of character. There stood the basilica, the fort, the Santo de la Alameda, the sanctuary of the Virgin and the grain silo, all skirted by the slopes of olives and fields of stubble. The fair would continue for another three nights at exactly the same pitch of intensity; then it would stop, the attractions would move on to the next pueblo, and Olvera would swiftly revert to normal, almost as if it had never been; there was a time and a place for everything.

If ever one wanted a community which functioned efficiently, commanded respect and gave satisfaction to its people, this was it. Ronda had burst out of these old bonds and lost this clear-cut quality. It had become diffuse, dispersed, unbuttoned, frayed at the edges, a bit of a mess. Olvera, therefore, had much to recommend it. But, as Don Juan Manuel had said, there were also the drawbacks of a closed society. Olvera posed and perhaps magnified the problem faced by all of us who seek the simple, classical refuge of the Mediterranean dream. Can we take it in its undiluted form (where this still exists)? Would we not in all honesty be better off in an urbanisation on the coast with tasteful villas in the Andalusian style? Perhaps. Yet the itch for the authentic remains extremely strong. On my score-card I gave Olvera Beta double-plus. That is a good mark in an exam, but not quite high enough when you are looking for a home.

5

THE ISLAND EFFECT

One thing that might have changed Olvera was the railway that never was. I had forgotten all about it until I stopped a kilometre or two out on the road to Pruna for a last look back. My eyes lit on the derelict railway station on the hillside down below the grain silo. On my ride to Osuna in the sixties I had crossed the phantom line several times, and had become so intrigued with it that I swore to follow it one day from start to finish – something I had never done, which goes to show the unwisdom of such pledges, especially when committed to print.

The project, conceived and begun under the dictatorship of General Miguel Primo de Ribera (1923–29) was for a branch line from Almárgen (on the main Madrid–Algeciras route) via Olvera, Coripe, Puerto Serrano, Bornos and Arcos de la Frontera to Jerez. The object was to give the economy of the sierras an outlet both towards the bay of Cádiz and the bay of Algeciras – thus linking it with the commerce of the great world. Alas, no train ever ran. The tracks, where they were laid, were torn up and sold; the cuttings and embankments slowly reverted to nature. But the long tunnels through the Sierra de Líjar and the Sierra Vaquera were presumably indestructible. Olvera's station too still stood, a little more decayed than in the sixties but with platforms and sidings clearly defined: platforms on which no red-capped stationmaster had ever unfolded his flag or blown his whistle, and the goods yard from which not a single item of freight had ever been collected or delivered. It was surprising they had not been pulled down, for they were a monument to a story of unhappy memory.

My first informant about the railway was an elderly barber who shaved me during my ride. The *golpe de estado* of Don Miguel took place, he recalled lovingly, on 13 September 1923. Those were good years, the best he could remember. Don Miguel enjoyed considerable popularity in his native Andalusia, not least as an all-too human statesman who would sometimes retire for two or three days to a shooting-lodge for a drinking bout with friends or an affair with a mistress before emerging, refreshed, to resume the conduct of the government. Don Miguel had made the roads, the barber continued, and provided work building them. Don Miguel had backed the railway. It was a beautiful idea, that railway; it would have been the finest scenic line in Spain. Then the politicians conspired to get rid of Don Miguel, whom they had always hated because he ran things so well without them; one year later they had got rid of the king as well. The work on the railway had been stopped when it was almost finished and never resumed under the Republic; the people of Olvera had been defrauded of their dream.

'Of course,' said the barber after a pause, 'they murdered him. They murdered Don Miguel.'

I looked at him, astonished.

'I always understood that he died in France shortly after his fall.'

'He was poisoned,' said the old man solemnly.

'By whom?'

'Why, by the politicians – who else? – who feared he might return and send them all packing. I have been told by people who know. There is no doubt they poisoned Don Miguel.'

If the railway had been finished and put into operation, it is an open question what effect it would have had on the economy of the interior. Olvera would probably have become even more industrious, thrifty and self-important, but the district's products would have remained essentially the same, and the local hegemony of Jerez was already long established. The result in Ronda, which did manage to get its station on the main line to Algeciras, was a small influx of tourists and lady watercolourists carrying their Baedekers, and of officers from the Gibraltar garrison; at the same time there was a large increase in contraband from the Rock, with the opposite effect on local industry to that desired.

Pruna is a curious place, flat but overhung by an old tower on a great crag. I knew it had a strong Communist element and that Communists had run the pueblo for some years, though I was not sure if they were still in power. I arrived on a Sunday morning. The church is 13 Plaza de la Libertad – deliberate malevolence of a Communist town council? It was well filled for Mass, mainly with women, though unusually there was a man at the back with a little dog, which escaped and went nosing around the pews. Its owner calmly retrieved it and returned to his seat, under which he obliged it to lie down for the rest of the service. Though the devotions themselves are solemn, the Andalusians treat their churches with pleasing familiarity. When the service was over a number of women remained chatting inside rather than brave the noonday sun. I circulated on a tour of inspection. The church is garnished with old altars and images, so presumably was not sacked. The pillars are – a rarity – of oval section. There are modern murals, including a Last Supper on the rear wall and a horrid painting under the vault of a great pink hand holding a slumped grey corpse in its outsize fingers: an unfortunate version of the Resurrection, if that is what is intended. The Virgin is robed in blue and treads a silver moon, very much in line with the old Inquisition ruling, which – though no longer mandatory – dies hard.

I had heard there was a famous *romería* from Pruna to a shrine in the hills above the town, and determined to discover more about it. The nearest bar, prominently displaying the hammer and sickle, did not look promising territory, so I moved on to the main bar where the buses stopped. Yes, said the landlord, there was indeed an annual *romería* to the Santuario del Navazo; it always took place on the first Sunday in May. He flicked through the calendar and calculated that next year's would be on 6 May. Everyone from the pueblo went, and people came from as far as Ronda and Osuna. I should make a point of not missing it. Which way was I going now? Towards Algámitas and El Saucejo, I said. Then I would pass the place; I could not mistake it. If I looked through the iron grille I would see a very realistic-looking tree with three stuffed doves. Strange, I said, for a wayside shrine to have no saint, only doves. He shrugged: the Virgin was carried up from the town and for the rest of the year people felt the doves were sufficient.

Having answered my questions helpfully enough, the man asked if I was German. No, I said, English. He had been in Germany for eleven years, he told me, working in a factory making aluminium window and door frames. Yes, there had been others from Pruna with him; that was what made it bearable – and of course the German foreman spoke good Spanish too. Germany was excellent in many ways, particularly for its health and social services, but the *ambiente* was cold, frigid. Eventually he had had enough of it: Germany for the Germans! But emigration had declined sharply all round, had it not? Yes, he agreed, though there were still many working in Seville, Madrid and Barcelona. Did they come back? Yes, they all came back for their holidays and many to retire. It remained to be seen what the next generation would do, but those of middle age and upwards were completely loyal to the pueblo. Population of Pruna? Four or five thousand. (I thought that sounded exaggerated.) Local administration? He grinned. After Franco they had had *Las Derechas*, the Right; then for eight years the Communists;

now the PSOE . . . but it was all the same. The only important thing was to have a good mayor who got things done for the pueblo.

Walking out into the main square, I saw that the *agrupación local* of the PSOE, the government party, had a bar in the far corner, in competition with the Communists. People probably drifted none too ideologically between these places of conversation and refreshment. A more important point about Pruna seemed to me its evident link with Germany – other pueblos I recalled had forged similar links with France or Switzerland. These small towns appeared to cling to a particular foreign connection, enabling groups of companions to go together and maintain a small expatriate colony. This obviously helped to preserve the unity and identity of the pueblo and to ensure its survival, which would have been more severely threatened by a wider diaspora.

The road from Pruna to Algámitas skirts the fortress hill and then climbs steeply to the Santuario del Navazo. Peering through the wrought-iron gate, one can see an alcove painted with clouds and *putti,* clearly intended to house a Virgin, but instead of her image there is only a mock tree, perhaps of papier-mâché, on whose branches perch the three doves I had heard of in the town. Pondering this, the explanation for it suddenly came to me. The best way to accommodate everyone in Pruna and to allow the Communists to join the annual pilgrimage (which was also a great community picnic) was to compromise on the doves, which were not only a Christian symbol but had been sanctified for the Communists by Picasso. What an imaginative solution! As to the patron saint with whom they toiled up from the parish church . . . well, she was the property of all, regardless of politics or belief or the lack of it, just as at Olvera. I was reminded of the anecdote of which there are many versions, Irish as well as Spanish, of the 'free-thinker' who proudly proclaims: 'Thanks be to God and his most blessed mother, I am an atheist.'

Turning from the sanctuary to the landscape, I saw that little if anything had changed in that respect in the quarter of a century since I had written from the adjacent Loma de la Cordillera:

> At each stop I looked over an ever-widening, more improbable panorama. The silhouettes and rock formations would seem exaggerated in illustrations to a fairy-tale. The whole area partakes of this strange air of fantasy. It starts really at Ronda with the *tajo* and the paper cut-out skyline of the peaks above Montejaque and Grazalema; it is continued at Pruna whose savage rock, crowned with broken fortifications, cows the dull village underneath; it is evident at Zahara, a rather better Pruna, whose fort shelters the tight agglomeration of houses like white chickens under its granite wing; it culminates at Olvera, whose outline of dark keep and twin-towered church, seen from any angle, almost defies belief . . . the crag is so sheer, the keep so pat on top of it, the basilica so perfectly in keeping with the aery fantasy of its surroundings that it barely seems to be anchored to the platform on which it stands.
>
> It is not only the works of Man but also those of God that defy the decent and the probable. Fangs, teeth, whorls, needles, columns of rock are everywhere protuberant like broken bones piercing the skin of nature after some frightful accident. God, in fact, it is who has led Man into all the curious extravagances with which the land is littered.

I think I should apologise for that. It is supposed to be bad manners to quote from oneself and in general I uphold that view. Also, I am not sure if my romantic effusion has lasted particularly well. However, it does serve to point up the contrast with the area I was about to enter, severely affected by economic blight and much less uplifted by dramatic scenery. When I rode this way in the sixties I suppose I was less affected by this decline from threadbare grandeur to real squalor because on horseback you always have your eyes on the track, and your mind is focused on the safe negotiation of treacherous paths or on the best reading of some inadequate old military map. Now, by car, the extent of blight and desolation was more swiftly grasped.

Frasquito had often spoken to me in the past of Algámitas as a favoured spot among charcoal-burners, who made their camps in the surrounding Sierra del Tablón and Sierra de la Rabitilla and treated the village as their metropolis. But that had all died the death administered by paraffin, butane gas and electricity, and there seemed to be no other activity to replace it. Algámitas today is a poor, spiritless, down-at-heel place, the gateway to 'Corbones Country'.

The river of that name is a sultry watercourse rising above El Saucejo and winding – often flagged by tough, gallant oleanders – between humpy foothills on its tortuous way to join the great river, the Guadalquivir. Along the valley of the Corbones most of the smaller houses and farmsteads are ruined and empty. Villanueva de San Juan, up on a bluff, looks brighter and more cheerful. In summer its population rises to two thousand souls, I was told at the *venta* on the road, due to the return of emigrants for the holidays. There is apparently a close link between Villanueva and Ibiza, where men and women from the pueblo work for six or seven months, returning home for the rest of the year. As a result of this contact with the hotel trade a local industry has sprung up: the cultivation and marketing of asparagus. Had I not seen the fern-like plantations down on the slopes along the river? Certainly I had. This confirmed my Pruna hypothesis of the special relationship between each pueblo and some distant employer.

But Villanueva is a beacon whose lamp plays over large stretches of country where human settlement is sparse and the means of livelihood tenuous. I pushed on towards the hamlet of La Romera, which I had passed through on my ride back from Olvera all those years ago, and stopped outside the rather grandly named Venta de los Cazadores (Hunters' Inn), a cottage whose front room contained a very basic bar. The owner was 'lying down', but his pert daughter insisted on fetching him. He appeared blear-eyed as if hung over, but did not seem to mind being roused. He had been in Germany, he said, for six years, until he couldn't stand it any more and had settled here with his wife and daughters. They had no electricity and had to go to the spring for their water. Even so, it was vastly preferable to the terrible precision and regularity of the Germans. I asked if the region hadn't become too depopulated for a *venta* to provide a living. Who were his customers? All but the largest *cortijos* seemed to be abandoned. Well, he said, they made a bit by cooking lunches for the *tiradores* who invaded the area on Sundays and often brought in their own rabbits or partridges to be prepared. Foreigners? I had heard there was some kind of a colony at La Mezquitilla, near El Saucejo. He grinned and downed a slug of anis. Yes, there were some over there, but they were retired elderly persons; three or four had come over to prospect in La Romera, but retreated in horror at the absence of piped water and light and had never been seen again. In fact, you had only to take your containers to the spring and you could fill them to the brim, if you were patient. If a proper well were bored, it would strike a plentiful supply. As to light, in his experience foreigners always managed to get it installed where Spaniards had failed. He retired to his inner quarters and resumed his interrupted siesta.

My next port of call was the Venta de Armijo. This was on the road to Morón, a little out of my way, but these gallant outposts in this wasteland seemed to me worth inspection. Although still extremely sparse in its amenities, Armijo's turned out to be a more substantial place, less of a shanty than the Cazadores. Armijo himself was a ruddy-faced, talkative elderly man; he sat down with me while his lively daughter of forty ran the bar.

'Between this business and the *huerto*,' he said, 'we manage to survive – at any rate in a good year. But we've had no real rain for several years now, the sort that renews the springs, and they say we are in a dry cycle that will last another three years. As things are, I can only irrigate a fraction of the *huerto*, which is a hectare in extent. Water is the key to everything . . . water and dung. With those two things you can grow anything.'

Despite the drought, he continued, foreigners were buying land. A German, or perhaps a Swiss, had come to see the ranch next door only two days ago. And then there was a whole colony of them outside El Saucejo. Perhaps I had heard of it? I nodded; these were presumably the timid old folk of La Mezquitilla. But for Armijo they might have been intrepid *conquistadores*, opening up new territories. His eyes gleamed as he spoke of them: the age-old dream, half indignant, half fascinated, of foreigners striking Spanish gold was upon him. If they settled in any numbers, water and light would follow – they always did – and the land would be revalued and revitalised.

This scenario seemed improbable to me, though I did not like to say so. Over 'Corbones Country' there hovers a curious aura of desolation, in which the only flickering lamps of civilisation (girlie posters, TV, a glass of wine and a *tapa* of cheese, a brazier in winter) are to be found in the wayside *ventas*, themselves only hanging on to survival by the skin of their teeth. In several hours I hardly met a car and saw no pedestrians except the odd *tirador* with a rabbit, probably poached, hanging from his belt. The big estates are all private shooting grounds, except 'El Roble', the Benítez Cubero ranch, which is devoted to the breeding of brave bulls. Later when I checked in Angus MacNab's *Bulls of Iberia*, I found he was not kind to the Benítez Cuberos: 'Large, heavy, sluggish, poor caste,' was his verdict. Did nothing flourish in 'Corbones Country'?

From Armijo's I decided to follow as far as possible, in reverse, the route I had taken on my return home from Osuna. This meant getting back onto the road to La Puebla de Cazalla. Just after La Romera this loses its metalled surface. For part of the way it accompanies the Río de la Peña, a tributary of the Corbones, which it resembles in every respect as it winds along its low dusty ravine, more generously endowed with rushes, clusters of willow and the ever faithful oleander than with water. Only the larger farm buildings have survived: those which presumably housed a tenant or a labourer are subsiding back into the earth from which their rubble and lime-mortared walls derived. But at least the immemorial holm-oaks are preserved, each spreading its wide crown over its own clearly-etched circle of deep shade. And the land is criss-crossed everywhere with old tracks and bridle paths, which would make for splendid riding were it not for the increasing prevalence of wire. Where the road crosses the Río de la Peña, there stands a welcome staging post, the Venta de la Peña, another of the gallant band, but I stopped only briefly to slake my thirst, as I still had a stretch of virtually cross-country driving ahead, which I wanted to put behind me before dark.

A few miles further on the road rejoins the Corbones, whose plodding course is briefly graced by a few tall groves of eucalyptus. Then comes a junction with an unsurfaced road signposted to Fontanar, which I took. There is a settlement called San Antonio del Fontanar, but the only buildings of consequence are those of the big farm of the same name, which somewhat resembles a Roman villa with all its dependencies. Outside these great agrarian barracks, themselves only thinly manned, the population hereabouts has dwindled almost to vanishing point.

Now came the tricky bit. From San Antonio I had to find the right dirt track for El Puerto de la Encina. At one point I went wrong but was lucky enough to come across a man delicately peeling a peach with a clasp knife outside a very run-down farm indeed; he was the only figure in the landscape. He showed me how to reorientate myself by a clump of cypresses. When I reached them I found they belonged to an old garden which had run completely wild, surrounding a ruined house which must once have been someone's rustic retreat; a faint trace of elegance and ease remained in a scalloped mock-Moorish window. I was now back on course, and came shortly to El Puerto de la Encina.

I vividly remembered stopping at this tiny hamlet on my ride back from Osuna in order to water my mount, Chico: there was then a deep well in the street, but you had to have your own bucket to get water. A kindly woman lent me her blue plastic one, which I had to lower some six or seven metres. There was no proper parapet round the top of the well, and while angling the bucket to get it filled I almost knocked a frail old lady, waiting her turn, over the edge. Now I had no one to water but myself. In the single shop (there was not even a *venta*) the youth behind the counter stopped serving a woman stocking up for the week, disappeared into the recesses of the place and came back with a glass full of ice cubes, over which he poured my lemon *refresco* with all the aplomb of a barman at the Ritz. I drank gratefully. Despite the reduction in the hazards and discomforts of travel since my last visit, I was heartily relieved not to have burst a tyre on those devilish *chinos negros*, sharp dark particles of chipped stone, which are the preferred surface for forest and farm tracks and even for parts of the road network. That is much worse than shedding a horse-shoe, upon which you simply dismount and lead your animal to the nearest smithy.

And so to Osuna. 'Corbones Country' was behind me; that river continued its sluggish progress through La Puebla, past Marchena and Carmona to emerge near Alcolea del Río, where it mingled its scant waters with the mighty Guadalquivir. Now I was down on the *campiña*, the shimmering vale of Seville, with the sierras only a smudge on the horizon. And there rising before me was the 'ducal city', as it likes to be known. The general effect is not as starkly dramatic as that made by Olvera, but there is something distinctly imposing about the regular conical mound covered with white houses and crowned with darker buildings of stone – the whole floating like an island above the delicate, unemphatic colouring and almost featureless extent of the plain. But there are many Spanish cities of this stamp, so why have I been moving crabwise towards this one ever since setting out from the *campo*? Am I not well off my beat? Was I not concerned with the sierras and their special characteristics, and looking for a retreat in the hills? Furthermore, is this foray not an annoyance to the cartographer and a puzzlement to the reader, requiring as it does an awkward-shaped map which will not fit neatly onto the endpapers?

To answer these charges I must summon up the motives behind my first trip in the sixties. By way of contrast to the simple charms of Arcadia, I had then felt a strong urge to investigate somewhere comparable to Ronda in its urbanity and the importance of its monuments. In the latter respect, Osuna probably surpasses Ronda. And Osuna confers its name on a dukedom, which Ronda, despite its petty Arab kings, has never done. Also, it was already becoming clear even then that Ronda's proximity to the Costa del Sol was likely to change its character very considerably; this seemed much less of a danger so far inland on the *campiña*, where agriculture still ruled absolutely. Thus the old graces and delicacies which Ronda was losing might still be preserved to some degree in Osuna; finally, a number of people had spoken of it as a goodly city.

In the event, I think it was the plaza of Osuna that most impressed me. The main square is of crucial importance to the character of every small town in the south. The Plaza de la Ciudad in Ronda has a fine antique savour, but its main buildings are all institutional or religious and it has no cafés or bars, no *vida*, no life; the Plaza de España by the bridge is bleak and windswept; the Plaza del Socorro is livelier but lacks architectural distinction. Other towns in Andalusia have fine plazas, for example Medina Sidonia (which we shall see) and Ecija (which we shall not). And the upper plazas of Marbella and Algeciras were worthy specimens before the tidal wave of tourism swept over them. With the possible exception of Medina's, the plaza of Osuna beats them all.

With such thoughts in my mind I drew closer and closer. The two main monuments, the Colegiata and the Universidad, loomed larger and larger above me. The access was no longer as simple as when I had ridden in on Chico along the *cañada real* which then (with the sole impediment of the railway line) led straight into the city's heart. Now one had not only to cross the tracks but to pass over a new motorway and then pick one's way through a thicket of signs before honing in on the only relevant one: *Centro Ciudad*. Once through a confusing periphery of the type in which planners delight, everything was very simple; the long white street flew straight to the plaza, which as far as I could see had not changed by so much as a leaf. It is rather longer than it is wide, with the *casino*, the club of the landowning and professional classes, occupying the top end; the town hall raised over an arch is on one of the long sides and the *plaza de abastos*, the municipal market, on the other; the lower end is formed by the high wall of the Convento de la Concepción. Most of the centre is occupied by an oblong promenade, shaded by acacias and oranges: this is a delightful place for courting couples, young mothers with children and old countrymen who jaw away on the tiled and wrought-iron benches. The plaza does not of course have a staggering view like that from Ronda's clifftop *alameda*; it is more enclosed, more sheltered, a civic centre *par excellence*.

I sought and got directions to the Caballo Blanco, a lodging that has been in continuous use since 1511. It has not been modernised and ruined. The place has a slightly seedy air, but the prices are very modest; Juan and his wife serve traditional food on the red-checked tablecloths in the *comedor*; there is no dreadful lounge and life revolves round the *comedor* and the *cocina*, into which you may well be invited for a glass of *fino* and a chat with the family.

The lure of the plaza is strong at almost all times of the day except mid-afternoon. It is not only a place of leisure but also still very much the town's business centre. In the club from midday onwards the landowners lounge in basket chairs, arms or hands resting on a long brass rail which runs across the tall open windows and prevents them from falling into the street; from here they survey the scene like bored spectators in a box at the theatre, while lesser mortals on the pavement below talk up to them in animated tones to which they half listen. A little to the left, outside the Caja Rural, are the brokers and dealers, alert to every movement of the local markets in land, produce, cattle; they wear cloth caps or black *cordobés* hats and carry switch-like canes to indicate their connection with stockbreeding. Others are bareheaded and in shirtsleeves, probably with nothing in particular to buy or sell and in the plaza simply because it is the nerve-centre of the town. Something similar still goes on in Ronda, though in a less concentrated way, spread out among the many bars and cafés of the Calle de la Bola.

Osuna's main square also gives access to the clean and spacious *plaza de abastos*, housed in two large arcaded patios. There is a different stall for each kind of meat – one for *ternera*, one for *cerdo*, one for *pollo* – and the fish hall displays great carcasses of *pez de espada*, swordfish, and its coarser relative *cazón*, along with all the other glistening slippery choice from squid to sprat. The fruit and vegetable stalls are also very handsome. The only trouble is that there aren't quite enough people to make the whole place hum. Spaniards are not romantics. If the supermarket is cheaper, that is where they will go. All the same, attendance is respectable. Stalls no longer in demand for food and produce have been taken over for perfumery and shoes. Possibly rents are kept artificially low by the socialist administration. One way or another the old market survives, a standing reproach to Ronda, which plucked out its heart by closing and demolishing its own marvellously lively equivalent in order to make way for a prestige *parador*, whose completion – if past form is anything to go by – may take years.

Osuna has other advantages over Ronda: next to the Caballo Blanco is a *talabartero*, or saddler, whose wares are much cheaper than in the capital of the Serranía. He says there are two or three riding schools, which train horses and riders in the Spanish style. The price of a middling mare? Ah, he couldn't say. But the horse dealers congregate in that bar over the street, the one with the large plate window. A little further along the same pavement is the hospital, housed behind the grand stone façade of the old county court. There are not many shops but prominent among them are the pharmacies (four in the Carrera de Caballos alone) and the hat shops: the latter of course go with an interest in horses – you cannot ride uncovered. There are two of these establishments almost side by side, the Antigua Casa Andújar and the Sombrería El Bombo ('The Bowler Hat') both carrying in their windows the same injunction: *'El sombrero viste'*, literally the hat dresses you, hatless you are not dressed.

I could find only one thing that jarred slightly in this part of town. In a principal street near the plaza is an old convent, which is now a school. The front courtyard has been restored not with paving stones and potted plants (which are the essentials of domestic gardening in Spain) but with four little squares of bright green grass on which sprinklers play. Grass is a corruption introduced from coastal swimming pools and has no place between marble columns behind an old ochre wall.

The Colegiata, the ex-collegiate church, soars above the old town. The west front hangs over a steep slope covered by a veritable army of *higos chumbos*, prickly pears. Normally they are strung out along a roadside or form a palisade round some very humble dwelling, and it is unusual to see them massed in such force, perhaps with the object of defending the great pile above them: certainly no one would attempt to seize it from this flank. Señora Rosario, the custodian, would be another deterrent to any invader. She is the daughter of a deceased official chronicler of the city: perhaps for hereditary reasons or perhaps because of a tendency to didactic pendantry which frequently affects educated Spanish women, she is a formidable incumbent of the post. The dates of the five Riberas the church possesses are at her fingertips and she shows an unflagging relish in reciting anecdotes connected with the Neapolitan painter who became such a favourite in Spain. It was 'The Martyrdom of Saint Bartholemew', she intones, which Ribera had hung out to dry on his balcony in Naples that attracted the attention of the Duke of Osuna, then viceroy, who brought it and the artist back to his country.

'That is the one in the Prado?' I ventured.

'No, that is another version. The one the duke brought back is now in Mexico.'

To make sure I had got that clear, she repeated the word, separating out its component syllables with the accent strongly on the first: '*Mé* ... ji ... co.' She watched me closely as I wrote this down, for I felt that she would only be placated by abundant notes.

The collection of paintings and other artefacts in the sacristy and adjacent rooms also includes works by Juan de Mena, Alonso Cano and 'Divino' Morales. Next you are taken down to the 'Pequeño Escorial' or mausoleum of the dukes and their consorts and ancestors. Careful explanations follow of the inscriptions on the plain stone coffins and the deeds of their occupants.

'The founder of the Colegiata and the university was not yet Duke of Osuna. He was the fourth Count of Ureña. It was *his* son, the fifth Count who was elevated to the dukedom by Philip II ...'

I continued dutifully writing all this down; the leaves of my school exercise book were beginning to run out.

There are certainly some fine items in Rosario's collection – for one feels it is hers – but the main glory under her care is the luminous hall-church itself, with its wide nave of flattened arches, flanked by round-headed arches of the same height over the aisles, all resting on elaborate composite classical piers. Yet, the side and end chapels have swirling late Gothic rib-vaults. It is a hybrid style which affords great height and light, and is much preferable to the tedious standard temples of the Jesuits which were to proliferate all over the Peninsula. A tremendous Churrigueresque *retablo* behind the high altar will make you shiver either with horror or delight according to your attitude to these elaborate constructions, which constitute the main contribution of the Spanish to the Baroque. All in all, Osuna's Colegiata rivals and perhaps surpasses its principal rival among the hall-churches of mainland Spain, that of Lerma in Old Castile; undoubtedly it is one of the finest churches in Andalusia.

The Osunas, however, were not only builders. Señora Rosario, pursuing her mission for that afternoon, which was to save me from the damnation of abysmal ignorance, was assiduous in reminding me of the patronage of Goya by the then duchess, rival society figure of the notorious Duchess of Alba; and of the Osunas' support for Pedro Romero, the founder of modern bullfighting, favourite son of Ronda. Goya's portrait group of the duke and duchess in 1789 gives one the impression of a good upper-bourgeois family of the Scottish Enlightenment by Allan Ramsay rather than of arrogant Spanish grandees – though the duchess's eyes are steely. But evidently a vein of extravagance ran in the family, as witnessed by the fabulous and luxurious embassy to Russia of the mid-nineteenth-century duke, recorded by the prolific author who accompanied him, Juan Valera. This seems to have been the final flourish. The title still exists, now borne more modestly. There is no resident duke in Osuna, any more than there is in Medina Sidonia or Medinaceli. The inheritors are Señora Rosario and the culture industry.

The Universidad, occupying an even more elevated position than the Colegiata, is a plain rectangular building with pinnacled towerlets at its four corners. Dating from 1549, it belongs to the period after the completion of the Reconquest when the great Renaissance cathedrals were going up; at the same time universities were founded in a number of small seigneurial cities (Baeza is another). The students of Osuna were especially bound to defend the thesis of the Immaculate Conception, but Cervantes is reputed to have said of their university that it was so bad that everyone passed. This was no doubt to ensure the triumph of the Virgin, now universally accepted by the Catholic Church but then still opposed by important elements within it, notably the Dominicans. However that might be, Osuna's university was suppressed after the Napoleonic Wars by Ferdinand VII, that extinguisher of even the feeblest lamps of learning, and now houses no more than the local *instituto* or secondary school. It is locked up except in term time.

Sitting on its steps, surrounded by cracked paving stones, broken beer bottles and dried-up flowerbeds, my attention was suddenly claimed by a few tiny shrivelled melons struggling bravely for survival. Their plight in this blinding light, under inhospitable scholastic walls, moved me, as a former melon-grower myself, to scribble them this little tribute. It is not worth translating; it was just a spasm in my exercise book. I record it simply as a small offering to Osuna:

> Acacias y naranjas en la plaza;
> en la cuesta de la Parroquia, la chumbera;
> y alrededor del colegio,
> el melón que no ha visto ni gota de agua
> echa menudita fruta y flor.

From the north side of the Colegiata a cobbled slope runs down to the Convento de la Encarnación, which has some treasured images, lovingly shown by a young Mercedarian nun, one of the two out of a community of thirteen who has special dispensation to emerge from the *clausura* to show visitors round. The Mercedarians, she said, were foun-

147

ded to redeem captives from the Moors in the thirteenth century; the present convent dated from the sixteenth and had benefited greatly from the bounty of the ducal house of Osuna.

The chief Virgin above the high altar of the convent chapel is from the eighteenth century; she is seated and looks rather like a fine lady taking tea. But the moods of the Virgin are many, and the museum also possesses a little Virgin of the Seven Sorrows by Juan de Mena and a large painting of her mourning over the crown of thorns, hammer, nails and other instruments of the Passion. It is this multi-faceted quality of Mary, I believe, which has made her so successful and popular a cult figure, a goddess for all seasons. The convent also possesses many little doll-like figures of the Christ child from different periods in different robes. The most striking is 'El Dormidito', the little sleeper, in which the chubby, smiling child is lying on an ebony cross, dreaming presumably of the crucifixion that lies ahead.

In the small archaeological museum further down the hill most of the 'Iberian' discoveries near Osuna (of the late 'Romanised' variety) are represented only by plaster casts. The originals are in the Archaeological Museum of Madrid. The curator is a charming and lively girl with the fine dark brows and eyes which have been incorporated in so many versions of the Virgin.

'Are you English or German?' she asked.

'English . . . well, British.'

She noted this down firmly under 'English' in her little book.

'Do you keep statistics of all the nationalities that come here? One Englishman, three Italians and so on?'

'Yes, I have to,' she smiled.

It turned out that by far the largest number of visitors were Spaniards spending their holidays seeing their own country. *Turismo nacional* has been much fomented by improved roads and by the interest of foreigners in Spanish art and culture.

... a goddess for all seasons

Coming down the final stretch from the *conjunto his-tórico*, I allowed my eyes to stray into every open doorway; I always find them hard to resist, but especially so in the south of Spain. Through one entrance I saw a man curled up asleep on a mat on the floor of the porch, his wife dozing peacefully behind him in a rocking chair; through another I glimpsed three girls, ranging from perhaps nine to fifteen,

149

all sewing diligently in the semi-gloaming which permeates the cool recesses of old Andalusian homes on hot afternoons.

Fine buildings in Osuna are not confined to the 'monumental' zone. Streets like San José and Huerta boast some very grand house-fronts: one with twisted Solomonic columns like a Baroque altarpiece; another with two almost life-size soldiers supporting the coat of arms; a third with a model of the Giralda of Seville framed by a broken pediment. These took me back to my years in the Casa de Mondragón in Ronda and stirred a certain weakness in me for that style of residence, though a warning voice whispered at the same time: you have been here before; such places can be dark and dank in winter and you may find nothing but a squalid warren behind that grand façade. My gaze dwelt affectionately, nonetheless, on that ultimate frivolity of the Baroque represented by the asymmetrical curlicued parapet of the Palacio (for 'palace' read ancestral town house) del Marqués de la Gomera.

At this point I recalled, almost with a jolt, a conversation on my previous visit. I was talking to some grain dealers from Estremadura in the *posada*, where we were all putting up. I asked if there were any big *fincas* in Estremadura. Not so big as hereabouts, they said. At this one of the local men began to talk excitedly. He was an elderly, unshaven, dissident sort of person.

'Here it is terrible,' he said. 'Every day worse.'

'Why?' I asked. 'With these good wheatlands and olives. I suppose you will say it is all divided between four *señoritos*?'

'Exactly,' he said. 'Three or four.'

'There are more,' said another. 'Say fifty or sixty.'

'Shut up. Those who count are three or four. Don Isidro López now has eleven farms. Each year he buys another for one of his sons. He has sixty tractors. And they have four cars in the garage. Don Eladio Bravo has ten *fincas* and his brother, Don Jesús, five. The money they make is badly invested. Either it is left rotting in the bank at 2 per cent or used to buy more land. Neither way does it provide any more work. When the people tried to take control, the Fascists moved in. And here we are, no better off than we were thirty years ago. You were saying Osuna is a fine city. I say the whole bloody place should be swallowed up in the bowels of the earth.'

'And the monuments and palaces of the Calle San José?' I asked.

He spat on the floor.

'Let them sink with the rest!'

Sobered by these thoughts, I was reawakened to the great bitterness that had ruled not so long ago, between the possessors of these mansions and the dispossessed. I turned my steps towards more modest quarters of the town. For there are other pleasing streets in Osuna. The Caballo Blanco is on the corner of the Calle de Granada, which runs right up to the edge of the town. Under a full moon after supper it looked like a wider and slightly grander version of a street in Olvera or in the Barrio de San Francisco of Ronda, with families bringing their chairs out onto the pavement and chatting with neighbours in adjacent houses or in front. Some little girls were playing at a bullfight, with a chunky one in glasses playing the bull very fiercely and the others running away shrieking while the girl-*toro* called out after them half derisively, half pleadingly: '*Faéname, faéname!*' This is almost untranslatable. The *faena* is the matador's solo work with the *muleta* in the final act before the kill. She wanted them to take this seriously. The burden of her song was, 'Fight me properly, please!'

Andalusians are torn between the delights of the street and the cool depths of their homes. On summer evenings the former prevail, but any observant traveller will be intrigued by the seemingly endless interiors behind quite humble frontages. I decided I could do without the coat of arms and the columns, but the lure of the porch and the patio and the inner rooms and no doubt a yard behind them remained great. The more I saw of the Calle de Granada, the more I liked it, so I asked Juan back at the Caballo Blanco how much such a house might cost.

'Few of them have more than seven metres across the front, but they are very deep; almost all of them run back thirty-five to forty metres from the street, if you include the corral. The current prices, depending of course on size and condition, are in the range of five to seven million pesetas.'

So, such a house could be had for say £30–35,000 – for which you couldn't get a one-bedroomed flat in Holloway. It was a tempting thought: our *campo* was worth more than that. Socialism notwithstanding, Juan hastened to assure me, Osuna was a very conservative place. The 'Ursaonenses' (the name derives from the bears supporting the ducal coat of arms which are a pun on *Urso*, the Roman name for the town) disliked change on principle: most returned from their studies or years of work abroad to settle in their home town. Building regulations were tight under the socialists, more so than under previous regimes. You couldn't build anything out of keeping. The more recent monstrosities wrought in Ronda by the Monte would have been impossible in Osuna. Here too the market place was still where it should be. And if you added in the shady plaza, the gentlemen's club and the equestrian bent, well . . . the pluses seemed to be stacking up against the minuses. Even the faint but persistent aroma of pure olive oil, which wafted up from the bottling plant down by the railway and hung like a rural incense in the streets, was not unpleasant. I fell asleep dreaming of a little 'palace' in Osuna, perhaps not after all in the Calle San José but a more modest version in the Calle de Granada.

In the morning, other considerations crowded in, as is their wont. I went to the excellent Mesón del Duque for coffee but found that the outriders of discord were present in Osuna too, with their 50cc displays of *moto-machismo* even on the cobbled circuit of the *conjunto histórico*. And then, in the Plaza de Rodríguez Martín, I noticed an extraordinary new mock-Greek birdcage in the shape of a column topped by an exaggerated Doric capital with a few feet of imitation marble at the base, the rest constructed of steel struts and wire mesh. Inside it canaries, budgerigars and other small birds hopped and fluttered or simply wilted in the hot sun, with hardly a patch of shade. It is strange how relatively minor things of this kind can have a disproportionate effect. The municipality must have gone out of its mind, I thought, recalling the perfectly decent and well-shaded aviaries of Ronda and Olvera. The minuses mounted another notch or two.

Back at the Caballo Blanco a handsome, grizzled man was taking a glass of *fino* with Juan, and I joined them. He was a son of Osuna who lived in Madrid: he had been a lorry-driver for twenty years and was now a 'transport administrator'. His family were completing their holiday at Sanlúcar de Barrameda; he himself had to return to work earlier and had stopped off for a night in the pueblo on the way north.

Señora Rosario's father's book? Yes, he had it on his shelves. It hadn't much substance. As a child in the thirties he remembered seeing copies of the local newspaper, *La Razón*, which carried a lot of articles about Viriathus and Trajan and Theodosius and so on – and that was a simple local weekly. But the book in question said almost nothing about those things of greater antiquity; it simply grovelled about the dukedom. There was a civilisation here long before the Renaissance and the dukes of Osuna.

'Will you retire here?' I asked.

'It would be bearable. But my family prefer Sanlúcar by the sea, and so, to be honest, do I.' He looked at his watch. 'I must be off. May I bring you anything from Madrid?'

I thanked him for his courtesy and hoped to see him on my next visit.

Before leaving, I decided to return to the Colegiata for a

final look at the lovely space and light of the interior. The big doors were open but the inner ones did not respond to my turning the latch. When I knocked I was admitted by Señora Rosario, who was smoking a cigarette. I was surprised at first, but reasoned that she was doing no more than most Andalusians: showing herself to be at home in church, where indeed she spent all day.

'You're alone *again*?' she asked, not best pleased to see me, as if I'd interrupted her in her office – which in fact I had; she had a desk and a bookstall just inside the door. 'I've had four groups this morning and I'm doing my accounts before closing. All right, come in then. I won't charge you. You have ten minutes while I check my figures.'

This time I made no attempt to do a tour of the rich fittings, but simply surrendered myself to the architecture of the building. On the way out, daring to again interrupt her in her accounts, I approached her.

'Forgive me, I'm afraid my notes are in a bit of a mess. When did you say the dukedom was created?'

She took off her reading glasses and looked up at me in some exasperation.

'The fifth Count of Ureña was created Duke of Osuna by Philip II in 1562,' she enunciated, dwelling on the stressed syllables of the date, 'mil quini*entos* . . . ses*enta* . . . y *dos*', as if addressing the slowest child in the class. Humbly and gratefully I corrected the scrawl in my notebook. Among the display of books and cards in her glass cabinet my attention fell on the *Guía Artística de los Monumentos de Osuna*.

'How much is that?' I asked.

'Mil cuatroci*entas* pesetas.'

It seemed rather expensive, but I said I would take it; I'd better bone up on these things before I saw her again.

'I'm afraid that's the last copy and I've lost the key.'

Señora Rosario didn't look as if she ever lost anything. But she sent me trotting off over the road to the Encarnación to see if the nuns had a copy. They had run out too.

'Look,' said the little sister, 'she has sent you here because our income is minute and we get a percentage on sales. She has a salary, so whether she sells one copy more or less doesn't matter to her. Go back and say we have run out; I bet she has a copy tucked away somewhere.'

I did as she bade me, but Señora Rosario was adamant. She *had* lost the key and anyway it was *her* copy (as if she needed it!), but when I came back next time she would be delighted to sell me one; it was being reprinted. She dismissed me with a brief if forgiving smile, presumably intended to mitigate her severity. Incongruously, I could not help wondering if there was a man in her life, for she is a fine-looking woman, the Vestal Virgin of the Colegiata of Osuna. But she is such a fierce custodian of its treasures that I am unable to be more erudite about them in this book.

I left Osuna with mixed feelings. Part of me was very much drawn to it; it retained not a few of the old charms that Ronda had lost. But the type of landholding in the surrounding *campiña* was against it. All the smaller farmhouses were collapsing; there would be no possibility of a smallholding; one would be confined to Osuna itself, where there could be no question of keeping animals other than pets and a horse, probably at livery. It would mean a firm decision to become a townee in a place where one had no roots. It would consign me to a life of idleness with vaguely literary and equestrian pursuits, to which I was sure I would not secure my family's consent. Even if I did, it would bring out the worst side of my nature: I would almost inevitably gravitate to the *casino*, so beguiling with its charming position on the plaza, and associate with men who, if not the architects, were the complacent accomplices of the sort of rural deprivation and depopulation to which the impoverished *ventas* bore witness. Land use in the sierras remained more diversified. There were still *huertas* of market garden size along the rivers; there were still cultivable clearings of an acre or two in the forests; and in the small pueblos the price of a house in the Calle de Granada would probably acquire not only a house in the village but a bit of land outside. Perhaps I would not be seeing Señora Rosario again after all.

I took the road back towards the hills. The fields were ashen; the powdery white streaks across them might have come from some giant peppermill dispensing fertiliser. The Corbones rose not far from here, but I was to see it no more. The zone known as Barrancos Blancos – after its white gullies and ravines – more closely resembled a series of chalky quarries. There were no trees, not even eucalyptus. So to El Saucejo, one of those large, unattractive Andalusian villages, unrelieved by interesting architecture or any other charming or arresting feature, whose original function was to provide a sullen pool of labour for seasonal work on the *latifundia* of the Guadalquivir basin. Into this category fall also Almárgen, Sierra de Yeguas, Campillos and La Roda de Andalucia. One understands why some of these used to specialise in the production of gut-rotting liqueurs such as *aguardiente* and dry and sweet anis. They are all 'white towns' with a vengeance, overpoweringly, blindingly so, yet not the sort that are included in the government's propaganda for the *pueblos blancos* and their folksy charms.

For all these reasons it was good to come down from El Saucejo, cross the N342 from Jerez to Granada, proceed through Almárgen without stopping and take the local road for Cañete la Real. Cañete had lodged in my mind as a gaunt, rough old place exposed on a bald sierra with little protection from the elements other than the spine on which stood the ruined castle. During the final century and a half of the Reconquest it was a frequent battleground. When Córdoba, Seville, Osuna and the rest of the cities and towns along the Guadalquivir were safely in the Christian bag, Cañete led a precarious life as an outpost on the border with the kingdom of Granada; between 1329 and 1492 it changed hands no less than six times. Something similar happened to Pruna, Olvera, Zahara and Cuevas del Becerro, but Cañete was the most subjected to warlike incursions of them all.

When I first came to Cañete by horse, the *posada* had the filthiest stable I had come across in all my wanderings. The strawloft was empty and it was hard to buy grain. The *casino* was a seedy bar. The balconies of the *fonda* were falling away from the walls and the beds were unmade at five o'clock in the afternoon. So overwhelming was the impression of stagnation and decay that I openly asked the cause, and was told *la emigración*. Cañete was the first place I had seen that showed what could happen when virtually the whole male labour force had been obliged to leave to find work in the north or abroad. I am bound to say the effects were less devastating in other nearby pueblos, for example Teba, which was very well kept, but Cañete was without a doubt a very demoralised place in the mid-sixties.

Despite all this it had, and has, a certain grandeur conferred by its buildings, which are not mean, its situation and its capacity for endurance. The squalor I remembered has been largely remedied. It was a relief, in fact a pleasure, to come up from the dull, sprawling, barrack-like villages of the plain to find a mountain pueblo that appeared to have recovered its self-respect. On the way in, the hallmark of the successful or at least viable pueblo was in place: the deep-blue municipal *piscina* with its grass surround, shade trees and throng of young people in the water and out. The plaza is not in the top league, being little more than a widening of the road with the town hall set back on one side and two cafés on the other, facing the dogleg bend that leads out towards Ronda. But everything and everyone that moves in Cañete must pass this point, and the cafés are always packed with sharp-eyed old countrymen. This is one of the windiest street corners in southern Spain, for Cañete is the highest town in the province of Málaga, with sweeping views over the Sierra de Ortegícar and Sierra de las Nieves.

The church is quite grand in a dilapidated way. The bell was clanking and women in twos and threes, arm in arm, were beginning to answer its summons. I followed them inside. It was apparently one of the days of the novena of the Virgin. Unusually for a pueblo the columns of the nave carry a tall entablature with an upper cornice from which the vault springs. There are old altars and images and a huge *Cristobalón*, the outsize mural of Saint Christopher with a child on his shoulder and a palm tree as staff, much like Ronda's. But the cynosure of all eyes is *la patrona*, the Virgin of Caño Santo with her silver penumbra and golden wimple and crown.

Back in the plaza I paused by a stone replica of the patroness, which jogged my memory. I went into the adjacent café. In conversation with the barman I said I seemed to recall there was a long-standing quarrel – perhaps there had even been a lawsuit? – with Alcalá del Valle, which also claimed the Virgin for its own. Wasn't there a sanctuary outside Alcalá from which she originally came and where a *romería* was held every year?

'Bah,' said a cheerful man drinking gin and Coke at a nearby table. 'That is a mere picnic. The real thing is the day of the Virgin here. Caño Santo is within the municipal district of Cañete, not of Alcalá. We are the only town in Spain to have her for our patroness. There are thousands of Virgins of the Rosary and Virgins of the Column and Virgins of what-have-you, but the Virgin of Caño Santo is unique – and she is ours. Shall I tell you how this came about? When she was discovered, as you say at the *santuario*, two hundred men from Olvera went to get her. But she wouldn't budge. Then four men went from Cañete – *cuatro Cañeteros* – and they brought her here and she has been here ever since. Don't talk to me about Alcalá del Valle. Don't even mention such a place in the same breath as Cañete la Real!'

In front of the town hall a wooden stage was nearing completion and being garlanded with bunting and evergreen branches. What was on? Had I not seen the posters? There was to be an *espectáculo* that evening. When? Ah, who could say, perhaps at eleven, perhaps at twelve. The *artistas* had not arrived yet. With some hours to kill, I went for a stroll round the town, lingering by the few big houses with armorial bearings, which slightly stirred the dormant *folie de grandeur* in me that I shall never quite eradicate; they must be cool and deep and quiet, with big patios. And this place with its rough, frank people might well be preferable to the more languid Osuna; also it was much nearer Ronda. But wasn't the whole object of the exercise to get away from the pull of Ronda? I was forgetting . . .

Eventually I settled at a table, ordered wine and *tapas* and watched the *paseo*: brooding single yokels, some wild-eyed; girls in smart split skirts and bolero jackets; the young-middle-aged mums in grand matriarchal patterned costumes parading their children, one or two as little bullfighters in country dress, another as a little sailor with a huge Victorian collar; and then the little girls with flour-white powdered faces and scarlet lips, wearing their Sevillian flounces. But perhaps the largest number were bronzed *campo* workers and small farmers in spotless white shirts and cloth caps with their decent, buxom wives. Suddenly a stir was caused by a dark, pert girl in a wide Ascot hat, who attracted all the attention she intended to. I watched profiles, coiled-up hair, antique costume jewellery (shades of the Phoenicians?) – all in constant animation and motion. Behind me, the elders of the town with their backs to the wall of the *casino*-bar slid their lizard eyes over the crowd and waited in silence, all prurient expectation. Expectation was the name of the game: let there by all means be an *espectáculo*, but not yet, Oh Lord, not yet . . . with the *paseo* only just getting into its stride . . .

At last, however, the 'Clásico Ballet Español' was ready to perform. The apologies of the masters of ceremonies for the delay were greeted with derision: what was he on about? What else was expected or desired? Four girls and a striking faun-like youth performed a hotchpotch of Ravel, Stravinsky, tangos and *pasos dobles* with considerable *élan*. An important citizen near me waved a waiter aside to get a better view; the municipal policeman and his wife sat down and sipped coffee among the elders; one of the latter clapped exaggeratedly but his spouse's handsome, haughty, desiccated profile was frozen with distaste beside him. Most of the audience of some three or four hundred stood crowded round the stage, their faces rapt. There were bursts of clapping at the more suggestive numbers, though one woman asked crossly why they didn't bring proper *cante flamenco* any more instead of this modernised mish-mash. The spectacle ended with whirling skirts, a barrage of castanets and a furious tap-dance by the male heart-throb. Almost immediately a tractor with a trailer-load of bales of straw began to move remorselessly through the crowd. Cañete had put on its glad rags and been regaled by a just passable show paid for out of its municipal coffers. What more could you ask for? Life must go on.

As we broke up, I bumped into a figure who had been familiar on the streets of Ronda for several decades: ruddy-faced, snub-nosed, bright-eyed, short and broad, cloth-capped and widely known as 'El Cañetero' or more simply 'Cañete', he seemed to epitomise his whole pueblo in his person. The first Christmas that Diana and I spent in Ronda, 1957 it must have been, 'Cañete' perambulated the main streets with a large basket of *cacahuetes*, monkey-nuts, which he sold in little cones of paper. On cold nights one could plunge one's hands into the depths of the nuts, which were still warm. He had many other lines. He was a baker. He bought a *huerta*. He kept a good mule and a string of milking goats which followed him along the track when he returned to town at night. He married and started a *campo* bar but his wife died and he sold up. He had a heart attack and survived, jaunty as ever. Nothing got him down. And here he was back in his pueblo, a bit grizzled and in poor health (blood pressure, he said) but still cocky.

'What are you doing these days?' I asked.

He grinned and rubbed his thumb and forefinger together, the sign for money; then he drew them both down his gullet, the sign that it came free.

'*Viviendo de Felipe*,' he said cheerfully.

This (from Felipe González, the prime minister) is code for a state benefit, whether it be *el paro* (unemployment); *la paguita* (the little payment, usually for some form of disablement) or *la vejez* (the old-age pension). Critics of the government say that this whole network has got out of hand and is little more than electoral bribery. But 'Cañete' was well and truly plugged in, and proud of it.

Descending from Cañete la Real next day, I paused at the cemetery on the outskirts, from where I could pick out the pink Moorish tower of the great estate of Ortegícar standing out clear against the slopes of olives that ran up to the base of the frowning sierra. Shorn sheep were grazing sunflower stubble. Other fields had been burned, leaving a pattern like a brindle hide. As I continued down, the road looped tightly round a decaying farmhouse with elegant bow-shaped grilles, inhabited only by a family of rat-like kittens. A stark white house in good repair on the right was sheltered by a single oak, a vestige of immemorial ilex forests, against whose massive trunk was piled a bundle of cut canes, gathered no doubt for shade or fencing. A row of almonds lined the crest of a hill. A little further on was a grander *cortijo* with pillared entrance, wrought-iron gates and a eucalyptus grove. From all these places there were fine views over rolling stretches of arable land, far more exhilarating than 'Corbones Country' because the grainlands were back in touch with the sierras. But where could you find a toehold in this great shimmering landscape? Abandoned buildings were not lacking but they would provide little more than a shelter, a mere shell, in a vast expanse from which life had flown, except when the great lumbering machines came in to sow and reap the crops or teams of men were drafted in to hoe. If you wanted to live hereabouts, it would have to be in the town. You would have to become a Cañetero...

◆

... or a Tebeño. Teba rivals Cañete in its antiquity and austerity. Richard Ford gives us the following stirring account of its recapture from the Moors:

> Andalusian Teba was recovered from the Moors by Alfonso XI in 1328. Bruce, according to Froissart, when on his deathbed, called the good Lord James of Douglas, and told him that he had always wished to fight against the enemies of Christ, and that, as he had been unable to do so while alive, he now selected him, the bravest of his knights, to carry his heart, after his death, to the Holy Land. As there were no ships going directly to Jerusalem, Lord James proceeded to Spain, and, thinking fighting the Moors in the intermediate time would be most agreeable to the wishes of the deceased, proceeded to the siege of Teba. He wore the royal heart in a silver case around his neck. In the critical moment of the battle, he and his followers were abandoned by their Spanish allies; then the good Lord threw the heart of the Bruce into the fiercest of the fray, exclaiming, 'Pass first in fight, as thou wast ever wont to do, and Douglas will follow thee or die,' which he did.

It would be a poor Scot, and even a poor London-Scot like myself, who, travelling in these parts, did not keep a sharp lookout for Bruce's locket: in my case especially so, for after Bannockburn in 1314 King Robert granted his companion-in-arms, my ancestor Sir Robert Boyd, the feudal barony of Kilmarnock, where our jurisdiction included powers of life and death until our forfeiture as Jacobites in 1746. From that misfortune, and the decline in our position which followed, my migration to Spain may ultimately derive.

Teba is grim of aspect from every side. The town occupies a fold under the great whale-backed hill on which stands the castle. No less ruinous than Cañete's, it is more extensive and its *donjon* is still the dominant feature of the skyline. The whole place is the paradigm of an old seigneurial stronghold, on the frontier between Christian and Moor. Far later, it acquired vicarious distinction through its countess, Eugenia María Montijo de Guzman, born in 1826. She was the daughter of a nobleman who had fought on the French side in the Peninsular War. The family lived not in Teba but Granada. When Louis Napoleon became president of the Second Republic in 1848 she went to Paris, and was married to him in 1853, just after he had become emperor, thus transforming herself into Eugénie, Empress of the French. In Teba there are few traces of her. As her Spanish home she preferred the castle of Belmonte in New Castile, where she carried out some unsightly alterations in an attempt to improve its comfort. After her husband's death in 1873 (followed by her son's in 1879) she became a *grande dame* in exile and high priestess of Bonapartism until her death in 1920. All this passed Teba by.

The main streets in the town run parallel to each other: Calle Alta; Calle Nueva with some grand doorways and the town hall; and Calle Grande which dips to the crossroads with the *casino*-bar on one corner and then rises steeply to the church. Most of the houses are neat as pins (and were so even in the sixties when Cañete seemed to have given up the ghost); there is a taste for *art nouveau* balconies, though there is one lapse from the general high standard in the shape of a fine but deteriorating Renaissance portico of different-coloured marbles which encloses nothing more than a cheap broken window in the façade of the Bar González up by the church. I was pondering this and wondering whether to climb up to the castle when a young woman with shining black hair pulled back above delicate ears, dressed in a well-cut black suit, came out of a side street and walked straight up to me. She looked like a company executive or a hostess at some business convention.

'Can I help you?' she asked.

'No thank you, I was just wondering whether I had the energy to climb up to the castle.'

'You can do it and you should do it. I will show you the way. Are you German?'

Teba, like Pruna, was evidently in the 'German zone'.

'No, English.'

As I have already remarked, I tend not to describe myself as 'British', which comes out pompously as *británico*, nor *escocés*, which tests some countryfolk's geography; *inglés* produces a much quicker understanding of where, broadly speaking, you come from; it also fits neatly into the German–English antithesis which war films have led people to expect.

'Isabel González,' the young woman responded, stretching out her hand. 'I live in Calle Alta No. 3, which is your house for whatever you require.'

I thanked her for that traditional expression of hospitality and told her my name in return.

'*Mucho gusto,*' she said with her hand still in mine.

She then described the route to the castle, and we parted with expressions of mutual regard.

I toiled conscientiously up the slope in the heat of the day. On my way down I lost my bearings and asked a handsome old man the way back to Calle Grande, where I had left the car. As he gave me directions, I noticed that he used the seventeenth-century construction *en llegando* (on arriving) rather than the contemporary form *al llegar*; in Teba they still spoke the language of Cervantes. It was a joy to hear.

When I stopped at a bar to refresh myself after my climb, it was a minor shock to find Isabel González at the counter. She again held out her hand and said:

'Isabel González.'

'Yes, of course,' I answered hastily. 'We have already met. Just an hour or so ago. You gave me directions . . .'

She overrode this.

'But I have seen you before . . . eight or ten years ago in Ardales. You came to our houses with two *señoras* and saw our pictures.'

I cudgelled my brains. Certainly I had been to Ardales, which was a few miles south of Teba, but not, I was sure, when she said and not with two *señoras*.

'Now I live here,' she went on, unperturbed. 'I am married. Look, here are my rings.'

She coughed; this turned into a minor convulsion and she asked for a glass of water, which was given her.

'I am not at all well, I must drink as much liquid as I can; my throat is an inferno.'

When she walked out after further handshaking, those standing around said she was touched.

'She is strange. She suffers from her nerves.'

There it was: the marvellously simple and definitive diagnosis of any kind of mental illness or instability, requiring no further tedious probing or analysis. But Isabel had nice manners, as did all the people I met in Teba.

I lunched well and very cheaply in the *casino*-bar: a huge salad, and excellent dish of assorted fried fish, crème caramel, wine and coffee. The TV was showing excerpts from a major bullfight the previous day. I got into conversation with the waiter about the widely held belief in Spanish cruelty to animals. He said that, on the contrary, Spaniards respected the dignity of animals. He retailed the opinion of a *torero* who had recently told an interviewer that for a fighting bull to be killed in a commercial slaughterhouse would be in his eyes the most enormous crime, as it would deny the animal the dignified death he had been bred for *and* the requirement for his killer to do it openly, in the sunshine, hiding nothing and risking ignominy if he bungled. As we spoke a piglet, two geese and various hens were brought through the dining room from the back yard, presumably to be sacrificed for some feast. At least they had been spared the indignity and degradation of factory farming.

In the afternoon I found the *parroquia* open. It is a spacious semi-hall-church with strange brown marble columns, each made up of nine roundels like superimposed cheeses with dark glossy rinds. Other features are the provincial Churrigueresque *retablo*, the sacristy with sumptuous vestment chests, a little vestment museum and the mausoleum of the Peñalver, Albarracín and Durán families (all prominent in Ronda). Several nuns were busy as good house-wives preparing the chalice and other utensils of the Mass against the arrival of the (peripatetic) priest: he turned out to be a fresh-looking young man who gave me a cheerful good afternoon as he bustled in.

Meanwhile, two men in one corner of the church were preparing a Virgin on a float for a procession later in the evening. Either they had lunched well like me or were nat-urally friendly, or both. The slim one at once took me for English. '*Alto y colorado*' were the essential clues: tall and red-faced. The fat one puffed contentedly at a stinking black cigar as he arranged the folds of the heavily embroidered robe. It emerged that he was the municipal police sergeant of Benaoján; but his native town was Teba and he always came to give a hand on feast days. He told me a bit about Teba and its products: agriculture in general, superb broad beans, the best olive oil in Spain (a frequent claim), leather goods and so forth. Tourism didn't figure in his list at all, despite the regional government's promotion of it. Neither here nor in Cañete was there a tourist or a souvenir shop or even a postcard in sight.

Winding down from Teba, I found myself beginning to develop a theory linking the manners and attractiveness or otherwise of a pueblo with its altitude: I don't simply mean altitude above sea level, though that plays a part, but more importantly above the surrounding countryside. For it was becoming clear to me that where a small town was built on an eminence or mound, so that the main road, filling stations and so forth had to be diverted round its base, that place conserved its integrity, intimacy and old-fashioned courtesies better than those into which the tides of progress and development swept more easily. It might be called the island effect. In Olvera, Osuna, Cañete and Teba the island effect appeared to be still strong. If you wanted something more streamlined and impersonal you would have to look elsewhere. But if you were in the business of outflanking

**. . . if you were in the business of outflanking the modern
world, it looked as if the high ground was the best**

the modern world, it looked as if the high ground was the
best. It would be interesting to see if this was borne out
when I reached the high-perched ancient cities of the hinterland of Cádiz. Meantime, however, I was beginning to feel
the tug of the Ronda heartlands, which I had deliberately
avoided so far but which should certainly not be neglected
– for they might still conceal some unsuspected haven from
which our local friendships could be maintained with less
disruption than if we made a bigger leap.

167

6

VISIONS OF UTOPIA

After a night in Ronda's comfortable Hotel Polo, I collected some fresh laundry from Ana and set off on my next circuit. My first stop was Arriate, only six kilometres from the capital of the Serranía. The normal way is to take the turning a short distance along the road to Campillos and Granada. This descends into the valley past a tennis club, one of the essential new amenities demanded by the Ronda bourgeoisie; the road then runs into the little town past the railway station at the head of the last great curve which brings the ponderous 'expresses' chuntering up from Algeciras to Ronda on their long night's journey to Madrid.

But there is another more intricate and interesting route off the Seville road, along an unsigned neighbourhood track which passes through a charming district called El Llano de la Cruz. Stretching along the upper valley of the Guadalcobacín (popularly Río de Arriate), this was the favourite retreat of the middle classes in the last century. Some of the houses on the gentle slopes are substantial farm buildings with a wing converted for the owners. Such are Santo Domingo and El Marqués, both with towers, and El Vicario, with a semi-secret garden. Most of them have a palm tree or two, maybe some cypresses, often a chapel. Others are more modest, just simple farmsteads with lofts which have been bought up, adapted and surrounded with wire by townees; then there are a few coastal-style villas sticking

168

out like sore thumbs – but not many of these yet. All this part of the valley is leafy with quinces and riverside trees, and many of the houses remain delightful, but it is much more suburbanised than when Hilly and I considered and finally rejected it for our country retreat in the early seventies. It is now less desirable than it was then, and much more expensive. Some of the finer and more elevated houses on the hillside are now confronted with the new raw side of Ronda, which was probably an inevitable development, but which one does not necessarily want to contemplate on a daily basis. Lower down, the lanes between cottages with orchards, which Hilly christened 'Devon', are becoming increasingly a prey to traffic.

Arriate itself, because of its proximity to Ronda, is the pueblo of the region most determined to prove itself no satellite of its grander neighbour. Ronda responds by denigrating the Arrieteños as *catetos*, bumpkins. Arriate hits back with the proud boast that its processions at Easter, Corpus Christi and on the Day of the Virgin much outshine those of its larger neighbour; and if this claim is not entirely well founded, certainly the pueblo is famed for importing prestigious and expensive brass bands – the army, the navy, the airforce, you name it – for these occasions.

Much of the pueblo's building is nineteenth-century, in that good plain style with few adornments save round the window grilles or over lintels which has dominated village architecture for centuries, regardless of fashion outside. Nowadays, however, shiny tiled dados are becoming more frequent on the façades of houses, while along the road out to Setenil you find crazy-paved walls, some wholly tiled fronts in sickly green or liver hues, and even impressive iron gates leading to small bungalows – or to nowhere. But these developments are still outnumbered by the traditional buildings; and the view of New Ronda exposes its much more brutal housing blocks under the crouching hump-backed sierra.

Arriate's success (it has increased its population, which

169

is the test) seems to have been due to three successive Communist administrations under the same mayor, who performed to perfection the main function of Spanish mayors, which is to get as much government subsidy and grant for the pueblo as possible; at the same time he also managed to encourage private investment. The small bourgeoisie were quite undismayed by their mayor's political affiliation; he did a good job for Arriate, and that was all that mattered. Now the socialists were in for the first time since *la democracia*: one would have to wait and see what they would do. The real Left was striking back with a massive poster campaign, from which the very word 'Communist' had been expunged; the end of the Cold War had filtered through to Andalusia. The new grouping with the Communists at the core was called Izquierda Unida, United Left.

The posters were plastered everywhere. They carried attractive pictures of the new Communist leader, Julio Anguita, looking like a handsome American professor of literature with his button-down collar and well-trimmed beard. Anguita had been a great success as mayor of Córdoba, where he was widely respected by all parties, including the Right. Alongside him on the poster figured the local candidate, who looked like a pleasant young bank manager in executive suit and tie. I wondered if Anguita, with the reputation he had built in Córdoba for clean government, would profit from the corruption attributed by the press to the socialist administration. His slogan, *Otra Forma de Gobernar*, another way of governing, was the eternal claim of the politician, usually received by the rest of us with scepticism. In view of the Communists' good record in Arriate, perhaps the voters would fall for it and elect the nicely-groomed young candidate. But whatever the colour of local government one thing seemed certain: Arriate would remain house-proud and aggressive, and would continue to splash out on its saints.

On the lower rim of the pueblo, right on the edge of the

country, rise the red brick walls and belfry of an old folks' home, the Asilo de Ancianos. I rang the bell and asked for Don Antonio Gamboa, once parish priest of the Iglesia Mayor in Ronda and now semi-retired as chaplain of this cool and spacious place. Round the patio sat or dozed some very elderly persons, some bright-eyed and fully aware, others with vacant gaze; a gardener tended plants along one wall; a sort of dolls' house contained a dozen canaries; some inmates peered down curiously from an upper gallery; a busy, smiling nurse-nun in spotless white garb with knee-length skirt showed me to the door of Don Antonio's apartment.

Twenty years before, Don Antonio had been a familiar figure to us, gliding in his soutane along the alleys of the *Ciudad* as if borne on a cushion of air, smiling and nodding at his flock, extending his hand for street urchins to kiss his ring. Now in clerical grey shirt and dog-collar with a pectoral cross, he looked (and probably was) smaller. He welcomed me warmly and took me to a little terrace at the back of his quarters, which overlooked a slope of stubble below wooded hills with a splash of green pasture high up on the skyline. A man with two mules was threshing grain with a wooden sledge. Two of the white-clad sisters were walking up the slope with some lay friends or relatives. There was nothing, except perhaps their hemlines, to suggest the twentieth century. Don Antonio apologised for the slight smell of drains rising from a leaky pipe in the leafy gully below; he kept on telling town hall but they did nothing; would I prefer to go indoors? The odour was minimal and the view delightful, so I said no. Then he went inside and brought back a tray with two cool bottles of beer and some cashew nuts.

The sisters, he said, were called the Hermanas de los Desamparados, sisters of the shelterless; their headquarters was in Valencia. They wore the white habit in summer and black in winter, and attached enormous importance to cleanliness. There were fifty residents in the home, all old, some physically infirm, others mentally disturbed. The nuns changed *all* their sheets *every* day, so that no finger should be pointed at any single individual for incontinence. And all the men were given a complete change of clothing, shirt and trousers, twice a week. The food served was simple and wholesome: did I know of Saint Teresa of Avila and her foundations? A little, I said. Well, she too had always insisted on good simple fare; when inspecting one of her convents her first demand of the nun in charge of the kitchen was always, '*Sopas de ajo . . . y bien hechas!*' Garlic soup . . . but well cooked!

Don Antonio went on to talk about the four foundations of the Marquis of Moctezuma: the Castillo and Santa Teresa schools in Ronda (my Jaime had spent a couple of terms at the latter), the Monte de Piedad y Caja de Ahorros de Ronda, and the Asilo here in Arriate. The object of the Monte was to put an end to usury. As the Monte is one of my *bêtes noires*, I could not refrain from remarking that it was often itself accused of usurious interest rates, expropriation and excessive favouritism towards its own employees, enabling them to buy up everything in sight. He would have none of this.

'Before,' he said, 'when a countryman borrowed two thousand pesetas to sow a crop, he had to repay four thousand. Those were medieval rates. The Monte changed all that. Also, the warm clothes that people pawned in summer were returned in winter, often regardless of the debt. Such accusations are made by socialist politicians keen to get their hands on its wealth for political purposes.'

I asked next about the role of charity in general, in view of the many tentacles of the welfare state.

'Charity,' he said with animation, 'is the greatest thing there is. Did not Saint Paul say as much? What is provided by those working for a salary can never compare to it. It is always rather cold, don't you think? They work for so many hours, and dish out determined measures of welfare, and that is it. There is no delicacy, no consideration of personal circumstances. Look, if I thrust this dish of nuts at you and say, this is your ration, take it, you recoil. You have just done so! But if I tempt you and say, please try another, you can gracefully accept!'

He put the dish down, smiling with delight at the success of his little gambit, before his rather hatchet-like face reverted to its solemn mould.

'You see,' he added, 'Ortega y Gasset put it well, or if the words are not his, he quoted from another: "Man is himself *and* his circumstances." You must not forget the circumstances, the difficulties, the afflictions.'

I suddenly recalled a snatch of conversation overheard from a call-box in Osuna: a man was talking urgently, perhaps to a creditor: 'But you must know, for Christ's sake, that man is man within his circumstances!' No one can say that Spanish intellectuals (unlike British) do not have some effect.

'Christ said, "Judge not that ye be not judged," ' Don Antonio went on. 'The trouble is that the state makes judgements. Probably it has to. But Christianity does not judge.'

He was eager now to turn to international affairs. The election of the new Archbishop of Canterbury had presented problems, no? The state had intervened? I did my best to explain the relationship of the government to the Church of England. Runcie had been too 'liberal' for Mrs Thatcher's taste; she had insisted on someone more ... I searched for the word, and came up with 'fundamentalist', although I was not entirely happy with it because of its current association with Islam.

'Evangelical, you mean?' he suggested helpfully.

Yes, I agreed, that would be the proper term.

But his real interest was reserved for the *rapport* between Gorbachev and the Pope. He brought out a magazine article and made me read it from beginning to end. Gorbachev had actually said that Juan Pablo II was an immense influence for good. A year or so before that would have been incredible, wouldn't it? The collapse of East European Communism also seemed incredible but was not really so: all powers collapsed in the end, except the Church of Christ. *'El que va contra el altar, se estrella!'* Whoever pits himself against the altar is dashed to pieces. He dwelt with satisfaction on this saying.

I asked about Spanish Communism, particularly in view of the widely acclaimed regime of the popular Communist mayor of Arriate. He smiled wryly.

'He did not do us much good here. He constantly refused to mend that *cloaca*, the great drain you can smell from here. And the socialists who are now in power are the same. But yes, he did some good things for the pueblo. You have to understand that this is not Leninism or Stalinism. It is a more humane form of Communism. They are even trying to change their name now. Everything that is good in Communism is taken from Christianity.'

'But surely most Communists are atheists, even the reconstructed ones?'

'Some,' he said, 'profess atheism from motives of pride or virility. But there are very few who believe in their hearts that man is just a little animal that rots in the earth.'

We turned to faith, which he said required no scientific proof and indeed could not live with one, because then faith would become meaningless; nonetheless faith was totally reasonable if you thought of it as had the French philosopher Pascal when he made his famous wager: 'Bet without hesitation that he exists . . .'

Don Antonio looked over my shoulder as I wrote this down in my exercise book.

'He with a capital H,' he admonished. 'We are talking about God. Anyway, Pascal went on, "If you win, you win everything; if you lose, you lose nothing." '

I asked about Spanish faith these days, especially among the young.

'Look,' he said, 'a few years ago the young became as thrilled with politics as children with new shoes. The politicians were delighted. "The young are ours!" they thought to themselves, and gave them the vote at eighteen. But the new recruits got bored and disillusioned, and now many don't bother to vote. You could say that without politics and without religion (for state education has not been favourable to religion at all) they have nothing left but the discotheque and immorality and pornography and drugs. But it is not as simple as that. It is true that they do not go to church, but they are nearly all believers. They have a great admiration for Jesus Christ. They are not lacking in values. After all, human values are *born* in man. Cold, atheistical materialism is like a slab of stone trapping those values in a pit, but they are still there and always struggling to get out.'

'You say the young admire Jesus Christ, but is not the real Spanish admiration reserved for the Virgin?'

'One must be very careful here,' Don Antonio said with a frown of concentration. 'The mother figure is always tremendously attractive. Men long for their mothers. Mothers intuitively understand the problems of sons. So the Virgin is above all a mediator. Christ came to save men, not to condemn them. Few understand that, so they turn to the Virgin in their distress.'

'Is it not the special genius of the Catholic Church to have understood this?'

'Perhaps. But we must be very clear the Virgin is a woman. She is not divine.'

'You would not think that from the processions.'

'No, you are wrong. If you look carefully at the iconography, there are few aspects of the Virgin that are not directly related to Christ. You said you wrote books. Look, I too have written a book. I will get a copy and dedicate it for you.'

He went out and returned with a paperback called *Olimpiada del Espíritu para Jovenes Inquietos*, Spiritual Olympics for the Anxious Young, which he put into my hands. The Olympic flag fluttered bravely on the cover; inside were pictures of young athletes which might have come from

175

Chariots of Fire. The text appeared to be a series of spiritual exercises cast in athletic terms, though one chapter was an interlude of relaxation with music and poetry including quotations from Saint John of the Cross and Antonio Machado. It was all a preparation for the 'great marathon'.

I returned it to him to write the dedication. When he had done so, he thumbed forward to the prologue.

'I thought of all sorts of important people I might get to write that,' he said, 'and then I reminded myself that I am a modest man with no need of such fanfares, so I got the goalkeeper of the Málaga football team to do it. Look!'

He held the page out to me with radiant pleasure; it was indeed signed, 'Fernando, Goalkeeper of CD Málaga'.

It was time for him to go about his duties and for me to leave. He guided me gently to the door. It was almost a shock to find myself back in the bright sun and busy street life of Arriate after more than an hour in that cool interior with a man animated and thrilled by the spiritual life. But the contrast is not really as great as it then seemed, for Spain understands how to absorb the influence of such as Don Antonio, even in pueblos on the make like Arriate.

I went next to one of the main bars, where I had arranged to meet Antonio Alarcón, brother of Rafael of La Mimbre. Antonio had suffered a back injury in the building trade and relieved the boredom of his life with a little activity as a *corredor* or broker in everything from property to livestock. There are still no estate agents in Ronda except for those promoting new developments. Antonio said he had a *huerta* outside Setenil which he was determined to show me.

From Arriate the road threads the loose necklace of houses forming the *barrio* of Los Prao (the pastures) and rises to a junction on the border between the provinces of Málaga and Cádiz. From this point a good earthen track (which I had often taken by horse in the old days) goes straight towards Alcalá del Valle. The motor road switches left towards Setenil.

To make conversation I began to speak of the politics of Arriate and the saintliness of Don Antonio, but my companion had no time for such topics. His interest was in the land.

'Look what you can see from here: Setenil, Olvera, Ronda la Vieja . . . *Que campos más alegres!*'

It was, as he said, a cheerful countryside. Once it had all been *dehesa* or *monte bajo*, rolling acres of holm-oaks and scrub ideal for the Andalusian black pig. Now grainlands have encroached, many mighty oaks have fallen and weekend 'chalets' have sprung up along the roadside – but each with its *huerto* of vegetables and a few fruit trees, representing the motorised bourgeoisie's tentative embrace of rural life. Though the oaks have been forced back onto the higher terrain, hugging the outcrops of the sierra, the views may well have been enhanced, sweeping as they do now over yellow stubble, rimmed by the dark residue of ancient forests and stippled by immense cloud shadows. The rootling piglets, banned for twenty years owing to 'African' swine fever (everything bad in Spain comes out of Africa) in favour of monstrous barrack-blocks of factory-fed sows, are at last back on the trot – wired in, it is true, but still free to forage and grow naturally without a revolting diet of whey and antibiotics.

Setenil has acquired something of a cult status because of its curious topography. It clings to the walls of a serpentine ravine carrying a rivulet which is little more than a drain except during occasional outbursts of furious spate. At more than one point on the rim of this ravine the tourist board has placed a bossy notice reading 'picturesque view', which indeed it is, but such supererogatory interference with one's own perceptions induces, in this traveller at any rate, a cussed sort of resistance and a general disposition to look very critically at the place. Setenil's claim to fame lies in its rupestrian dwellings with neat white dolls'-house façades, whose roofs are formed by overhanging ledges of rock. The effect is strangely fungoid: white stems under

177

mushroom eaves, leading to thoughts of old crones weaving spells or pursuing other minor forms of evil. The ruined Arab fort and the parish church occupy a bluff above these troglodyte streets. The church has a late Gothic vault whose swirling ribs are pleasing, but the westernmost bay has collapsed and been replaced by an extended portico, giving the building an oddly lopsided shape; the congregation is made up mainly of women – perhaps some of them witches from the cave-houses down below.

But Setenil's real hub is the *cafelillo* in the little plaza, where the stern concentration of men playing dominoes or hunched over cards creates an atmosphere so intensely self-absorbed as to be almost impenetrable to strangers; you feel yourself repelled by some psychic force when you try to push your way in. The square is always packed with cars, though the most intricate pilotage under arches and up or down gear-wrenching slopes is required to get there. At one end is a sizeable house entirely clad in green-and-white lavatory tiles, exuding lustrous bourgeois disdain for the cave dwellers along the river bed. Here Antonio left me contemplating more posters bearing Anguita's handsome and discreetly bearded face while he vanished to fetch his relatives who owned the *huerta*. Eventually he returned with a man and a lad, who climbed in behind us, and I managed to extricate the car from the coiled and knotted streets, not without relief.

Just outside Setenil we took a track which brought us down to the Arroyo de Alcalá a little above its passage through the town. Several slopes on the way were covered with what my companions called *sidras*, which looked remarkably like canteloupe melons to me. They were indeed nothing to do with cider but rather a type of melon whose fibrous flesh was turned into 'angels' hair', a filling much used in cakes and pastries. In conversation I noticed that Antonio and his relative referred to each other not by name but as *compadre*, which reflected the close tie formed by the marriage of Antonio's daughter to the other man's son. Nonetheless, as they were not blood relatives they retained the formal third person and were reserved in their speech.

We soon stopped at a small farmhouse, where we left the car. The 'Huerta Flor', Flower Orchard, our destination, faced us across a stream which we crossed easily on foot, for it carried little water at this time of year. With a Land-Rover, they said, one could drive up to the house. What about in winter, if the river was in spate? No problem, they said, it would be easy to build a concrete bridge of tubes. Looking at the sandy banks, I wondered. The house, on first sight, was a disappointment; it had a corrugated-iron roof. But this could always be tiled. Everything else was pure enchantment. A patch of garden on a platform with a few old-fashioned unpruned rosebushes hung over a half-moon of flat land which followed the curve of the stream (and was no doubt subject to flooding). But the bulk of the land was contained in a re-entrant or subsidiary valley, watered by its own spring and flanked on one side by a steep wooded ridge with ilexes, walnuts, gall-oaks and wild olives, rising to a clear crest marked by a dry-stone wall and sharply silhouetted trees. Beneath this were some cultivated olives and a little swathe of arable land, shaped like a horn, over whose inner curve rose a miniature cliff of the same formation as that which harboured the cave dwellings in the town. Concealed in this rock-face was another spring, like a tiny subterranean lake, running into a hand-made trough, where women used to bring their washing; next to this was a stone bench.

'Here,' said the owner, 'they could sit and chat in the shade before carrying their washing back to the house. Look, the bench is sheltered from both sun and rain by the overhang of the cliff.'

'Here,' enthused Antonio, 'it is so sheltered you could plant an orange grove.'

I tried to sort out the existing trees. There was one small orange tree, but the slope was mainly occupied by a motley collection of such old Spanish favourites as *madroño* (arbutus, the emblem of Madrid), medlar, apricot, pomegranate and persimmon. There were also unkempt roses like those in front of the house. These few grace-notes together with the natural setting combined to create a rustic bower in which I would have lingered longer had the others not beckoned me on. There was more to see, they said.

The tip of the horn met the dry-stone wall. Following this, we came up onto a small plateau of grazing land with holm-oaks and views round the compass: over the property; down into the stream where there was a large abandoned flour mill; outwards to the cemetery of Setenil with its avenue of cypresses; and beyond that to the great tilted tableland of Ronda la Vieja with its slab of Roman masonry like a giant milestone.

'We have had some wonderful picnics up here,' said the owner, 'with that view of the Roman fort.'

'Fort . . . or theatre?' I hinted, knowing it to be the latter.

'You may be right,' he acknowledged cheerfully. 'I have never been up there.'

His brown piglets had escaped from their run and we followed their tracks where they had rootled and scuffed. He was quite unperturbed.

'They never stray far,' he said.

We had come full circle and were standing looking down on the house. Because of the intricacies of its configuration the place had somehow seemed larger than the nine hectares or twenty-two acres which was its official measurement. As we slithered down, he drew my attention to the irrigation tank, jauntily painted blue to bring it into the swimming-pool family; and he pointed out where he had sown maize or chickpeas in previous years. Finally, he showed us the chicken-run and the abundant supply of firewood.

'Here you can grow anything,' he said. 'You make the kitchen garden wherever you want and plant your tomatoes and peppers and so forth there. Then if you sow potatoes and chickpeas, and with all the fruit there is on the place

– and if you kill a couple of pigs – why, you have everything you can possibly want. You need buy nothing but bread!'

When I asked him if he had ever kept cattle to graze the upper plateau and the slopes, he said not.

'For one thing I don't understand cattle. Then they might fall over the edge and that is a lot of money gone. But really, you know, I don't like the great blundering things. With pigs and hens and vegetables and the odd goat, if you like, you know where you are.'

He had conjured up, most compellingly, the age-old dream of self-sufficiency; he had rubbed the lamp and the genie had sprung out of the bottle. It took me back to the heroic days on our own *campo* when Hilly and I had tried it, with very limited success. So, though he had managed to enthrall and enmesh me yet again in the dream, I was sceptical of his claims that the Huerta Flor could exist as a little autarchy. He himself had a business in the town and his strapping son was in that too, not working the land. Indeed, it was clear from the rudimentary arrangements in the house that they had never lived there, much less lived off it. For all its earthiness, the Huerta Flor was a prosperous shopkeeper's *recreo*, of which for some reason he had now tired: perhaps he needed the money for his business, perhaps he wanted to buy or build a villa somewhere more accessible.

And yet . . . and yet . . . if anyone had the will and sufficient skills to rehabilitate Arcadia, this was the place. Classical antiquity would have approved the adherence to the old crops and herds which were the staple of the Homeric world. In the dark or middle ages a family would have survived well on such a plot. The Renaissance would have waved a literary wand over it. The eighteenth century would have approved the feathery outline of the trees and the rustic nooks and crannies apt for languid hours; the nineteenth century would have liked the ingenuity of the irrigation system, and the twentieth century . . . well, I might not be representative, but for me it was an idea to flirt with, the stuff of daydreams, though not, I knew in my bones, for me or mine. Yet that did not mean it would have no takers, for that crescent of land beckoned like an enticing finger from long ago.

Later, I asked Antonio what he thought was the rock-bottom price his *compadre* would accept. He said ten million pesetas, or approximately sixty thousand pounds. This could seem cheap or expensive according to means and expectations. But if any reader of this book with more youth, energy and resources than myself would like to look at it, I will gladly put him in touch with Antonio (that is suggest to him in which bar in the Calle de la Bola in Ronda he might be found), who will I am sure take him out to see the Huerta Flor. Possibly it has not yet been sold. Not every buyer will want to build a bridge which may be swept away by the first flood. And even if it has a new owner, it might well be sold again. In rural Spain there are no agents' boards. If you like the look of a place, you can ask if it is for sale and, if the price is right, it may well be. It is the mission of the *corredor* to stimulate such deals. The buyer I have in mind for the Huerta Flor is in his thirties or forties with a bonny but sturdy wife, two lively children and a modest private income. The important thing is that he should not view it as a cheaper substitute for a place in Marbella with sprinklers on the lawn, but rather see himself as an apostle of the New Arcadia.

Hardly anything could be further from the crabbed cuteness of Setenil than the grid of straight white streets which make up Alcalá del Valle, its nearest neighbour. There are several Alcalás in Andalusia. Alcalá la Real, de Guadaira and de los Gazules are all picturesque in their different ways. This one is the ugly duckling. But let it not be thought that Alcalá del Valle is without its appeal: despite its plainness I hold it in some affection and, having left Antonio with his relatives, I headed towards it.

Years back, I had adopted Alcalá as an occasional bolt-hole from Ronda. It was just the right distance for a good ride and an overnight stay at the *posada*, the Parador de Basilio, which had a well-found stable and served a good supper for man and beast. The journey took some three hours via Arriate and Los Prao, then served only by a dirt road, and on to the provincial border; from there a thumping good track (the one I had passed with Antonio en route for Setenil) led through the oak forest to Alcalá itself.

The first time I did this, riding along at a hand canter, I came up behind what looked like a riderless mule with loaded baskets but no one in charge of it. As I drew level, a blanket-covered heap on top of the packsaddle stirred and a boy unfurled himself from sleep. In the baskets were boxes of fish, as I could tell by their smell. The boy looked about twelve, but was probably fifteen. He said he went to Arriate every other day to get the fish off the slow train, the *corto*, and bring it back to Alcalá, a round trip of about twenty-five kilometres. What was unsold by his father in the pueblo he took on the next day to Algámitas, a further thirty kilometres there and back. He slept all through Sunday and till midday on Monday, then started his round again.

Hearing me cajoling my mare in an attempt to keep her to the pace of his mount, he asked me what was that name I was calling her.

'*Golondrina*,' I said, which means swallow.

'We do not name our animals here,' he said. 'We say the grey, the bay, the black, the mule, the donkey.'

'That's not always so,' I said, delighted to be able to correct him. 'There are many names for mules. I know only a few. Often they are called after bullfighters or singers, for example *La Paquera, La Pastora, Boticaria, Bombita, Machaco* . . .'

These were all names Frasquito the woodman had told me. I paused and asked the boy what his mule was called.

'*Mula*,' he said.

When I reached the town, I soon found the *posada*, and was unloading my things when I realised that my *alforja*, the double saddlebag of thick grey material with a slit between the pouches to fit over the high chairback of the saddle, was no longer there. It held my extra sweaters, shoes, shaving kit and camera. The last place I remembered consciously checking on it was back among the oak trees just before I met the fish-boy. Cursing myself for not having secured it properly, I went back at a fast trot, anxious to cover the ground before dark. The first person I met outside the town was a little old man, tanned and toothless, leading a donkey.

'You haven't by any chance seen a grey *alforja*,' I began, then saw the object itself laid across the donkey's panniers.

His face broke slowly into a delighted grin.

'It's lucky for you it was *I* who found it,' he said, 'for it might easily have been someone from Arriate or Ronda, and those people can't be trusted.'

I agreed I had been supremely lucky it was him and thanked him profusely.

'Look first,' he said, 'to see that nothing is missing. I have not even looked inside. I do not know what the *alforja* contains.'

He waited eagerly for me to examine the contents, which I refused to do, saying that I had not the slightest doubt they were intact. He seemed a little disappointed that his honesty could not be paraded to those who were now gathering round.

'Very well then,' he said, 'take it. My name is Pablo Navarro, always at your service. Just over the bridge on the right is my house, which is your house also.'

I gave him fifty pesetas, which he was bound by honour to refuse the first time, but when further pressed he accepted the note with evident satisfaction. I rode back to the *posada* in a much better mood than I had left it.

That evening I met a handsome young man of twenty-five or so, unemployed and rather drunk, who spoke very bitterly and scornfully of the town.

'In this town,' he said, 'nobody rules but Don Mierda. I don't care if he has a capital of four or seven or ten million pesetas: he is still a *mierda* and they are all *mierdas* who have capital and why we should have to respect and obey them for their money and call them Don Fulano and Don Mengano is a mystery beyond my understanding, for they are all *mierdas* and full of *mierda* and deserve nothing but to eat their own *mierda*.'

Mierda means shit. His companions apologised for his condition but obviously agreed with his sentiments, and from that day I realised that Alcalá had a strong, pungent, proletarian personality of its own.

Though toned down by greater affluence, Alcalá retains its proletarian flavour today. The houses are neat and white and stark with no flowerpots or window dressing. There are no coats of arms over doorways. The grandest housefronts are in plain toasted brick or modern coloured tiles. The town hall in the upper square has had a post-modern facelift that might have come straight out of London's Docklands. Lower down there are brash pub-disco-bars along a new esplanade. Some of the walls of the raw new buildings are still unwhitewashed and plastered with political posters, many bearing the beguiling and ubiquitous features of Julio Anguita. The only noticeable refinement in this district is that the streets are named after the most delicate poets: Federico García Lorca, Rafael Alberti, Vicente Aleixandre. That is not sufficient to have secured the regional government's accolade of inclusion in the touristical *Ruta de los Pueblos Blancos*; but I did not get the impression that this was of burning concern to the people of Alcalá.

I walked first up to the church. I had been told that during the August feast days the patron saint, San Roque, was still brought out in procession and I wanted to see this, for I wondered how much clout the patron still had in this radical pueblo. The church was shut. I consulted a group of old men sitting on a wall; they thought it might be tomorrow – or the day after – but they couldn't be sure. I next tried a bar. The barman and those on either side of me at the counter disclaimed all knowledge of any such event. It was only when I looked over my shoulder and saw that the whole wall behind me was painted with a rising sun on which was stamped a red sickle (but no hammer) that I realised I had wandered into a Communist den, which would naturally abjure all such superstitious practices.

Back in the street, I saw a man carrying an Andalusian flag – a white bar between two bars of green – which led me to suppose he had something to do with the festivities. I quickened my step and caught up with him. When I put my question to him about the procession of San Roque, he looked at me crossly over his shoulder.

'I have no idea. How should I know? I am an atheist.'

He entered a compound where men were whitewashing and hammering and hanging flags, bunting and paper lanterns. It turned out to be the *caseta* or club tent of the Communists. They suggested I should try the official *caseta municipal*, which might know more about such bourgeois fetishes as saints. I then came upon the entrance to a discotheque, guarded by a sinister-looking youth in a T-shirt and dark glasses, smoking a cheroot. When I told him of my quest, he burst out laughing and summoned his friends to join in his mirth.

'Sorry,' he said when they had all laughed their fill at the foreigner in search of the old pop culture of religious processions, 'but I really can't help. That's not our scene. You'll have to ask the priest.'

Following their directions to the priest's house – despite their scepticism they knew well enough where he lived – I again passed the church. It has no tower to speak of but shelters behind an unusual stepped façade with a large clock in the centre, giving it the look of some official building, or a railway station. This time the door was open, and I slipped in. However secular the air outside it was immediately dispelled; here was a veritable repository of images. I swiftly identified Saint John the Baptist, the Virgin of Sorrows, the Sacred Heart of Jesus, the Assumption of the

Virgin, a Virgin and Child enclosed in a silver penumbra, the Three Marys and Saint John, and finally San Roque with the dog who brought him little loaves of bread in the wilderness.

At this point a small, neat man in rimless glasses and shirtsleeves came up to me. He was bearing keys, and said he was about to close. I had just moved on to study a wooden panel in high relief, perhaps of the seventeenth century.

'That,' he said, 'is the Virgin of Caño Santo appearing to a herdsman, whose cow she has just saved from the pit into which it had fallen. But perhaps you have not heard of the monastery of Caño Santo?'

I said I had ridden there many years before. I knew it had been founded by the dukes of Osuna but had fallen steadily into ruin since the sequestration and sale of the monastic lands in the 1830s; when I saw it it was a mere shell.

'Then it is more so now,' he said. 'There is talk of restoration, but nothing has happened. In the meantime, the gypsies who deal in antiquities have removed everything portable, including the bell from the belfry.' He paused and added slyly, 'Following their example, I took the holy water stoup you see over there. Why should they have everything?'

'Is there still a *romería*?' I asked.

'Very much so. We take the Virgin out there every year on the first day of May, because that is when she was discovered.'

'But I was told in Cañete that the real Virgin is theirs. She is after all their *patrona*.'

'They are very ignorant and credulous up there,' he said with a superior smile. 'It must be the altitude. The truth is there was a dispute. Eventually the image was divided in two, but the head and shoulders which went to Cañete were burned by the Reds in the Civil War, since when, obviously, Cañete's image lacks authenticity. Ours is at least partly original.'

This was so different from Cañete's account that I would

have pursued these arcane matters further, but the man was jangling his keys, so I asked about San Roque's procession.

'That will be on Saturday.'

Addicted though I was to Alcalá, I could not see myself hanging around for three days. I asked if the people were not turning their backs on their images, particularly here.

'San Roque is still very popular,' he said carefully.

We were now on the doorstep. Thinking a donation would be appropriate, I proffered a hundred-peseta coin, asking him if he was the sacristan.

'No,' he said, accepting it. 'I am the parish priest.'

I apologised profusely: 'Seeing you in civilian clothes . . .'

'Don't bother. I am a Galician from the north. I do not stand on ceremony.'

'How do you feel about the Andalusians?'

'*Hombre*, I've been here for twenty-two years. I am half *andaluz* by now.'

'They are good people here, on the whole?'

He smiled with wary tolerance.

'Like all God's children, they fall into errors. But let me suggest something to you. Come back on May Day and you will see an event of great interest marked by much popular enthusiasm. The whole town accompanies the Virgin on the *romería*. Even the Communists.'

Back in the lower town the Communist *caseta* was now in full swing, apparently the most popular of all the tented pleasure domes along the main concourse of the fair. Despite the new look epitomised by Anguita, posters of Lenin, Che Guevara and La Pasionaria hung behind the long zinc counter, from which the citizens of Alcalá were ordering long, strong *cuba libres*, gin and tonics or clinking tubular glasses of *tinto de verano*. Some young girls round a table were clapping and singing (in mid-August) an old Christmas carol, '*Los peces en el río* . . .' A plump but exquisitely grey-hatted and accoutred *caballero* minced by on his neutered dapple charger, maned *à la* Velázquez, leading the shirtsleeved municipal band towards the portable ring which had been erected beyond the esplanade for the evening's bullfight.

'I gather the socialists are in power now,' I said to the barman as he mixed *cuba libres* under the picture of Guevara.

'Yes,' he acknowledged. 'Of the thirteen councillors we have six and they have the rest. But we shall get back.'

'But aren't you finished – after Eastern Europe?'

'Not at all. There is still much to be struggled for which the PSOE can't deliver.'

'I get the impression that the PSOE are doing quite well. There is a lot of new building. They must be spending money on the pueblo.'

'Yes, they are spending all they can. Many people now pay taxes who didn't. Particularly if you are on the payroll as an ordinary working man, you now pay tax. The trouble is the landowners and doctors and other professionals still avoid it; they don't pay their share.'

'I thought the government was going after them.'

'Bah, they have clever accountants . . . those people always have their ways and means . . . besides, there are very many vested interests which the PSOE doesn't dare tackle because it relies on them. Only we can do that.'

At the next bar along the concourse, the ruddy-faced man who served the drinks said he would be going back to Germany again after the fair – he hoped for the last time, after twenty years working abroad. What was his job? 'Butcher,' he said grandly. This turned out to be a job in the slaughterhouse. On the tax question, he agreed there was much evasion. But life was undoubtedly better. After forty years of *abandono*, in a mere eleven or twelve years the Spanish people had pulled themselves up by their own efforts. The government couldn't do everything, but it had done much; the houses and roads were there for all to see. He had bought this bar with his earnings abroad; he would do one more spell in Germany because his employer, who doted on him,

Alcalá del Valle a Sus Emigrantes

had begged him to. But that would be that. No, the Communists would not get back.

Along the road, in a little bit of dusty garden with wilting oleanders, stood a stone statue inspired, it would seem, by Soviet social realism. The cloth-capped, shirtsleeved figure, at once chunky and mawkish, represented a man on a platform with two suitcases; these were suggested by one stone slab placed at a slight angle on top of another. The most interesting thing about it was not the work itself but its inscription, which ran: *Alcalá del Valle a Sus Emigrantes.*

190

Licensed, in effect forced, emigration was arguably the most cynical policy of the Franco regime. The Spanish social historian A. M. Bernal has written of 'the image of the emigrants, stretched out on station platforms, transported like herds of beasts, carried off – aided in their passage, as the official jargon went – to countries whose language they could not speak, confined to ghettos, maintaining themselves in isolation, alone, accompanied by nothing but a simple wooden suitcase.' Bernal calculated that roughly two million Andalusians were forced to emigrate, with government connivance. This is the perception that lies behind the statue in Alcalá.

Bernal's view forms the basis of the Left's position on this issue, which is that people were deliberately marginalised so that they would present no threat during Spain's twenty-five years of much-acclaimed economic development. They were conned into believing that they would acquire new skills abroad for the brave new world coming into being in their own country, but were in fact employed in slaughter-houses, hoeing beet and the like. When they could no longer be afforded by their host countries, because of the oil crises of the seventies, they came back to unemployment and stagnation worse than when they had gone obediently into exile in semi-slave conditions in the national interest. To crown it all, they were blamed by the authorities for coming back home where they were surplus to requirements. This goes some way towards explaining why 'booming' Spain still has the highest unemployment rate in Europe.

There was, however, a second wave of migration on the back of the Spanish boom, which took place somewhat less traumatically *within* the Spanish frontiers: notably to Catalonia, where a million Andalusians have formed their own community and districts, maintaining their identity and language in the face of strong local promotion of the Catalan language and culture. They even have their own deputy in the Catalan parliament. Finally, there is a continuing demand for labour to satisfy tourist demands on the coasts.

All this might be thought to sound the death-knell of the Andalusian pueblo. But the pueblo has fought back fiercely. Julian Pitt-Rivers remarked on the Andalusian desire to live in compact communities, and this persists. Whether from abroad, from Catalonia, from Madrid, from the Costa de la Luz, the Costa del Sol, the Costa Dorada or Ibiza, the sons and daughters of the pueblo return whenever possible to their source. The experience of forced labour in foreign parts and of the Andalusian ghettos in Spain itself have, if anything, fortified the belief in the pueblo as Utopia.

The special attachment of the *andaluz* to his homeland is attributed by the archetypal Spanish intellectual, José Ortega y Gasset, in his *Teoría de Andalucía* (1927), to the 'vegetative ideal'. The Andalusians, he says, are one of the oldest peoples in the world, and they know themselves better than any other. Though neither aggressive nor separatist, Andalusia is the region of Spain that possesses the most radical culture of its own. That culture is founded on the exceptionally propitious qualities of the climate and the land, which is 'the last residue that remains to us of paradise'. Its roots are agrarian and it lives by 'amputation of everything that is heroic from life', in contrast to the warlike culture of Castile. The olive is the symbol of peace. Ortega likens Andalusia to China, another ancient pueblo, which has submitted to wave upon wave of conquerors but has always ended by subverting them to its own ways. Four thousand years of idleness cannot be swamped by a mere horde of Mongols or Visigoths. To be an *andaluz*, born in the most favoured corner of the planet, is an extraordinary stroke of luck; to a few select sons of Adam paradise has been given back – with no conditions. This explains the peculiar enthusiasm of the *andaluz* for his *patria chica*.

Ortega's analysis may strike some connoisseurs of Andalusia as being defective in one or two important respects. During the Reconquest Andalusia was repopulated by settlers from the more bellicose north: from Navarre, Galicia, León and Old Castile. Even in this benign climate it was not easy to find people to farm the land when the Muslims (who indeed thought it paradisaical by contrast with the desert) had to be replaced. Though geographers since Strabo and travellers since Ibn Batutah have sung the praises of Andalusia as a land of milk and honey, and this has seeped through into folklore and popular belief, it is not entirely borne out by the facts. Overall, soil in Spain is of poor quality. According to Alison Wright, by Mallada's calculations only 10 per cent of the land can be described as being of good quality, and most of this is to be found in Galicia, the cereal lands of New Castile, parts of Catalonia and the coastal plain of Valencia. In Andalusia only the three-crop-a-year *vega* of Granada enters this league. Everywhere else agriculture has always been and remains very tough. For this reason herding has always been more prestigious than husbandry in the south. The techniques of irrigation which the Moors brought to perfection are still practised, as in my own valley, but the acreage which benefits from their system is small and the new techniques of sprinkling large expanses of plain depend entirely on the reservoirs, which depend on God. The bond between the Christian Andalusian and his soil is thus not always of the idyllic kind described by Ortega. Gardens are a matter of a few (admittedly charming) flowerpots. Few will be found to prune or harvest the olive. Ploughing is a chore; reaping is another; hoeing is the worst. Anybody who is anybody lives in town, preferably with a coat of arms or a religious symbol over his door.

But other things in Ortega ring true still: the economy of effort to produce the desired result and no more; and the modest cuisine. Of the latter Ortega remarks wryly, 'Socialist sensibility has brought to our attention innumerable times that the Andalusian country labourer hardly eats and is tied to a simple diet of *gazpacho*. That is certain but the observation is false because it is incomplete. The truth would be approximated more closely if it were added that in Andalusia everyone eats little or ill, not only the paupers . . . A day labourer in Azpeitia eats more and better than a rich swell of Córdoba or Jaén.' The virtues of light Andalusian fare have become more apparent in a diet-conscious age, but basically the idea of minimum effort requiring minimum fuel remains. You eat as much as you need to perform the labour necessary to assure the optimum amount of leisure. Leisure is the great good, to be whiled away as you wish; that is the gateway to paradise.

The penchant for leisure leads to an attachment to the *fiesta*, the most visible demonstration of leisure (and of a little money in one's purse). Industrial holidays are all very well, but are extremely boring if spent lying on a beach where you know nobody and are not known, and when you are bronzed by toil anyway. The pueblo fair is much more amusing, and there are dozens of saints in the calendar around whom some kind of local holiday can be fabricated. As a result of this attitude, Alcalá del Valle, population just under five thousand, on the borderline of viability, runs to seven days and nights of fair – two more than the larger Olvera – including three days of taurine spectacles: a comic one, a serious *novillada* and one for very young novices.

This passion for *ferias* and *fiestas*, Ortega says correctly, leads the foreigner into the erroneous idea that the *andaluz* is orgiastic. Nothing could be further from the truth. Rather the tempo is *adagio cantabile*. 'The *fiesta*, the Sunday, spills over into the rest of the week and impregnates it with festivity and golden repose. But, also, vice versa, the *fiesta* is less orgiastic and unique, the Sunday is more Monday and more Wednesday than among the northern races. Sevilla is only orgiastic for tourists from the north; for the locals it is always slightly festive and is never so entirely.' The bulls, the fair, Holy Week, are to be taken in one's stride. The nearest thing to a Spanish orgy is the *romería*, which may give rise to drunkenness, fights and riderless horses; the supreme example is the famous one to the Virgin of Rocío, which involves three bacchanalian nights. But the ordinary fair grants no such licence.

Ortega also writes very well about the flummery of Andalusia. 'That which is admirable, mysterious, profound in Andalusia is far beyond the multi-coloured comedy which its inhabitants put on for tourists.' The Andalusian, quite distinctly from the Castilian or Basque, is perfectly happy to make a spectacle of himself for foreigners – without, of course, giving his soul away; he is simply exaggerating a tiny bit what he would be doing naturally. In effect, a subtle, ancient people, who know themselves very well, can take themselves off a little and make a little money on the side without touching the innermost core of their lives.

How does Ortega's theory stand the test of time? I think it remains valid, but it requires important modifications. He could not, for example, have foreseen the tourist boom, that most *immoderate* explosion of nordic frustration. Coinciding with a profound change in the economic equation, this has led to a greater and more cynical exploitation of the *quincalla*, or 'ironmongery' as he called it, of the Andalusian scene than he would have approved of. But the more important point that almost undermines his whole theory of vegetative existence is that, in terms of modern expectations, it has ceased to supply even an attenuated livelihood. His land of milk and honey, his paradise (not even 'demi' in his view) cannot supply cars and *cuba libres* to the young or even, unaided, a dignified retirement for the old. This is where a major revision of the theory is required. The values are much the same; the pueblo is still Utopia (though there is an unresolved query as to the attitude of the young when they themselves become mature). But the terms of survival have changed drastically, for the native economy of most pueblos with under say five thousand souls is pretty marginal to the needs and requirements of its citizens. Thus we come to the essential new ingredient, the preservation of the pueblo as an act of political will.

It is no coincidence that Spain has opted to have a 'regional policy' of the type now out of fashion in Britain; otherwise the country would have split up, leading perhaps to another military dictatorship. The new constitution of 1978 set up another expensive layer of government, *las autonomías*, within the Spanish unitary state. One of the roles of these seventeen 'autonomous' regional governments (including the Junta de Andalucía) is to secure the survival of places like Setenil, Alcalá and many others through a combination of subsidies: regional subsidy of infrastructure and jobs, and central government subsidy via the social security system. The third leg of the economic tripod is provided by the remaining but diminished remittances from abroad of the emigrants honoured by Alcalá's statue, and by some more local earnings on the coast. The large public-sector contribution explains the popularity of the Left and Centre-Left parties pledged to deliver these benefits. I see it all to some extent as the pay-off for the failure of agrarian reform.

It is striking that *la reforma agraria*, the great rallying cry and burning issue from the mid-1830s to 1936, which even induced the Franco regime to set up its rural settlement agency, the Instituto Nacional de Colonización, is no longer on the agenda of the working class. The tremendous bitterness and violence that it engendered have passed into history (though I shall have occasion to refer to it again in certain places where it has left an indelible mark). The big placards that you see in many parts of Andalusia announcing schemes of agrarian reform by the Junta in conjunction with the European Community have nothing to do with the original aspirations of the reformers. They are all large-scale irrigation works for big farms, some of which may be co-operatives though the majority will not, whereas the old-style reformers' demand was for a plot for everyone.

These days, in lieu of the plot people have settled for the *paguita*, the 'little payment' from the state. Though pueblo life remains simple, because the requirements of Utopia are simple, its preservation is costly. It cuts right across unfettered market economics, and stern critics will dismiss it as the fruit of unhealthy nostalgia. All the same, the urge to preserve the pueblo springs from deep cultural roots. There is a widespread conviction that it is worthwhile, that it is part of the proper order of things that fine, bronzed old men should be able to sit around on public benches in the plaza of say Alcalá or Montejaque, while the mature males employ their leisure hours in dominoes and cards, and the young disport themselves at the municipal *piscina*. Unlike Castile, there are no abandoned pueblos, however small, in Andalusia, nor are there likely to be as long as the leading politicians of the day – Felipe González, Alfonso Guerra – come from the deep south.

Too long a diversion to spin out from a naive statue in Alcalá del Valle? Perhaps. If so, I apologise. Maybe I should have tried to enliven it with some such device as Hemingway's when he invented the old lady to listen to his explanations of the bullfight and ask awkward questions, thus breaking up the text with dialogue. But there has already been a lot of dialogue in this book, and there is more to come. We are not going to lack conversation; we may even get sick of it. Also, these things about emigration and local economies had to be said somewhere. It was the statue to the emigrants in Alcalá that set me off, and I think I can say I have shot my theoretical bolt . . . for a bit.

From Alcalá to Cuevas del Becerro is a short drive, crossing the railway line near the station of Setenil, which is several kilometres from its pueblo. If Alcalá is plain, Cuevas is plainer. No aspiring building punctuates the unambitious skyline strung out along a low ridge above the Ronda–Campillos road. Its church is so simple and unpretentious that by comparison Alcalá's is a cathedral. Richard Ford, punning on its name, which means caves of the calf, called it a 'den fittish for beasts'. When I first knew it, it had more bars per metre of street front than any other place in the region. The men of Cuevas were quick to invite and pay. The standard rate of consumption of little thimble-shaped glasses of white wine was about a dozen an hour.

This time I found that it too was in the throes of its fair. In order to accommodate the standard industrial summer holiday, many older and more widely-spaced dates have been junked, and literally dozens of pueblo fairs are packed into August on either side of the feast of the Assumption. Emigration from Cuevas appeared to have yielded dividends: the local link here is with Switzerland, and there were a surprising number of BMWs and similar marques parked outside the lowly houses. Otherwise there were few changes. Cuevas is a long, thin pueblo, and the people seem to have decided very sensibly that theirs is a horizontal rather than a vertical townscape; there are no attempts at tower-blocks to ape the disasters in Ronda; a few crazy-paved dados and garishly-tiled housefronts might offend a visiting aesthete, but then not many aesthetes visit Cuevas del Becerro.

The fair was taking its usual course. Awnings were stretched over some sectors of the main street, where café tables occupied the road and the traffic was diverted; the girls were out in their Sevillian flounces; little paper flags strung on lines (Andalusia, Spain, Europe) rustled constantly in the evening breeze; the municipal band, seated outside the town hall, puffed and sawed and thumped its way through popular favourites. Many doorways were open. Some houses preserved their old studded doors and salient windows from which a twitch of the curtain allowed the inquisitive eye to rake the whole street. Others had glossy tiles and dados, mock marble floors and the latest three-piece suite on offer from the emporium in Ronda. But whatever the taste or content, most homes were on frank display, with the older members of the household sitting on the step or bringing their chairs out onto the pavement.

I ran into a male nurse I knew, once a pillar of the Ronda hospital, now living in Algeciras. His wife was from Cuevas and they came every year to the fair. He told me you could still leave your car unlocked here, whereas it was more than likely that when he got back to Algeciras he would find his flat burgled. The principle of *honradez* is crucial to a pueblo's self-esteem. Customary corruption is tolerated. For example, a village mayor ordering sand for some building work will be asked 15,000 pesetas a lorry-load. He will say this is too much, whereupon the sandmen will say all right, 14,000 then, to which the mayor will assent. But he will ask for a receipt for 15,000 and pocket the difference. That is a recognised perk, and everyone knows the rules. Privileged treatment over bureaucratic requirements such as building licences is acceptable too, because almost everyone has a little bit of graft through a relative who has a friend who knows Don Fulano etc. But stealing (except by those whose profession it is, such as gypsies) is wrong and intolerable in a small community and can only be explained by malign external influences such as drugs. However much the government's policies on health or education or social security may be approved, there is almost universal condemnation of what are seen as socialist laws which are more on the side of the criminal than of the police.

Deciding to check on the Communist *caseta*, I eventually found it in a large shed. As at Alcalá there were posters featuring Guevara, La Pasionaria and Lenin (here beardless and wearing a neat American-style collar and tie with pin). Marx himself and the Sandinistas also qualified for this pantheon, but not Anguita. Conversation with the barman was difficult in the hubbub. He confessed there was a split in the leadership, which was damaging: they were down to six seats on the council and the socialists had an overall majority – a similar line-up to Alcalá's. I waited while he served a large round of drinks. Would a change of name help? No, he didn't think so. As far as he and his friends were concerned, the PCE, Partido Comunista Español, was an old party with an honourable tradition, and there were no grounds for changing the label because of the Italians or East Europeans or anyone else.

Cuevas has a main road strip of a few hundred metres with

199

the filling station and some more bars and the main *venta*, which has turned itself into a hotel in anticipation of 1992 – expected to be a boom year because of the completion of the Common Market, the World Fair in Seville and the Olympics in Barcelona. I spent what was left of the night here and set off in the morning for El Burgo. Rather than return to Ronda, I took the back route via the hamlet of Serrato and over the Sierra de Ortegícar. I knew the council of El Burgo was still Communist-controlled and I was armed with a letter of introduction to its mayor, Eduardo Carbonell, who I had reason to believe would prove a new-model Communist.

This impression had come about through an earlier conversation with Julián de Zulueta, an ex-mayor of Ronda in the socialist interest and a highly cultured man with a wealth of historical knowledge. It had thus been natural for me to consult him on the phenomenon of village Communism before taking off on my travels. Julián was still intrigued by the Anarchists. Before one talked of Communism, he said, there was a prior question: where had all the Anarchists gone? They had once been the strongest force in Andalusia but now no one would admit that their father or grandfather had been any such thing. Of course the Anarchist killings of landowners and business people in Ronda during the prelude to the Civil War, followed by an equal and opposite White Terror, had made it extremely dangerous for many years to talk about these events. Even now that political comment and action were free, it was still hard to find anyone who would acknowledge Anarchist connections.

Julián's theory about the roots of Andalusian Anarchism derived from the fact that its strongholds were all to be found in 'Muslim' Spain, where resentment at the bad faith of the Catholic Monarchs and their successors had smouldered for centuries. There had been the famous rising of the *Moriscos*, nominally converted to Christianity, in the Alpujarras and Serranía de Ronda in 1568–1570, followed by further violent protests against the decision taken in 1609 to expel them altogether. The villages around here were of Berber stock, and even after the expulsion not a few remained, particularly in the valley of the Genal. These were the areas where Anarchism was later to take root. The fury against the Church, the image-burning (the main church of Grazalema was still gutted) and the killing of Civil Guards could all be traced back in Julián's view to the merciless imposition of Castilian culture on these reluctant and resentful tribesmen. These days, as he had been saying, there was no sign of Anarchism anywhere, but it was unlikely that so strong a current would simply disappear.

I wondered if the Communists could be the inheritors. It was difficult to see the connection, Julián thought. The ideology, the mentality, the programmes were so different. Some Communists were extremely entrepreneurial these days – witness Arriate, whose boom had started under a Communist mayor. All that would have been anathema to the Anarchists. It was improbable that they had simply switched allegiance. Well then, could their disappearance be linked to the removal of agrarian reform, their strongest plank, from the political agenda, as much of the surplus labour had migrated to the cities and any residual land-hunger had been bought off by the welfare state? Had not all this made the Anarchists' vision of a redistribution of the earth's surface simply irrelevant?

Julián agreed that could well be part of it, but it remained something of a mystery. What was certain was that the Communists still had a piece of the action. There had been some outstanding Communist mayors, notably Anguita himself, now leader of the PCE, from which Santiago Carrillo had split off. Because of the schism the Communists were not doing as well as they might, given the existence of a substantial body of opinion well to the left of the PSOE. He could not say how far the proposed new grouping under the banner of Izquierda Unida would flourish, but the person

201

to talk to was Eduardo Carbonell, who had done much for his pueblo.

Cupped in a hollow under the frowning sierras, El Burgo is as compact a little burgh as you will find, rising neatly on its hump with prickly pears covering the slope between its old walls and its trickle of a river. It is a place I have always found a little daunting, precisely because of this compactness and air of self-sufficiency. At the entrance is a grove of tall eucalyptus trees shading a low wall on which old men sit sharply scanning everyone who passes. Driving over a little bridge, I pulled in at a bar on the left, planning to leave the car there and proceed on foot. The landlord gave me directions to the town hall but then restrained me; I would not catch the mayor till later, if at all; in the meantime he had something right here which I had to see.

I reluctantly allowed myself to be conducted to a door at the back of the bar, which the landlord opened with a flourish, flicking a light switch at the same time. I found myself in an elaborate cork-lined discotheque, equipped with booths with plush upholstered banquettes and decorated with tropical love scenes painted in black silhouette on gold panels; beyond was a large secluded patio with an outdoor bar repeating the decorative motifs inside. It was not the first such establishment I had been in but it was still a peculiar experience to walk straight from the largely medieval aspect of El Burgo into this cavernous wonderland, of which the casual customer dropping in for a beer would have no suspicion.

A response was clearly expected, so I said the place must be a great boon to the young. The proud owner agreed. The young folk here, he said, were warm and welcoming and well-behaved: no one under eighteen was allowed into the disco and any troublemaker was permanently banned. The people as a whole were *gente noble* – which had nothing to do with nobility of birth, but rather of character (a horse is also said to be *noble*, if it refrains from kicking and does not buck its rider). It had always seemed to me an interesting question whether the Spanish people are an inherently noble race: the behaviour of Arturo in our early *campo* days seemed to support the claim, but others had shown a meaner streak. As far as my host was concerned, it was eminently true of the people of El Burgo; good behaviour towards strangers was a vital ingredient of nobility, and in this they excelled. If anyone fell short of these standards, he was cold-shouldered by the others until the *oveja perdida*, the lost sheep, rejoined the *rebaño bueno*, the good flock.

As regards work, he went on, there was the usual mix of agricultural products, but nearly three hundred men were working in *la construcción*, half of them on the coast. These did not commute daily but would hire a flat between a dozen of them and cook their own *guisos* or thin stews and drink only water during the week, in which fashion they could live for five or six hundred pesetas a day. On Friday afternoons they returned to the pueblo and put all their wages in the hands of their wife or *novia* for the house or car they were buying or for general household expenses. This was another instance of the nobility he had referred to: that they were prepared to work under such conditions for the family's good. On Saturdays, apparently, they liked to divert themselves, and they did this in their own way with their friends in their own pueblo and not on some amorphous stretch of coastline, which was simply where they earned their wages. Saturday night, I gathered, was very lively right into the small hours. The folk then slept in on Sundays, but religiously went to bed not later than midnight in order to be ready for a dawn start on Monday. This, according to my informant, was the manner of life of El Burgo, which was a good, warm, friendly place, where the population of some 2800 souls all lived in harmony together.

It was time to be off to the town hall. The landlord said I would be more likely to catch Eduardo the mayor in the

Hostal Sierra de las Nieves, where he always lunched, as his wife and family lived in another town. He then gave me a warning: the mayor only lunched there because it was near the town hall. The food was in fact much better here under his own roof, where his wife served a proper *cocina familiar*, family cooking, none of your international muck. If I decided to stay in El Burgo, I should have no hesitation in returning and they would look after me far better than in the *hostal*. I noted that even in Utopia there were some rivalries.

When I presented my letter at the town hall, I received a reply after some time that the mayor was occupied for the rest of the morning and then had an engagement for lunch, but if I cared to join him later in the *hostal*, he would be happy to talk to me over coffee. I duly appeared at the appointed time and my quarry was pointed out to me sitting in the restaurant with another man; they had clearly been talking business but I was beckoned to join them.

Eduardo Carbonell turned out to be short, bearded, and slightly exophthalmic; his companion was a firmly fleshed, youngish man, dark haired and complexioned, slightly flushed and drinking *cuba libre* – which appeared to be the ideological drink in Communist townships. It was the companion who set the conversational pace. He was a building contractor living on the coast and employing two hundred men, but he was also a *nacionalista* of El Burgo, from which he drew most of his employees. Of course, the name had been Al Burgís in Arabic, he assured me authoritatively, for was he not half Moroccan himself? His great dream, he went on, was to convert the fortress into a *parador*, and he began to expand on this . . .

As soon as I could get a word in edgewise, I asked Eduardo some political questions. How was the council composed? It consisted of seven Communists, two PSOE and two Independents, which meant to say Ecologists. Why was Communism so much in the ascendant here, when it had lost ground elsewhere? Well, he said, it was a very modern type of Communism: the appeal was to a region which was still very poor but whose inhabitants wanted their own houses and cars and good schools – which he supported and was doing something to provide. Now there was one car to every three or four of the population, whereas a few years ago there had been only four cars in the whole pueblo. As to the decline of his party, which had lost control of a number of town halls, one had to remember that there was still very strong representation in Arriate, Alcalá, Setenil and Cuevas, and they might well get back next time round with all the scandals that were affecting the socialists. Anarchism? No, that had totally disappeared except in Barcelona and Cádiz. Had ex-Anarchists become Communists? He couldn't say, but certainly they had no muscle since the demise of the famous Anarcho-Syndicalist union, the CNT. I nodded. Reverting to the PCE, Partido Comunista Español, would it not have to change its name, as the Italians had done? Possibly, he agreed. The slogan on everyone's lips these days was Izquierda Unida, United Left.

Coffee and brandy had now been put before me. Raising my glass, I said there was much admiration abroad of how the Spaniards had come through the transition to democracy. Eduardo said, yes, the transition had been precarious, especially at the time of the attempted coup by Tejero in 1981, but thank God they had come through. I asked if it was true that Anguita, his leader, when mayor of Córdoba, had only been able to rule through the support of the Right.

'Absolutely!' said the entrepreneur, determined to have the floor again. 'And the same goes for Eduardo here. He could not be mayor without the support of the Right in the pueblo. I am of the Right myself... well, really I am nothing, I am not political, I am a businessman. But I love Eduardo and respect him for what he has done for the pueblo, so we remain good friends. You should see the culture centre I am building for the young, for everyone here. *Una obra faraónica*, on an Egyptian scale. There is nothing like it in Ronda, I can tell you. Of course, I hope he will pay me, but mainly I do it for love . . .'

'Shut up,' said Eduardo good-humouredly. 'You have a perfectly good contract and you talk too much. I have to go shortly and this man wants to ask *me* questions.'

'What about the idea of *turismo del interior* . . . *turismo rural*?' I slipped in.

'That interests me very much,' Eduardo said. 'People are getting fed up with the coast. We must give them something else – nature, trekking in the ecological reserves, the authentic Spain.'

'But they'll still want some entertainment,' said Pharaoh irrepressibly. 'That's where my culture centre comes in: the accordion . . . dances . . . *cante jondo* . . . flamenco . . .'

He snapped his fingers in the air.

'I can see two big problems,' I said. 'First, the language barrier. Second, the attitude of the pueblo. I am sure you have good people here, but they have been isolated for a long time. Will they welcome foreigners in their midst? There's going to be a pretty big culture gap.'

'Culture is becoming globalised through television,' said Eduardo. 'That's universal. You can't get round that. And then the sierra folk are by nature very hospitable.'

I pondered this. It had not always been so on my rides in the old days.

'What about village houses for letting?'

'There are none at present. But we want to work on this. We have built a new *barrio* on the outskirts . . . you have seen it?' I nodded. 'Or rather the people have built it themselves with government help: this is the pueblo with the highest percentage of self-built homes in Spain – two hundred of them. Anyway, this means that some of the old houses are falling vacant, and they could be modernised for tourists. That is something we must stimulate. After all, they are building artificial *pueblos andaluces* on the coast but we have a *pueblo auténtico* here, already in existence with all its ancient savour, and it can be adapted at a fraction

'... they are building artificial *pueblos andaluces* on the coast, but we have a *pueblo auténtico* here ...'

of the cost. We have the labour to do it right here. Those who used to be in agriculture have learned.'

'Absolutely!' said Pharaoh. 'I am the largest single employer here. I can vouch for the workers of El Burgo.'

'But what about the young? If they leave en masse, the pueblo will die, with or without tourism.'

'The demographic profile is a problem,' Eduardo acknowledged. 'But the young have two discos ... and it is the young marrieds who are settling into the new *barrio*.'

'And with my culture centre,' said Pharaoh, 'what more can they ask?'

'Do you have a drug scene?'

'Only soft,' said Eduardo promptly. 'There may be a couple of dozen users in the pueblo.'

'Is decriminalisation the answer?'

'For cannabis, certainly.'

With another *cuba libre* for Pharaoh, a brandy for me and a *ponche* for the mayor the talk became more general.

'The *andaluz* is very stoical,' said Eduardo. 'Dozens of cultures have rolled over him and he has assimilated them all. Now, we have competitive individualism, based on envy. He will digest this too.'

'It is precisely the criticism made by many people of Mrs Thatcher's Britain,' I observed.

'Well, it is much more acute here,' Pharaoh pronounced. 'Here we have envy glorified as a principle. Spain is the most envious country in the world . . . and the most affectionate.' He grinned and looked round to observe the effect of his paradox.

'Stop your foolishness,' Eduardo rebuked him. 'Spain is a fiction invented by historians to describe something that never existed. Here we have Galicians and Catalans and Basques and Navarrese and Castilians and Andalusians. The "Spanish miracle" is that despite the hopeless way we run things we continue to move forwards.'

'Fiction indeed,' said Pharaoh cheerfully. '*El Señor Alcalde tiene razón* . . . Mr Mayor is right. But is not fiction divine? I myself shall write it. Alongside the *parador* in the fort I shall create with private money – I am not asking him for a penny – my ultimate fiction in the shape of a Moorish palace, which will add much lustre to the upper town and will be a temple of entertainment complete with *houris*.'

'I never imagined,' I said, 'that in El Burgo I should discover the city of a thousand and one nights. Perhaps the tourists will flock here after all.'

They both heaved with laughter at this. Encouraged, I went on:

'But surely the Ministry of Culture will come down heavily against these fantasies and tell you that you must stick to the original . . .'

Here they could contain themselves no longer.

'He is right! Of course Don Fulanito, the exquisitely cultured and purist Don Fulanito, will come from the ministry with his equally aesthetic deputy Don Menganito, and they will say that the *casco antiguo* of El Burgo must be preserved in all its authentic grimness! Quite right, exactly so. *Este inglés* knows us better than we know ourselves!'

There was much patting of my back and clasping of my hand and insistence that we should drop the formalities and use the familiar *tu* and meet in Ronda on the first possible occasion.

I left in a warm glow, beguiled by their flattery and tickled by their ebullient projects. It was only later I realised I had failed to ask half the serious questions I had jotted down.

'Ah well,' I consoled myself, 'I am not a sociologist.'

It was time now to get some feel of how the landowners were making out under a socialist government. From El Burgo I had rung my friend Paco Hinojosa in Ronda, on whom I was relying for a re-entry into landowning circles. Don Francisco Hinojosa Bohórquez, to refer to him a little more formally, is a bachelor landowner with an interest in rural property development. The landowning class is not a homogeneous one; it is made up of a number of strands. It includes the old aristocracy, the haute bourgeoisie who were the main beneficiaries of the nineteenth-century sales of monastic and municipal estates, as well as – more recent arrivals – the owners of the very large agro-businesses (in which the two former categories may also be involved). The aristocrats accord a semi-mystical respect to the rural working class as the repository of the true virtue of the pueblo in its broadest sense – somewhat akin to that accorded by intellectuals to the kulaks in old Russia. But more modern employers are less tinged by such romanticism. How, I wondered, was all this working out in the Spain of Felipe González?

Paco told me not to return to Ronda in pursuit of enlightenment but to meet him at midday next day in the *venta* at Cuevas. He arrived almost on time, much to his credit, as he had been up till 4 a.m. and was suffering from a hangover, which he attributed to his man of confidence and henchman, Barea, who had a prodigious capacity for devilish drinks in frosted glasses. But Paco was too much of a gentleman to default on our engagement. His charming crinkled face was just a little more crinkled than usual and his eyes narrowed to mere slits as he stepped out of his vehicle into the judgemental sun. The plan was that we would go first to Ortegícar, the largest farm in the neighbourhood. He had arranged for the administrator to meet us here. Meanwhile he was much in need of coffee. I should explain that Ortegícar has long been of special interest to me because it was there, years back, that I first met the exquisite *caballero andaluz*, Don Mariano Gómez de las Cortinas.

I was riding back from Teba to Ronda, along a fine dry track between stubble as far as the Cortijo del Salado, a farm on the main road. Following the directions of a woman who emerged from the farm, I crossed the road, forded a stream and kept along the edge of an olive grove, above which there suddenly loomed a large, square, brick Moorish tower, its battlements crowned with pointed merlons. I selected a path that seemed to lead towards it, but had not gone far when I found myself confronted by a gentleman on horseback riding out of the olives in my direction. His animal was tall, glossy, high-stepping, its head drawn back by a martingale – the antithesis of my cob-like Chico. His saddle was less bulky than mine, but his feet rested in the same type of heavy stirrup. He was casually dressed in an open-necked shirt, jersey and grey flannel trousers with an outside seam over unpolished half-boots. He was bare-headed and his face was mildly distinguished; he had blue eyes.

'Can you tell me the way to Cuevas del Becerro?' I asked.

'Certainly. I am the owner of this property. Please follow me. Are you English?'

'Yes, I am.'

'On tour in these parts?'

'Yes, a little tour, but I live in Ronda.'

'Ah then, you are Mr Boyd. You once gave a poodle dog to my brother, Rafael. I am Mariano Gómez de las Cortinas. May I invite you in for a drink before I put you on your way?'

I assented readily. The tower, a massive structure, turned out to stand free in the middle of a large farm compound. As we approached, a man in a flat-crowned cockaded hat with a holstered shotgun attached to his saddle rode up. My host dismounted and told me to do the same.

'The guard will take the horses. We can walk round this way.'

Grand country houses, with which England is peppered, are a rarity in Spain; in fact they are almost non-existent. Instead, one finds big *cortijos*, usually inhabited by a bailiff and his family with perhaps a floor for occasional visits by the owner. The large landowner with his fleet of cars, like the peasant on his mule, prefers if possible to sleep in the pueblo. Ortegícar seemed to be something of an exception. The family spent some months in the country, Don Mariano said, moving to their Granada house for the winter and their house in Ronda during the great summer heat.

Leaving the farmyard, we passed through a garden of privet hedges, medlars and magnolias to emerge on a terrace, where a man was sitting at an easel painting the landscape; this was Rafael, who remembered me in connection with the dog; he gave me a friendly nod and continued his absorbing task in pursuit of a satisfaction never quite achieved. The family quarters, far from occupying a mere floor, seemed to fill the whole of a large three-storey wing. The three or four main rooms on the ground floor bore some resemblance to those of an English or perhaps a Scottish country house. They all had the same high barrel-vaulted ceiling; they were all furnished in a bulky, comfortable, shooting-lodge style; and there was a great display of antlers and boars' heads on the walls.

The family circle consisted of my host's wife, mother, sister-in-law, Rafael the painter and various small children who were playing round the fire. Most impressive of all was the old lady, a stylish and composed matriarch presiding over a scene which enticingly blended old wealth and young promise. A maid brought drinks. I had only just caught them, I learned. In a few days they would be moving back to Granada. I was so entranced by this way of life, which seemed to me as near perfect as could be devised, that I had never forgotten the hour or so I spent that day with Don Mariano and his circle. Today I hoped to find out how this charmed existence had fared under *la democracia*.

As I processed these memories, Paco Hinojosa restored himself with black coffee. Soon we were joined by a bright, professional-looking man of early middle age, by name José. He was the son of the old bailiff of Ortegícar and was the current administrator. With 1600 hectares (some 4000 acres) it had been the largest property in an area where holdings were not huge. When the old lady, the matriarch died, it had been divided in Andalusian fashion into four lots. The heirs had not gone in for a company with shares, nor a co-operative, but for separate managers and machinery with some centralised administration to achieve economies of scale and for tax purposes: this was the job done by José, who, forsaking his father's horse and holster, had become a businessman at a desk. Of the four present owners, one of the sisters had nine children, so in the next generation that portion would degenerate into parcelisation. This principle has been criticised throughout Spanish history as leading to a constant redivision of political units, but who is to say it is not fair and reasonable among private citizens? It does of course create a class of smaller and smaller *rentiers*, to the point where none can survive on his holding, but they in turn get jobs in banking or insurance or the army and possibly come back into the market again as purchasers of land. It is not obviously worse than primogeniture, which is a great disincentive to effort, imagination or investment. And it is of course fairer.

More coffee was called for, and we turned to the local impact of the European Community. Paco said Felipe González had sold Spain down the river to his friend Mitterand by agreeing to defer the full integration of agriculture for several years in order to protect Continental Europe from an influx of early produce from Andalusia. More positively, 'Europe' seemed to have stimulated the demand for olives; the doctors too had lifted their ban on health grounds and they were selling for the first time for many years at sixty to seventy pesetas a kilo. Those who had grubbed up mature olives with government grants were beginning to regret it.

'The ancients knew more about land use than we do,' said José. 'The land that was good for olives is still best employed for olives, and we are rediscovering this. Similarly, in Estremadura they uprooted all the old ilexes, and now they are replanting them.'

Somehow, perhaps inevitably, we got onto politics. They were both scathing about the local administrations. The mayor of Grazalema was paying himself 180,000 pesetas a month, with not much less for his deputies; the mayor of Ronda, who had an active career as a doctor, was getting 300,000 pesetas, although he didn't reach the town hall till one o'clock after his hospital work and then did nothing but sign a few papers. These jobs were previously done for honour, with only a few expenses. I asked how this new bandwagon had started. Paco answered that the socialists were trying to catch up and get rich quick wherever they were in office. Conservatives had never shown such greed, or such nepotism and corruption. What was more, the PSOE remained in power mainly by means of the gigantic patronage it exercised through *el paro*, unemployment benefit, which went to three million people, two thirds of whom were working; if you added together their votes and those of their families you had a body of support that was almost unbeatable.

I immediately recalled 'Cañete', when I bumped into him at his home-town fair, proudly proclaiming that he was *viviendo de Felipe*. Wherever people were doing this, they would undoubtedly be *Felipistas*.

José said that whatever one thought of Franco, he had never taken any steps to enrich himself or his family, in evidence of which his widow had recently been reduced to selling some not very valuable jewellery. Paco thought it remarkable that, as a dictator with a love of shooting and fishing, Franco had never even awarded himself a country estate. José weighed in again with the assertion that many of the bright middle-aged socialists with good jobs in the town halls and in the central administration owed their careers to the 'salaried scholarships' that had been awarded them under the Franco regime. He personally saw Franco as a 'right-wing socialist'.

I asked if there had been no corruption in those days. Less than now, José said. In fact, so sick had people become of socialist malpractices in Córdoba that the Communist Julio Anguita had come in, supported by the Right, on a pledge to run a clean administration. When Anguita's official car was lying idle he sent the driver away to do something useful and said he would use his own vehicle if he needed to go anywhere. This bore out what I had been hearing in some of the pueblos. Something similar, José went on, had happened in Jerez, where the Right had put Pedro Pacheco of the Partido Andaluz in power. Clean government was becoming a more important factor than the political label of aspirants to office. Even so, I couldn't help wondering whether Anguita's proud slogan *Otra Forma de Gobernar* would ever make much headway against more deeply entrenched 'Spanish practices' – to which other nations were no less addicted.

Eventually, at about one o'clock we set off for Ortegícar.

It was only a short drive and when we arrived it seemed an even more glorious place than I remembered. Although the land had been divided up, the house had been left in its entirety to Rafael, the painter; Mariano had received the Ronda house, while the sisters shared the one in Granada. On greeting us, Rafael said he had not even been as far as Ronda for a month; he would have to show his face at the fair to prove he still existed. He introduced us to a glamorous niece surrounded by three or four dachshunds in the library, then showed us a collection of flower paintings he was preparing for an exhibition: his easel this time was set up in the large drawing room with its tall windows and faded tapestry chairs. Thence, via the 'old' chapel, just a little oratory really, we emerged onto the terrace platform with one of the finest views in Andalusia.

Over on the left reared up the harsh Sierra de Ortegícar (whose other face towered above El Burgo); this was still the habitat of the shy ibex and, some said, the lynx. Moving clockwise, the Sierra de las Nieves raised its crouching flanks behind Ronda; then came the Sierra de Grazalema with its jagged peaks and high shoulders mantled with pines. To the right Cañete la Real, or one tip of it, was just visible under the crest capped by its ruined castle. But the general effect was not grim, for in the near and middle distance the land was pleasantly varied with olive groves running up to the rock-line, standing crops and stubble on the lower slopes, and poplars and other riverside trees following the course of the Guadalteba.

I asked if I might climb the great tower. Rafael said that as a boy he had spent whole days on its roof with music and books, but he hadn't been up for years; he begged to be excused. Paco volunteered to accompany me but wasn't best pleased by the bird droppings which clogged the steep stairs – for the grand old keep was now just an enormous dovecote. Rising above this, I tried to keep my mind on its history, for Ortegícar was an important stronghold in the fourteenth century. It was captured by the Christians in 1331, immediately after the taking of Cañete and Teba, but was soon lost again and not recovered until it was seized in 1410 by the Infante Don Fernando, grandfather of Ferdinand the Catholic, on his way to capture Antequera. Like all strong places in the vicinity it led a turbulent and precarious life in those centuries. The landscape would have been more wooded and less well-tended. Sustenance would have come mainly from flocks of sheep and goats, with some vegetable gardens along the river. Under Christian control the pig was introduced as the main staple of the family larder. The large grain fields and the orderly lines of olives came later.

From the parapet of the tower I could survey the whole complex: farm buildings, owner's wing, olive-oil factory and the corral in which the *yeguada* – consisting of thirty or forty brood mares – was enclosed to keep them off the crops until the harvest was in. When we had clambered down, we were shown the 'new' chapel. This was a bit of an afterthought, set up in the yard to accommodate the Virgen de los Dolores, imperiously brought here by Rafael's late mother from Granada, where it had once been the object of a public cult and procession but presumably failed to maintain its popularity among so many competing images. The Virgin's hands were clasped round three twisted nails representing those extracted from the cross. Family baptisms, weddings and first communions were celebrated here under her absorbed and downcast gaze. I thought that a Virgin in one of her less disconsolate moods would have been more appropriate.

Walking back to the house, something nagged at me, which at first I couldn't pinpoint. Then it came to me: this place seemed much more than a mere Moorish-turned-Christian fortress; it had the scale and completeness of a Roman villa. This impression was enhanced by some details: a shallow pool shaped like a Roman bath and not painted a vulgar blue, and some lapidary inscriptions in Latin round the garden. Roman, Moorish and Christian threads seemed intertwined, imparting a great sense of continuity – which was evidently shared by the staff. Rafael was still addressed as 'Señorito' in the old style. José's father, still in service, wore a leather sash with a polished plaque bearing the legend *Guarda Jurado*, sworn guard, which appeared to confer on him a sheriff-like authority for dealing with trespassers and poachers. The farm children gambolled about in the yard under the indulgent eye of their patron. Many of the signs of a very ancient patrician and paternalistic regime were still there, albeit in attenuated form.

How much longer would it last? With the land divided and likely to be further splintered when the next generation inherited their shares, the supporting economy needed by a great house would quickly fall away. In England it might have become a country-house hotel. Here perhaps in due course it would be a rural *parador*? Meanwhile, I hoped fate would be kind and allow Rafael to live out his life with brush and canvas in his childhood paradise.

As we took our leave Rafael said to me, 'When Mariano heard that Paco was bringing you here today, he wanted to be here too, but he was called away on business. He says you are to ring him when you are in Ronda; he will be very happy to see you there.'

I now had to decide which way to jump. The amiability of Paco was such that he would take me to see other estates and their owners in the area if I so wished. There were also many more pueblos awaiting inspection; I had not yet touched the valley of the Genal, much less the inland foothills of the province of Cádiz. But a priority asserted itself. Rafael had been charming, but he was so absorbed in his paradisaical way of life that it had not seemed right to press him on the condition and future of his class and such intrusive matters. It therefore seemed all the more important to take up the invitation of his elder brother. That, I decided, should be the next move, while he was in the vicinity, for I knew he had other interests which might take him away for weeks at a time. Once again Ronda stretched out its long arm and claimed me.

7

RETURN OF THE SPY

The telephone is not as useful a tool in Ronda as in London. People do not like to make their arrangements or do business over it; all this is done *en la calle*, in the street. The first time I rang Don Mariano, he was 'withdrawn', that is to say he had not yet emerged from his dressing room; the next time he had gone out. The strategic place to take up position for an encounter in the street is at a table outside the *casino*, because anybody who is anybody in Ronda crosses the Plaza del Socorro some time between the hours of twelve and three, after which they all go home for lunch.

The *casino* is not what it was. It never had the languid Sevillian elegance of Osuna's, but it is larger, and had a sort of seedy grandeur when I first belonged to it. In those days the presiding genius of the place was a long-retired Civil Guard, by name Policeto, a magnificent figure of a man endowed with rugged good looks and unusual height for his race. He sat at the foot of the main stairs observing the large patio and listening for the telephone – which did occasionally ring with an enquiry as to whether Don Fulano or Don Mengano was there. Policeto held in his memory exactly which members were in the building and in which room doing what, but he would never disturb anyone who was doing something important like playing chess or cards.

'How are you keeping, Policeto?' I used to say.

He would slowly rise to his great height and answer cheerfully, 'Not so well as your honour.'

'Anything new?'

'No, all is as usual here and I am in my customary place like the good artilleryman at the foot of his cannon.'

If for some reason I failed to greet him, he would stretch out as I passed and take my arm in a vice-like grip.

'So the rich will have nothing to do with the poor, eh?' he would chuckle in my ear.

In the old days the *casino* had eight hundred-odd members, consisting of the landowners, the doctors, the lawyers, the bank officials, the larger shopkeepers, the teachers, the more important *corredores* or brokers, even some gypsy patriarchs who had switched their business from the declining wool trade to antiques – in short almost everyone who was not in the artisan or manual labouring class. Now the numbers were down to some three hundred, due to competition from the new tennis and country clubs, the lack of appeal of such a frowsty old building to the young, and the high cost of membership, which rose in more than inverse ratio to the fall in subscriptions, as a result of the mounting repair bills and debts. In any case, the bar giving onto the plaza was open to the public at large and even the members tended to have their coffee there, as the service was better than if you ordered in some inner sanctuary from a shambling waiter who would take half an hour. Nonetheless, there was still a hard core of worthies who kept up their subscriptions for the privilege of sitting at the terrace tables to the right of the door, which were reserved for them (there will always be people who like sitting in special places); and there were still private rooms for chess, billiards and cards, though the roulette wheels and baccarat tables had been consigned to the attic in 1936 and never brought down since. If you climbed the grand staircase, at whose foot Policeto used to keep guard, you came to the rather splendid ballroom. The *baile vermut* (Spanish equivalent of a *thé dansant* with a slightly alcoholic edge) which used to take place weekly in the patio was long past, but the ballroom still came alive annually when Ronda flocked to it to see the old year out and dance the new year in.

After an hour or so at a table outside the bar with coffee and the papers there was no sign of Don Mariano. Becoming restless, I decided to take a turn down the Calle de la Bola. I looked in first at the tiny bookshop, which had changed very little over the years: school books, Asterix, accountancy, whitebound missals for first communion, comics . . . these were still the staples of the trade, though the shop window was a little more daring these days, with translations of George Orwell, a treatise on Anarcho-Syndicalism, the works of Octavio Paz and so forth – none of which would have passed muster under Franco.

I picked up a publication of the University of Granada on Ronda and its region. It had pieces on archaeology, demography, urbanisation from the fifteenth to the nineteenth centuries, local songs, a local poet, a local dominie of renown, Ronda in the Peninsular War, rural deprivation and other more abstruse matters. The essays had long footnotes and poor-quality photographs, which I found just as riveting as the expert but sterile studies, exploiting stark light and shade, which filled so many *de luxe* coffee-table books on Spain. The page fell open at a picture of the Casa de Mondragón and the alley leading down to Villa Paz, which gave me a sudden jolt. Angelita, the tall, graceful woman who had served in the shop for many years, was looking over my shoulder.

'Diana loved that house,' she sighed. 'Such a pity. She was so beautiful.'

'Yes,' I said, 'she was.'

'I shall always remember her. I never forget that party you gave in the Villa Paz garden. It was such a romantic place.'

This must have been just after our arrival, when there were so many hopes not subsequently realised. I did not wish to be unresponsive to Angelita's nostalgia or disloyal to my own past; but nor did I wish to be tugged so far down memory lane. I was rescued by the bookseller himself. He had small, neat, sallow features under a bald domed crown – reminiscent of a seventeenth-century portrait by Pacheco.

'*Carramba, chico!*' he said when he saw me. 'Come in and sit down.'

He waved aside a crony who was occupying the only other chair and I sat down at the little round table the bookseller used as a desk. It was draped with a cloth, under which an electric brazier would glow in winter to warm his own toes and his visitors'; in the old days it was a real pan of well-stoked charcoal. The walls of the sanctum were lined from floor to ceiling with box files, educational paperbacks, local history and legends, dictionaries, encyclopaedias, course books, all evidence of the Spaniards' reverence for knowledge as a packaged commodity. (I recalled a girl studying philosophy whose whole set reading had been encompassed in one volume the size of a telephone directory.) There was nothing much that could be classified as a 'good read', except possibly a translation into Spanish of *Swann's Way*.

'When did you arrive?' the bookseller asked.

'I've been here for a month or so.'

'That is rather a long time before coming to see your friends.'

'Well, you know I have a little place in the *campo*. I have been down there, and visiting quite a lot of pueblos.'

'Yes, I know you have become a countryman. The people say you always come to town these days dressed like a reaper.' He smiled. 'When you first put on that garb, they thought you were a spy.'

I smiled back.

'Yes, wasn't that absurd?'

'Of course. But then you wrote that book about us. I remember I had some copies here in the window. The language barrier prevented me from reading it. I understood from you that it was in the folklore *genre* but afterwards I was told it was very satirical.'

'Well, I suppose I had a bit of fun at the expense of the

In the bookseller's den

landowners and the Church and the Monte.'

He raised a finger gravely.

'Criticise the proprietors. Say what you like about the Church. Ridicule the town hall. But never in Ronda attack the Monte de Piedad.'

Founded early in the century by the Marquis of Moctezuma as a non-profit making institution with the object of providing rural loans at less than medieval rates of interest, the Monte de Piedad y Caja de Ahorros de Ronda became in due course the main local developer and patron for miles around. It had some positive effect on the labour market by creating jobs in banking, in building, and in property development. But its effect on architecture in the town was disastrous, while in moral and cultural terms it had always exuded a sort of unctuous materialism that I found distasteful. Nor was it free from accusations of that very usury it had been founded to eliminate. The town hall had for decades been one of its largest creditors, and it was supposed to be a recipe for harmony in Ronda when there were close links between the two bodies. For example, for some years

222

the son of the director-general of the Monte was mayor. But this was not possible with a socialist municipality, especially as the government was intent on moulding the reluctant Monte and similar institutions to social purposes of its own.

'But I thought the government itself was attacking them,' I said. 'Is it not trying to curb the power of the Monte and other savings banks by requiring them to be run in the public interest in return for their tax privileges?'

'Curb *their* power?' echoed the bookseller. 'And who needs curbing more than our disastrous local administration? I tell you, I no longer supply them with a single sheet of paper, because they will not and cannot pay. The debt of our socialist council to the Monte is nothing short of scandalous. Just to service it, the town will have to sell the cork forests it has owned since the Reconquest.'

'Well, that does sound a pity,' I acknowledged, 'but it is a local matter, and surely the government in general has done rather well . . . fantastically well considering all the prognostications of chaos or repression after Franco. And there seems to be no serious challenge from the Right.'

The bookseller lowered the dome of his head towards me; his tone became confiding.

'The trouble with us,' he said, 'is that all Spaniards are egoists. Therefore, political life is less civilised than in England. The predominance of Felipe (which I believe to be disastrous) and his henchmen in the provinces is due to the fact that the Left, being needy, will always unite to a greater extent than the Right. The Right, being better off and already economically more powerful, will form factions and squabble over who should be the leader.'

'I always thought the Right closed ranks to defend property.'

'Not here,' said the bookseller. 'It was not until the terrorists of the Left started to haul them out of their houses and *shoot* them that the Right came together at the outbreak of the Civil War. Now the Right is splintered again and socialism is rampant, including the grossly incompetent brand of it we have here.'

The telephone rang. As he picked up the receiver, he pushed a book towards me, which I saw to be one of recollections of Old Ronda. I opened it and glanced through it as he spoke. When he had finished his conversation, he came back on a different tack.

'The trouble is, we have lost *convivencia*.'

'But if that means a sense of community, how does it square with the innate egoism you are talking about?'

'It is the necessary cement. *Convivencia* is especially necessary for the egoists. Now there are no values other than instant gratification and the three-piece suite. But before people lived together more closely and with greater mutual respect. In that book' – he tapped the volume he had placed in front of me – 'one of the contributors recalls how the shops were open all day from eight in the morning to eleven at night and the women would go four or five times a day to the shop not only to buy a packet of this or an ounce of that, but also for conversation, for human contact; in addition, they would help one another with whitewashing, dressmaking and so forth. For the really poor there were communal kitchens run by the nuns.'

'But wasn't this virtuous co-operation a function of poverty?' I suggested. 'Do you really want to force people back to those days in order to recover a lost innocence? Because there was another side of the coin – look here!' While he was on the telephone I had come across a different sort of passage in the book. 'Here is someone, a retired local government official, recalling the single-storey houses with their big corrals where you had to defecate because there was nowhere else ... and the public fountains where women had to queue with their pitchers ... and the smallpox and typhus and sleeping sickness that were rife ...'

'No,' said the bookseller, 'I don't believe you can put the clock back. People will never surrender their cars and their three-piece suites. And public health is certainly much better. At the same time we are in grave danger of losing the social cement that we Spaniards in particular need if we are to survive these temptations. We are not moderate pragmatists like the British. We may yet revert to extremes. There are some glimmers of hope, it is true. The religious brotherhoods, the *cofradías*, are attracting more members, particularly among the young. But on the whole I am not optimistic, as long as we have socialism which encourages the worst and the most lax in society. But with your pinkish tendencies you won't of course agree.'

'Pinkish? I am a stalwart centrist!'

The bookseller smiled craftily.

'But *pas d'ennemis à gauche?*'

'Not at all,' I said. 'For example, what is called the Loony Left in our country. But I have been taking a little look at your village Communism out here, and it is pretty clear the old Stalinist brand is doomed and the new wave is turning into something quite different.'

'Ah, then you have fallen for the vogue enjoyed by Señor Anguita. Well, I must warn you to beware of that too. It is a passing spasm without a future . . .'

The telephone rang again and I got up to go. He raised his eyes to me as he began taking down an order.

'Anyway, look in again whenever you wish and we will discourse on the sacred and the profane. Next time we'll go out for a coffee.'

As I was leaving, Angelita smiled her wistful smile.

'Don't desert us again for so long.'

'I won't. Your esteemed employer wants to talk about the sacred and the profane. That is irresistible. Booksellers don't do that sort of thing in England.'

Keeping a weather eye open all the while for Don Mariano, I continued up the street. The bookseller had reminded me of a curious episode in my life, and this propelled me next into the ironmongery and drugstore owned by Paco Montecorto. Paco is a retired secret policeman. He is a nice-looking fellow with a small military moustache, neat white teeth and an infectious laugh. His wife is plump and pretty as a partridge. For years I had bought a number of basics from them when I came up to town from the *campo*; notably 'Sotal', a very strong disinfectant for use in chemical loos, paint, whitewash, firelighters, candles and insecticides. But I went there for another reason too: Paco had a sense of humour, and we shared a private joke.

'Here comes the spy!' he always cried delightedly when I entered the shop.

I had recently been to Montecorto, the tiny settlement where he had been born; I told him how pleasant I had found it. He made a face.

'You never took to country life?' I asked.

'The country?' Paco grinned. 'I can't even stand the sight of a flowerpot.'

'So the secret police was a much more congenial occupation?'

'No comparison.'

'Even shadowing people like me? That must have been rather boring.'

'Not at all. There was much speculation about you in those days. It was my job to find out the truth. To establish the truth or falsehood of something is always interesting.'

'But all we were doing, as you very well know, was riding around the countryside, visiting villages and looking at ruins, plants, birds and so forth. It was just part of our romantic affair with Old Spain.'

'Yes, I remember how elegant your first wife looked on a horse,' he said. 'But you always carried a camera and she binoculars. That was suspicious.'

'You can't record ruins without a camera or watch birds without binoculars. Are you telling me it was seriously thought that we were sending back reports to our masters on the state of the mule tracks in case of war over Gibraltar? Or investigating the stockpile of nuclear weapons in the cave of La Pileta?'

'I see you have captured the Andalusian irony,' he said with approval.

'We do have a native brand. But now, let's be frank after all these years. Surely these things weren't taken seriously?'

'Well,' Paco smiled, 'perhaps not as a threat to the state. There are degrees of seriousness. But the region round Gibraltar has always been a sensitive area for us, as you well know. And then more recently people have wondered why you suddenly left Ronda and went to the country and started dressing like a peasant. When you first came, you dressed as an English gentleman.'

The bookseller had picked on this too.

'I happen to like the country and to get on with peasants,' I said. 'They interest me more than English gentlemen. It's as simple as that. As to Gibraltar, I have always been in favour of returning it to Spain with appropriate safeguards.'

'Maybe, but the authorities didn't know that.' He paused and added slyly, 'You know, it may have been my favourable report on your characters that saved you from expulsion at one point.'

'I'm sure it was very helpful,' I replied cautiously, not wishing to sound too beholden.

'Curiously enough,' he went on, 'I came across a copy of it only the other day.'

His watchful brown eyes scanned me intently to see the effect of this revelation.

'I'd like to see it,' I said casually. 'Just for the historical interest, of course. Presumably it's no longer secret?'

He looked at me mischievously, knowing he had whetted my appetite.

'I'll see if I can lay my hands on it. You know how it is with *papeles*. It is always the same. You can never find them when you want them . . . and then you come across them when you are looking for something else.'

I didn't suppose I would ever see his report, even supposing he had actually written one. It was a bait to keep me in play. He didn't give a damn whether he sold me anything or not but he loved to reminisce, and suspected rightly that I would return to winkle more out of him. I took my leave, saying I would be back in a week or so.

'*Adiós, Espía!*' he called out genially as I left the shop.

I now turned my steps towards the Bar Jerez, where the *señoritos* often gathered for a glass of sherry before lunch and where there was some hope of finding Don Mariano. As I passed under the large awning stretched over the outside tables, I was hailed imperiously and fraternally by a great voice:

'Ali!'

I stopped and immediately spotted Pablo Arahal and his apple-cheeked wife Antonia. Though he had suffered a thrombosis which cost him a leg, he was as ebullient as ever and insisted on ordering me a large *tinto de verano*, which is a mixture in a tall glass of red wine, ice, pop and a slice of lemon.

Pablo had been a lieutenant in the Republican army *por idealismo*, not just because he had been caught on that side by the outbreak of the Civil War. Trained as a teacher, he had lived for years after the war under suspended sentence of death and under virtual house arrest; altogether he was disqualified from teaching for twenty-four years. So he became an artist, first working from a table in his brother's café, later branching into ironwork and ceramics with a small electric kiln of his own. When he was at last allowed to return to his profession, it was only to a backward pueblo, where his views – it was thought – would not find any significant outlet. But he covered his schoolroom walls with huge murals and was adored by his pupils; much that was missing from the arid and tendentious textbooks of the time he supplied out of his own experience and imagination. Finally, in retirement, he had been rehabilitated completely by the new regime and proudly produced his identity card which bore his restored military rank.

'Also,' said Antonia, 'he has been allowed to count all his

wasted years as a teacher towards his pension, so for the first time ever we are not pinched. It was only justice.'

I said how glad I was the wheel had turned at last. But not everyone seemed content, and I reported the disillusion of the bookseller (and other shopkeepers I had chatted to) with the socialist government.

'Bah!' said Pablo. 'There is no choice in this country but to be on the Left. The Right in Spain has always behaved beyond the pale. Of course, the Church and army are much weaker now but financial power still lies where it always did.'

'Is there any danger of a return of reaction?'

'I don't think so. The people have tasted freedom. But you always have to remember that the *instincts* of the Right never change.'

I asked him what had changed most in Spain.

'Well, undoubtedly things are much better. Justice has been done to those of us who fought for the Republic. We have been treated well. And it is nonsense to say the socialists have run riot with expenditure. They may be a bunch of incompetents here in Ronda but nationally income tax is still only 16 per cent. What is wrong is that the landowners, lawyers and doctors – those who can afford accountants – don't pay it. Of course, they never did, but Felipe has not done enough to bring them into line. That's what ordinary people resent and why there is some discontent. But if you ask me what has changed most since the days of *la miseria*, I'm afraid I have to say it is loss of *convivencia*.'

I was struck that exactly the same sentiment had been expressed by the bookseller, from a right-wing perspective. I wondered aloud whether this had not been the most distinctive quality of the Spanish people, both reactionaries and revolutionaries. If so, what chance had it of surviving the onslaught of prosperity?

'That's right,' said Pablo. 'When in misery or danger we hang together like heroes. When victory is won, or justice done, each goes his own way.'

'But the young still have ideals,' Antonia protested gently, 'and I believe they always will. One idealism goes, another comes. Our son and daughter-in-law are passionately – what do you call it? – ecological, and want to save the earth. They are not political, but . . .'

'You can't save the earth without politics,' said her husband, who was political to the core. 'But Spain will never go "green". There are too many vested interests.'

'But isn't it the mission of socialism to dismantle vested interests?'

'Yes, in theory, but socialists are not immune to the corruption of power. Like other political parties they value power above all else.'

'Then perhaps Anarchism really was the answer for Spain?' I ventured. 'Free-standing self-governing municipalities and all that.'

'That was a pipe-dream of innocent and oppressed people. It could never have worked. Socialism is the only creed suitable for struggle. Then it is very good and strong and clean. But when the struggle is over' – he spread out his hands – 'human weakness creeps in.'

'But it is still better than what went before?'

'Oh yes,' he said firmly, 'a little corruption in a democracy must be better than a tyranny of any stamp, which will always be more corrupt and where the corruption will not come to light. Much has been achieved. Do not underestimate that.'

'But loss of *convivencia* is the price that has had to be paid?'

'I am not sure it has been lost,' said Antonia. 'I think that under the surface it is still there.'

Her husband patted her hand.

'Antonia always thinks the best,' he said. 'But yes, on the whole I still have faith. It is just that there are dangers in good times as well as bad.'

At this point our conversation was drowned by two or three youths revving up their 50cc bikes again and again before roaring off at full throttle.

'Idiots,' Pablo growled. 'If they think that shows man-hood, they should have seen the real thing in '36.'

'They have never heard of '36,' said his wife. This time it was her turn to pat his hand. 'It is just the exuberance of youth.'

Suddenly I spied Don Mariano coming out of the bar followed by several companions. Excusing myself, I left the table and went up to him. With elaborate courtesy he begged my pardon for not having been available when I telephoned. If he had had a number for me, he would have called back. But this encounter was most fortunate, for now we could fix a time. Alas, this afternoon was impossible and so was tomorrow morning . . . but he would have great pleasure in receiving me tomorrow evening say at six o'clock in his house in the *Ciudad*. I knew where it was? Good, then he looked forward to that very much indeed.

'What do you want with the *señoritos*?' Pablo grumbled when I rejoined him. 'When you have so many good friends here, why mix with that bunch?'

I explained that in trying to discover if and how Ronda had changed, I could not afford to neglect any social class; Don Mariano had always been friendly to me, and he seemed the natural person to consult.

'You could have saved yourself the trouble,' Pablo said. 'You won't find any change there.'

With more than twenty-four hours to kill until my date with Don Mariano, I decided I should seek out a younger view of the contemporary scene. It was unlikely that either solid shopkeepers or old socialists were representative of the opinion of anyone under forty. The person who immediately came to mind was Ana Mari Segura, once a pupil of mine. She had ability, looks and charm but was also marked by *inquietudes*, a certain mental restlessness, which set her apart from the crowd and enabled her to observe it from a little distance. I knew she had secured a well-paid job in the Monte but had left it because she couldn't stand the atmosphere of bourgeois conformism and tale-bearing. Subsequently she had tried out several things, including a herbalist's shop in Málaga, which she ran for several years. Now she was teaching English and living with her friend Alonso who did the same. They had taken a flat with a marvellous view in the *Ciudad*; in order to afford this they went without a car or telephone. Last summer they had spent two months in Devon and Cornwall and loved it. Bed and breakfast places were cheap, they thought, by Spanish standards, and pleasant to stay in. They spoke warmly of Tavistock and Polperro.

In the afternoon I went in search of them. I found them at home and they welcomed me in. We sat in a room with a huge wall-to-wall window view. It took me right back to my early days in Villa Paz, from which the prospect had been almost identical. There had been little apparent change. Ana Mari served camomile tea. Knowing some of her interests, I asked if the ecological movement was making any headway.

'Well, young people are concerned. There are various groups and publications. But you can hardly call it a movement yet. At the practical level it has achieved very little. There was a demonstration the other day about the filthy state of the river. This is very important for Ronda and the shops were going to close in protest, but in the event none of them did and only about a hundred people turned out with placards in front of the town hall. The press had been alerted and clearly took away the impression of a totally apathetic and lethargic pueblo . . . which is what we really are. Because, if you'll excuse the term, it means that whenever we eat anything that comes up from the valley we are eating *mierda*, literally, and we put up with it. It makes my blood boil. *Yo soy muy luchadora.* I am a fighter. Installing a new water-purifying plant is an absolute necessity, yet all they can think of in the idiotic town hall are grand projects like a tourist *parador*, while neglecting the most elementary necessities of life.'

'Would you say Ronda suffers from a sort of permanent personality crisis?' I asked. 'I mean, provincial capitals know what they are for, which is bureaucracy, and so do coastal resorts, which are for tourists; also, some of the pueblos have a clear sense of purpose, for instance Olvera . . .'

'Yes, or Teba, or Cañete.'

'Precisely. They have a clear conception of their identity and more modest aspirations, whereas Ronda is always flirting with fantasies and suffering delusions of grandeur. I think it all goes back to those rather brief periods as a semi-independent Arab fief, which conjured up visions of an independent kingdom. Then when the modern provinces were formed, Ronda saw itself as the natural capital of one which would include Algeciras, Tarifa and a great swathe of the coast, but the government of the day bundled it into Málaga – which it has always resented.'

'I think that's true,' she agreed. 'You remember the old *copla*: "If Ronda had a sea, what a sea it would be!" That sums it up.'

'It is actually surprising there isn't a project to bring the sea to the mountains,' I suggested.

'Absolutely!' she smiled. 'But there have been many others.'

'In my memory,' I said, warming to the theme, 'there have been the funicular railway, the golf course, the aerodrome, the headquarters of the Foreign Legion . . . and now, as you say, the *parador* . . . none of which have come to fruition.'

'And not long ago,' she added, 'there was an Englishman who came and enthused everyone with a project for a university on two sites: Ronda and Marbella. It was all mixed up with lots of other things like breeding pure Arab horses and sports of various kinds, I don't remember all the details. Anyway, he managed to interest a lot of people, including the town hall. But it turned out he had no capital and no serious backers. He wasn't exactly a fraud. Apparently he'd been a professor of planning somewhere. But the scheme was a non-starter, and the bubble burst.' She paused. 'The point is he only got as far as he did because it was the sort of thing people wanted to hear.'

Neither Ana Mari nor Alonso was as critical of the socialist government as of the municipality. Though 'not political', they were in favour of the government's works, in particular the Universidad Popular, which was not a grandiose scheme but a sort of adult education project using existing buildings; they also thought Felipe was doing a good job for young people.

'They come in for a lot of criticism from their elders,' I said. 'They are blamed for the collapse of morals, particularly the drug addicts.'

'They are the victims of the consumer society,' said Alonso fiercely. He had red ringlets and pale blue eyes and, I think, some Irish blood.

'Maybe,' said Ana Mari, 'but you have to distinguish a little. Drug addicts belong to all social classes. They include some of the young with right-wing tendencies who boast of their parents' position in society and are very vicious. But usually they are very ignorant and with a low cultural level, or they are very restless and weak, with a huge dose of insecurity. They can't haul themselves out of the well of horror into which they have fallen. They are responsible for much of the crime – to feed their habit.'

'Agreed,' said Alonso, 'but it is the condition of society that has put them in that well.'

'The Old Guard would say: "Not at all, it is the collapse of values," ' I interjected.

It was Ana Mari who now came out fighting.

'What collapse? What values? Were the old values so great? Did they not support *caciquismo*, corrupt politics, *señoritismo*, toadying to the privileged, and widespread hypocrisy – the last being perhaps the greatest Spanish value of all?'

'Were there not prostitutes and bawds and pimps and abuse of all kinds long before the young fell for hard music and drugs?' Alonso asked.

'Of course,' I said. 'You are talking of the oldest professions. But though you are telling me what was wrong with the past, you are not giving me much hope for the future, and I am sure there is some.'

'Oh yes, I think so,' Ana Mari said. 'There has been a great advance for women. Possibly that has been the greatest change of all. Women are beginning to own their lives rather than act as slaves to their husbands and families.'

'But I always thought of the Spanish woman as a very powerful figure behind the scenes,' I said. 'After all, Spanish society is often described as matriarchal. Are women now attempting to exchange one form of power for another? If so, are they not in danger of losing their traditional influence without gaining parity with men in other fields?'

'That is a myth,' Ana Mari answered, 'which I don't accept. I don't see that influential figure quite so clearly. Certainly, women have always shown a degree of astuteness at managing relationships within the family circle; but in the outside world they have had neither voice nor vote, and only the man has crowed. Women have always been resigned and psychically prepared to put up with almost anything. Their little revenge has been confined to the occasional seduction through feminine wiles. The modern woman in general is more aggressive and more direct in her relationships with men. Some, of course, have gone too far with their *machismo* and have lost whatever charm and naturalness they had. On the other hand, there are many households in which there is greater understanding of the woman by the man. These men help in what were considered female territories like shopping, cooking, washing up, caring for the baby and so on. This may be less common in Andalusia than elsewhere; here the men are less open in this sense, particularly in the pueblos. Nonetheless, I have friends on the coast and in Madrid who live together as couples on equal terms and conditions in every way and conduct their lives in liberty and mutual respect, which is what I really like.'

'What about marriage? Will it not decline as an institution?'

'It is still very popular, though I don't believe the young accept all the old family values. They participate in the rites of the Church; they baptise their children and see that they take their first communion, but it is all a matter of habit and custom.'

'But is that such a bad thing? It has always seemed to me a great strength of the Catholic Church that it is part of the fabric of everyday life and does not require excessive religiosity. Many people complain to me that consumerism has weakened the social cement. If the Church helps to keep the edifice together, what is wrong with that?'

'There are other forms of social cohesion,' said Alonso, 'which do not require religion: for instance respect for the environment and the crusade to save the planet.'

'I don't think the Spaniards have lost their instinct for social living,' Ana Mari mused. 'I think that would survive the death of religion.'

'Something that hardly seems in prospect,' I said, 'if you think of the cult of the Virgin.'

'That cult is still very strong in Andalusia,' she agreed. 'Even some who never go to Mass are devoted to the Virgin and have great faith in her. In Ronda Holy Week is still very much alive. It is an occasion for people to exteriorise their emotions, so that it becomes a kind of catharsis . . . which is probably good for the mental health of the pueblo.'

'But really you think it is rather childish?'

'Not exactly, because there is a sense in which we are all children. But I do think there are other paths of spiritual development. There are people coming back to religion but with a different conception of what Christ means. There are short courses in Christianity being run now, on which people, above all ordinary people, discover a much more humanised Christ than we were taught about as children; a great atmosphere of brotherhood and togetherness is created on these courses, which later flows out into the private and family lives of those who attend them – who then live a more direct and human type of Christianity.'

'It sounds like Protestantism.'

'Well, I do actually believe there will be a return to puritanism and simplicity when people have exhausted the pleasures of consumerism. It doesn't look that way at present because everyone seems to want to possess more of what is on offer: money, fame, prestige . . . whatever. The trouble is, Spain has advanced too rapidly for people to know where they are. It will take a long time for them to realise that the consumer society will not ultimately give them personal satisfaction. At the moment it is all showing off this, that and the other acquisition. They are still enjoying the great leap into prosperity.'

'But you are suggesting that people will move through this phase and then return to their natural puritanism?'

'Yes, I am.'

If that sounded paradoxical in a Catholic country, I reflected, it was worth remembering that Spaniards of all classes had traditionally been austere in their personal 'lifestyles', strangers to luxury and enemies (as Ortega said) of orgy.

'It is happening already,' said Alonso.

But not very fast, they both agreed.

In the evening I drove Ana Mari and Alonso down to the Llano de la Cruz to meet Siegfried and Gisela Leckenbusch. Siegfried is an artist with a wide technical repertory who became fascinated by Spanish artifacts such as millstones, horseshoes, the toothed wheel of threshing sledges . . . and turned them into haunting and frequently ironical constructions which were cunningly sited in his old garden. He is a charming, humorous and self-deprecatory man – a great self-parodist. Gisela is his handsome Brünhilde. It was she who wanted to make contact with the ecological groups in Ronda.

We sat on the cobbled terrace with the shadows gathering round Siegfried's sculptures. Wine and generous German *tapas* were served – more substantial than the Spanish playthings for the palate. Gisela dashed off to put her hens to bed; she had to contend with foxes and other predators. When we got down to business, Ana Mari said there were small gatherings of women in Ronda, concerned mainly with women's problems – diet, the purity of foodstuffs and so on – and she thought Gisela's best way in would be to join in such a group and perhaps give a talk to it. There was also a more general ecological movement, but that was being infiltrated by politicians and she did not recommend it. I said it was all very well, but politics, especially local politics, was bound to play a part. What about the Coto Doñana?

This, of course, has become an international *cause célèbre*. The 'great marshland . . . the biggest roadless area in Western Europe' in Jan Morris's words, with all its teeming wildlife, is now the battleground of developmental interests versus conservation, the test case for Spanish greenery (which the regional government, the Junta, espouses – at least on paper) against a multi-million project for a tourist complex to accommodate 30,000 visitors a year. Most of the little group on Siegfried's terrace felt that the development (which would drain the marsh) might well be halted partly because of the decline in Spanish tourism, partly because of the international outcry, and partly because the prime minister himself had a retreat within the Coto and it would look bad if he was seen to give in to local political pressures which would benefit his own party. I was less sanguine that any of this would prevail against the intense desire of the local branch of the PSOE to satisfy and benefit electorally from the greed of the villagers of Ayamonte, who were tired of living modestly on the edge of a swamp.

Nearer home, Ronda's polluted river was discussed again.

Gisela had heard that the environmental department had
come up with half the cost of a new sewage farm, but it
was rumoured that the debt-ridden municipality had simply
swallowed this up for other purposes. I said I thought it
most unlikely that the Junta would put their money on the
table until the matching funds were there too. If Ronda
could not come up with its half, then presumably the plan
would fail. Ana Mari shared my scepticism about Ronda's
ability to come up with its share, but she was less pessi-
mistic about the Spanish response to the environmental
challenges in general.

'TV is a big influence,' she said. 'There are more and
more wildlife programmes. I never used to like animated
cartoons, but now they all tend in a direction respectful of
nature, plants and animals. This is all being lapped up by
the young.'

'And taught in schools?'

'Much less that it should be,' Alonso said with his usual
vehemence. 'Conservation ought to be an obligatory subject.'

'But it's not only the educational material that counts,'
Ana Mari said. 'There is the other side of the coin, which
is the capacity to assimilate. Now, the Spaniard – because
he is so much alive – takes things in quickly. I noticed
it particularly when I worked in the Hotel Victoria: the
foreigners were thicker, slower to understand things, even
when I explained in good English.'

I sat back and looked at her in admiration. I found her
capacity to surprise me one of her most refreshing characteristics.

'That is fascinating,' I said, 'because it goes dead against
the conventional wisdom of the rest of Europe concerning
Spain. Most Europeans, at any rate till very recently, would
still have thought of Spain as the most Catholic, reactionary
and backward country in the Western world – nice for holidays, but not strong on ideas. Of course, I recognise that
this goes far back to the Inquisition and the "Black Legend"

that grew up about Spain, which still casts a very long shadow . . .'

'What is this "Black Legend"?' asked Gisela.

'That is best answered by reading those who tried to refute it, particularly Juan Valera in his essay published in 1868, I think, called *Concepto de España*; and *La Leyenda Negra* by Julián Juderías, written early this century. The latter tries to show that the Spain of the Counter-Reformation was no worse than its contemporaries, no more fanatical or cruel than they were, and that the English burned as many witches as the Inquisition did heretics . . . and so on. Valera is much more subtle. He says Spain has formed its own concept of itself very largely in response to the calumnies of foreign writers and the condescension implicit in such sayings as "Africa begins at the Pyrenees". The response has taken two forms. One is to take refuge in past glories and talk of nothing but Lepanto, Pavia, El Cid, Pelayo, Cortes, Pizarro, Numancia, Zaragoza and the like. The other celebrates poverty and backwardness as virtues because it is the simple life which makes people saintly and good. Valera amusingly describes a solemn eulogy of the humble *garbanzo*, the chickpea, as the symbol of wholesome simplicity, delivered by a distinguished pedant to some learned academy. In the case of Andalusia those who lead the simple life are doubly blessed, as their land of milk and honey allows them to live at ease, in contrast to the unfortunate peoples of the north whose unfriendly clime and sterile soil obliges them to rely on industry and cunning inventions for survival. Either way, Valera says, whether the Spanish apologists adopted the high bombastic line or preferred to stress simple virtues, they felt no need to bother about the march of progress: desirable advances such as trains or telephones could easily be copied. Américo Castro, the historian, later said that Spaniards were adept at this, but it was Unamuno who coined the immortal phrase, "Let others do the inventing!" '

'Very impressive,' said Ana Mari ironically, 'with all those quotes from grand intellectuals. But where does it all lead to?'

'It leads back to your contention that the Spaniards are exceptionally quick on the uptake – which does not quite seem to square with either foreigners' perceptions of Spain or Spaniards' perception of themselves. Even if there is some truth in it, it would appear to be an imitative rather than an inventive quickness of mind, as Castro implies. If that is so, is there much hope of a specifically Spanish conscious-ness about contemporary issues such as the environment?'

Ana Mari pondered this without taking umbrage.

'I don't think the old perceptions of us were wrong at the time,' she said. 'We were undoubtedly dragged down by hypocrisy and lethargy and ignorance. What has happened is that we have changed fast. It can happen. Look at Eastern Europe. We caught the tide at the right time. If Franco had died in 1950 or 1960 rather than in 1975, the time would not have been ripe, because a new generation without mem-ories of the Civil War would not have been there. So the change would not have been so profound. But democracy coming when it did has released skills, energies and strengths which may yet surprise our old critics.'

'You think then that we can bury the "Black Legend" once and for all?'

There was silence round the table. Dark had fallen. A dog bayed, emphasising the marvellous stillness under the stars, like the underlining of a word. Ana Mari and Alonso, embodiments of a New Spain, looked at each other; a flash of complicity passed between them.

'We are hopeful,' she said.

When I went to call on Don Mariano, I seemed to step back into the Old Spain that Diana and I had first known. The house in an alley of the *Ciudad* was distinguished by its reddish stone portico surmounted by a coat of arms. In the *zaguán*, or cobbled porch complete with drinking trough and mounting block, I found the hall porter smoking a cigarette; he scurried back into his den and re-emerged without his weed to admit me through the front door. The owner then came out from one of the salons surrounding the patio; after some discussion as to where we should be most comfortable, we settled on wicker chairs in the patio itself. In deference to my Englishness, whisky was offered, but I declined for it was still only just after six on a hot afternoon. The daughter of the house then very charmingly brought a tray of soft drinks, nuts and cold beer, after which she retired discreetly.

Don Mariano is the *beau ideal* of the *caballero andaluz*: neat of figure, small of foot, bright of eye, firm in opinion but modest in expressing it, punctilious but not stifling in courtesy. We began by recalling our first meeting in the sixties, when I was riding across his land at Ortegícar: I on my stocky little mount, Chico, somewhat overburdened by me and saddlebags; he astride the high-stepping bay on which he had emerged from the olives by the Moorish bridge and conducted me to the house.

He was still, perhaps more than ever, above all a country-lover. He believed one lived better in the country and that those who lived on it and off it, however poor, had in Andalusia at any rate possessed great *educación* – by which he meant good manners. Today the young were ill-educated in that sense; in the town swear-words proper to a man in certain settings had become common usage among girls walking in the street. People were much less courteous. But there were certain minimum courtesies that had to be preserved; this did not mean that you had to be so hypocritical as to tell an ugly woman that she was beautiful, but there was a balance to be struck.

Thirteen to fourteen per cent of people in the Ronda area still lived from agriculture or herding, Don Mariano said, which was high by European standards. One of the reasons was the resurgence of the olive, which was labour-intensive. Things went in waves of fashion, didn't they? Condemned for its cholesterol content by comparison with other inferior vegetable oils, olive oil had now been rehabilitated and recovered its prestige. Something similar could be said for the whole Mediterranean diet. All the poor man's foods – chickpeas, lentils, broad beans – previously frowned on by 'informed' medical opinion and dismissed by intellectuals like Ortega were coming back into favour. It was being shown that there was less incidence of cancer on this modest diet . . . though God knew what would happen to the population at large flocking into the cities and subsisting on atmospheric pollution and junk food.

As to Ronda itself, Don Mariano most regretted the architectural barbarities that were springing up, despite the fact that when pulling down a house you were required to take a photograph of the façade and reproduce it. Even if this was complied with, which it often wasn't, the old irregular lime-washed surfaces, a palimpsest of many coatings collecting both light and shade, were being replaced by plumb-line concrete walls, on which the whitewash was dead and dreary, not subtle and alive. In terms of other deteriorations of the urban ambience small motorbikes ranked high. There was a legal limit of decibels, which was never enforced and was probably unenforceable. I told the story of the Japanese manufacturer who had found a way to produce quieter engines but had been required by his dealers to re-noise-up his bikes for the Spanish market. Don Mariano said the more powerful and expensive the bike, the less noise; some were able to satisfy their *machismo* through almost silent power, but that did not solve the problem of low income leading to poor-performance technology. If Spain became richer, would the problem solve itself? Don Mariano doubted it. Probably only if the government imposed more stringent standards.

We had shot our bolt on bikes and I wondered what would follow. I had not long to wait. The conversation shortly changed gear when my host introduced the subject of that august body, the Real Maestranza de Caballería de Ronda. At this point he insisted that whisky be brought in: it was

J&B, a pale variety which we drank in tall glasses with ice and water. After a lawsuit against Seville in the reign of Alfonso XIII, he said, the Maestranza of Ronda was confirmed as the senior of the five in Spain, the others being those of Seville, Granada, Valencia and Zaragoza. Their original object had been to promote the management of the horse as a machine of war. Ronda's motto was, and remained, *Dios, Patria, Rey*. There were about a hundred *maestrantes* of Ronda and Mariano himself now had the honour to be their *hermano mayor*, or elder brother. The president was Don Juan de Borbón, the king's father, who had been present at a meeting in this very house. All five Maestranzas met together once a year, alternating as hosts; it had been Ronda's turn two years back.

Qualifications for election? Yes, lineage was important, but it was not necessary to be a great aristocrat; it was sufficient to be a *hidalgo* and able to live decently from a worthy profession; you were not ruled out by working as, say, a bank official. It was true that the original requirements were linked strongly to the great sixteenth- and seventeenth-century Spanish obsession with *limpieza de sangre* (pure non-Jewish, non-Arab descent) but nowadays personal merits, above all *el sentido de la caballerosidad*, the sense of chivalry, were equally important.

How, I wondered, did the Maestranza pursue its aims in the late twentieth century? Well, as was to be expected, the breeding of horses had always formed an important part of its activities, and still did. Did I know that the famous English thoroughbred had a touch of Spanish blood? He himself kept a *yeguada* of mares. Mercifully, he had been spared the dreaded equine fever which was ravaging the south, but the ban on the movement of horses across provincial boundaries had made it impossible to sell his foals and he had suffered considerable loss.

Then, the Maestranza as a body maintained a *picadero* for breaking horses in; and it paid the wages of two blacksmiths. It was also in the process of building a new range

244

Entrance to the *picadero* of the Plaza de Toros de la Real
Maestranza de Caballería de Ronda

of stables with sixteen loose-boxes behind the bullring with
the object of providing free stabling, but not maintenance
costs, for horse-lovers who had no country property of their
own. This project was particularly close to his heart because
horsemanship in Ronda had declined sadly in recent years.

How was all this financed? Ah, here the Maestranza of
Ronda, like Seville's, was fortunate in possessing a source
of income in the shape of the bullring which it had built
in 1784 and still owned. The old rings of the other three
Maestranzas (Granada's had been the oldest of all) were
pulled down in the last century and replaced by modern
arenas from which those Maestranzas derived no revenue.
In Ronda the present impresario of the *plaza de toros*, the
retired matador Antonio Ordóñez, paid a rent which allowed
him to put on as many *corridas* or other taurine spectacles
as he wished; horse-and-carriage competitions also took
place. With its earnings from the ring the Maestranza was
able to pursue the activities Don Mariano had described and
also to carry out some acts of charity: the social security

system left many lacunae and charity was still important.

Politically . . . well, as a body the Maestranza was apolitical and would collaborate with a town council of any colour over arrangements for the fair and so forth. Personally, Don Mariano was a conservative, and he supposed that most members were too. The trouble with politics these days was that people went more for a leader than for principles. The great sin of socialism was that it subsidised unemployment (much of it not genuine) on a vast scale; also it was just as corrupt as other political creeds, if not more so. I said that the rest of the world had been agreeably surprised by the way Spain had handled its political 'transition'. Don Mariano agreed that the Spaniards had been a violent people but, with the exception of 'the cancer of ETA', they were now more civilised. Much of this was due to the king. He had been *un gran moderador* – more important really in the process than the politicians.

Returning to the Maestranza, I asked if there was any danger that its income would dry up through the collapse or decline of bullfighting under external European or internal green or ecological pressures. He agreed these pressures existed, but thought they would not prevail. Rather than declining, bullfighting was experiencing something of a renaissance; it had pulled itself up from its low in the late seventies, when it had been aimed by unscrupulous promoters at ignorant tourists. There was still a good deal of criticism of the breeders for producing bulls of fine appearance which collapsed on their knees as soon as they were worked tightly with the cape. People said this was because they were artificially fed rather than roaming free and putting on muscle on the ranch. It was true that the ranches, the *dehesas*, had been reduced in size through the tendency to convert the flatter parts to more lucrative cereals. But he was sure that most breeders were conscientious; after all, they could not survive constant humiliation in the ring.

A much more serious criticism, Don Mariano believed, could be directed against the manner of placing the *pica*:

the picador on a horse with its padding, weighing 1000 kilos all told, was like a tank against cavalry. No, he was not in favour of removing the padding, because he did not want to see a horse trailing its guts round the ring (the spectacle that had so tickled the old lady in Hemingway's *Death in the Afternoon*). But in the old days the unprotected horse had obviously been lighter and more exposed, and the picador had needed to lean out and place the lance properly before impact rather than waiting for the bull to hit the padding and then jabbing and twisting the steel point from above. That should be penalised. Personally, he went on, he was only an *aficionado mediano*. What he most liked about the bulls were the *faenas en el campo*, especially the *acoso y derribo*, when horsemen chased and overturned the young bulls with lightly-tipped poles; the selection of the future seed bulls would then be made from among those who did not flee but stood their ground after the *voltereta*, as their somersault was called. This was very fine to see and indeed was turning into a spectator sport in its own right.

If he was only lukewarm about the *corrida* (except as the main source of income of the Maestranza), had he any stronger *afición*? Yes, Don Mariano said, he was passionately addicted to that other great Spanish blood sport, which like the *corrida* was practised under strict and ancient rules: he referred naturally to the *montería*, in which the hunter's principal quarry were the roebuck and the wild boar. The ecologists, of course, were against it. In a gentle dig at Julián de Zulueta, the ex-mayor and an ardent ecologist, who accused the hunting fraternity of merely breeding to kill, he said it was just not true that they enjoyed the suffering of animals for its own sake; what they enjoyed was the skill of the chase. Furthermore, Julián and his friends quite failed to distinguish between *cazadores*, hunters, who loved and respected animals and conducted themselves according to the rules, and *tiradores*, who blasted off at everything that moved, whether quails, starlings or even *tórtolas*, turtle-doves. The *cotos de caza*, the private game reserves, actually preserved species rather than eliminating them. Four or five wolves had been sighted on his estate in the province of Jaén and he had given strict orders they were not to be shot; every time he read of the killing of one of the few remaining wild bears in the Cantabrian mountains it deeply saddened him.

I wondered about the new so-called 'natural parks', like that of Grazalema, now coming into being under public stewardship, presumably with the idea of opening up the countryside to the people – albeit with fierce restrictions. Was this a good thing? Don Mariano said it was desirable to protect flora and fauna, though he doubted whether this was best done by unleashing hordes of townees on the environment. But the main cause of concern was what was happening, or was likely to happen, on the Coto Doñana. This had become an international scandal, in which socialist minsters were deeply implicated. It would not only be immoral but absurd to build yet more tourist facilities in one of the great nature reserves of Europe at a time when tourism was *declining* in Spain, due to rising prices, increasing noise, diminishing courtesy and competition from the Caribbean, the Pacific and Asia. In these circumstances, the threat to Doñana was little short of criminal. Here at least, I thought, the traditionalists and the ecologists seemed to be of one mind.

Where intervention was required, Don Mariano continued, it was lacking; while in the newly protected areas I had referred to there was excessive interventionism by competing and sometimes conflicting official agencies. Who after all had maintained the natural habitat to date? The landowners, of course, and now they were being told they couldn't sneeze on their own land. There was AMA (Agencia del Medio Ambiente) and IRYDA (Instituto de Reforma y Desarrollo Agraria) and ICONA (Instituto de Conservación y Organización Nacional Agraria, responsible for state-owned lands), and IARA – one couldn't even recall what IARA stood for, there were so many damned acronyms these days! He knew a few good agronomists and engineers in these bodies, but for the most part it was all a vast job-creation agency.

All bureaucracies, I agreed, tended to become bloated, especially in Spain where such jobs were the dearest aspiration of all mothers for their sons. But on the positive side wasn't the Junta de Andalucía attempting to improve the economy of the interior by stimulating rural tourism, and wasn't that a worthy aim? Again, Don Mariano had reservations. You had only to look at the picnic sites to see the litter of cans and paper and plastic left behind. Did I know that the humble torch battery was the most non-biodegradable thing ever invented and would take centuries to disappear? This might seem trivial compared to the crime of arsonists who burned down great swathes of old forest or new plantation out of malice, but one should not forget the no less devastating involuntary arsonists who were cooking a paella and thoughtlessly let fall a match. Rural tourism was a nice idea but it had great drawbacks – not least that the animal species which had fallen back onto ever rougher terrains would eventually, pursued by the inquisitive human being, have nowhere left to go.

He paused and refreshed our glasses. Did I know the Sierra de Cazorla? I said I had only skirted it. Well, that had been one of the greatest areas for wildlife in all Spain. But gradually it had been degraded, first by the national rail company, the RENFE, cutting down woods for railway sleepers; then by re-afforestation schemes with their grids of tracks and firebreaks, *rompiendo la corteza de la tierra*, breaking the earth's crust and causing landslides into the rivers which became silted up. At the same time, the indigenous animals – the wolf, the ibex, the boar – had been driven out and replaced by such importations as the moufflon, a wild sheep native to Corsica and Sardinia. And this in its turn was forced to retreat as the villa developments climbed up the hillsides . . .

All these concerns – which Don Mariano expressed in an

even, gentle tone of voice – were based on his over-arching respect for what he called the *bienes de Dios*, God's gifts, with which the Almighty had so richly endowed Andalusia. I found myself harking back to Ortega y Gasset's theory of the vegetative ideal, which it seems to me all Andalusians, great and small, high and low, are striving intuitively, if sometimes confusedly, to preserve. But there the common purpose splinters: the aristocrat not unnaturally feels that things worked better under the old paternalistic order, while the newly mobile common man wants his share of the action but lacks or has lost the ancient knowledge of nature's strengths and frailties. Thus, there is a real danger of a Left–Right split, on the lines of the fraternity of the footpath versus the owners of grouse moors in Great Britain. This would be a great pity, because the Left is not always right and the Right is not always wrong: as Don Mariano had pointed out, it was the socialists who were threatening the Coto Doñana.

Our whiskies were almost drained, and Don Mariano had another appointment. We had been talking for two hours. Once or twice, on his side and on mine, we had abandoned the formal *Usted* and slipped into the familiar second-person *tu*. A path had thus been opened towards greater *confianza* or intimacy and he hoped very much we should proceed further along it. I gathered that he was not inviting me to an orgy of familiarity but that he would be happy for our relationship to be conducted in the more intimate mode. I realised at once that what to others might seem a simple step was to him, with his fine sensibility, a matter of some moment. I said I should count it a privilege to fall in with his suggestion.

I do not want to dwell excessively on this, but these nuances have their fascination. There is a rather heart-warming tendency among Spaniards in the south to go directly to the second person if they consider you to be on their social level. Thus, grandees and local gentry will slip quickly into *tu* with an English 'gent'. It was also the usage that came naturally to my one-time neighbour Arturo, who aspired to a strictly egalitarian Utopia. Some of the Ronda bourgeoisie use it to me out of old acquaintance or shared intellectual interests (the bookseller, teachers, doctors, lawyers). I use it to the middle and younger generations of my 'mafia' but not to the elders, Ana and Mateo. The thing to avoid above all is an ill-balanced relationship in which master talks down to servant as *tu* but expects to be addressed as *Usted*. With the exception of a few boors even the *señoritos* are punctilious about this. Moro, the fish-porter, embraces me and we use *tu*, because we know in our hearts that we are not much more different than grains of sand or ears of corn.

Mariano – as I must now call him *tout court* – is an expert in the fine-tuning of these matters. In him there is neither brash *bonhomie* nor rigid formalism. He had invited me on this occasion towards the lower foothills of friendship and I do not deny that this gave me some satisfaction. We British have virtually abolished our verbal inflections and relegated the third person to archaic and ceremonial purposes, thus depriving ourselves of the more intricate and subtle possibilities of what Spaniards call *tratamiento social*. We may say it is more democratic to have bulldozed these awkward social humps. Most Spaniards would disagree. They would say we have deprived ourselves of the superb intimacy and ultimate democracy of using *tu* to both God and king.

8

MORISCO COUNTRY

Until recently the valley of the river Genal was one of the most isolated rural districts in southern Spain. On one side, the (then) hazardous road from Ronda to San Pedro de Alcántara poked short, brittle branches down to Parauta, Cartajima and Igualeja. On the other side, the road to Algeciras, sweeping along the crest of a high ridge, touched the pueblos on the valley's upper rim – Atajate, Benadalid, Algatocín and Gaucín – but left several others nearer the river sunk in leafy obscurity; some of the latter had no motor road at all. In effect, the two trunk roads, like the arms of a pair of dividers with their hinge in Ronda and their points on the coast, enclosed a secret and secretive world that seemed almost embalmed. To the south the sturdy mass of the Sierra Bermeja was a bastion standing in the way of coastal influences. The only way out of this strange, hushed triangle was by the small bus or communal taxi which juddered its way daily from most of these settlements into Ronda, bringing a sprinkling of the valley folk to do their shopping or transact their business in the metropolis. These days, the spread of car ownership and a much improved network of mountain roads have lessened the isolation without as yet affecting the picturesque charms of the Genal pueblos or bringing any significant signs of 'development' to them. Why then did I not start – and perhaps end – my quest in what may sound a close approximation to paradise?

It is a 'good question', as hearty politicians and panellists say, and deserves a less evasive answer than they usually give. The essential starting point is that these villages are of Berber origin and were caught up in the great revolt of the *Moriscos*, Muslims nominally converted to Christianity, in 1568–70, and likewise in the further uprising against the decision of 1609 to expel them from the country altogether. According to Julián de Zulueta (see pages 200–201), the failure of the Catholic Monarchs and their successors to keep their word with the vanquished after the completion of the Reconquest caused a smouldering resentment that was never quenched and resurfaced centuries later in rural Anarchism.

From the apex of the 'dividers' I set out along the right-hand arm, the road to Algeciras, whose first stretch runs through an especially bleak and bald expanse of sierra. After ten kilometres or so it reaches a junction with a narrow road on the left. This tilts down across a waste of boulders and stones, somewhat relieved of its grimness by the enormous views of wooded hillsides to the south. Then comes a series of loops, followed by a hairpin bend, delivering one into Alpandeire.

I have long had a soft spot for Alpandeire. It is dominated by an imposing twin-towered Jesuit-style church which seems quite out of proportion to the size of the place, but is also reassuring: such labour would surely not have been lavished on an ill-favoured or ill-natured pueblo. The few streets, mostly steep, bear out this first impression. Embellished with bougainvillaea and hydrangeas, they have an unusual sweetness for these altitudes; most of the dwellings have charming open lofts and quaint chimneys; along the main street are a few more substantial houses built no doubt for the doctor, the lawyer and the small gentry.

Leaving the car by the church, I walked down to the plaza, one side of which is formed by a little esplanade with a miniature bandstand and a terrace overlooking the plunging ravines and gullies below. From here other dazzling white pueblos are visible, perched under their crags or folded into the wooded hills. I had known all their names for years and had visited most of them but could never recite them in the right order because they disconcertingly changed position from each different vantage point.

'That is Benalauría,' said an old man who had suddenly materialised beside me. 'Those two are Benadalid and Algatocín. The furthest you can see is Benarrabá, which is bigger than it appears because you can only see the tip of it over the trees.'

I thanked him and rolled their names over under my breath . . . and of course there were others that were not in sight: Atajate, Faraján, Jubrique, Genalguacil and half a dozen more whose names all whispered mysteriously of their Berber past. I knew that the most poetic moment to contemplate them was after dark, when they resembled coronets or necklaces of light glinting against the dimmed folds of the landscape . . . when you were less than ever certain which was which.

When I entered the main bar, it took some time to catch the eye of Miguel Bullón, the landlord. He is a thick-set, sturdy, almost chubby Spaniard; fair in colouring and soft-spoken with the sort of physiognomy that often goes with the gentle craft of the baker. Eventually I managed to ask him, as he served me, whether there were any houses for sale in the pueblo. His first response was 'no', followed shortly by 'maybe'. He is a dealer at heart, and his blood runs faster at even the remote prospect of a transaction which could bring honour and satisfaction to all parties and a nice fee for the intermediary. There were always the Morenos, he said, whose house was too big for them and was shut up; the old lady lived nearby in a smaller place. He would slip out for a moment as soon as there was a lull at the counter but at present as I could see . . .

He continued serving his customers with benign paternalism.

'What? A camomile tea? And it is already one o'clock!

What a thing to ask for when the others are all taking wine or a nice cold beer! María, one camomile please!'

Someone asked him for a *tinto de verano*.

'With ice?' he asked, using the old country word for ice, *nieve*, literally snow, which derived from when *pozos de nieve*, snow-wells, were dug and filled on the hillsides and then covered with earth and scrub; in summer their contents would be disinterred and brought round the villages by muleteers, packed in straw and rushes and sold to households and bars.

Neat cubes of refrigerated ice now tinkled in the customer's glass, but it was still *nieve* in Alpandeire.

My immediate neighbour at the counter lived and worked in Estepona. His wife preferred the coast, but he came up to the pueblo whenever he could.

'I get a kick out of my house and a bit of land I still have. Agriculture is finished because of the high wages but I can manage a few trees on my own. You should see my damsons. And there is a market for almonds.'

After a while Miguel beckoned from behind the bar. He led me just round the corner. A little old lady, bright as a pin, admitted us through double doors into a cobbled yard. We decided to start at the top. The whole *cámara* or upper floor was unpartitioned, like my loft in the *campo*. Chinks of light showed through the rafters but the roof tiles were so cunningly slanted by her brother, the old lady assured us, that not a drop came in. As usual in these upper storeys designed as huge larders for hams and other produce, the windows were tiny: if enlarged – she was quick to point out – they would give splendid views over the hills.

The ground floor consisted of the main parlour with a handsome fireplace and three dark bedrooms off it; there was also a kitchen and a small yard, formed on one side by living rock. The front patio was very pleasant with its overhead vine, a bay tree and a good-sized room along one wall which would make a fine study. From the patio a wide shallow flight of steps led up to a terrace, while a cobbled ramp led down to a large semi-basement stable with its own door onto a side street. A mare was munching at a manger; there were several cages of rabbits and a goat; half a dozen more horses could have been fitted in. The original purpose of the house now became plain: it had been the *posada* of the pueblo, providing lodging for men and beasts, before entering its present owners' hands in 1942.

As to price, I had no idea whether I would be asked half a million or five million pesetas. Having extolled the iron and woodwork, which were not exceptional, the old lady said proudly that the property had been accurately measured and contained nearly four hundred square metres. Real-estate notions from the coast had clearly begun to creep up into the sierras. There was also, she said, a gentleman from Marbella who was interested. She then added demurely that she and her brother had been thinking of asking four and a half million pesetas.

Miguel, with his instincts for a deal, began to talk her price down then and there. There was no house in the pueblo which was worth that much. Why, even the doctor's on the corner of the plaza had gone for only two and a half – and her property was in need of much more repair. He started flaking plaster off a wall with his clasp knife, scratching it down to the brick.

'You should have seen this patio,' she said, 'when it was freshly whitewashed. Then it looked very different – white as a dove. It hasn't been done for four or five years, but when it is done again . . .'

'That's not the point,' said Miguel, sharply for him. 'The point is that you will never get that price.'

Afterwards in his bar he talked the place up to me: its size, its basic soundness; the girth of its structural pillars, the thickness of its walls. His idea of a proper price was three million. This set my mind ticking. It would need as much again spending on it, but for little more than thirty thousand pounds all told one could have a marvellous retreat with access to a telephone and medical services (an important consideration as one grew older). Animals were not ruled out as they would be in county towns like Ronda or Osuna. Most of the backyards I had looked down on from the loft had hens, and no doubt there were pigs too. The roomy stable would comfortably accommodate any horse or horses we could conceivably want, and though the countryside was very irregular, it was still criss-crossed by the old bridle tracks.

'Could one buy or hire a bit of pasturage?' I asked, mindful of Hilly's yearning for a mare.

'With time that could be arranged,' Miguel answered in his soothing and assured way, perfectly crafted to banish all anxieties. 'When you are here – we can talk to one or two people. There is always a solution.'

In Miguel's world there was virtually nothing that could not be arranged. And in Alpandeire as a whole there was nothing raucous; it seemed to breathe an air of rustic gentility. It was all rather tempting. I said I would consult my family and let him know shortly.

'Well, don't leave it too long,' he said evenly. 'That house has other *novios*.'

Despite his love of a deal, I got the feeling that this was the nearest he would ever come to hustling anybody.

Before leaving I had another thought.

'How well are your people disposed towards strangers?'

This was one thing that clearly couldn't be arranged. Miguel pondered it seriously and then said simply, 'Here they are *canela*.'

Canela is cinnamon, a bland spice often used in southern parlance to denote something simple, easy, sweet.

'But the old violence from the time of the Moors – and the *Moriscos* – that has all gone?'

'What are you talking about?' he said with derision. 'Here we are all Christians since the Flood. Do we not have our native saint or *beato* at any rate? Have you never heard of Fray Leopoldo de Alpandeire?'

He pointed to the beatified father's calendar hanging on

the wall: it showed the luxuriantly bearded monk who had been a local celebrity at the turn of the present century. There, surely, his gesture implied, was a potent talisman against any of the nonsense I was talking about.

'But in other pueblos,' I suggested, 'there is another tradition, is there not?'

He shrugged.

'In other pueblos, who knows? Some may be more abrupt socially or have more closed mentalities but you will not find any of that here, where people are open and noble.'

I did not pursue the matter. I had no doubt he was right. But Alpandeire was not, I suspected, typical of the region. It had closer and less tortuous access to Ronda than most of its neighbours. I still recalled the palpable hostility that had greeted travellers in the Genal valley in the not so distant past, which seemed – on reflection – to give some colour to Julián de Zulueta's theory of a crypto-Islamic world nursing age-old resentments against its conquerors and oppressors. I wondered if I should find any vestiges of this as I penetrated further into the labyrinth.

Faraján is a rougher and less visually delightful place than Alpandeire. But the atmosphere was lively, for I arrived during the fair. I had free drinks and *tapas* in a busy bar by courtesy of a cheerful man I had unintentionally jostled while struggling to the counter. French cars were much in evidence and two of the company tried out on me the French they had picked up as emigrant workers. It was execrable, but they produced it with pride and it was applauded by everyone like some amateur conjuring trick. The landlord too had worked in France.

'Everyone comes back in August,' he said. 'People don't leave their family and friends for longer than they can help. There is something about *la tierra de uno, aunque sea mala*, one's own patch however bad, that nowhere else can match.'

'Do the young feel that?' I asked.

'Oh, they have a good time here, don't you worry! You

see those girls playing pool there? They are from Seville; their father was born here and has a good house. They come every summer. They go to all the fairs. And the music we have nowadays is all for their tastes.'

In the small pueblos I detected a special anxiety for the young – a deep concern that they should not be bored or alienated and therefore desert the old soil and hearth – and I found this touching. Old men were prepared to put up with night after night of the most appalling heavy-metal music in fair-time, if that was what the younger generation wanted. This was in marked contrast to the sanctimonious denunciations by the Ronda bourgeoisie of the vices of modern youth.

Of Júzcar, the next tiny pueblo (population 279), I was able to form little impression. It was sunk in the somnolence of mid-afternoon; not a dog stirred, not a soul was in sight. Rather than linger until it stirred to life, I pushed on towards Cartajima, as I wanted to try and identify the scene of a violent episode described in Moreti's *Historia de Ronda*. According to this source, one Meliche, a *Morisco* bandit and outlaw, was pursued in 1570 by Bartolomé Gutiérrez Duarte and his four brothers, all famous warriors. In a skirmish, in which Bartolomé lost a brother and a nephew, he badly wounded Meliche, who had himself carried to the 'puerto de Cartajima', a pass through which the Christians would have to make their way on their return to Ronda. Here a hole was dug and he had himself interred in it up to his armpits in order to keep himself upright. With two loaded guns he waited and, when the Christian cavalcade came within range, shot Bartolomé in the head; the stricken man died later in Ronda. In Moreti's words, 'The Moor was immediately torn to pieces.'

When the rebellion was over, Bartolomé's widow and family were awarded confiscated lands in the vicinity. But the *Morisco* cause was not dead. A new bandit leader, called Tajarillo, arose, and rallied resistance in the Serranía to the edict of 1609 expelling all the remaining *Moriscos* from Spain. One day in 1610, Tajarillo and his men lay in wait for Francisco Gutiérrez, a grandson of Bartolomé. They fell upon the young man and escaped with his gun. Francisco tracked Tajarillo to a shepherd's hut and in the ensuing tussle the weapon exploded in Tajarillo's face and killed him. Francisco then cut off his head and took it to Ronda, where he paraded it through the streets in a procession with drums and fifes, accompanied by the local authorities and nobility; he was subsequently awarded more lands for this heroic feat.

It was hard to tell from Moreti's account where these events had taken place, but I thought that some recollection of them might have lodged in folk memory. Enquiring in the main café of Cartajima for someone familiar with the history of the pueblo, I was directed to the *bar de los ancianos* higher up, hard by the church. This was marked by no sign and looked like a private house from the outside, but I could see two or three thronged tables through the window and heard the click of dominoes. Everyone looked up as I entered. Those playing the card game *tresillo* were keeping their scores with chickpeas from a pile in the centre of the green baize cloth. After a short scrutiny of the stranger all returned impassively to the game in hand.

A hefty young man was serving behind the counter; he had recently returned from the coast to take charge of the bar. Someone with a knowledge of local history, Meliche and such-like tales? The trouble was that all the archives had been burned in the Civil War. But the very gentleman standing next to me knew a lot. He was a fine-looking old man of seventy or so. Nothing loath, he started on 'the time of the French'. He had the right dates but had never heard of the 'Peninsular War' or even the normal Spanish term 'War of Independence'. On the Moors he was extremely vague and spoke of the chieftain of a tribe of bandits who had long ravaged the locality; also of a cave and hidden treasure.

Here the barman chipped in: 'In Marbella, next door to where I used to work, they have built a mosque and it has a great library. The Arabs from there have been up here looking for treasure.'

There did not seem to be any resentment against Islamic millionaires prospecting for their roots, or even for treasure, in the sierras. How many people of Moorish stock had in fact remained in these labyrinthine hills after the 'final' expulsion? Rafael Aguilera, the leading amateur of local history in Ronda, whom I had consulted, had no doubt the number had been considerable: you could still detect their influence in the speech rhythms. That there was a remnant and some interbreeding with the dominant community is accepted by most historians, but they differ sharply on its importance and extent. Some children were left behind and brought up as servants or apprentices by Christian families; some of these later contracted matrimony with 'Old Christians'; some people of Moorish extraction were protected by landowners to work their land; slavery was still rife and there were Moorish slaves; and last but not least there was a reverse flight from Barbary of *Moriscos* who had received less than a warm welcome in Africa and risked life and limb to return to their native land – of which the most famous instance is Sancho Panza's encounter with the *Morisco* Ricote in *Don Quixote*.

But the old men's bar in Cartajima was not the place to air such speculations. Talk soon turned to the local economy. The chestnut, as I had no doubt seen, had everywhere replaced the vine. Several assertions were made of the high quality and alcoholic content of the must that was still produced by a few local growers. However, the chestnut had undoubtedly taken over as the main product. This meant twenty days of unremitting activity in October: a few ripe conkers fell from the crowns of the trees, already free of their prickly husks, but the majority had to be prised out with knives and gloves. The chestnut producers were mostly smallholders; there were only a few larger proprietors. The Genal chestnuts commanded a good price because they were early; in other areas the harvest was not till November. But everyone, large and small, was swindled by the middleman. This was said with total acceptance, as if it was a law of life. All the same, I got the impression that it was important for the pueblo to be identified with and rally round some form of production, however marginal economically, as evidence of its continuing vitality. Some pueblos gain more than others from their local industries, but in all of them the symbolic value of that activity is as important as the economic, and in some cases more so. Without it the inhabitants would feel they had surrendered completely to the international industrial juggernaut. Thus, in Cartajima, the importance of the chestnut was much talked up.

Yet the juggernaut undoubtedly provided most of the income. There were some four hundred registered inhabitants in the place, said the barman: virtually all of the able-bodied ones were down on the coast, apart from half a dozen youths employed on make-work schemes by the Junta de Andalucía. Some had settled down there and only returned for the holidays; others went down on Mondays at dawn (like the men of El Burgo) and returned on Friday afternoon. A self-confident man in a blazer, standing near me, had a flat in Marbella but was never happier, he said, than in the pueblo.

'You see,' he said, 'it's easier for us to get home now than it was in the days of Franco when most of the emigration was *abroad*.' He paused and added with pride, 'Spaniards have stopped being guest-workers for richer countries.'

This took me back to Alcalá del Valle's statue to the emigrants who had kept it alive throughout those years. Of course it was good that Franco's mass exportation of labour to remove pressure on the labour market and diminish dissent was over. In a curious way the coastal corridor, which was such anathema to the purists, had become the life-support machine of the mountains, allowing the sons of

Cartajima to work from home-base, returning at the weekends with money in their pockets. This had an additional
spin-off for the traveller, for there was no doubt these pueblos had become more open and tractable as a result of their
contact with Sodom and Gomorrah. The great question was
how corrupted, if at all, they had been by the contact. I
could not very well ask this directly, so I probed about the
continuance of old customs.

'You should see the day of the Virgin of August,' said he
of the blazer. 'That is when Cartajima lives.'

'But the real patroness is the Virgin of the Rosary,' said
the old man carefully. 'Her proper day is in October. They
moved it to August . . .'

'To fit in with the holidays of the emigrants, of course,'
said the barman. 'Everyone can come then.'

I thought how sensible it was that the saint's day should
be moved to suit the needs of the flock, and said as much.

'Why not?' grinned the barman. 'After all, she's *our* saint.'

'One thing they haven't been able to change,' said the old
man stubbornly, 'is Easter Sunday morning. That is very
fine. You should come back for that.'

I said I would do my best.

When I came down to Parauta, a pretty place tucked into a
chestnut slope, facing the more martial Cartajima, I went
first to the bar by the bus stop. Over the counter were the
usual girlie posters. I asked for the wise man of the place
and was directed, as at Cartajima, to the café where the old
men gathered. This faced onto a charming little plaza, in
which an ambulant tradesman had set out his wares and
was treating the population to wave upon wave of ear-
splitting music from the loudspeaker on his van. I had to
shout my enquiry but was soon escorted politely to the door
of him I sought, Diego Sastre by name.

Diego had a calm, contemplative, relatively unlined face
for his age; I felt he never spoke unnecessarily. We stood
in his passage while we talked. Rather than volunteer

information, he would simply answer questions. But on one thing he was emphatic. Parauta had never been Moorish. There had been a Moorish settlement near by, which he called Benacín. No, it no longer existed; there were no traces. From its beginning Parauta was the place where the Mass was celebrated and the converted Moors had joined the new village. Parauta had always been Christian. The old patroness was the Virgin of the Conception, whose proper day was in December, but she had recently given way to the Virgin of August. It was the same story as elsewhere: the saint's day had been adapted to the industrial calendar.

The chestnut crop, Diego said, was the staple here too. The trees were divided among a number of small owners. Sales were effected through a co-operative of three pueblos: Parauta, Cartajima and Igualeja. These were the earliest chestnuts in Spain, ahead of Huelva by a month. Certainly the brokers charged steeply for their services, but they drove a hard bargain also with the buyers, and a better price was obtained this way than any individual could hope to obtain on his own.

Inhabitants? Perhaps 260 or 270. Diego was the first villager I had met to agree that his pueblo might die. No, Ronda folk were not buying village homes; they preferred the new chalet developments – and the young wanted only noise, diversion, bustle, crowds. When I suggested that tranquillity and repose might come back into fashion and people might then seek out the pueblos of the Serranía, he was politely sceptical. Indeed, as I walked back through the plaza the salesman's loudspeaker was still pounding its din; reverberating round the old lofts and eaves and grilles; and rebounding presumably from the special noise-proof mem- ·brane which I have always supposed to reside within the Spanish ear.

Dusk was falling. Igualeja was next on my itinerary. I knew it boasted a *fonda*, where I planned without much enthusiasm to spend the night. I drove up from Parauta onto the San Pedro road, turned right and shortly switched again onto a well-surfaced but narrow and precipitous mountain road winding down to my destination.

With over a thousand inhabitants, Igualeja is the largest and most prosperous pueblo of the upper Genal valley. Its people are reputed to be tough and ruthless. The biggest farmer in my own valley is a son of Igualeja; he has achieved success by converting to cereals and savagely cutting his workforce; he is respected and indeed fawned on, but not loved. Business acumen is of course no crime, but I was aware also of certain fearsome acts of violence associated with Igualeja. For example, years before I had been told on good authority of a father and son from the pueblo who had fought all day with axes over the ownership of a single olive tree; the son killed the father but was terribly maimed himself and later died in prison. 'Two lives for an olive tree!' I remember exclaiming to my informant. 'Yes,' he said with some pride, as if this proved that Igualeja (of which he was a native) was a serious place. 'Yes, precisely: two lives for an olive tree.'

More recently, Rafael Alarcón from La Mimbre had revived this memory. I met him one afternoon on his way to Ronda in an unwonted suit and tie for the memorial Mass of a friend killed a year before. 'He was the same age as my brother and me,' he said, 'and he was bailiff of a farm on the other side of Ronda. One night a madman from Igualeja came and demanded shelter and work. Our friend said he had no authority in such matters, which were for the owner to decide; upon which the *loco* upped and battered him to death with a stone; a few days later he hanged himself in prison.'

None of this made for cheerful expectations of the place. Also, its location is somewhat lugubrious. Many of the pueblos of the Genal are dramatically sited on crest or spur; others like Parauta are pleasantly tucked into a fold of the hillside. By contrast, Igualeja is strung out along a gully overshadowed by steep wooded ridges. It is near the source of the Genal itself and its most gracious feature is a series of ponds separated by shallow weirs, from which the town and its *huertas* receive their water. But the streets have little charm until you reach the plaza, which is agreeable enough, but no more so than many others. The church is modern, in the neo-fascist style of the Franco period.

In the event my evening in Igualeja had its compensation in an encounter with Alvaro, a Ronda schoolteacher whom I knew slightly. I bumped into him in the *fonda*, where we supped together. It turned out he was the producer of an important annual happening in the pueblo, its Passion Play in Holy Week. The origin of this is curious. Perhaps because of the ungodly tendencies of the place the parish priest at the beginning of the century decided to involve the people directly in the representation of scenes from the Passion of Christ. He wrote the verses and directed the performance, which took place over the Thursday and Friday in the streets and in the church. But he was fond of wine and women, had a mistress and several children, and was moved by his bishop in 1920 or thereabouts to a larger pueblo where he would be less his own master. The inhabitants did not have the spiritual drive to continue the play after his departure, so it died. But after the war the script was located in the municipal archive of the town to which he had been posted. A theatre group in Ronda got to hear of this and decided to revive the play in its place of origin, where it had now been re-established for several years.

I found it strange that intellectuals from Ronda should devote so much effort and thought to imposing on Igualeja a religious spectacle that had no ancient roots; equally strange that enough of the inhabitants should come forward to fill the roles for no tangible reward – for no one was paid. Taken together with the tough reputation of the pueblo in the outside world, it contributed to an unusual atmosphere of dualism that I found disturbing, almost sinister. I did not add Igualeja to my list of potential retreats, though I did promise Alvaro that I would do my best to attend the Passion Play when it was performed again next year.

The following morning a short drive took me to Pujerra. Hydrangeas were blooming against whitewashed walls. I asked three girls standing on a hump-backed bridge where the track to Jubrique began. Though the road died here, there was said to be a way through. They confabulated together for a while, then their spokeswoman said they didn't know, after which they all dissolved into uncontrollable giggles.

The landlord of the only bar was one of those balding Spaniards with a doormat chest and pronounced views which brooked no argument. A dispute arose about sherry. A young man who had worked as a waiter in Doncaster and longed to return (but preferably to Brighton, which was more fun) insisted that Dry Sack was the best brand of all. The landlord snorted with derision. He wouldn't let such pap pass his customers' lips – La Ina and Tio Pepe were the only sherries fit for men. The anglophile insisted that the English had virtually invented sherry, and went to fetch a book to prove it. He read out the relevant passage; the book also said that the Italian Barolo was the prince of red wines; neither proposition went down well with his fellows. I said the word sherry did indeed owe its origin to the inability of the British to pronounce *Jerez*. This set the landlord off on an extraordinary paean of praise for Hitler, who had wanted all Europe to speak the same language – and wouldn't that have been a fine thing? I retorted that Hitler had had all sorts of less desirable aims, even supposing that this was a good idea. He then asked me if I had known him. Not personally, I said, though I had been for a short time in the army which was fighting him. He looked at me suspiciously, then started bullying his wife through the serving hatch before turning once more on Doncaster Man to belabour him further for his apostasy.

When I asked for directions to Jubrique I was subjected to a cross-fire of conflicting advice. One said it was a few kilometres; another that it was more than twenty, which was more plausible. One said you had to bear left at such and such a point and thereafter always right; another contradicted him about a particular turning but the first said that was not the one he had meant . . . *coño!* And so it went on. Between the young girls who didn't know at all and the men who thought they knew but disagreed on crucial links in the route, Jubrique might have been on another planet. Pujerra is a pretty place, buried in hushed, leafy and undulating countryside; one might think the search for a refuge from the industrial world was over. But this very remoteness breeds fantasies and prejudices which are not always attractive: mine host was a case in point and, however secluded a dwelling one might find in the forest, it would be difficult to avoid his influence, for the village store adjacent to the bar was his too. By comparison, Tomás, who fulfilled roughly the same function in Alpandeire, was a prince of diplomats.

I left Pujerra on a good dirt track. Whenever I came to a junction I relied on my gut instinct in deciding which branch to follow. It was a beautiful drive; the slopes were steep and thickly wooded; interspersed with the chestnuts were the pale cinnamon-coloured stems of freshly stripped cork-oaks. At a high point above the dense green valleys and ravines I came across a gypsy-like woman who spoke Spanish with a German accent, encamped with several vehicles in a grove of umbrella pines. She gave me far better directions than I had got in Pujerra and before long I emerged on the Jubrique–Estepona road.

Having reached this point, I changed my plan and decided to continue south on the narrow ribbon of road which leads over the spine of the Sierra Bermeja towards the coast. Unwinding along a series of gullies under the ever-present woods, this road climbs to the pass of Peñas Blancas, a windswept platform from which it commences its descent. Rather than tip down coastwards, I took the forest road to the right which continues upwards to the highest peak of the range, Los Reales, at 1452 metres above sea level. A little below the top I found a campsite with a *refugio* consisting of a log-built bar and restaurant. The young man in charge is a nature-lover, enthralled by all its moods. In February, he said, there had been a tornado, unheard of in the Mediterranean: children had to clutch the lamp-posts down in Estepona; rubbish-trolleys ran riot; a great crane was lifted up and deposited elsewhere; there were hailstones the size of ducks' eggs; and then to crown it all snow fell on 19 May from Peñas Blancas upwards and it was impossible to get through to the refuge – which was unprecedented only twelve days short of June.

'The atmosphere seems to be changing,' I said.

'Or we are changing it,' he countered darkly.

I walked up through scrub and heather to the peak. From this height the coastal strip – rather than some monstrous excrescence on the 'fabled shore' – seemed but a puny development, a thread of fragile settlement that might easily be left derelict by the flight of the tourist, the rising of the sea level or a new age of typhoons. Hardly more than a couple of kilometres wide, it was confined tightly between the beach and the first hummocks of the foothills, a bumpy terrain of umbrella pines and firebreaks below which the developers had pitched their tents, halted apparently in their advance towards the commanding heights.

On a clear day the view swept from Málaga to Gibraltar and across to Africa and the mountains of the Rif. Today there was a haze. All the same, the formidable reddish wall of the Sierra Bermeja stood out sharply enough: running east above San Pedro and curving round to join the Sierra Blanca above Marbella; declining to the west of where I stood towards Casares and the Genal valley before rucking up again in the direction of Gaucín. This was a vantage point from which, if anywhere, one could sense the reality of the Moorish presence in this corner of Spain right into the seventeenth century and the corresponding weight of

Christian fears. Along the shore still stood the signal towers that warned against raiders from the 'Barbary Coast' just over the water, lost in the haze. Inland in the villages and hamlets of the sierras were the *Morisco* inhabitants, unwilling converts to Christianity, with their backs to the sea from across which they hoped desperately for succour from the kings of Tunis and Algiers. At the far end of the Mediterranean loomed the presence of the Turk, already in Cyprus, from whom Philip II's Spain still feared another Islamic invasion, reversing the eight centuries of Christian endeavour invested in the Reconquest.

Why had the Habsburg monarchy doubted the loyalty of its *Morisco* population in such an event? It all went back to the terms of the Capitulations of Granada in 1492, which had been constantly eroded, first by forcible conversion and then by persecution. The pluralism of the Middle Ages was dead and buried. In 1501 there was a serious revolt in the Serranía de Ronda and Sierra Bermeja, in which Alonso de Aguilar, one of the most distinguished Christian captains of his time, perished. When it was suppressed, large numbers crossed over into Africa but, according to H. C. Lea, 'they left multitudes behind to brood over their wrongs and to detest the faith they had been compelled to profess'. In 1526, at the time of the revolt of the Germanías, Charles V ordered all *Moriscos* in Aragón and Valencia to be baptised, thus gaining another 160,000 extremely reluctant converts. Religious tensions continued to run deeply and damagingly throughout much of Andalusia and the Levant, with the Inquisition playing a pivotal role in the perpetuation of discord. A vicious circle was set up: the Inquisition derived large revenues from confiscations and fines imposed on lapsed converts; the Crown received valuable subsidies from the Inquisition; therefore there was no wholesale expulsion of the large *Morisco* minority but rather connivance in uneasy and sometimes violent co-existence.

During this period there were many provocations on both sides. Christians enjoyed making ex-Muslims eat pork; in

Ramadan in particular they would smoke out recusant families by issuing them with social invitations which they were extremely reluctant to accept. A refusal to eat eggs fried in lard would point to someone whose Christianity was but a veneer. *Moriscos* were also said to steal children and Moors were widely regarded as *cocos* or bogeymen. They were accused of hiding their own children from baptism and washing away the sign of the cross from those forcibly baptised and renaming them in their own tongue. Pirate raids, which were frequent along the Mediterranean coast, were often masterminded by *Morisco* renegades who had fled to Algiers. So, the *Moriscos* were seen as heretics, bandits and pirates, and basically disloyal.

At the same time, their position was not enviable. They enjoyed none of the respect accorded to the *Mudéjares*, who had been allowed to practise their religion under the early Christian kings and had become integrated into a pluralistic society as craftsmen, builders and husbandmen. The case of the post-1492 *Moriscos* was entirely different. Their self-expression was confined to such secret and illicit acts as that of one old man who had practised all his life a religion which wasn't his and finally – apprehensive for his soul – summoned a learned Muslim to his deathbed and died in the faith of his ancestors.

In the 1560s the discontent of the *Moriscos* swelled again, stimulated by the appointment to the Presidency of the Chancellery of Granada of Diego de Deza, with instructions to enforce a new *pragmática* or edict against the Moors. This was in effect a draconian set of requirements which finally overturned the last vestiges of the settlement of 1492. The new rules banned speaking, writing or making contracts in Arabic after a moratorium of three years; Moorish dress might not be worn after existing clothes had worn out; women must go with their faces uncovered; betrothal and marriage ceremonies must conform to the usages of the Church; Moorish names and surnames were no longer to be employed; and perhaps worst of all – because it removed a cornerstone of Moorish culture – all public and private baths were banned and were to be destroyed.

From the beginning of 1568 there were rumblings of revolt, including a failed plot to capture the Alhambra on the eve of Easter. The rebellion proper broke out in the Alpujarras, the southern slopes of the Sierra Nevada, where a certain Fernando de Valor, a descendant of the old caliphs of Córdoba, reverted to his Arab name of Aben Omeyya and was proclaimed king under an olive tree. In the words of Diego Hurtado de Mendoza, its aristocratic chronicler: 'The beginnings of the war were small. At the outset it was a mere rebellion of bandits and outlaws; a peasant rising, a conspiracy of slaves; a pother of rivalries, hatreds and low ambitions which was compounded by delays, shortage of money, and by muddles, bad faith, want of trust, incapacity and weakness on the part of men whose job it was to understand these problems, make the decisions and manage the king's affairs.'

Most of these reproofs refer not to the Moors but to the initial response of the Christians. What began as a 'peasant rising' eventually involved thirty thousand rebels under arms and became a civil war. The truth is that Philip II needed all the strength he could muster to put down the *Moriscos* in the mountains, poorly armed and equipped though they were, and lacking any significant support from their co-religionaries across the sea. After other seasoned generals had failed Philip had to call in no less a military expert than his half-brother Don John of Austria to take over the conduct of the war.

Throughout 1568 and 1569 most of the action was in the Alpujarras and over towards Almería. Then the conflagration spread in 1570 into the Serranía de Ronda and caught up in its flames all the pueblos of the Sierra Blanca above Marbella and of the Sierra Bermeja – both on its coastal flank and on its inland face along the valley of the Genal. Don John ordered detachments from all over Andalusia to gather in Ronda under the command of Don Antonio de

Luna, an experienced soldier from Antequera. According to
Moreti, Pedro Bermúdez, head of the Ronda garrison, was
then sent out with five hundred men to take 'the positions
of Jubrique' in the very heart of the broken terrain I had
just passed through. Many of the *Moriscos* had fled up into
the high sierra with their flocks, women and children, leaving the Christian soldiery to sack their pueblos and slaugh-
ter or take prisoner those who remained. The infuriated
Moors then descended like mountain goats from the heights
and put the 'imbecile soldiery' to flight.

In this engagement Pedro Bermúdez lost forty men. At the
same time, some Christians who had fortified themselves
against reprisals in the church of Genalguacil were burned
alive in it by the Moors. On their return to Ronda Bermúdez's ill-disciplined militiamen refused to turn in their pris-
oners, and auctioned them for profit. All this was in direct
contravention of royal orders, and Luna had to go to Seville
and give the king an account of himself for this botched
operation. He blamed the poor quality of the troops he had
been given, and was exonerated but nonetheless replaced by
a local magnate, Cristóbal Ponce de León, Duke of Arcos,
who was put in charge of the whole area of the Serranía.

It is worth noting here that, despite the rebels' tiresome
refusal to lay down their arms, Philip's policy was not yet
to expel between half a million and a million (estimates
vary) of his subjects, many of them peaceful and hard-
working, out of a total population of some eight million.
That would come later. He wanted rather to remove them
from what were considered the sensitive coastal regions of
Almería, Granada, Málaga, and the Serranía de Ronda and
resettle them far inland in Estremadura and New Castile.
The Duke of Arcos, like others of the major nobility, had
many Moorish vassals and was thus in favour of a negotiated
settlement. Accordingly he proceeded to Casares, a fortified
township within his own domains (and only hidden by a
spur from the peak on which I stood). From here he made
contact with the two main Moorish chieftains of the region,

El Arabique and Ataifar, whom he persuaded to capitulate on the king's terms.

Most of the *Moriscos* were now prepared to surrender; some had not even taken part in the uprising. But a turbulent character, an outlaw called El Melque, went among them castigating their leaders as traitors who had sold them for Christian gold; he also painted a horrendous picture of their fate once they fell into Christian hands. Despite this attempt to discredit the negotiators, the people of Benahavís (nowadays a choice retreat for those in whose eyes Marbella has become too vulgar) decided to accept the king's terms. Armed with a safe-conduct from the duke, their emissary, one Barcoqui, went down to Marbella to deliver their letter of submission to the garrison commander. But the people of Marbella, or some of them, in Hurtado de Mendoza's contemptuous words, 'greedy for the spoils that would be theirs if the Moors did rise, in which case they would be able to loot their possessions, brushed aside the guard and murdered El Barcoqui'. This of course appeared to confirm what El Melqui had been saying, and the dying flame of the rebellion was yet again rekindled.

The final act, in the military sense, took place not long after when the duke came down from Ronda with a large force and surrounded El Melque, who had withdrawn with three thousand men, including two thousand arquebusiers, into a strong natural fortress above the Río Verde, not far from Istán and some way inland from Marbella. The silent deployment of the Christians was given away by the premature discharge of a firearm by a soldier from Setenil; the assault almost miscarried but in the end was successful; El Melque was killed and those of his followers who escaped were scattered in small bands in the sierras. There remained the mopping-up operation which consisted of *correrías*, armed raids, by *cuadrillas* or patrols from the various garrisons that the duke left in many of the pueblos, including Istán, Ojén, Monda, Guaro, Tolox, Cartajima, Jubrique and Ronda itself.

It was one of these Moor-hunting *correrías* that led to
the incident I have already described outside Cartajima, in
which another Melque or 'Meliche', possibly the son of the
duke's opponent, died, having first revenged himself on the
Christian Captain Bartolomé Gutiérrez. Such are the epi-
sodes with which local historians delight to spice their otherwise turgid accounts of civic, commercial and religious life
in their cities. But they may well be seen as the red herrings
of history. For every picturesque desperado there must have
been dozens of ordinary *Moriscos* who wanted a peaceful
settlement. Yet Philip's eviction order applied to the rebel-
lious and submissive alike. Gathered at various Andalusian
assembly points, the *Moriscos* were marshalled into columns of 1500 men, women and children, each of which was
to be escorted by two hundred men on foot and twenty on
horse. All this Philip, ever a stickler for detail, had decreed.
In these formations they were to be marched to their new
abodes on the harsh plateau of central Spain, a far cry from
the paradise of Andalusia. But this meticulously planned
operation did not go quite as intended. 'It was a most piti-
able departure,' Hurtado de Mendoza tells us, 'for those who
had known them well off and established in their homes;
many died along the roads from labour, from weariness,
from grief, from hunger; killed by the very ones who were
supposed to guard them, sold as captives.'

No less a person than Don John of Austria, itching to be
freed from this inglorious civil war in order to take command of the great armada against the Turk (which was to
earn him enduring fame at the battle of Lepanto the following year), fussed in a letter to the king's secretary, Ruy
Gómez, about the wretched condition of the dispossessed.
The last party sent that very day, 5 November, from Guadix,
was assured of dreadful tribulation, for there was such a
tempest of wind, rain and snow that the mother would lose
her daughter on the road, the wife her husband and the
widow her infant. It could not be denied, the monarch's
half-brother added, that the depopulation of the kingdom

was the most pitiful thing that could be imagined.

Small wonder that there was unconcealed mourning among the surviving *Moriscos* when the Turkish seapower was crushingly defeated by Don John (of whose more delicate sentiments they were not aware) in 1571, or that there was rejoicing when the Turks captured Tunis in 1574. However, those who had made it to their new and less congenial locations were so industrious that within ten years they had repaired their position and through their own exertions and thrift were beginning to excite the jealousy of their Christian neighbours. This of course had an adverse effect in the long run, for it was one more factor in the demand for the Moors' total expulsion from the Peninsula. The real tragedy was that, whether deported from Andalusia after the rebellion of 1568–70 or expelled from Spain altogether after 1609, these people always felt that they were being hounded from their fatherland. Ricote, the *Morisco* in *Don Quixote*, says to Sancho Panza, 'the desire that almost all of us have to return to Spain is so great that most of those (and there are many) who know the language, as I do, return there, and leave their women and children helpless: so great is the love they have for her.' And this, as Sancho points out, was on pain of death.

Coming down from Los Reales, I thought I had begun to fathom the brooding sadness which, for me at any rate, hangs like a pall over the otherwise enchanting valley of the Genal. Retracing my route in part, I came to Jubrique, not to be confused (though it frequently is) with Ubrique, a much larger and more industrialised hill town thirty kilometres or so to the west; to avoid this it is sometimes called Jubriquillo. Clinging like most of its neighbours to a steep hillside, it is now a very quiet and reserved place: probably its last great event was the bungled assault in 1570 when Pedro Bermúdez lost forty men. Today it has a boarding house and is remarkable for the cheapness of its wine and *tapas*, but I did not linger as I wanted to push on to the

**Moorish influence in a Christian shrine
near Jubrique**

reputedly delightful Genalguacil.

The names are undoubtedly part of the magic. The river Genal was probably for the Arabs 'Ouaddi Genna', the garden river or river of paradise. Genalguacil was 'Genna-al-Wasir', the garden of the vizier or magistrate. With a population of just over a thousand, Genalguacil is a splendidly situated pueblo which has máde a serious attempt to adapt to the modern world. Not long ago it won the provincial prize for 'beautification': climbing plants hang in picturesque festoons across the narrow main street, the houses are all immaculately whitewashed and some have become gentrified holiday residences. In the neat municipal swimming pool with its shady trees and grass verges I watched a teacher tending small charges at the shallow end; her perfect Iberian features reminded me of the famous Dama de Elche in the Archaeological Museum in Madrid. A young Adonis was keeping a sharp eye on safety. He said young people came from Madrid and Barcelona and all over the place to spend a fortnight or a month with their relatives; no, they were not in the least bored; the proof was that they came back again, because it was a cheerful and a beautiful pueblo. It was evident that Genalguacil had managed to build up quite a reputation for itself as a hill station. Despite the bright new face, I could not put out of my mind the horrendous burning alive of Christians in its church or the many other similar events in the neighbourhood during the rebellion. That was all a long time ago? Yes indeed, but then there is no time limit on the activity of ghosts.

From Genalguacil the road plunges to the bed of the Genal. There is an inn on one side of the bridge and a campsite on the other. The place is popular in summer for picnics and shallow bathing and paddling. Apart from a ford between Júzcar and Pujerra higher up, this is the only point where the public has ready access to the secretive river running always through a tunnel of trees until it flows into more open country below Gaucín.

Climbing again, still through thick woods, I emerged after a few miles on the Ronda–Algeciras road at Algatocín. The 'Al-Atusín' of the Arabs is a slightly larger place than its immediate neighbours, with over 1300 inhabitants. Though the church tower is neo-classical, it is covered with a blue-tiled cupola which appropriately gives it the air of a minaret. I paused here, for a decision had to be made whether or not to extend my journey southwards to Gaucín and Jimena de la Frontera, both of which at one time or another had fallen within Ronda's fief. I knew from reports that a number of foreigners had settled in and around Gaucín, from which Gibraltar was reassuringly visible. There were further pockets based on Jimena and Castellar. I wished them well, but I had to remember that my remit did not extend to foreign colonies. Curious though I might be as to how they were faring, a little mystery blurring the edges of my map would do no harm. It would simply have to carry the legends: 'Here be British . . . Here be Germans . . . Here be Danes.' Some other inquisitive explorer might then be emboldened to investigate the condition of these invading tribes – an interesting task perhaps for a social anthropologist? At all events, Benalauría beckoned. So I pointed towards Ronda and took the first turning on the right which wound steeply down again into the woods.

Romantics have wanted to derive Benalauría from 'the Daughter of the Houri', but the greater likelihood is that 'Ibn-al-Uria' or ' -Auria' was named after a founding paterfamilias. What is not in doubt is that it was an *alquería* or fortified farmhouse dependent on the larger Benadalid. The entry by car into the tiny plaza, which has parking for a maximum of three vehicles depending on size, is extremely tricky, and extrication can be even trickier. The church is poor in altars and images; presumably it was sacked. An eerie *rosario* was being sung in the evening led by the recorded voices of a priest and female assistant on tape.

In the plaza some tables had been set out for dominoes; a number of elderly men were sitting on benches under the acacias. Approaching one of them, I said I believed the pueblo had celebrated a fiesta with a mock battle of Moors and Christians earlier in the month.

'Yes, it was the 4th of August this year. But it varies a day or two each time round. It has to fall on a Saturday or Sunday.'

'I suppose it commemorates the Reconquest?'

He shrugged.

'That you will have to ask Don José Antonio.'

It turned out that Don José Antonio Castillo Rodríguez was a son of the pueblo who had become a teacher in a much larger town near Seville. He still had a house here, and returned for the holidays. A little later I was lucky enough to have this courteous savant pointed out to me. When I explained my mission, he welcomed me warmly and we repaired to the Casa de la Cultura, a bar and leisure centre on the plaza.

Benalauría, Don José Antonio explained, may have been an outpost in Roman and earlier times, but it was not permanently populated until after the Muslim invasion of 711, being close to the road that led from Algeciras via Jimena, Gaucín, Benadalid, Ronda, Teba . . . and so on to Córdoba. Though it was an oversimplification that the Berbers had settled only in the mountains and the Yemenites in the plains, it could be deduced from the place-names and the similarity of the climate and terrain to the Rif that the settlers of Benalauría were Berbers. It appeared that they had provided a contingent in support of Abd-el-Rahman I of the Omayyad dynasty, when he severed himself from Baghdad and declared himself the first independent Emir of Córdoba after the massacre of all his clan in Damascus. Throughout the Islamic years silk, dried fruits, the olive and the vine were the principal products. After the Reconquest, Benalauría and Benadalid passed into the seigneurial jurisdiction of the dukes of Alcalá, while Algatocín, Benarrabá and Gaucín were allocated to the dukes of Medina Sidonia.

I asked about the *fiesta* of Moors and Christians. Did this relate to the Reconquest, or the suppression of the *Morisco* revolt, or what? On this he became animated. The current text of the event seemed to belong to the late romanticism of the end of the nineteenth century. It had been revived in that form after the Civil War – but much of it was absurd. He was himself working on a new version. Did I know the plot? Well, it was as follows. The first part, enacted in the morning, was called 'The Captivity'. The Moors had disembarked in Algeciras but, finding their retreat cut off, had pushed on into the sierra and laid siege to Benalauría. In the fray they captured the patron saint, Santo Domingo, while the Christians captured two Moorish princelings. The invaders then advanced on horseback to the saint's empty shrine, where they deposited a cash offering to pay for the *fiesta*. The second part, which took place in the afternoon, was called 'The Rescue'. An attempt was made to negotiate an exchange of hostages, the princelings for the saint, but the Moors reneged on this. Thereupon the Christians assaulted the Moorish positions and liberated the saint – as a result of which the infidels were converted *en bloc*.

This simple tale, said Don José Antonio, was a perfectly acceptable framework for the *fiesta*, but the history was ludicrous, bringing in Napoleon and the French excesses during the War of Independence, also introducing 'Selim the great, the far-renowned, the unvanquished and outstanding monarch' along with such terms as 'Ottoman' and a type of Turkish gown which had nothing to do with the Andalusian Arabic tradition. In short, it was an arbitrary hotch-potch, in which arguably the most important event, the *Morisco* rebellion, was not even mentioned. And worst of all, this nonsense was presented in a pompous, grandiloquent, balladic style, which led him to suppose that it might have originated in a patriotic-nationalist attempt to drum up enthusiasm for the colonial wars with Morocco at the beginning of the century. However that might be, he had started to rewrite the text and was determined to turn it into something much more relevant to the history of the pueblo than the mere slogans of a recruiting drive; and the *Morisco* revolt would figure prominently. The *fiesta* should certainly be preserved, because no other pueblo in the area had one quite like it, but it must no longer be a travesty of the truth.

I applauded his zeal. Of course, few people in the audience of a village spectacle would carry out an exhaustive textual exegesis, so it could easily have been let ride on the basis that its main thrust – the triumph of Catholicism over all comers – was perfectly acceptable, and there was no need to fiddle with the details. Spaniards have often been accused, with some justice, of turning their history into propaganda. But it was evident that a new and more rigorous spirit of self-examination was abroad and that many of the old myths and clichés were being questioned. Even in so tiny a place as Benalauría, here was an intellectual anxious to put the record straight. I congratulated Don José Antonio and wished him luck, and hoped to return to witness his revised version of the *fiesta*.

'I wish I could know as much of your country as you know of mine,' he said as we parted. 'It has been an honour and a pleasure to help you, however modestly, in your noble task of writing about my homeland.'

This was gracious of him and gratifying to me, especially as in the past I had sometimes felt my curiosity about all things Spanish was resented as unwelcome interference.

Climbing back to the main road, I came very shortly to Benadalid, a more substantial place with a roadhouse and swimming pool. Lower down are the pretty church square and the cemetery, thriftily installed inside the neat ruins of the castle. Wanting to collect my thoughts on the Genal before heading back to Ronda, I sat for a while on the promontory beneath the castle walls and watched the dusk rising like a mist from the cavities of the valley and the lights of other pueblos suddenly signalling their position in the gathering dark. I do not claim any hyperactive sensitivity to the redolence of history, and yet – despite the undoubted allurements of places such as Alpandeire and Genalguacil and Benalauría, as well as the leafy charms of the countryside – I could not rid myself of the intimations that had come to me on the summit of Los Reales, whispering of sorrows still lurking in the shadows, discords still unresolved and ghosts unlaid.

Why so? Why such feelings? It came to me forcibly that the time factor was important, and the watershed was 1492. From the battle of Las Navas de Tolosa in 1212, which opened the way through the Sierra Morena, there was sporadic warfare for nearly three centuries. First, the victors took the spoils of the great cities and grainlands of the

Guadalquivir; in the next two centuries the strongpoints of the sierras like Olvera, Cañete and Teba succumbed; eventually the last redoubts, among them Setenil and Ronda fell, followed shortly by Granada itself. Throughout that long period war was waged on a more or less chivalric basis between rival states: when the Moors were defeated, they withdrew further into their heartlands, but Islam was not, either in its own eyes or the Christians', a lost cause. In fact, this was when a taste for Moorish things caught on among the Christians: when the fabulous mosque of Córdoba was thought suitable for a cathedral; when Peter the Cruel attempted to emulate the Alhambra in his rebuilding of the Alcázar of Seville; and when the Trastamara kings John II and Henry IV affected Moorish dress. This was the beginning of the glamour of Moorish Spain, which so enthralled the Romantics and which is now the staple of the tourist trade in Andalusia.

While this period lasted, the Christian advance was achieved in open fight, in hot blood rather than bad blood. The Cross was triumphant but the sons of the sickle had not yet been driven into their last hiding places; those who remained in the reconquered territories continued practising their religion and were encouraged to use their skills in the service of their new masters. Christianity was victorious but not ungenerous, confident enough to harbour Muslim populations and to dally and trifle with Moorish art and artefacts. All this has had a lingering effect. Where Islamic power was blown away earlier and the dominant culture successfully established, there is to this day a difference of atmosphere. If the great swelling fields of the province of Córdoba or the rolling uplands to the north of Ronda still expand the lungs and cleanse the mind, this is not only because of an exhilarating landscape but also because they were captured in clean fight and before the emergence of that crabbed, obsessive spirit which led to the *Morisco* revolt.

After 1492 everything changed. A settlement was made

with the defeated religion, but was never adhered to. Medieval pluralism went by the board. The parts of Andalusia most affected by the new intolerance were Almería, the Alpujarras, the Axarquía, the Serranía, the Sierra Bermeja and the Genal. These were in the main peasant areas, where there were no great cities to be disputed, no worthy rivals and no honours to be won. A recusant population smouldered. When blood was spilt, it was not in equal combat but in low cunning and squalid bitterness. The great captains called in to quell the Moriscos knew they were engaged in an ignoble task. There can be no comparison between the glorious action of Don Rodrigo Ponce de León, Duke of Arcos, in seizing Alhama de Granada from under the enemy's nose in 1482 and his direct successor Don Cristóbal's mopping-up operations in the Serranía nearly a century later. It is hardly surprising that Don John of Austria could not wait to be off to higher things.

Of course, there were the geopolitical considerations I have mentioned, not least Spain's fear of some unholy alliance between the Protestants and the Turks. I believe this was neurotic. There was admittedly some piracy along the coast and the menace (soon to be demolished) of the Turkish fleet. But the threat of a strike into the heart of Europe, as when the Moors reached Poitiers in 732, was non-existent. Even after the disastrous Armada of 1588 there were no nibblers at the Spanish landmass; on the contrary, Spain had recently absorbed Portugal and did not face rebellion and secession there till 1640. She was thus left to decline in her own time and in her own way.

In his book *The Moriscos of Spain: Their Conversion and Expulsion* H. C. Lea ventures the following opinion:

> When we compare the inconsiderable number of the exiles
> with the original large Moorish population of the lands
> recovered during the Reconquest we can realise how great
> a proportion of the Mudéjares must have become
> Christians and been merged indistinguishably with their

conquerors. Medieval toleration had won them over, and its continuance would in time have completed the process. Not only would an infinite sum of human misery been averted, but Spain would, to some extent, have escaped the impoverishment and debility which served as so cruel an expiation.

Some might quarrel with this sanguine view of the feasibility of reconciliation and ultimate assimilation of the *Moriscos*. Nonetheless, the refusal to make this final effort hangs heavy round the neck of Spain, and nowhere is this more apparent than in the old Berber villages of the Genal, which languished for centuries in a crypto-Islamic twilight and where the ghosts of that unhappy past have never been laid.

9

TOWARDS THE SILVER BAY

To close the circle around Ronda there remained only the lands to the south-west and west. The distances to be covered were rather more than hitherto and I prepared for this trip with some of the excitement associated with going abroad. The main places I wanted to visit were all down in the foothills of the province of Cádiz, on the edge of the coastal plain, and thus at some remove from the sturdy mountain pueblos – in relation to which they almost qualified as foreign parts.

I left Ronda on the road that follows the Guadiaro for a few miles before swinging up to the little town of Benaoján, famous for its hams and canning factories. From here there is a further climb under the flank of the Sierra de Líbar, past the palaeolithic Cueva de la Pileta, before the switchback swoops down again to the station of Jimera de Líbar. With its cluster of little villas wreathed in bougainvillaea and morning glory, its riverside *playa* and abandoned hotel, this modest settlement was a popular place for holidays before the Spaniards followed the foreigners to the sea and before the ice-cold waters cascading out of the Cueva del Gato a little way upstream were contaminated by sewage flowing down from Ronda.

These little railways stations, lying hundreds of metres below the high villages whose names they bear, form a fragile chain linking Ronda with the bay of Algeciras. In earlier times their canopied platforms, adorned with flowerbeds and equipped with a *cantina*, provided the main focus of life for the inhabitants, as well as the spice of contact with the famous contraband route from Gibraltar. Then swarthy women carried precious coffee in the lustrous coils of their raised black hair, while others were swollen to abnormal girth by layers of pure wool cardigans; then packages of tobacco were thrown out of carriage windows and retrieved by men who strapped them onto dogs specially trained to transport them through the hills and woods, eluding the Civil Guards, to the remote pueblos of the sierras. That was an activity that gave rise to much profit and enjoyment, to say nothing of welcome bribes to the forces of law and order. Those were the great days of the railway!

Recently rumours have been circulating of a plan for yet another huge dam which would submerge the line, consigning the stations of Jimera, Cortes and Gaucín to a watery grave under the glassy surface of a reservoir. It appears that the RENFE and the Junta's environment department have so far won (the Junta alleging that an additional large expanse of static water would change the micro-climate of the region) against the national water board, but the latter is powerful and may strike again. The stations have been reprieved, but I wouldn't like to bet on their long-term survival.

From Jimera the road rises again to the shelf occupied by the pleasant, airy pueblo of Cortes de la Frontera. With a population of some 5000 it presents the standard dazzling white façade, with the exception of its distinguished stone-faced town hall from the period of that enlightened despot Charles III (1759–88); it also boasts a small bullring of proper masonry (it is a matter of civic pride not to have to sink to a portable circus-style ring) and a fine *alameda* or public promenade. The latest amenity is, of course, the municipal swimming pool: sunk in a landscaped slope with trees and flowers, this is one of the most attractive in the area. The burgeoning of these bathing facilities in out-of-the-way places always acts on me as a wry reminder of the suppression of the Moorish baths which was such a major incitement to the *Morisco* rebellion. Now no self-respecting Christian pueblo can survive without its *piscina*.

Cortes is a relaxed, frank, open town, more friendly and communicative than many mountain pueblos. This may be due at least in part to its relative wealth, deriving from its extensive cork forests which stretch far away to the south and west. I knew that cork was harvested on a nine-year cycle; when the bark was ready in a certain section of the forest it would be stripped; that area would then be left untouched for the following eight years until its turn came round again; during those years the strippers would successively tackle other sections of the forest. But I had never watched this process and was determined to do so.

The harvest was now under way and in the bars I received a variety of directions how to find the *corcheros*, as the cork-strippers are called. But at least they all pointed westwards, so I took the road which leads eventually to Arcos and Jerez. This winds through a seemingly endless expanse of pines, *quejigos, alcornoques* (the cork-oaks) and other smaller fry, covering many thousands of hectares and stretching as far westwards as La Sauceda and southwards to Castellar and Almoraima, where it verges on the ranchlands of Los Barrios and Algeciras. Though large stretches of this belong to private owners, much of it is the patrimony of certain town councils, which somehow escaped the forced sales of municipal lands in the 1850s. The largest forest domain of all belongs to Jerez, one of the richest towns in Spain; Cortes is a substantial owner; Ronda is there too – its zone marked by little stone obelisks carrying the legend *Montes Propios del Excelentísimo Ayuntamiento de Ronda*. But this is the estate that will have to be sold off, according to my indignant bookseller friend, to pay the debts of the profligate socialist administration of our ancient, noble and loyal but despoiled city.

After some miles I turned onto the forest road to El Colmenar, as the station of Gaucín is called, far below on the valley floor. About halfway down I branched to the right along the contour of a hillside and fancied I was getting warm. Suddenly on the edge of the track there rose up, almost like a stage fortification, a great wall of stacked pieces of bark shaped roughly like large Roman roof tiles. It must have been seventy or eighty metres long and six or seven metres high. This must be the camp and loading bay of the *arrieros*, the muleteers who collected the smaller piles left by the *corcheros* on the hillside and brought them down for weighing, stacking and loading onto lorries. The *arrieros*, I had been told, moved about a fortnight behind the *corcheros* to avoid overlapping and treading on toes or tails. Often they didn't know where the *corcheros* had reached in the enormous woods; they simply followed the trail blaized for them, moving their own camp and the depot when necessary.

The chief of the *arrieros* was a dark, handsome man in his thirties from Cortes.

'Are you English?' he asked.

'Yes.'

'From Gibraltar?'

'No, from England.'

'Why don't you give us Gibraltar back?'

'Because the Gibraltareños don't want it. Our Foreign Office would be happy to come to an arrangement, but as long as the inhabitants are against it . . .'

'But surely the Queen with a stroke of the pen . . .'

'Our Queen has no power over such matters these days.'

'It must cost the British government a lot of money. If that were cut off . . .'

'It is not so much, and it has been reduced. Personally, I think Gibraltar would be wise to join Spain, which passionately wants it, and leave the UK to which it is an embarrassment. You would shower financial benefits on it. But it is up to you to persuade the people.'

'Why should we when it is ours anyway?'

'Perhaps you should invade, then,' I suggested flippantly.

'Yes, I would favour that,' he answered seriously.

I pressed on with my search for the *corcheros*. I found their cars and bikes about a kilometre further along the track, where I parked also and started to climb. I sweated up an irregular, slippery, leaf-strewn slope for twenty minutes, following more or less the boundary between the peeled trees and the untouched trunks, but it was not always clear-cut. The forest was punctuated by outcrops of rock and more than once I climbed one of these and through cupped hands called out to the *corcheros*. Nothing greeted my cries but the rustling of the treetops. The immemorial forest betrayed not the slightest sign of men secreted in its depths. I began to think I had not only failed to locate my quarry but was now so lost that I might also fail to get back to the car. Then I spotted a pale cinnamon-stemmed tree, the first I had seen for a while. I clambered towards it and resumed my march, still calling, until I almost bumped into some rolled-up bedding hanging from a branch; beyond this I came into a wide clearing with a great tarpaulin shelter and a number of tents and rustic tables. There was still no sign of life until there emerged from under the tarpaulin an urbane-looking, balding man with a high domed forehead and the features of a bank manager, to whom I explained my business.

'They're just down there,' he said, 'beyond that next clearing. You can't miss them.'

He was wrong there. I stumbled on. Soon I was lost again. I paused and listened in vain for the clunk of an axe. I was about to retrace my steps to the camp when at last I heard voices; a few more paces and I had walked right into the middle of a group of men who were lying or sitting on the ground. Feeling an intruder, I was in doubt how to proceed when I saw to my relief that one of them was Roque, a man from El Colmenar to whom I had once given a lift; he was good enough to vouch for my character and I sat down among them. I wondered if I had arrived too late to see any action, but after a couple of minutes the haunting sound of

The *corcheros* at work

a horn, blown by their foreman, brought them to their feet and they resumed work.

The technique is for incisions to be made, maybe a yard long and a foot across, in the trunk and along the main branches. The axe is then applied quite gently to prise away the piece, if possible entire, so that it falls to the ground in the curved tile-like shape I have attempted to describe. Big trees require a short iron ladder, shaped to the trunk, and of course more incisions than smaller ones. Incising and prising so that the stem of the tree is unwounded are special skills; when practised properly it is like removing a garment and leaving the flesh intact. A team of ten or twelve men

291

moves through the forest, leaving piles of cork behind it, with surprising speed. But the forest is very big, and the task, as I was to be told more than once, is endless – like painting a huge bridge or ship.

When the horn sounded again, it was for the lunch break and we all scrambled back to the camp. The balding bank manager turned out to be the cook. The *corcheros* dispersed to their various tents and bundles of bedding. Some took a swig of wine or beer; others drank water from rough cork containers. I went with my mentor Roque and his friend Gregorio to a sort of wigwam of branches. As elders of their craft, they ate separately from the rest. Roque went for a bowl of gazpacho with floating pellets of bread and another of *garbanzos* and potatoes which constituted the main course called *la olla*. He brought these back to our shelter and placed them on a table of rock. Gregorio then made me a seat out of two stones with a cork cushion, lent me a spoon, and we three ate communally from the same dishes – something I had not done for twenty-five years, though it used to be common in *campo* households.

All the other *corcheros* assembled with their spoons round the cooking pots, which the chef had set out on a trestle table. They were a mixed bunch: an elderly man with a paunch and belt and braces; one or two grizzled men in their fifties; a roguish fellow with a handkerchief round his forehead; some young men in military forage caps. Each of them advanced every couple of minutes with his spoon and hunk of bread, took a spoonful from one of the pots and withdrew, to be followed by a companion, and so on in a curious ritual resembling a very slow dance. There were no fixed turns but no collisions either, so perhaps there was some underlying pecking order which dictated the choreography. A dozen or so men plus the cook and the foreman thus ate their fill on foot without plates around the big pots in the dappled glade. In the background one of the younger men squatted brewing coffee. It was the most unusual buffet lunch I had yet attended, so I left the wigwam and advanced with my camera. The response was enthusiastic.

'Take Anselmo, he's the old one with the belt and braces. *Muy típico!*'

'Take Juanito . . . for his *novia* . . . so that she may repent!'

'Take me, as I wield my spoon!'

'If you give me the camera and show me what to do, shall I take you?'

When they dispersed, the cook was left alone: he sat on a boulder and ate a slice of watermelon, looking grand and civilised. I went back to the shelter, where I shared their dessert with Roque and Gregorio. It was notable that their frugal meal had contained no meat or cheese and there had only been one *trago* of *vino* when we first sat down. Gregorio was concerned that I had not eaten enough and kept pressing on me more bread or *olla* or fruit; I must not hold back for them; they had eaten to their satisfaction.

'How much longer is this job going to take?' I asked when we had thrown away our rind and other leavings.

'We shall finish this stretch by the end of this *quincena*,' said Gregorio. 'Then we move over to La Sauceda on the other side of the forest. We shall require two *quincenas* there . . . perhaps more.'

The *quincena* is a fortnight, consisting in their case of thirteen days of work and two of rest. The routine is invariable. The men start at seven and work till ten, when they stop for an hour for *las sopas*, a kind of broth. Resuming at eleven, they work through till three when they break for two hours for *la olla*, the repast we had just enjoyed. After this they can relax, sleep, play cards or do as they wish till the last shift, which runs from five till seven. The shifts are themselves punctuated by a short break of five minutes every hour. All work is begun or dropped in response to a single ululating call on the foreman's horn.

'The work is hard,' Roque said. 'Nine hours flat out would be impossible. That is why the day is divided as I have described. In this way it goes in a flash.'

'And there is a two-day break between *quincenas*?'

'Yes, the first day of rest is paid and the other is not. But that is our choice; we prefer the extra leisure. That is how we make the contract.'

'Wouldn't you prefer to be permanently employed?'

'No. For one thing the town hall, which owns the forests, couldn't afford it. For another we are free to engage for the season or not, according to our needs. We contract our own labour freely – or do not – in accordance with our circumstances.'

'And when the cork harvest is over?'

'There are always jobs in the forest,' Gregorio chimed in, 'what with the firebreaks, or the roads and tracks, and now with the *brezo*.'

Brezo, I had discovered, is a tall Mediterranean heather forming much of the scrub on these hillsides. It is cut with a hook or sickle and is all the rage for rustic shelters and umbrellas round swimming pools; in Cortes there is a small factory where it is trimmed and wired onto steel frames.

'Yes,' said Roque, 'the *brezo* is a new industry which also has some importance. Myself, I do not need that work. I have a little *huerto* with its own *casita* near the pueblo, which I have to attend to. Though of course my home is in Cortes itself.'

I smiled to myself. Those working in the woods did not want to live in them: that was for the Germans and Danes who were apparently buying up the leases of the few witch-like dwellings with a bit of land that were scattered here and there in the forest.

'Does harvesting the cork run in the family?' I asked. 'Will your sons follow in your footsteps?'

They both shrugged.

'The elders pass on the art to the young folk. Some make use of it, some don't . . . but the work is endless . . . the forest is eternal.'

The sense of continuity that they conveyed, and of confidence about the shape of the world around them, was very strong; fashions might change, the young might crave new experiences, but the forest and its work would always be there – waiting.

That evening there was a *novillada sin picadores*, an apprentice bullfight without picadors, in Cortes. The ring was packed to capacity, which amounted to some seven hundred people I guessed. The inner circle of the arena was painted laterally in green and white, the Andalusian colours; the *burladeros* behind which the *toreros* and their assistants can slip out of danger were still in the traditional red and yellow of the Spanish flag. Through the good offices of a friend I was placed in a *burladero* along with the local photographer; from time to time one of the young aspirants or his *banderillero* (and minder) would squeeze in beside us as the bull tried out its horns on the planks of our little palisade.

The three *toreros* all came from the school of Málaga. Their ages were sixteen, sixteen and fifteen respectively. Their opponents were two-year-old bullocks weighing 130 to 150 kilos each. There had been no *novilladas* in the Cortes ring for some years, I gathered, but now they were being subsidised by the town hall with the assistance of the regional government. The first lad, fair and snub-nosed, managed some decent passes with the right hand but could do nothing with the left. The difficulty of killing a bull that has received no thrust from above by a mounted man became apparent: it will not stand still. But when the boy plunged in, he was lucky, dropping it dead on the first *estocada*, and was awarded two ears and two rounds of the ring. The second *torero* looked more the part, offering elegant capework and long slow passes with the *muleta*. He hit bone on his first attempt to kill but his second was sufficient and he received an ovation, while the dead animal earned a round of the ring drawn by nine men in lieu of the usual mules (or of a fork-lift truck, which I have also seen, a deplorable development).

On and off during these two encounters one of the

banderilleros in charge of the boys was standing beside me in the *burladero*, hissing advice and instructions: 'Give him space . . . keep your hand down . . . show him the rag properly . . .'

He told me the law required them to carry on their normal education, but they devoted all their spare time to learning the art, either in the corrals at the back of the Málaga ring or out on the bull ranches during the winter months. 'It's a profession that requires much sacrifice,' he added, 'but these are good boys and those were two good little animals.'

The third lad was out in the ring by now making a tremendous hash, first with the cape because he attempted *chicuelinas* which he could not complete, and then with the *muleta*, when essaying *manoletinas* which did not come off either. His whole *faena* was chaotic and he was disarmed at almost every pass. But he had placed his own *banderillas*, which is always well-received, and when he lined up to kill he was amazingly fortunate: the bull charged and impaled itself on his sword, giving him the prestige of having killed *recibiendo*, or strictly speaking *aguantando*, which is the absolutely correct term when the bull's charge is unprovoked. On the strength of this he was awarded an ear.

The fourth bull was not good and was efficiently despatched by the blond lad. The fifth was not good either, and had a depressing tendency to sink to its knees, but the young classicist, Paquito Arijo by name, had sucked in a lot of bull-lore in his sixteen years and extracted a respectable *faena* out of it, which he crowned with an honourable kill. To the knowledgeable this was probably the best performance of the day; he received a well-merited ear for his labour with a disobliging animal.

Finally, a very small bull about the colour of a brindle bull-terrier rushed into the ring to be greeted with hisses and catcalls. Modern Spanish audiences hate anything other than glossy black bulls, though it was not always so. Young Ricardo de Alba, aged fifteen, received it with a *larga cambiada*, the great show-off pass in which the matador on his knees whirls the cape over the bull's horns as it charges past. The rest of the performance was as chaotic as before, but when he was knocked over and nuzzled on the ground for the third time by his peppery little adversary, he got so angry that he kicked off his remaining slipper (having already lost the other) and hurled himself into such tricks as turning his back and calling out from over his shoulder like El Cordobés or provoking the bull while gazing up at the gods like the great Litri. He killed again with one stroke and stalked away from the carcass in the gloaming, every inch the cock of the walk, collecting up flowers and hats and wine-skins from the sand.

In the bars afterwards, as is usual in Andalusia, scepticism prevailed over enthusiasm. But the connoisseurs were agreed that Arujo was the one to watch. The fifth was really a non-starter until he turned it into something. Did I know the legend of the fifth bull? I said I had heard it, but was there anything in it? Certainly, they said: statistics over many years showed that it had been the vehicle of the greatest triumphs. It is worth remembering, even on the worst afternoons of bulls, to reserve judgement till the fifth.

Westwards from Cortes the road skirts the fringe of the great forest as far as the isolated *venta* of Puerto de Galis, where it divides. The branch to the left winds for many more wooded miles via La Sauceda to Jimena and Algeciras. The right-hand route leads down to the ancient cities of the province of Cádiz and the ranches where the brave bulls are bred. I took the latter. After skirting the grim Sierra de Cabras, the road enters undulating country, recently ravaged by a vicious forest fire. Soon the old stronghold of Alcalá de los Gazules becomes visible on its mound. On either side of the road large numbers of white cattle egrets flop and hop their attendance upon sunken-backed, wide-horned domestic herds, which introduce a whiff of Africa into the rippling plain.

The hub of Alcalá is the Bar-Restaurante Pizarro. The

town has a mayor and council of course, and a town hall, but this is where it is run from. It is also a place of generous *tapas* and mighty meals. Two *tapas* with bread are plenty for lunch, and if you think that *consomé al Jerez* and *huevos a la flamenca* are a light supper, you will have to think again. The presiding genius is Paco Pizarro, an exquisite person – sleek black hair, quizzical circumflex eyebrows, swift brown eyes – who performs beautifully with all his customers, even the most domineering ladies. A busy and successful restaurateur, he also finds time to go to art classes in Cádiz two nights a week and plans his first exhibition for 1993/94.

Paco can fix anything. When I told him of my interest in the future of the *corrida* and my desire to meet some *ganaderos* or breeders, he said that some of the most important *ganaderías* in Spain were in the immediate vicinity: those of Torrestrella, Antonio Gavira, M. Vázquez and Diego Romero to name only a few. Their owners were all his friends and clients and he would certainly set something up for me, despite the short notice. True to his word, no sooner had he finished serving – weaving elegantly among the tables, no passive majordomo he – than he was on the telephone, and he soon came up with an arrangement for me to visit the Gavira ranch, Vega Blanquilla, that afternoon. Unfortunately Don Antonio would not be there but his employees would look after me. He detailed his own son, Juan Antonio, to accompany me.

The estate consisted of low-lying *vega* or meadowland with shoulders of rock and little hills of oak and oak-scrub. As we drove in on the long dirt track, we came across a complete *corrida* of six bulls enclosed in a paddock, munching bales of straw. They had long straight backs running from head to rump with little sign of the *morrillo*, the great hump of bison-like muscle into which the picador drives his lance. They looked heavy without the neatness of quarters which is the hallmark of the fine fighting bull.

'I don't like them much,' said Juan Antonio. 'They have

no elegance and little *trapío*. And the *cornadura* is not wide enough.'

Trapío is the general presence and condition of a good caste bull; *cornadura* is the spread and effectiveness as a weapon of the horns. Having said this, Juan Antonio had second thoughts; he seemed to think he might have let the home-team down to a foreigner.

'But they're strong bulls, good bulls, brave bulls nonetheless,' he added.

Two enormous umbrella pines heralded the approach to the farmhouse, which had a seedy air with touches of *douceur* such as a palm tree and a little stretch of formal garden with privet hedges.

Two men were standing in the doorway. One was tall, handsome with long slit eyes, over which his peaked cloth cap was pulled down, giving him a slightly sinister look. He was the *conocedor de toros*, an alternative name for the more common *mayoral*, the man in charge of the bulls. He lived closely with the bulls, fed them, selected the cows to be tried for courage in a *tienta* and sent the rejects for meat; it was he also who selected the *lotes* of six bulls for a *corrida* and accompanied them to the ring. He was the chief technician, and taciturn to boot. When I began to question him, I got minimal answers. Extent of the estate? He really couldn't say. It was big? Yes, biggish but neither one thing nor the other. The number of the herd? I would have to ask the owner. Value of a fighting bull? It varied; Don Antonio dealt with all that. I might have been a tax inspector.

His companion, shorter and older with a military moustache and more welcoming demeanour, was the *capataz* or farm manager, responsible for crops, machinery and feed. He obviously thought the other's lack of sociability had gone far enough and invited us inside. He was not going to pass up a rare opportunity for *conversación*.

Yes, the bulls we had seen were four-year-olds, the minimum age for a full *corrida*. And they had to meet a minimum weight, 470 kilos wasn't it now? He looked at the *conocedor* who remained as evasive as ever: the authorities had changed the weight more than once.

'But it was 570 kilos before 1928, wasn't it?' I asked.

Ah, the *conocedor* could not say; he was not a historian. How many *corridas* would the ranch supply each year? Probably from five to seven, some thirty-six to forty-two bulls. These were the first numbers he had vouchsafed. Price? He glanced uneasily at the *capataz*, who said the range was between half a million and a million pesetas per head . . . but with all the costs and the rejects it certainly wasn't a goldmine . . . it had to be done for love.

When I mentioned the criticisms I had heard of *ganaderos* for stuffing their bulls with artificial meal rather than grazing them properly, the *conocedor* showed his first sign of animation. As far as he was concerned, the animals had to eat. When there was little or no grass, as during the droughts of recent years, their diet had to be supplemented. You couldn't present an emaciated *corrida*.

They were both agreed that the *fiesta* would not die. In line with most other people I talked to, they gave as their first reason the unique nature of the fighting bull. Here they had history on their side. He is the descendant of the giant aurochs of antiquity. His full name is *Bos Taurus Africanus*. Some say he was first introduced into Spain by the Carthaginians; others that he came earlier, brought by Minoans to the Cretan colony of Tartessus. Either way, he has been in the Peninsula for a very long time and belongs to a distinct and rare branch of the bovine race, quite different to domestic cattle. He is barely edible and would certainly not flourish in a zoo.

'There is no other function for him,' said the *capataz*. 'The ecologists and all that lot, whatever they call themselves, can't deny that his pleasure is to be fierce; when he charges he enjoys it; it is his nature – *es lo suyo* – he is doing what comes naturally. Domestic cattle cooped up in pens and cages lead much worse and much shorter lives and meet a much more degrading end. Or that at any rate is my opinion. Furthermore, if the *corrida* were banned, many jobs would be lost. In these parts it is an important industry. There are also signs that *afición* is on the increase.'

Talk turned to horses and equitation, which had also been on the increase until the recent *peste equina*, the devastating equine epidemic that had come some said from Egypt, others from Morocco, carried by the polo ponies of unscrupulous Arabs who had evaded the veterinary laws; this had driven many Andalusian horse-breeders to ruin through the extinction of their export trade. We touched also on cockfighting, which I assumed had died out. Not a bit of it. It was still alive and well around the bay of Cádiz, especially in Cádiz itself, El Puerto de Santa María, Puerto Real and Chiclana.

I recalled a cockfight in Jerez twenty-five years before. The ring was tiny, perhaps four or five metres across. Chairs surrounded the low wooden *barrera*. Sherry circulated. No sooner had the contestants been weighed in than a rapid cross-fire of betting began, not by book or tote, but by individual wagers yelled across the miniature arena. The first five minutes of each fight were the liveliest, with tremendous attacks and flurries of wings on both sides. The artificial spurs attached to equalise the birds were hardly used; almost all the action consisted of swift repetitive jabs with the beak to head and neck, the two beaks sometimes locking in a clinch. Before long one bird usually managed to establish superiority over the other, and it was then a war of attrition. The losing bird would sometimes stagger and fall, but victory was not established until it sank down unable to rise again, with the victor still stabbing away until it was collected up by its owner and carried crowing triumphantly from the ring. A draw was awarded if the weaker bird managed to stand the whole of the allotted time without going down for the count. In the mess of blood it was impossible to see what damage was done, though eyes were often lost. Even so, the damaged bird might fight again with one eye and a handicap and would in any case serve for breeding;

301

good losers apparently made good breeders. Those were my recollections. The others confirmed that the sport still flourished; there had been one or two rule changes but in essence it was the same.

'It's curious,' mused the *capataz*, 'but the bull, the horse and the fighting cock go together. You might call them a trio. Certainly, many *toreros* go in for all three. Fighting cocks, like fighting bulls, are naturally brave. Even if you leave them alone, without pitting them against each other in a ring, they will fight to the death.'

As we drove away, chance had it that we came across a couple of three-year-old bulls with their horns locked in combat. Heaving, shoving, gaining and yielding ground, twisting and reversing position, they were oblivious of the car which they spattered with pebbles and dust as they crossed the track right in front of us. It was a full ten minutes before one of them broke and backed off. They had not been competing for females; it was the wrong time of the year and none were in sight. They were, to borrow the phrase of the *capataz*, just doing *lo suyo* – what came naturally. If bullfighting was banned – or so the argument went – the species would soon become extinct, as there would be no commercial reason for breeding it; the heirs of the aurochs would vanish from the earth.

On our return I reported to Paco the cagey reception we had received from the *conocedor* at Vega Blanquilla. I had hoped to meet a *mayoral* who would be more forthcoming. Paco said they tended to be a silent breed. He would make sure I met one of the leading *ganaderos* as well, but that would take a little more time. In the meantime, on the subject of *mayorales*, he told me the following tale. A certain Ortega was a matador who had had plenty of opportunities but had never risen above the mediocre. He married a dancer, Tana, and when he retired from the ring he fulfilled his dream and hers by becoming a *ganadero*. But things went badly. They had five years of drought and had to buy in enormous amounts of feed. He had bought his bulls on tick and couldn't even service the debt, let alone repay it. Through all these vicissitudes his wife insisted on maintaining her style and her pretensions as the consort of a *torero* and *ganadero*. When she came into Alcalá, she would enter Paco's establishment in her fur coat, tossing her hair, and call out to him for all the world to hear, '*Paco, prepárame una mesa . . . que vienen los mayorales a comer . . .*'

'She wanted everyone to know she was going to lunch her *mayorales*,' Paco said, 'but she only had one and couldn't pay him!'

I murmured something about *folie de grandeur*.

He nodded and then added, '*Pero hay grandeza en los toros . . .* there is greatness in the bulls, you know. This creates an atmosphere of expectation, of illusion if you like. That is what Ortega and his wife fell victim to. He ended up in prison for it.'

When Paco excused himself to attend to some clients, I started chatting to José the barman. The population of the pueblo, he said, had shrunk from eleven or twelve thousand to six and a half. The charcoal industry and the cork factories had disappeared. There was talk of making it up by tourism, but that was hopeless. The odd bird of passage like myself might stop for a meal and climb to the Iglesia Mayor and the castle, but we could be counted on the fingers of two hands. Two new hotels were being built – not for tourists but for the overflow of the emigrant families who flocked back every year between July and September. It was the same story as almost everywhere; it was the nostalgia of the natives in exile which was keeping the pueblo alive. There were second-generation emigrants, José said, who had never seen the place until they had become enamoured with it on a trip with their grandparents, and now returned regularly without fail. In the summer the town was transformed. Did I not see the *paseo* already building up outside? I did indeed. Well, that would go on till four or five in the morning . . . and even later in the fair.

José was right. It is not easy to sleep in Alcalá on a summer's night. Abandoning the attempt, I rose early and went out to see the town while it was still cool. Irregular windows pierce the old patched Moorish walls above the steep promenade that circles them on the northern side. They must command a fine view of the hills swelling up towards Puerto de Galis, I thought. Perhaps an eyrie, a perch in that wall would not be a bad place to end up? The promenade is somewhat vitiated as a tourist amenity by the rubbish tip below the parapet. But there are compensating charms: lambs, goats and hens in byres and shelters formed by the remnants of an outer line of fortifications; then the road unrolling between cattle pastures back into the highlands.

As I reached the top, the cracked bell of the Iglesia Mayor spoke out. Down the slope went men on their 50cc motorcycles, sputtering out of town with adzes in their esparto saddlebags, on their way to some country labour. On their return in the evening they would bear sacks of produce; properly loaded, a *moto* can carry as much as a donkey, and more willingly.

The keynote of the Plaza de San Jorge, which crowns the town, is grandiose decrepitude. The weatherbeaten portico of the Iglesia Mayor is a fine piece of Isabelline-Gothic; in the tympanum Saint George slays the dragon watched complacently by the Virgin. Stubby columns joined by chains stake out the area of sanctuary afforded by the church in earlier times – just as round the cathedral of Seville. The town hall straddles a wide arch over which runs the inscription *Casas Consistoriales de la Muy Noble, Leal e Ilustre Ciudad de Alcalá de los Gazules.* Somehow dilapidated Alcalá has managed to get one up on Ronda in the honorifics league. Noble, loyal *and* illustrious are distinctions not claimed, to the best of my knowledge, by any other of the little cities with long histories in this part of the world.

The archway leads to a labyrinth of narrow streets with

steps and ramps, mostly impassable to cars. A pale blue-grey is the favoured colour on the woodwork and dados of the flat-roofed Moorish-style houses; this is sometimes combined with a gilded knocker or handle on a door painted the colour of French mustard. Many of the dwellings give onto a little courtyard, usually graced with a lemon or bay tree. This is not a picturesque district of the sort beloved by the brochures, smothered with grilles and geraniums and bougainvillaea. Its secret is that a little goes a long way. A single geranium in a tin, a shaft of light falling on the dark, polished leaves of a plant, a hen-run made up of railway sleepers in a backyard, an old stone doorway framing a deep pool of shade – these are the threads, some gleaming, some dusky, running through an ancient, well-worn fabric of life.

At the bottom modern life is more obtrusive. There is the Casa del Pueblo or club of the governing party, the PSOE. There is a church with posters bearing the message 'Inject life, kick drugs!' under a picture of a broken syringe and a desperate-eyed youth with wild spiky hair. The idea is that you change your fix and get hooked on Christ. There is a whole string of cafés and bars along the main concourse; Pizarro's is the smartest, having recently been relined with a Sevillian *azulejo* dado, as good a design as it was five hundred years ago; others are mere dram-shops with a zinc or hardboard counter. Facing Pizarro's is an establishment with an awning carrying the legend 'Drift Gin', a rather delightful name for a drink that does indeed – I have tried it – cause one to cast off from the moorings of reality.

In the outskirts seediness abounds, not in a sad, negative way, but rampantly. Shanties, rubbish, prickly pears and a blithe unconcern with municipal neatness are the order of the day, encouraged perhaps by a climate favourable to all creeping, climbing and straggling plants such as morning glory and clematis, which run riot everywhere, covering a multitude of sins. And so it goes over the hummocky hills and tawny plains as far as Los Barrios and Algeciras and Barbate, all unbuttoned places with a raffish atmosphere, to

which 'Drift Gin' is the ideal accompaniment. By comparison the mountain pueblos seem almost prim. This is what
makes the mountain-dweller feel abroad down here.

When I returned from my tour of the town Paco Pizarro
came up to me with quiet satisfaction: he had pulled of
another coup. On no account was I to wander off again,
because at two o'clock or thereabouts the well known *ganadero*, Don Diego Romero, was coming to meet me. I thanked
Paco warmly for his good offices, opened a newspaper and
settled down to wait. This was the time when anyone of
any consequence in Alcalá assembled round Paco's counter;
this was where the town's business was done. The landowners, the vet, the main functionaries all dropped in. The
custom was for two or three of them to share half a bottle
of La Ina accompanied by little earthenware dishes of tripe,
trotters and chickpeas or some delicacy of the season. The
professionals and officials wore white pleated jacket-shirts
with a handkerchief displayed in the breast pocket, over
grey or fawn trousers and neat tasselled pumps. The country
interest affected khaki tones and unpolished half-boots,
showing them to be true sons of the soil. One or two smoked
lethal black 'Faria' cigars.

I knew when Señor Romero had arrived, because there
was a ripple among them; hands were pressed; arms were
laid lightly on his shoulders; but he did not linger, and came
straight towards me. Paco treated him with respect and
introduced him as 'Don Diego'. There was something
immediately impressive about this medium-sized figure
with ruddy, mobile features, an amused eye and a distinctive sharp peak of hair like a raised vizor over his strong
brows and nose; like Arturo's, it was an Iberian or Numantine warrior's face. He wore a buff-coloured leather jacket,
open-necked shirt and corduroy trousers with big turn-ups
over his boots. I felt at once that here was a man of authority
and expertise in his own world; also that he was calm and
assured in his centre. We stood at the counter. Paco poured
a *copa* of Tio Pepe for me and called for a coffee for Don

Diego, who had already eaten.

I did not like to take notes, so I listened to him very intently. The future of the *fiesta nacional*? Well, like all living things, it changed and evolved to survive. Before you had the romantic story of the ragged *maletillas* with their bundles over their shoulders going from ring to ring in the hope of an opportunity. Now you had the schools in Málaga and Jerez and elsewhere. He himself took a personal interest in the one at Jerez. They sent their novices to the small pueblo rings: Grazalema, Olvera, Ubrique and so on. I had seen such fights? Good. Then I would know that some of the lads were promising and all put their hearts into it. Yes, there was usually a subsidy from the town hall; such things could not be self-financing. But the schools themselves organised the *cartel*, who was to appear and the supporting cast, in fact everything. It was a big move forward.

'So there is more opportunity than ever before?'

'There is opportunity.'

'If there are more aspirants coming onto the scene, how are the breeders responding? Are there more *ganaderos*?'

'No, about the same number.'

I took the bull, as it were, by the horns.

'You must have heard the criticism that the fighting bull is no longer reared as previously, roaming on the *monte* with his natural diet supplemented by real grain, but kept in more confined spaces and fattened up on artificial feedstuffs which make him look glossy and handsome but undermine his strength. Is there anything in all this?'

Don Diego chewed on the question.

'Look, the *toro bravo* is like a sportsman. He needs his proper regime if he is to perform to maximum effect. There is no *ganadero* in the game who wants to see his bulls falling to their knees and himself humiliated. Whatever people may say, this is not a cynical business. The *ganadero* wishes to triumph. But what you cannot have is a regular factory product. Each *ganadero* has his own type of bull but even this will vary. The seed bulls are not all equal, nor are the cows which they cover. It has to be a variable product with no mathematical certainties.'

He spoke straight and it sounded good; I did not have any sense of special pleading or vested interest.

'What about the anti-bullfight lobby?' I asked.

'Nobody obliges anyone to go to the *corrida*. That is its great protection.'

'Yes, but there is opposition, isn't there?'

'I know that it exists. But I also know that in France they are putting up a statue to a Spanish matador, Ruiz Miguel, and that there is talk of *corridas* for Japan. I am not concerned with those things. I only note them in passing. My concern is with the Peninsula. If the *corrida* were banned here, you have to think of the many, many people who would lose their work: the employees of the impresarios and of the breeders and of the *transportistas*; and then of the *banderilleros* and sword-handlers and all the entourage of the matador; to say nothing of the horse-copers and carpenters and ring-attendants. Taken together, they would amount to thousands, many thousands, without counting their families. Why, here in the province of Cádiz alone we must be sixty or seventy *ganaderos*, between the first and second categories, creating several hundred jobs just in the triangle formed by Alcalá, Medina and Vejer. And this is only a small corner of Andalusia, which as a whole has more *ganaderos* and more bulls than the rest of Spain. Note the last point, because you can have small *ganaderos* with few cows, who are also listed, but here we have not only more *ganaderos* but more bulls also. So you can see that if it all folded, it would be a disaster for the region. Of course we could convert to more cereals, but they are much less labour-intensive.'

I digested this.

'What is the ideal size for a *ganadería*?'

'Some have five hundred cows, which in my opinion is too many. You don't have enough control. You need many *sementales*, seed bulls, and you don't know what will be produced. Others have only a hundred or so cows, which is too few. There is a halfway house.'

'Which you have?'

'You could say that.'

'And what is the value of a mature *toro bravo*?'

'The value of a *corrida de toros*, that is to say a lot of six prime bulls, has to be put in the region of six million pesetas.'

'Do you have any preferences about where your bulls go – locally or further afield? El Puerto de Santa María or Madrid?'

He smiled.

'You know, it is curious, some breeders are obsessed with local triumphs; others prefer to sell their bulls as far away as possible. I am prepared to send a *corrida* anywhere: Seville, Madrid, Bilbao or on my doorstep. I will send my bulls anywhere.'

'What about the future? Is the *fiesta* gaining ground or losing it, or more or less maintaining its position? You have talked about the enthusiasm in the schools, but if there is eventually no public, what then? Most of the people I have talked to are in the game. They tend to believe what they want to believe. I would particularly value your judgement.'

He was too canny to be drawn into predictions.

'I am in the game too, so my judgement is no better than theirs. But I would say that the *fiesta* tends to respond to the emergence of a great figure who dominates a decade: a Belmonte, a Manolete, an Ordóñez, a Luis Miguel, a Cordobés. *La feria se enfoca mucho en el cartel*, if you understand that. The quality of the cast is important. Although there are now some good *figuras* and some good *novilleros*, there is currently no *maxima figura*. This has an effect. You have to have a great deal of *afición* to go to the bulls as a simple spectacle – playing no part in the action – with the risk of coming away disgruntled or disappointed.'

'The elders go partly through habit, don't they? But if the young drop off, then surely the *fiesta* is as good as dead?'

'... the *fiesta* tends to respond to the emergence of a great figure'
(Alvaro Domecq, Rafael 'El Gallo' and Juan Belmonte
in retirement)

He smiled again, rather subtly.

'We too were young. In my case I was born *dentro de la fiesta*, right inside it, because of my father. *Afición* does tend to descend from father to son. I don't know why that should change. We are obsessed with change. There are many things which continue.'

'So you are an optimist?'

'Cautiously so. There is also a development which I haven't mentioned. Many of the young are drawn into the *fiesta* through the *peñas*, which are very important.'

A *peña* is a circle or club, usually devoted to some cultural, artistic or sporting theme; or it can be the fan club of a particular football team or bullfighter.

'The interesting thing,' said Don Diego, 'is that they are growing fast now that they are admitting women – even girls – to full membership with voting rights in what was exclusively the province of the male.'

'Do you approve of that?'

He hesitated slightly; it was the only time he was a shade evasive.

'*Hombre*, it is good up to a point, if it helps to keep up the traditions.'

'But that *is* a big change, isn't it?'

'Yes, but of course it is part of something wider. It is happening not only with the bulls. It is happening also in the religious brotherhoods.'

These are the lay bodies, called *hermandades* or *cofradías*, pledged to a specific Virgin or patron saint, whom they bring out in procession, principally at Easter or Corpus Christi or on the August feast-days. Women had always dressed the images and society ladies in *mantillas* would follow them as dames of honour, while poorer women came behind as penitents; but it was the men who ran the show, and no woman walked in the robes of the brotherhood.

'You mean that girls are coming out as Nazarenes, wearing the pointed *capirote* with holes for the eyes, like the men?'

'Not only that. They are carrying the floats too. How long is it since you have seen an Easter procession?'

'Some years.'

'Well, do not be surprised if the next time you attend one and it stops for a rest and someone removes their *capirote* for a breath of air, it is a beautiful girl. That is what I am telling you. The young are rallying to the traditions.'

Our conversation turned to horses and the *peste equina*. He knew a breeder who had been selling eighty or ninety stallions a year and could not now sell a single one owing to the disease and the quarantine regulations; he was ruined. So there would be no horses at Rocío next year when the pilgrim caravans converged at Whitsun on the famous shrine near the marshlands of the Coto Doñana? Don Diego was not so sure. Rocío had a powerful emotive pull and there were many important vested interests behind it. *Hermandades* came from as far as Barcelona and Santa Cruz de Tenerife. There were a number of routes of entry: one from

Sanlúcar, another from Huelva, another from Osuna and
Utrera, another from Estremadura and so on. And then they
had to wait to go in, because the *hermandades* entered
strictly in order of seniority. It was very fine; he himself
was a regular. As he spoke, I vividly recalled Hilly cantering
on our black horse Babi through the torchlit, firework-
spangled dusk of Rocío when she was pregnant with Jaime.

On cockfighting, Don Diego confirmed what the *capataz*
had told me. *La pelea de gallos*? Yes, certainly, El Puerto
and San Fernando were important centres, so were Jerez and
Seville. No, it was not prohibited. The *reñideros*, as the
rings were called, were all authorised. It was true that earlier
practices such as artificial spurs were now frowned on. And
the export trade to South America had gone down. But there
was still money in *los pollos*, the chicks, which some people
bred as a second string to bulls or horses.

At this point we were joined by Don Diego's wife. She
was wearing trews and the obligatory unpolished half-boots,
like her husband, but she also had immaculately lacquered
black hair, painted lips and flashing eyes. Seeing them
together – him with his ancient Iberian potency; her dash-
ingly accoutred as the breeder's spouse – I felt the enduring
strength of the world they represented, a world compounded
of important financial interests and genuine *afición*, which
found both its symbolic and its practical expression in the
trinity of the bull, the horse and the fighting cock. It was a
world with deep and tortuous roots, some pre-Christian,
though now closely allied to the cult of Mary. It would not,
I sensed, be easily swept away by Eurocrats or animal rights
groups or even by the government in Madrid, if it wished
to retain the votes of the Andalusian people.

Paco Pizarro was full of stories with an unusual twist. That
evening he told me about the beggar he had befriended, as
a young man, and installed in a room behind his father's
bar. This was much criticised at home, for Paco's protégé
was a German, and odd in his ways. But the stranger had

great culture and intelligence. Before long he insisted that Paco took him to where he could get clay. He began to make figures of men and animals which left everyone who saw them overcome with admiration. No longer the 'beggar', he became the 'sculptor', from whom Paco derived no little kudos. Some months later the sculptor said to his protector, 'If ever I leave, my sculptures are all for you.' Paco didn't take this too seriously, but one day the German was not to be found anywhere. Paco sought him high and low. Yes, he had been seen in such and such a street, then on the high road, but when Paco followed up the clues there was no trace of him. He had vanished as suddenly as he had appeared. Recalling the verbal legacy, Paco became convinced he had gone for good. But Paco's father, who was extraordinarily legalistic, would not allow him to keep the sculptures, in case the wanderer or his heirs should return to claim them He insisted on their being deposited with a judge, who took them off to Seville.

'I have never seen them since,' said Paco wryly. 'Nor, I believe, has anyone else.'

Despite his exacting day in the restaurant and the constant claims on his attention, Paco would sit far into the night at a table in the bar, talking. That night he spoke to me of his 'enormous restlessness'. He practised, he said, 'mental gymnastics' in order to concentrate the powers that he felt in himself. For example, by concentrating on someone's back he could force that person to turn and face him. Though he tried to develop these powers, he was also alarmed when they worked. This had been so particularly on one occasion when he tried to make his own image disappear from a mirror . . . and it did! We talked of the bright and dark sides of sympathy. I urged him to hold back from witchcraft and praised his undoubted gifts as a hotelier and restaurateur, in which role his capacity for entering into other people's minds had, I suggested, found a healthy and constructive outlet. He sighed and said it did not add up to fulfilment. Was that why he went twice a week to art classes in Cádiz? Yes, he supposed so, and believed he would succeed in that too; he had this capacity for success. But, I said, there were surely no horizons in art. It wasn't just a question of 'succeeding' in art and then casting about for something else. Painting alone should give him ample scope for self-expression for a lifetime. He listened to me politely but in his mind, I could tell, he was still dabbling with the occult.

The sanctuary of Nuestra Señora de los Santos, patroness of Alcalá, lies about five kilometres outside the town. Its most striking feature is the very fine domed *camarín* with glass-lined walls set in Rococo gilded wood trimmings. Raised above the high altar, this is the Virgin's chamber or boudoir, into which her image can be rotated for her clothes to be changed. She is less than life-size, standing barely more than a metre high under her silver baldachino with a fully-robed and upright Christ child held presentation-wise in front of her stomach. Here there is no lulling on the lap of a joyous babe but the display in hieratic posture of a future monarch who will triumph through his sorrows – for she also clutches the three nails of the Cross in her right hand.

But perhaps the most moving objects in the little church are the naive ex-voto paintings which cover the walls and bear witness to the Virgin's miracles in lieu of the usual collection of dolls' limbs and other gewgaws. One, dated 1972, shows a young man knocked down by a bus and apparently dead – but as he had commended himself to Her before he set out, he revived. Another of 1859 shows a mother on the point of death in a very lumpy cottage bed; she is saved by the prayers of her kneeling daughter to the Virgin, who appears clad in her stiff robes, borne on what is intended as a crescent moon but looks like a boat in the sky.

There is an arcaded and galleried patio with tile pictures of Saint George and Saint Isidore of Seville, a charming and peaceful precinct. In the outer courtyard a ceramic plaque is let into the wall with a facsimile reproduction of some lines of verse by the ageing and self-doubting humanist intellectual José María Pemán, on his eighty-second birthday, in which he leaves his heart whose 'song is out of tune' with devotion to God for the succour of his saints. One feels he has come in rather sadly from the cold.

Machines were flattening out a stretch of ground just below the sanctuary; great pyramids of yellow sand waited to be spread. Apparently a portable bullring was to be erected for a fight to coincide with the *romería* in honour of the Virgin on her day, which fell next month. I asked the custodian if he thought it a good idea that the *novillada* should take place not only in the Virgin's honour but also right under her nose. Goodness, he said, why on earth should I suppose she would raise her hands in horror? Were not many *fiestas taurinas* organised to support her cult? Did not many bullfighters owe their lives to her? The only question in his mind was whether there would be sufficient parking space.

Leaving the security of the sanctuary, I set off on the bleak drive to Benalup de Sidonia. The land was flat and ashen in colour. What little surface was left on the road was being rapidly chewed up by an endless procession of lorries carrying rock for the construction of yet another dam and reservoir, designed to capture the headwaters of the Río de Barbate: a joint effort, according to a placard, of the Spanish Ministry of Works and the European Community. There were also large self-congratulatory notice-boards along the roadside, erected by the Junta de Andalucía, proclaiming this to be a *Comarca de Reforma Agraria*.

All this propaganda about agrarian reform suddenly struck me as an ironic comment on the failure over more than a century to implement any such thing. The running sore of the Spanish body politic, source of much violence and bloodshed, which no government from the 'liberal' administrations of the nineteenth century down to the Republic of 1931–36 had managed to cure, was now being poulticed by great irrigation schemes long after the issue was dead. The old slogan of rural communities, *el campo para quien lo trabaje*, the land for those who work it, had long faded out of political parlance and into history under the influence of industrialisation, emigration and tourism. The residual workforce would notice little or no change, because the new exploitations would be large agro-businesses; the main difference from the past would be that the men would sputter out to the fields on 50cc mopeds rather than going on foot or by mule. If only agrarian reform had come in the 1890s rather than the 1990s, how different the modern history of Spain might have been!

Benalup de Sidonia, with such a pretty-sounding name conjuring up some medieval village, comes as a distinct shock. It is a grim, depressing place on a slight mound, with flat-topped houses, many of them mud-coloured without even the healing balm of a coat of whitewash. The only vertical feature is the mast of the local radio station; there is not so much as a modest belfry. The pueblo overlooks fields of cotton, that most horrible crop to pick, and rolling ranchlands with African-looking cattle. The road in is lined with cactus, prickly pear, canes, yet more canes, a rubbish tip . . . and nothing more dignified than the odd umbrella pine. Benalup is the epitome of rural blight and desolation.

Small wonder. For behind the fancy new name lurks the notorious Casas Viejas, scene of perhaps the most widely known incident of Andalusian rural violence, which took place in 1933 under the Republic. The Anarcho-Syndicalist union, the CNT, had called for an armed uprising, to coincide with a planned railway strike; it was to be triggered off on 8 January in Barcelona. Local sections were to rise as soon as they heard this action had been successful. The workers in low-lying Jerez would then cut the electricity supply at night, which would be a signal to elevated Medina Sidonia, whose people would rise themselves and light a beacon as a sign to the surrounding pueblos like Casas Viejas, then without electricity or radio, that the insurrection had begun. This did not work out. The Barcelona rising failed. The lights were not extinguished in Jerez. No beacon was lit in Medina. But somehow a written message from Jerez got through to Casas Viejas, reading, 'At ten o'clock at night, no matter what the consequences.'

Though some of the elders demurred, the younger hotheads decided to act. They dug a ditch across the main road and posted guards at all the principal points of access to the village. Then they fired on the small contingent of Civil Guards, who retreated into their *casa cuartel*, which combined the functions of married quarters and barracks. When the sergeant and one other man unwisely appeared at a window they were shot and mortally wounded. Next day the insurgents paraded through the streets with banners, pillaged the church and burned the saints. Reinforcements arrived that afternoon from Medina; the insurrection collapsed and the workers took refuge either in the country or their homes.

The violence might have stopped there, had not the Guards forced the door of a suspected man's house; one of them was killed and another wounded as they attempted entry. A contingent of forty men, newly posted south from Madrid, then arrived on the scene. Their commander, Captain Rojas, called on the occupants of the besieged house to surrender. They refused and he ordered it to be set on fire. Seven people died. Next day twelve men were arrested, only one of whom had been active in the events of the day before. Rojas ordered them to be taken to the burnt-out house, which he told them to enter to see what they had brought about. Then he shot them one by one with his own pistol. The total casualties were by now three Guards and twenty villagers. Thus did the people's armed forces subdue their own people.

Why did this incident escalate and accumulate such a toll of deaths? The explanation advanced by John Corbin in an illuminating essay, 'Insurrections in Spain: Casas Viejas 1933 and Madrid 1981', is that honour was impugned: political action moved from *la calle*, the street, where it was legitimate, into *la casa*, the home – whether the Civil Guards' barracks or the workmen's dwellings – where it was not. More widely, he suggests, the whole working-class movement was activated by the loss of honour implicit in the status of its members as wage-slaves, employed only half the year at that. The word *vida*, life, means for Spaniards self-determination, which goes far beyond the lesser forms of life represented by plants and animals. Honour in *la calle* means the ability to dispose of one's own time in stalwart effort or absolute repose as one chooses, rather than being at the beck and call of a farm bailiff. Each domestic unit should ideally be self-sufficient; hence the call for the redistribution of land to enable each family to sustain its members with its own labour and its own property. Dependence on employment by others violates this principle of autonomy.

If this is accepted, it helps to explain why working men in Spain are – or were – motivated more by considerations of personal honour than by improved living conditions. It certainly fits with the southern Spanish temperament which values leisure, *visible* leisure in clubs and bars (not hidden away and wasted at home) as the pinnacle of self-determination. In these public places each man is self-evidently his own master, measuring out his life with coffee spoons. Nor, despite the difference in context, is it entirely out of line with Veblen's classic *The Theory of the Leisure Class*, in which he wrote: 'The early ascendency of leisure as a means of respectability is traceable to the archaic distinction between noble and ignoble employments. Leisure is honourable and becomes imperative partly because it shows exemption from ignoble labour.' Among the noble pursuits of archaic societies in their predatory phase hunting (which leaves lots of time for leisure) ranked high. It still does among all classes and across the political spectrum in Spain, where it enables the working man to rival or even surpass the gentility of his social superiors. It is in recognition of these things that the Spanish state recognises every Spanish male as 'Don' (as it might be 'Esquire') and is careful to use this in its correspondence with its citizens – other than in bourgeois Catalonia, which will have nothing to do with such obeisance to the ancient world.

From doom-laden Benalup I scuttled towards Medina Sidonia, whose mound, visible for miles around, is almost perfectly conical and the highest in the region. Little is left of the castle, so it is the parish church tower that makes most of an impression on the horizon. The Plaza Mayor is one of the finest small town squares in Andalusia. It is oblong and flanked by almost irreproachable buildings, all deferring to the splendid town hall which occupies one end; at the other is the pleasant nineteenth-century marketplace round two arcaded patios. There are no lodgings other than the Pensión Napoleon and the Fonda Reyes just behind the market. Old-fashioned hardware and clothing stores and pharmacies predominate among the shops. There are a number of gracious streets, notably Padre Felix which runs downwards from the plaza, flanked by sizeable houses all dazzling white with tall Cádiz-style window grilles coming down to the pavement. Despite the height there is a whiff of the sea, the same tang as that which rose no doubt with ambiguous appeal to the nostrils of the seventh Duke of Medina Sidonia, a poor seaman, when he reluctantly obeyed his king's summons to take command of the Great Armada.

I climbed up to the castle, consisting now of only a few stumps of masonry; yet it is worth it for the views of San Fernando, Cádiz and Jerez. The latter is about thirty kilometres off, but I could see clearly how a blackout by the insurgents there in 1933 would have been immediately apparent up here. On the way down I stopped at the Venta del Castillo, run by a handsome bold-eyed woman who was offering *tapas* of venison or wild boar. The *venta* was spotless but across the street was a crumbling corral littered with every conceivable kind of non-biodegradable waste, round the edge of which a municipal dustman in a green boiler-suit was sweeping fastidiously. Along one of the walls of the corral were tethered three or four lean greyhounds, the very image of the *famélicos galgos*, the famished hounds which bayed to the moon in Antonio Machado's poem on the proud old city of Soria in *Campos de Castilla*. Perhaps, I thought, there is something Castilian about Medina: so high and wind-scoured and aloof above the plain.

In the Plaza de la Yglesia Mayor the church, devoted to Santa María la Coronada, is the usual pleasant patchwork of tastes and periods found in these ancient towns. The tympanum over the entrance sports a Baroque version of the Virgin treading the ubiquitous crescent moon; above her float a couple of jolly cherubs placing the celestial crown on her head. The interior has some hybrid Gothic-Plateresque features somewhat reminiscent of the temple of that most potent of all Spanish goddesses, the black Virgin of Guadalupe. Here there is a fine Renaissance retable in dark wood and the central Virgin figure seems dusky too in the half-light. I wondered if she likewise had green fingers for fertility.

From these exposed heights the streets all run sharply downwards past houses with little courtyards and old columns. The street names are heavy with sanctity: Misericordia, San Juan, Sacramento, San Vicente de Paul, San Francisco. In fact Medina has an altogether more religious aura than Alcalá. Almost the only variant on this sacred nomenclature is provided by a street named curiously after a Dr Thebussem, whom I imagined as the bearded medical director of some old-fashioned spa with magical healing powers. I later discovered that the name is a slightly germanified anagram of the Spanish word *embustes*, meaning tricks or fibs, and was adopted as his *nom de plume* by a celebrated local humourist, bibliophile and eccentric who wrote the first book in Spanish on philately.

For this arcane piece of information I am indebted to Señor Antonio Orellana, an enthusiastic amateur anti- quarian, who runs an electro-domestic shop and videotape library. After showing me his collection of coins, all minted locally, the good Señor Orellana treated me rapidly, off the cuff, to a veritable tide of knowledge and speculation about his home town. Some said the name derived from Sidon; hence the Roman Assidio Caesarina, from which the inhabi- tants to this day are called Asidonenses. The Arabs added the Medina, thus Medina Sidonia. There was a Visigothic bishopric here and I must see the Hermita de los Santos, which had been dated as early as 608 and was very impor- tant. Medina began to lose importance after the Reconquest about 1250. Yes, there had always been a strong link with the sea, not always a fortunate one, as was demonstrated in 1588; the Spanish naval commander at the time of the loss of Cuba had also been from Medina. But these – or so his tone seemed to imply – were minor setbacks in the town's long and varied history.

When the English sacked Cádiz, the year before the Armada, the duke wanted to move the bishopric back to Medina, which he thought suitable because of its many churches and its strategic position; that project sank too with the Armada. The present duchess, the so-called *Duquesa Roja*, lived in Sanlúcar de Barrameda and they never saw her. She might be the twenty-second or twenty- third of her line, Señor Orellana couldn't recall which, but there was now virtually no link. Medina today was a quiet and agreeable place; but it was also in effect the capital of the interior of the province, which prevented it from becom- ing too much of a backwater. Drawbacks? Hardly any. The *Levante Rondeño* and the *Levante de Tarifa* could be tire- some winds but they did dry the atmosphere, which would otherwise be too humid from proximity to the sea. Advan- tages there were many: the pueblo was open, sympathetic and tranquil. Anyone you approached would be helpful 'within the limits of his knowledge'. Medina was also famous for the pastries made by its nuns and, of course, for Dr Thebussem . . .

The further mention of this genial polymath reminded me of the fine-looking houses I had seen in the street named after him, one of which appeared to be for sale. How much, I asked, would such a dwelling cost? Property, said Orellana, was very reasonably priced in Medina, ranging from three or four million pesetas for a modest home to ten or twelve for a mansion. I am bound to say that his praises of his birthplace, coupled with my own observations, had begun to work rather favourably on me. I could imagine worse fates than browsing in my library, in the manner of Dr Thebussem, behind one of those dignified façades, then strolling down to the main square for an aperitif at the Restaurante-Bar Cádiz, from where one could contemplate the fine town hall with its inscription proclaiming that this city like Ronda was *Muy Noble y Muy Leal*; though it did not qualify for the third honorific *Ilustre* boasted by Alcalá, it was decidedly more substantial and less dilapidated than its 'illustrious' neighbour.

There were other objects worthy of contemplation too, not least the women passing by on their way to and from the market place, many with striking features of Phoenician mould under their fine brows and eyes. All in all, Medina seemed to combine a number of attractions, including – as at Teba and Cañete – its elevation, which confined the highway culture of the transport café and the filling station to the roads which circled its base. But here there was another element, the sea: not the degraded pond of the Mediterranean, but the Atlantic. Beyond the bay of Cádiz stretched the ocean; between Cádiz and Tarifa lay long stretches of silver sands where Spanish beach life had staked out its territory with its *chiringuitos* serving fresh-caught *boquerones* and sardines and great slabs of *tortilla* with rough red wine; there foreign tourists scarcely ventured, deterred by the long trail from any airport and by tales (with some truth in them) of whiplash winds which drove you scurrying indoors.

The whole culture of these foothill towns was impreg-nated with Atlantic airs and legendary tales stretching far back to Tartessians and Minoans and even to Atlantis. On these coasts trading stations were set up by the Phoenicians, worshippers of Astarte, precursor – some said – of the Virgin Mary. You had only to slip down the hill and over a few undulations to savour all these influences. Once there you would exchange Machado, grave Don Antonio, bard of the inland plains and cities, for the faun-like poet of the gleam-ing bay, Rafael Alberti, ardent advocate of its myths and grace and luminosity.

With my head slightly turned by all this, and more than half an intention of coming back to investigate further, I drove out of town in the direction of Arcos. Then I saw it. As when a slender and shapely woman turns and the drawn curtains of her hair reveals some unsightly blemish, so I suddenly became aware of a hideous new building, still under construction, which had been invisible from the south (whence I drove in) and whose horror had not been fully apparent from the castle – though I should have been warned by the telltale brooding crane. Ronda has done some pretty awful things, but nothing as crass as this. The style is something between 1930s Odeon and the superstructure of a transatlantic liner. I thought at first it must be a new hotel or conference centre, but when I drove impulsively right into the middle of the site, I was blandly informed by a foreman that it was to be a health clinic.

Almost anything else could probably have been success-fully attacked on aesthetic grounds, but this alas was on the side of the angels, and would be stoutly defended not only by officialdom but by every charitable and welfare organisation on the grounds that 'Our old and infirm deserve no less . . . this is a temple of health with all the latest facilities' and so on. The culture department must have been completely outgunned by the apostles of the caring society. The result was that this stranded liner, a debased modern Ark on Ararat, from which healthy animals would not walk out but infirm human beings would walk in – for whom equally good services and facilities could surely have been provided in some other spot. When I reached the main road and looked back up, I saw that it was if anything worse than I had feared. When completed, it would clearly steal the skyline from the high church of La Coronada. Alas, Medina, I thought . . . *adiós*, Alberti . . . farewell, good Orellana. For I knew that I should not be settling in the street of Dr Thebussem after all.

And so to Arcos de la Frontera, titular seat of the Ponce de León family, dukes of Arcos, who were prominent in the last stages of the Reconquest and in the suppression of the *Morisco* revolt. Raised on an inland cliff above the river Guadalete, boasting an impressive (and inhabited) castle and two grand parish churches, Arcos is a rival to Ronda on the tourist circuit. However much you deprecate the effects of your own local *turismo*, you tend to support the home-team, so I have always approached Arcos with a critical eye.

My first experience of the town was not of a confidence-building nature. I came with my first wife, Diana, in the late fifties. We had been plied by Anita Richmond with tales of interbreeding and madness, of witchcraft and covens still active in the old city – of which she claimed special knowledge through a family connection with the castle folk. We discounted most of this as the product of an overheated imagination. But no sooner had we arrived, found a lodging and climbed to the high plaza than we realised we were being followed by a strange, blubber-lipped individual with long lashes and dark eyes; falling in beside us, he pressed his services on us as a guide. Armed as usual with the appropriate books, I assured him we had no such need. This did not deter him and we could not shake him off. Eventually, we turned into a bar to escape him, but he followed us in and continued pestering us, to the extent of sitting at our table and waiting for us to finish our drinks.

The barman, a blond foxy fellow, observed all this closely. All of a sudden he came out from behind his counter and tried to hustle our persecutor out into the street. On this, blubber-lips drew a clasp-knife and slashed him quite deeply in the arm. The barman retreated, cursing and holding his bleeding limb. An ambulance was called. Blubber-lips ran off. The police arrived and soon cornered him in a cul-de-sac.

Shortly after this we were escorted to the Civil Guard post to give our account of the incident. Somewhat to our consternation we were ushered into the same anteroom where the accused man, unguarded, was waiting his turn. We were seen first, and our deposition was painstakingly recorded on an ancient typewriter. As we left, blubber-lips smiled faintly, conspiratorially, as if some sort of bond had been forged between us. He was out and about on the street later that same evening. For many years afterwards he performed the function of carpark attendant, with the authority vested in him by a uniform cap, in the upper plaza. More than once I was obliged to confide my vehicle and its contents to him. When our eyes met, his were always perfectly blank, but I could tell from the faint smile on his great lips that he had not forgotten.

Seen from afar, Arcos, like Ronda, has changed greatly, as the glaring white modern tenements tend to outshine the grizzled old battlements and the mottled and lichened stone walls of the churches. Within the old quarter, however, almost the only innovations are the government *parador* and a few ceramic shops and art and craft galleries. Without squabbling about the rival merits of one city's artistic heritage as against another's, there can be no doubt that Arcos possesses two impressive churches. The architect of the Baroque portico of San Pedro must have had more than a nodding acquaintance with the cathedral front of Murcia, while Santa María in the main square is of most unusual quality.

The fine Isabelline-Gothic west entrance of the latter is

a grander version of Alcalá's. It has swooping late Gothic vaults over nave and aisles and is rich in side chapels and images. But above all it rejoices in a magnificent Renaissance retable in the Berruguete style occupying the whole east end above the high altar and featuring as its centrepiece a coronation of the goddess that puts Medina's in the shade. This church's impact on the skyline is made by its imposing tower-belfry, which stands out a little from the main body of the building but appears from a distance to bestride it, like a rider on a horse. On the Sunday evening when I arrived, the citizens were answering the summons of its bells in goodly numbers, lured not least perhaps by the promise of a recital on the newly restored organ after the Mass.

Yet, the dark side of Arcos has not been totally eclipsed. As the citizens were mounting the steps and thronging into the church, a trumpet sounded further down the street, and shortly a little troupe of four appeared: the trumpeter himself, a gypsy in a shirt of many hues leading a black goat, a woman and a girl child. The gypsy stopped right outside the church entrance and unfolded a small stepladder he was carrying over one shoulder. The trumpeter sounded a fanfare and the gypsy ordered the goat to climb the ladder, which it did. Then, obeying a series of taps with a baton, the animal was induced to mount, hoof by hoof, from the narrow platform onto a wooden knob on which it balanced and slowly turned full circle, while the trumpeter blew a triumphal peal on his instrument and the woman and the girl circulated for coins. During the collection the goat remained poised on its pinnacle. Though rendered slightly ridiculous by a couple of artificial red carnations pinned between its horns, nonetheless it seemed to offer a mocking challenge to the service which had just begun. Indeed, the trumpet quite overpowered the opening words of the lesson. The devil was still patently abroad in Arcos de la Frontera. When his troupe moved on, the little girl led the goat.

Others, however, find nothing sinister in Arcos – or perhaps turn a blind eye to it. The pleasant woman, Mencha by name, who runs the Hotel Marqués de Torresoto just round the corner from Santa María, is a *Madrileña* who came in search of peace. She says the only thing left now is to *buscar rincones*, look for quiet corners. She and her business partner, Andrés, have turned this small seventeenth-century 'palace', which was in a ruinous state, into an agreeable restaurant with four or five rooms for guests. In the evenings before serving dinner she plays cards with her young son and their friends at a wicker table in the corner of the patio. Outside the door the traffic passes intermittently along the one-way system but is not troublesome except for the occasional irruption into the narrow alley of a moped which peppers the patio with a fusillade of sound. Mencha winces; the game goes on; this is the nearest you can get, even in a small provincial city, to the ideal *petit coin*.

Mencha's partner, Andrés, who takes the morning shift, is a native of the province of Jaén. He worked for twenty-two years in Barcelona. He is a refugee from *la sociedad del colapso*. For him society is literally collapsing. Madrid, Barcelona, Valencia are becoming intolerable through their traffic congestion. The authorities in some major Spanish cities are now handing out really punitive fines for parking offences – up to £200–300 a time. But still the traffic pours in and the metros are more and more crowded and inadequate.

'Do you seriously see Spanish motorists giving up their sacred rights?' I asked. 'The British government believes it would be political suicide to tamper with them.'

He shrugged.

'When it takes two hours to get to work from a suburb or you have to sit in a ten- or twenty-kilometre tailback returning from holiday, people are bound to begin to think. There's plenty of time for thinking in a traffic jam.'

'But is there any party taking up the anti-automobile cause? Greens, Ecologists, the Andalusian Party?'

'Not with much energy. As you say, the idea is not popular yet. But there are other groups, pressure groups. And of course the intellectuals are writing more and more about collapse. This has an effect, a slow one perhaps, but it filters through.'

Ah, the intellectuals, God bless them! They are always there on the Continent, always to hand even in Spain – but never in Britain, or not in that guise. We have our party think-tanks, independent think-tanks, policy analysts, management consultants, forecasters, political academics, political columnists, but never – perish the thought! – intellectuals. Intellectualism as a word, as a concept, as a way of examining the world, is simply not British. If mentioned at all, it is in a derogatory sense, as when the right-wing press sneers at 'left-wing intellectuals' or the Left hits back at 'ideologues of the New Right'. But that's about it. Even our heavyweight pundits are first and foremost journalists. We have had and shall have no Unamuno, no Ortega y Gasset, no Sartre, no Camus, no Servan-Schreiber, no Havel . . .

In the eyes of Andrés ours is the loss. For he is in little doubt that intellectuals – in the long run – are the only people capable of preventing the total collapse of society. In the meantime, co-managing a small hotel in Arcos de la Frontera is about the nearest you can get to earning a living without being driven to distraction.

While in the Hotel Marqués de Torresoto I read the little volume on Arcos in the series 'Pueblos de la Provincia de Cádiz' published by the *Diputación* or provincial council. The whole series has a socio-economic slant and is not at all hooked on heroic history or monuments, so it is not recommended reading for tourists. The thing that interested me about these books was that whether the subject was Grazalema or El Gastor or Alcalá de los Gazules or Arcos itself, there was always an almost identical section with a few minor local variants on the appalling rural situation between 1836 and 1936 and the total failure of any government of whatever colour or whatever intentions to do anything significant about it.

Roughly, the story is as follows. As lands were reconquered, they were awarded either to the military orders – meaning the knights of Santiago, Calatrava or Alcántara – or to individual nobles in a regime known as *de señorío*, or seigneurial jurisdiction, with very considerable powers reserved to the local lord who owned much of the land. However, there were also communal lands, generally wood and pasture, for the people. It is fashionable among historians to say that the feudal age properly speaking never existed in Spain because of the communal lands and the absence of serfdom. Be that as it may, most people worked on the lord's land and were almost totally dependent on him; *and* the system lasted into the nineteenth century!

The ministers of the 'Enlightenment' under Charles III (1759–88) tried to bring about the reform of land tenure and to create new agricultural colonies, but without much success. In 1780 the last Duke of Arcos, Francisco Ponce de León, died, without heirs and the *señorío* passed to his cousin, the Countess-Duchess of Benavente, who was married to the Duke of Osuna (among the grandees it was, and is, a small world). She acted rather more liberally than her predecessor as far as the municipal and common lands were concerned. There was a shift from livestock – sheep and wool in particular, due to the collapse of the wool trade – into cereals, olives, vines and horse-breeding with mildly increased job opportunities. Even so, 80 per cent of the working population remained landless labourers. The Constitution of Cádiz, passed in 1812 by the goverment in exile during the Peninsular War, declared against the *señoríos* but it was not until the Liberal triennium of 1820–23 that they were finally dissolved and their regimes abolished.

But Spanish 'liberalism' turned out to be a very different kind of animal from what we understand by the term. It was 'progressive' in one sense: it believed in railways and trade. Yet it aimed at highly centralised powers and was far from devolutionary; in the 1830s it adopted a provincial system modelled on the French with civil and military governors rather than prefects. But the most famous act of the Liberal establishment was the *desamortización* or disentailment and sale of Church lands, started in 1835. This enormous acreage of property was almost all snapped up by lawyers and businessmen who could raise the funds needed by the government to pay its debts. The result was a new type of *latifundismo* or concentration of large estates in a few hands, perhaps to an even greater extent than under the discredited religious and seigneurial regimes, which had been slightly tempered by the obligations of charity and *noblesse oblige*. The number of landless labourers did not fall, but increased. The first law of *desamortización* was followed from 1855 onwards by a second wave of *desamortizaciones*, this time of municipal lands, including the communal forests, woods, pastures and grazings which had previously been let to small farmers or were open to all. These too were auctioned off to the highest bidder. Privatisation of utilities and housing in Britain in the 1980s undoubtedly widened share- and property-ownership. The Spanish privatisations of the mid-nineteenth century, in a still largely rural society, had the opposite effect.

Thus we come back to the age-old bitterness in the south, based on the paradox of 'rich land, poor people'. The fact that much of the land was second or third class and the agricultural goldmine largely mythical had little effect on popular perception, when the few clearly lived well and the many did not. This was when Anarchism took root and began to spread rapidly. Unrest and uprisings took place in 1855, 1862, 1868 and 1869. Anarchist cells grew up in Arcos and in the surrounding towns and villages of Algar, Bornos, Espera, Prado del Rey and Villamartín. The majority of the labourers, who as a class formed the vast majority of the population, were lucky to work 160 days a year for a miserable wage.

Despite their idealist philosophy, the almost sub-human

conditions in which they lived tended to fuel violence among the Anarchists. Anarcho-Syndicalism, less idealistic and more political, eventually won the day in the south and established itself firmly in Arcos, as in Jerez. Palliative attempts were made through irrigation works in the first two decades of the twentieth century but they had little effect on the ordinary labourer. Jerez boasted one of the most important concentrations of capital in Spain, with the worst social record. Under the dictatorship of Primo de Rivera, himself an Andalusian, major public works were undertaken, which mopped up a good deal of labour. But the great hopes pinned on 'the railway that never was', designed to open up the interior trade and commerce, were disappointed. Primo's fall was followed the next year by the exile of the king. The third Republic came in 1931. As we have seen at Casas Viejas, alias Benalup, in the matter of agrarian reform the Republic failed too. In this respect it performed no better – one could say worse, owing to the expectations vested in it – than its predecessors.

Such is the background. Small wonder that consumerism has found ready takers, undeterred by prophecies about the *sociedad del colapso*; the intellectuals will have to work hard to get that one across. Since 1965 Arcos has been the beneficiary of a reservoir, which has given rise to a good deal of development: there are flats and villas with lawns running down to the edge, restaurants, a palm-shaded *merendero* or picnic site, a paddle-steamer and aquatic sports. As a result the river Guadalete has been reduced to a mere trickle, but Arcos has been happy to swap a meandering stream for these new amenities. The Pantano de Arcos, as it is called, is linked to the much larger Pantano de Bornos, completed in 1961. Bornos is the next town upstream.

The so-called *playa* of Bornos has a slightly evil feel to it. It is a stretch of much-littered and well-trodden grass, breaking off abruptly where the water has ebbed a little from the submerged fields, leaving a muddy strand. Here all the contradictions of modern Andalusia are assembled in peculiar and poignant juxtaposition. There is a disco-pub, which is a sort of round-the-clock nightclub; there are two or three *chiringuitos* or shanty-bars; cows graze and rub themselves against almond and acacia trees in a wired pen next to the carpark. Across the glassy surface of the lake rise the peerless mountains of the Sierra de Grazalema, looking just as if they had emerged fresh from a romantic watercolourist's brush.

Running up from the waterfront are streets of single-storey fisherman-type houses which were there, curiously enough, before the unexpected bounty of the lake arrived. Men in cloth caps, T-shirts and braces exchange jests and ribaldry between one doorway and the next. Gypsies squat playing cards on the pavement, or mending a bicycle, or clapping their hands as if to conjure up a vanished song. It is a town of dogs, too: skeletal greyhounds, matted poodles, half-breed Alsatians, pert pets and scavenging strays, as many dogs as humans . . . or so it seems. Nearer the centre is the club of Comisiones Obreras, the Communist trade union. It is a bare room with a few chairs and tables, a pin-table and a portable zinc-topped bar supplied by Coca-Cola.

Early in the morning each Bornos housewife waters the pavement outside her door. The dogs are out and about, sniffing at refuse sacks, until scattered by the municipal rubbish lorry zooming up the street like a tank with its attendant infantry, who load up their unsavoury cargo with every appearance of good humour, for at least they have a job. In the *cafelillo*, where the men gather, documents are studied and deals made. An old man at the counter dunks his *madalena* in his coffee; a companion enters, lays an arm across his back and wishes him 'Buen provecho,' to which the other answers, 'Gracias, amigo. Usted quiere?' In all these towns the traditional courtesies apply. Your breakfast, or any other meal for that matter, must be offered to who-ever sits down at your table. 'Buen provecho,' which accompanies the no less obligatory refusal, is a utilitarian version of 'Bon appétit' and means: May it do you good! These two phrases neatly illustrate the difference between French and Spanish attitudes to food.

Though Bornos today has a strong proletarian atmosphere, it too was an old township within the seigneurial system. Its overlordship changed hands several times. It was sold in 1362 by Juan Ponce de León to the master of the military order of Calatrava, who sold it to the Ribera family in 1398. The Riberas were also lords of Alcalá de los Gazules. Don Fadrique Enríquez de Ribera, first Marquis of Tarifa and builder of the superb Casa de Pilatos in Seville, left it to his nephew, the first Duke of Alcalá and Viceroy of Naples, in whose line it continued till it fell by marriage to the dukes of Medinaceli – with whom it remained until the final extinction of the señoríos.

Bornos can thus recite a rollcall of great names, which are of little help to its present condition but add a whiff of faded grandeur, to which Spaniards are seldom averse. Though it is low-lying and offers no dramatic silhouettes in the style of Ronda or Arcos, several of its buildings testify to those aristocratic connections. First and foremost is the 'palace-castle' of the Riberas, a rambling pile in poor repair with crenellated walls and some signs of past magnificence, as in the finely carved Plateresque decoration round the windows. Across the plaza is the parish church of Santo Domingo, with a good tower of 1792. The interior – whose walls, columns and cupola are all, unusually, painted plain white – provides a gracious and luminous setting for the great gilded retable. Otherwise there is little decoration and there are few saints; these were presumably destroyed in some outburst of 'Spanish fury'.

Higher up stands the convent of Corpus Christi. Expensively restored as a 'social work' by the Jerez Savings Bank, it is now a vocational education centre. The sixteenth-century cloister has been given the purist treatment and stripped back to bare brick and white columns. The spacious austere lecture halls, equipped with steel and plastic chairs with spatulate arms for note-taking, look business-like. The young twitter and flutter like starlings on the grand entrance steps and then troop dutifully in to get their qualifications. The pedagogic tradition of dominie and disciples is still strong here: old-fashioned perhaps, but Spain is creeping up the European educational league table. In the tug-of-war between this ex-conventual training centre and the disco-pubs and *chiringuitos*, the latter may have the stronger pull, but at least Spain does offer vocational education in buildings that can vie with Winchester or Eton.

The real jewel of Bornos, however, is hidden behind the walls of the decrepit palace. It is described in the history notes provided by the town hall as a 'Renaissance garden'. Though it undoubtedly has some Renaissance features, it struck me much more as a particularly charming example of an old Spanish garden of Moorish inspiration, on the lines of the Alcázar gardens in Seville. It is not as large as those, of course, confined as it is on three sides by crenellated wall and on the fourth by the run-down mansion. In the centre there is a pagoda with benches of sixteenth-century tiles. The beds, framed by low hedges of box or privet, contain masses of chrysanthemums, shaded by orange trees, oleanders and miniature palms – an unexpected combination. Also, less surprisingly, the *manzanilla* or camomile plant abounds around the bases of straggling, floppy roses, which are not pruned back as in England to produce the perfect bloom. The paths are of yellow sand or of small narrow cobbles laid in the mosaic style which dates back to Roman times. Among the bigger trees are some enormous magnolias, carrying a sort of soft cone after the shedding of the flower; and tall palms of course; and acacias, medlars and cypresses.

The Renaissance is evident in a blind arcade with empty niches, clearly designed for the antique statues that the Ribera or Medinaceli families planned to bring back from their diplomatic or viceregal missions to Naples or Rome: whether they were ever filled and then despoiled I do not know. There is also a lily pond presided over by an unconvincingly alarmed virgin, clutching her robe to her breasts; and a grotto suggesting the influence of Mantua or Verona.

The walls of the building overlooking the garden are simply those of an old Spanish *caserón*, a warren-like family dwelling with little palatial about it except for such touches as the Plateresque windows. The roofs are like those of a large farmhouse, with pigeons clustering on the tiles. There is an element of grandeur in the main courtyard with its upper gallery resting on a lower arcade of highly stepped arches – but this extends round only two sides, and it is all in bad repair. In the tunnel-like *zaguán* or porch, through which carriages once rolled, live the municipal dust-carts. Sooner or later the Beaux Arts zealots will move in and spruce it all up; in the meantime the genuine aroma of old provincial Spain still pervades this place.

The opening hours are regular and strict: nine to one and three to six in winter, stretching to seven on summer evenings. Why couldn't they be longer? How lovely to linger here under the giant magnolias in the summer dusk! The custodian shook his head firmly. If it stayed open any later, the young would abuse and vandalise it. I could see no sign of riotous youth. One couple of *novios* were taking snapshots of each other in an empty niche of the Renaissance screen. Otherwise the precinct was left entirely to some elders from the adjacent old folks' home ... and myself. I said as much, but the custodian was adamant.

'You can't trust the young,' he said. 'They respect nothing.'

I reflected on the fear the middle-aged always have of the young, from which perhaps none of us is quite exempt.

Ejected from the magical garden, I returned to the *playa*. Its unashamed squalor and its superb view would, I thought, help to concentrate the mind. A *chiringuito* produced squid and red wine. Some of the mistrusted young were doing the *macho* motorbike routine; others were quietly fishing.

What was it, I asked myself, about these towns which I

found titillating, yet faintly sinister, as if I were on the brink of addiction to a drug? Of course, they varied a bit, but there were common characteristics. Alcalá, Medina and Arcos were all oriented to a greater or lesser extent towards the Atlantic. The palimpsest of torn bullfight posters on their walls and hoardings spoke of the renowned bullrings of the bay: San Fernando, El Puerto, Sanlúcar, all bywords for fastidious fans who despised the fraudulent showbiz fights of Puerto Banus and Marbella. In all these old towns of the hinterland one savoured a sense of the authentic . . . a smell of the tawny fields . . . a tang of the sea . . . a whiff of paganism . . . a glint of Alberti's sparkling poems. Bornos, contemplating its own deadpan lake, also felt the tug towards the ripples and the spray, as evidenced by its parody of a beach. But here there was a corresponding pull from the dusty satellite towns around Seville, such as Utrera and Carmona with their grainland economies.

Whichever way they faced, however, whether towards the sea or the valley of the great river, these old seigneurial towns had adapted to the modern world with outward conformity but some kind of inner scepticism. This had its attractions. *Le cafard* . . . *l'ennui* of the French found their apotheosis in Andalusian *aburrimiento*, the art of spinning out the day without false expectations. They were thus not bad places for a weary expatriate content to dabble in their past and gain a limited entrée to their society and customs. In any one of them such a person could decline gently and with some respect, becoming part of the process of disintegration, the leafmould of history . . .

I raised my eyes just in time to the sharp-spined crouching mass of the Serranía. In its folds were the mountain pueblos with their rawer climate, fresher air and sterner attitudes. The mood that had been stealing over me began to recede. Of course, one must beware romanticising the highlands as much as anywhere else, but I felt suddenly that it was time to answer the call of the hills.

◆

Choosing a different route back, I skirted Arcos and headed for Algar, on whose edge I stopped at a *venta* for lunch. The landlord was full of talk and bombast. His great-great-great-great-grandfather had been an aristocrat, member of the select Maestranza de Ronda, designer of the *plaza de toros*, count of this and that, a grandee of Spain and goodness knows what else besides. He produced a photograph of a portrait of his ancestor which, he said, Ronda longed to get its hands on. He himself had been mayor of Algar for several years. Many people were dissatisfied with the present administration and were putting pressure on him to stand again. He just might, but he doubted if he would be persuaded. During his term of office he did many things for the town: he began the road from Algar to El Bosque; he also completed the upper terraces of the bullring, which had stood unfinished ever since its founder, the then mayor, was stabbed to death with fourteen wounds outside its entrance on the outbreak of the Civil War.

'Fourteen dagger thrusts,' he repeated with relish, as if this proved that Algar was no mean pueblo.

It is in fact a harsh little grid of a place: two thousand inhabitants, straight streets, neat houses, proper little square, no quaint corners – not inviting. But its countryside is pleasant and rolling. The ex-mayor's unmade road to El Bosque winds between ilex-crowned hillocks, on which sheep browse while their shepherds sit with their staves by the roadside – in some cases they are only children. Arcadia immediately springs to mind. Is this it? Have we arrived? Where is its capital?

El Gastor (as I have suggested) has abdicated the role. Algar is not in itself attractive. What about El Bosque, with its winsome name (the Copse)? The track continues, following the pine-clad verge of the Embalse de los Hurones, another great reservoir dating from the early sixties. Creeks nuzzle up to the roots of the trees, forming dappled pools under the overhanging foliage. When one leaves the lake there are more undulating pastures, with horses and a stud farm. It all looks promising. Perhaps this is journey's end? Alas, there is something not quite right about El Bosque. It possesses most of the attributes of the ideal *pueblo blanco*: nice setting, gleaming white houses; a proper bullring; and additional amenities such as a three-star hostelry and a fine municipal *piscina*. Also, it houses the office and information centre of the Parque Natural de Grazalema, from which useful maps and leaflets can be obtained. It can thus lay claim to being the capital of that *turismo rural* which the regional government earnestly strives to promote and which must surely be a good thing in economic terms for the pueblo and in human terms for those who need to escape from the *sociedad del colapso*.

With so much going for it, what's wrong? Where's the rub? It's hard to put a finger on it, but the architecture contributes: El Bosque's houses are squat and smug; the town hall, rebuilt in the Franco period, intends to be imposing but has mean drainpipe columns supporting its arches; forbiddingly fenced chalets, some with guard dogs, surround the core. Yet, more important and insidious is the sense that the place is not candid about itself, is holding something back. Despite the information centre, gift shops, souvenirs, postcards, local 'crafts' (mainly hideous leathergoods from neighbouring Ubrique) and similar aspects of the consumer-friendly face – despite all this, there is a pervasive impression of concealed lives, doorways less open than elsewhere, watchful eyes behind shutters, possibly of congenital madness confined in small back rooms. Towns and villages, like people, have distinct personae, and the atmosphere here has neither the unashamed vulgarity of the coast, nor the open decadence of the hill towns round the bay, nor the bluff innocence of, say, Cañete or Teba. And nobody is beautiful.

But that is a jaundiced and prejudiced view, I can hear someone expostulating, which also smacks of snobbery. Why should the egoism of the *soi-disant* 'traveller', self-appointed connoisseur of native culture, deserve more

consideration than the simpler and less pretentious requirements of the tourist or the economic interests of the district? Are not these folk striving, with a bit of government
help, to build a thriving economy? Be off with you and your
fine disdain and fancy notions about Arcady! Get you to
your run-down, ramshackle, rickety mountain pueblos and
expire of boredom in them if you so wish . . . but leave
honest, up-and-coming places free of your puffed-up sensibility and aesthetic sermonising! Spare us your condescension! Leave us in peace!

Thus spoke El Bosque. I bowed my head and fled. No
capital of Arcadia this! I found myself driving rather faster
than was wise up the next stretch of road, thoughtfully
edged in green by Michelin to indicate a 'scenic route'.
Down on the left nestled Benamahoma, which I knew to be
a sweet place – much patted on the back for its old market
gardens, trout farm and cottage industry of rush-backed
chairs. But I wanted to get up higher; the summons of the
sierras was strong within me. As I swung up towards the
Puerto de Boyar above Grazalema, my first acquaintance
with this pass came back to me vividly.

My cavalry officer friend, Johnnie Watson of the Blues,
and I had toiled up on our grey mares from Grazalema,
protected by our Metropolitan Police capes which spread
over our mounts' wet flanks and rumps; we were heading
into a sharp west wind and peering through mist with a
visibility of just a few yards; the unsurfaced road petered
out short of the Boyar pass. We had only an inaccurate
military map and the lie of the land to guide us. An abandoned hut provided a welcome shelter for a short halt and
a long pull at the brandy flask. When we reached the top,
there was a sudden rent in the clouds and liberated rays of
sun came leaping and dancing down glen after green glen,
turning them briefly to gold, against a background of dark
purple hills and yet more hills, all under a bruised and
turbulent sky. Then the mist swirled back, the vision vanished and we toiled on . . . to reap our reward three days

later in the shape of steaming baths, a fine dinner and much self-esteem at our exploit in the best hotel of Jerez.

Now it was all brightly packaged. Two or three campsites, gay with red, blue, yellow tents, were crammed; jolly repasts were enlivened by electronic music at rustic tables under the pines. Cyclists and backpacked roamers contended with a fair flow of cars along the road. Wire fences kept everyone without a permit well out of the *pinsapares*, where the millenary pines were guarded with archaeological solicitude. Frequent signs warned of forest fire. I recalled Don Mariano's view that the landowning class had been nature's true friends, and that when the urban masses were let loose on her fair face there would of necessity have to be severe restrictions: few would be criminal arsonists, but many would be careless and almost none would have the familiarity with country lore that was inherent in aristocrats and their retainers. Restrictions or no, however, newly mobile urban man was on the move that day, swarming over those portions of his inheritance permitted by the authorities.

Emerging on the Seville road, I turned towards Ronda. I coasted down the serpentine curves between Sanguijuela's steep wooded slopes and the table-mountain, topped by the farm of El Cupil, which hangs over our valley. Reaching the valley floor I crossed the railway and began to climb towards the very noble and very loyal city, encased in its new battlements of concrete. Shortly I switched onto the Benaoján road and started to sink again . . . past the Legionnaires' camp . . . past the rural school . . . past the *tienda*, the universal shop-cum-bar of Paco el Bueno . . . down through the scattered settlement of La Indiana . . . back over the railway track twice on unguarded crossings . . . and so to the *campo*. I had come full circle. But I had reached no conclusion, and was suddenly aware of this.

Paco's cart and mules stood a few yards from the house. Their owner and his son Antonio were sacking maize cobs and piling them on board. He came forward with his hand outstretched and a broad grin. I had not seen him for some weeks.

'Well, well,' he said, 'home is the traveller. How was your journey?'

'Good,' I said. 'Very good. I have seen a lot.'

'You should have taken me with you. You know how I love to see other pueblos, and never do because I am a slave here to your land and mine. But I doubt if you have seen anything preferable to this?'

'I am not so sure,' I answered. 'I have seen some very fine places.'

'But not Cádiz way, I warrant?'

He touched his right cheek just under the eye to indicate that all Cádiz men are homosexuals.

'There are fine places there too,' I said evenly, 'fine old cities near the sea.'

He shrugged; there was no accounting for tastes. Would I be staying for the fair?

I said I certainly would. The September fair was the climax of Ronda's year and I had not coincided with it for some time, so I was determined to participate to the hilt. Who knew? It might be the last fling.

'Good, then we'll have a *copa* or two in the *feria*,' Paco said. 'Now I must be getting on.'

I watched him depart with his crop, his beasts and his son. Whatever our disagreements, I could not help admiring him, a peasant of the old school, tough, cunning, skilled in his own way. If we stayed in the *campo*, Paco or someone very like him would always be our lot. That must be clear in our minds when we made our choice.

10

FUN OF THE FAIR

The *feria* is the main secular event in the calendar of all Andalusian pueblos, large and small. Traditionally it consists of three interlocking spheres of action: the livestock fair or *mercado de bestias*, the funfair, and the bullfight or series of bullfights. Though *los toros* are sometimes associated with religious celebrations, for example on Easter Sunday, at fairtime in most pueblos religion takes a back seat. This secular impulse goes right back to the medieval monarchies, and was encouraged by Philip II. Fairs then required a royal licence. These were intensely lobbied for by municipalities, their attraction being that goods brought into or out of a city during the relevant period – which might be ten days, twenty, or even a month – were exempted from the crippling royal taxes called *alcabala, peaje, portazgo*, etc. It was a good way for the Crown to reward loyal and favoured cities – and later to ask them for hefty subsidies out of the proceeds.

Ronda still has two fairs of ancient origin in May and October. But since 1954 a new fair, the *Feria de Pedro Romero*, which takes place in September, has far outshone the other two. This was designed to commemorate the bicentenary of the birth of the great matador who virtually modelled the *fiesta nacional* as we know it today. The main bullfight is called a *corrida goyesca* because it is fought in the period dress in which Goya painted some of the principal bullfighters of his day. There is thus a strong flavour in the September fair of bulls and the virility and symbolism associated with them.

Of the other two prongs, the livestock market has become by far the weakest. This was when the *campo* used to come to town, and the owners of herds and flocks demonstrated and exchanged their wealth. But as the town has grown, the livestock area has been thrust further and further onto the periphery. At the same time, there has been a dramatic reduction in the number of draught animals, coupled with bans on animal movement, first because of 'African' swine fever, which confined pigs to their farms for almost twenty years, and then to the more recent outbreak of the dreaded *peste equina*. So animal markets are not what they were, though they still take place in an attenuated form in evidence of a continuing if reduced rural economy.

The third prong, the funfair, has if anything grown and prospered with the arrival of dodgems and dippers and the railway of horror and palaces of science fiction. Ronda's funfair, like Seville's and those of all larger pueblos, is a temporary township set up for a week in a *campo de feria* on the outskirts. It is complete with streets, booths, bars, amusements, *cafeterías*, *chocolaterías*, *pizzerías* and above all with the *casetas* of the various clubs and professional and workers' associations.

You can't plunge into all this cold. There is a warming-up process, which takes place in the main streets and squares of the town. Under awnings and paper lanterns temporary zinc bar counters are set up on the pavements with tables and chairs in the roadway, denying access to all traffic. The hundreds of permanent establishments do not seem perturbed; they are packed too. The Plaza del Socorro is the hub. I took up position on the *casino* terrace. Some striplings sauntered by in *traje corto*, the uniform of the ranch consisting of flat-crowned hat, bolero jacket, cummerbund, striped trousers and half-boots. Their dads may have owned no more than a chalet and a swimming pool, but this was the way you strutted into town. Upper-class girls, and

343

Why do respectable females exhibit themselves like this in public?

mature ladies too, were parading in *traje de gitana*, gypsy dress with tight bodice and a flamboyant pattern of large dots on bright colours, hugging the thigh and then frothing out into many flounces. Why do respectable females exhibit themselves like this in public? Some say that gypsy costume, music and dance provide a mask which permits wilder and more shameless behaviour than is the norm. At the same time, the element of fancy dress suggests that the shamelessness is assumed, not deep-seated or real. The lid is not off the pressure cooker but a valve is provided for the escape of some steam.

The fraternity of the horse arrived next – a dozen or so

all told, composed of young bloods, the *picador* or riding instructor of the Maestranza, an old swell with a girl up behind, some cut-throat-looking gypsies behaving like kings on horseback, and a couple of bourgeois children who had been taking lessons and were proudly escorted by their parents on foot. All of the group displayed cool horse management in the crowd. The adults also managed a stirrup-cup, a tulip-shaped glass of sherry, with aplomb; this was the fount of *alegría*, the spirit of the fair, but you did not drink it all; you returned it to the waiter with a thimbleful undrunk; there were several more days to come; excess was bad form. The old swell, bulky, lizard-eyed, coaxed his mount into dancing a few steps to the music that poured out of the loudspeakers; then the little cavalcade moved on.

The Calle de la Bola, apart from the paper lanterns, was much its usual self. The *paseo* is always a conspicuous display of leisure, heightened a little during the fair, when it is also more democratic, because everyone who has two pesetas to rub together takes part and looks smart. Proceeding in a stately fashion through the throng came Don Pedro Sánchez Castillo, an ex-mayor, now suffering from poor eyesight, conducted by a retinue of sons and relatives; he stopped every few yards to greet and be greeted.

'Don Pedro, what a joy to see you! How are you?' I said.

'Mister Boyd, I too am overjoyed. Frankly, I am not too well. My sight is not at all good. But I manage. With the help of many kind friends I get by.'

He and his entourage moved on, but were stopped five paces further on by someone else. Later I saw him comfortably settled with his court at one of the *casino* tables.

I moved in the direction of the Bar Jerez, where the *señoritos* gather. There indeed they were: two or three landowners, a dentist, a doctor, an influential official, all interrelated. They opened their circle to include me.

One of them to whom I had once taught English, Eduardo by name, said, 'Mister Boyd, *tu eres una institución ya en Ronda.*'

345

Mister Boyd, thou art – formalism and intimacy on a collision course! I reflected, not for the first time, on the appalling disadvantage of having a Christian name with no equivalent in other tongues. That is why I called my son James ... Jaime ... Jacques. There are other good names too, like Philip and Martin and John. Alastair, get thee to thy Celtic mists!

Round the corner I was plucked into the Bar Mediterráneo by an ironmonger's assistant, with whom I often exchanged bullfighting gossip. He called at once for a glass of *manzanilla*, the delicious light, fresh relation of sherry from Sanlúcar with its hint of the sea.

'Are you going to the bulls this afternoon?' he asked.

'Yes, of course. Have you seen them?'

'Yes, they look good. With plenty of *trapío*.'

'Let's hope we're lucky then.'

'Yes, let's hope so.'

I went next in search of my regular bullfight companion, Rafael Valiente of La Mimbre. I soon spotted his Roman profile under a peaked cap. He was standing back on the pavement and surveying his new building under construction in the Calle Sevilla; it was to have six dwellings and a lift.

'So the *campo* is still prospering, despite you farmers' complaints!'

'It is very hard to make money,' said Rafael. 'One has to be mechanised. I have my tractor, the harrow, the long rake. I only lack a baler; I hire that. And of course I have the milking machine, which is essential – you have seen it, haven't you?'

I had indeed. The gleaming apparatus with its tubes and coils lurked like an alien in Rafael's dark old stable behind his Spartan farmhouse.

'Now, look at my hands.'

He held them out, They were smooth, without calluses, and the nail of his left little finger was longer than the rest to indicate that he was no mere labourer. I said they were better kept than my own and he smiled with satisfaction. His builder arrived and I left them to an earnest discussion on costs, having agreed that we would meet for lunch at the Peña de Pepe Luis Martín.

This *peña* is the fan club of the *torero* of that name, whose strong supporter Rafael remains, despite his lack of success in landing contracts since he became a full matador. There is a bar and a restaurant and you can read the taurine press and watch the *corridas* in other towns on television. The boy who serves the bar is against the bullfight.

'We have no right to do such things to animals.'

'You should be working in a football or a tennis club, then.'

'I don't agree. My opinions have nothing to do with my work behind the bar.'

'But surely you must have seen Pepe Luis fight?'

'Yes, I have watched him on the TV.'

'Did you watch him take his *alternativa* (graduation ceremony to full matador) last year in Málaga?'

'Yes.'

'Was he good?'

'Superb. Considering he drew the worst of the lots. The second bull, from which he cut the ear, was very difficult. But he knew how to manage him. He is a born *torero*. Look!'

He took me over to a wall plastered with photographs. In one the baby Pepe Luis was being baptised, cradled in a matador's embroidered parade cape.

'His father was a *novillero*,' the barman went on, 'who became deaf as a result of an infection that went wrong in the army, so he had to give it up. Now he is a taxidermist – he stuffed and mounted that fox over there. Is it not lifelike? But he was determined that Pepe Luis should become a matador. Now, look over here.'

This time it was a picture of Pepe Luis aged three and a half with a *muleta*, provoking the charge of an older boy holding a pair of horns in front of him.

'So he was brought up to fulfil his father's dream?'

'Absolutely.'

'And you don't object to that?'

'Why should I? Each one follows his own calling.'

'But how many share your opinion about bullfighting in general? Do you think it will continue? What do the young think?'

'They don't like it. They don't go like their parents did. They are not enthusiastic.'

'So you think it could wither away?'

'Perhaps eventually. I think it should. But it is tradition, it is custom. You can't imagine Spain without it. If it happens, it will be very slow. It will take a hundred years.'

Nicolás Aguilera, a horse-fancier and retired *rejoneador*, had just come to the counter and was listening.

'There is a movement against the *fiesta*,' he agreed, 'but so far it is a small minority, mainly *ecologistas*. And there have been some rumblings in the European Parliament.'

'There is no European jurisdiction that I know of,' I said. 'Also, it would be extremely difficult to abolish as long as bulls are fought in the south of France and the authorities turn a blind eye to it.'

'Precisely. There was talk of abolition under the socialist government way back in the days of Belmonte, but it came to nothing. Ultimately the *fiesta* will survive or die not by edict but through its *aficionados*.'

I put to him the same criticism of the breeders that I had put to Don Diego Romero. How long would the public stand for rotten bulls?

Nicolás looked grave.

'That is the crux. The fighting bull is the foundation of the *fiesta*. They are not all rotten. There are still some good breeders. You should have seen the bull of the Conde de la Corte in the last breeders' concourse in Ronda; it was frankly magnificent. It tore down a whole *burladero* and splintered it to matchsticks. But Carlos Nuñez, Domecq . . . the so-called "bulls on wheels" . . . you can forget them. Therefore, there will have to be a reform of the *fiesta* if it is to survive in the long run. First, the artificial feed must be cut and the pasturage revived. Then the *suerte de varas*, the picador's act, must be changed. When a 500-kilo bull, already weakened by bad diet, charges the man and horse weighing 1200 kilos all told, he takes too much punishment. Smaller horses and shorter steel points on the *puya* will have to come.'

I recalled Don Mariano's view to the same effect. But I had also read old accounts of spectacular *corridas* in which, to take one instance, five out of six bulls of Graciliano Pérez Tabernero (the other was a coward) charged the picadors twenty-nine times between them, overthrew the picador several times and killed one horse – even though the *peto*, the mattress-covering of the chest, right flank and belly of the picador's mount had already been introduced. Going further back, there were recorded instances of an individual bull charging the mounted men eleven or even thirteen times. Clearly the animals we were talking about were pale shadows of these, even though some of the same blood might run in their veins.

'And what is the likelihood of getting your reforms?' I asked Nicolás.

'I shall preach them,' he said, 'as long as I have breath in my lungs. But I am not a breeder. I am not Alvaro Domecq. The trouble is that seventeen generations of bulls have been denatured since the Civil War and you can't produce a new strain overnight. It'll take time.'

'But are the breeders willing to put their house in order?'

'If they don't, it will be their fault, not Europe's or the ecologists' or anyone else's if the *fiesta* dies. And then indeed Spain won't be Spain any more.'

That phrase, that refrain, took me back to Diana's and my hesitant and then total conversion to the bullfight. It was simply the most different, the most dramatic, the most foreign thing about the new way of life we had adopted; it proved to us, if anything did, that we had stepped into another world, and helped to maintain our sense of wonder at the change. We were determined almost as a matter of duty not to be squeamish. We saw some very bad fights, in fact some disgraceful ones. But we also followed the rivalry between Luis Miguel Dominguín and Antonio Ordóñez . . . and then Ordóñez's masterly lessons in the classic style in the early Ronda *goyescas*, exquisite but emotionless, with the bulls carefully selected for their almost hypnotised obedience to the magician. By way of contrast we saw Miguel Baez 'Litri' (senior) in his apocalyptic four-season career: he would challenge the bull from twenty or thirty paces to an *estatuario*, in which he would gaze up with his Cyrano-like profile to the gallery and the gods while the beast plunged past his tasselled tunic, on which it left its blood. The celebrated *tremendista* El Cordobés with his jerky, awkward, risk-taking stunts never equalled this. One year we made a minor cult of a lesser figure, Gregorio Sánchez, who led the top league for that season I think. Gregorio was an in-fighter if ever there was one: not suave and smooth like Ordóñez, nor effortless like Luis Miguel, nor a stuntman like El Cordobés, but determined to extract the last ounce of fight out of his enemy, however unpromising. Up and down the land he got stuck into everything that came his way, and fought it valiantly and killed it well. He was especially popular in the small cities around Madrid, where there was no other entertainment but pigeon-fancying and cockfighting and where the great event of the year was the bulls. I remembered Gregorio in the dust of Talavera de la Reina . . . and of Aranjuez . . . and of Guadalajara, where Diana and I got hopelessly drunk in his honour and had to be conveyed back by taxi to the Gran Hotel Velázquez in Madrid, where we were staying beyond our means. The demeanour of the grand commissionaire in his cockaded hat, who greeted us at the imposing entrance, was magnificently impassive.

Though we had some notion of the historical development of the bullfight, in which Ronda had played an important part, its anthropological significance was of little concern to us then. It was clear from early days that what we were witnessing was not a sport but a ritual, and that very demanding criteria governed its correct execution. Yet it was not till much later – through reading authors such as John and Mary Corbin and Garry Marvin – that I became interested in the latent symbolism.

Personal honour and heroism are of course important. But the opportunity for their exercise would not arise were it not for the deeper requirement of the bullfight, which is to symbolise the domination of 'culture' over 'nature'. Paradoxically what we call 'barbaric' is in terms of Andalusian culture 'civilised'. The bull is brought from the countryside, the world of nature, to the urban centre, the place of culture where civilised people dwell. His very wildness is the product of human effort and ingenuity, because he is bred from stock specially selected for aggression. Among matadors it is not the fearless exhibitionist who is most admired but the one who conquers his own fear; to succumb to fear is to give way to the beast within, the baser side of human nature.

The contest is between males. The suit of lights exaggerates the shoulders and moulds the genitals of the man; the bull's impressive anatomy is there for all to see. Man and bull each seek to penetrate the body of the other, the matador with an artificial extension of himself, the sword; the bull with his horns which are integral to him. If the matador is gored, he is emasculated and eclipsed into the shades where he is tended by women until he recovers or dies. To avoid emasculation the matador must penetrate the bull successfully and honourably, going in over his horns, having first lured him and worn him down expertly and prepared him for death. But the most important point to be proved is the mastery of humanity over animality, of culture over nature. The matador may achieve high honour and riches for himself, but there is a sense in which he is also Everyman; there is no cult of the body in the bullfight; few matadors look like Greek heroes and their assistants are sometimes absurd; the great Belmonte's physique was so poor that sometimes he could barely shuffle a few yards on the sand; as in many Spanish activities the spirit is the thing. Therefore, it is not true that the *corrida* is a spectacle in which a primitive people gloats passively over blood-letting; it is a bad kill if the bull bleeds from the mouth; the blood is incidental, and the less of it the better. What is true is that the honour of the public is on the line, and they share in the matador's triumph, just as they feel self-disgust at his failure. That is why it is called the *fiesta nacional*. Without any element of international competition, it is the confrontation in which Spain looks at itself.

High-falutin'? Maybe. But if so, it is necessary to ask why the bullfight continues unabated and indeed is on the increase in the major fairs. Most of the explanations I heard on my journeys are fairly unconvincing: namely that it is traditional; that without it there would be no role for the brave bulls; and that it employs a lot of people. As regards tradition, military coups were also traditional, but they have been abandoned; as regards the bulls, many *ganaderos* would be better off if they converted to cereals or domestic livestock; as regards employment, the redundancy of a few thousand people would be as nothing compared to the massive shift from the land to the cities and the huge emigration of recent years – a mere ripple on the labour market. No, these are marginal interest-group considerations and clearly insufficient to keep the *fiesta* alive. Those who say that Spain would not be Spain without it are nearer the mark, and it is probably some sense of its deeper roots in the Spanish psyche that animates both apologists and opponents when they agree that bullfighting will last at least another hundred years.

But there is a final question. If the anthropologists are correct, why do Spaniards need to demonstrate mastery over nature by these archaic means rather than as other nations do – by science, invention, industry and so forth? It is worth remarking that though Spaniards admire medical doctors (representing the triumph of culture over nature) they have little respect for scientists (who hold that all matter is governed by the same principles and who deny the spirit). This is because the Spanish view of the cosmos is essentially hierarchical, a matter as it were of layers: thus plants have more life than things, animals more than plants, humans more than animals, and God more than humans. This is not far removed from the medieval cosmology based on concentric spheres, in which the ether beyond the moon, inhabited by angels, was purer than the sub-lunary domain of men and creatures. Man occupies a unique position in this order. He has links with both the spiritual and the material worlds. He is the link between the superior and inferior orders. He has his being in cities and pueblos where his temples and buildings attempt to reflect the harmony of the universe. His spirituality differentiates him from animals, especially through the exercise of autonomy, the pursuit of honour and the ability to rise above material considerations as do the mystic and the saint; but these qualities are threatened by his animality, 'the beast within', whose worst manifestation is fear, the slinking away, followed by humiliation – the opposite of honour, which is an expression of the spirit. In the bullfight both possibilities exist. Hence the drama. There is no question of delight in cruelty to the animal. That is not the aim, not the focus. The fervently desired outcome is the apotheosis of the man; and if like Belmonte he is too physically weak to run away from the bull or to jump over the *barrera*, so much the more glorious.

Still no sign of Rafael. Where on earth had he got to? Presumably still haggling with his builder. I stretched for the papers. The bullfight critics, I had noticed recently, were being very tough, especially in the national dailies, as opposed to the specialist journals which were more venal and more prodigal with the benefit of the doubt. I picked up a back number of *El País* in which there was a withering critique of the *corrida* of 20 August during the Bilbao fair. Under the headlines *La Mas Absoluta Invalidez* their correspondent wrote: 'The Cobaledas were nice-looking but short of breath. The Cobaledas seemed to be made of butter. Not when they came bounding into the ring. Finely presented, they no sooner emerged from the dark than they galloped eagerly, rushed fiercely at the capes, snorted menacingly, then all of a sudden – *catapum!* – turned into total invalids.'

Later in the same piece he changed the metaphor even more damagingly. 'Veterinary science should study the case of bulls which appear in the ring as cockerels and, suddenly, become hens. From enraged bull to broody hen in two minutes thirty seconds: that was what was happening to the Cobaledas. The metamorphosis of the fighting bull into the broody hen is one of the most common events of modern tauromachy.'

By now I was a little unnerved. If things had come to this pass, what on earth were we going to see this afternoon? I wished Rafael would come, so that we could discuss these dreadful reports. At this moment he walked in with his peaked cap perched jauntily over his high brow, beaked nose and lively eyes; he was full of *bonhomie*, greeting everyone. When I pushed the newspaper towards him, he brushed it aside. The bullfight like everything else had its ups and downs. Some breeders were more scrupulous than others. He had seen some exceptional performances over the last year or so; he did not believe we should be disappointed today.

During lunch we reminisced over *goyescas* good and bad. Some of the early ones were superb, Rafael said, when Ordóñez was in his prime. But later, I reminded him, they had become more and more contrived and more and more expensive. Finally, towards the end of the Franco period I had found them rather nauseating. A bevy of young society ladies in period costume were drawn round the ring in a landau and deposited below their box. When they were seated, Don Fulano de Mengano, a huge toady of Antonio Ordóñez, would come out onto the sand and present the famous matador with a luscious great spray of flowers in plastic, fit for a *diva*. Then the 'bulls on wheels' would be launched from the *toril* and Antonio, followed by his son-in-law or some other favoured youth, would do their stuff in an expert mannerist style quite devoid of any sense of conflict. The bulls either did what they were told, in which case the matadors did some pretty passes, or were speedily despatched if they were disobedient, without any attempt to correct their asperities. It was all a far cry from the guts, grit and sheer determination to get something out of his opponents that Gregorio had displayed on those afternoons of dust and sweat in Guadalajara and Talavera de la Reina.

By this time the *corrida* seemed at such low ebb that I was on the point of deserting it entirely. Then in September 1978 the *goyesca* bubble burst. Antonio was now licensee of the ring. His politics were of the Right and he wanted to have the *corrida* later than usual, on 16 September, this being the date on which Franco's troops had 'liberated' Ronda in 1936. The recently reconstituted Left, led by Antonio's cousin, Juan Harillo, protested that the sixteenth should be a day of mourning, not of celebration; they warned the mayor and the civil governor that if the bullfight went ahead on that day, there would be civil disorder. Antonio was invited to choose another day, and refused. In the event, a *corrida* without any big names was laid on during the normal period of the fair and was boycotted by all the more prosperous citizens; the ring was a quarter full and the afternoon was a fiasco. Harillo was much criticised for pricking the big, beautiful bubble of an occasion on which Ronda gloried in its ancient ring, its favourite son, the large influx of prominent Spaniards and tourists, and its slot on television. But in fact it was a turning point. For the next year, Harillo, by now mayor, organised a decent quality *corrida* at reasonable prices, which was not a flop.

'Do you remember 1979,' I asked Rafael, 'with bulls of

355

the Conde de la Corte?'

'Yes,' he said, 'they were very uneven. The *toreros* were middle rank. Paco Ojén, I think it was, did not shine.'

'True,' I countered, 'but what about the fifth which fell to José Luis Galloso? He was small and fast with splintered horns and there was a wind, but despite all that Galloso did a full *faena* working him very close; he lost the *muleta* once but went right through the repertoire before ending with a series of *manoletinas*; then he delivered a great *estocada* which doubled the bull up and earned him a standing ovation and two ears. It was a good honest fight. It revived my faith . . .'

'Yes, *chico*,' said Rafael soothingly, 'but that was all a long time ago and we have a bullfight to go to this afternoon, remember? I like to get there in good time. Let's be off.'

We sat on the *pilastra*, the stone parapet which carries the columns supporting the gallery; our feet dangled into the *callejón*, the circular passage between the auditorium and the *barrera* into which the bull sometimes jumps. This row of seats is unique to Ronda. It is not patronised by the Maestranza, which has its own boxes, nor by the other *señoritos* who prefer the more expensive *tendidos*; it is where the knowledgeable small farmers and mechanics and artisans go. Though we had had a full lunch with coffee and brandy afterwards, Rafael was provided with his wine-skin and – like everyone else except the toffs – with his *bocadillo* or salami-filled bread roll for half-time. He kept on slipping down into the *callejón* to greet someone further round or chat with some policeman or official of the ring, with all of whom he was on familiar terms.

As he had predicted, it was a good afternoon. The bulls of Joaquín Buendía of Seville *dieron buen juego*, as the critics say: gave a good account of themselves. Of the matadors, I had hoped more of Roberto Domínguez of Valladolid, an elegant pedagogue of tauromachy, who on this occasion was lackadaisical except for a superb kill which sent his second opponent rolling and earned him an ear. Joselito of

Madrid, who had taken on himself the challenging trade name of Belmonte's great partner and rival, drew the worst lot and despatched them efficiently. It was Emilio Muñoz of Seville, whom I favoured least, who stole the show. Emilio exhibited, *par excellence*, the Sevillian style: hunched shoulders, predatory stance; his whole frame poised on the balls of his feet; the right leg slithering forward with the lure extended on that side; then the arrogant advancing of the slim belly to ensure the obligatory smear of blood on the pearly-white, black-piped, eighteenth-century costume when the bull charged.

In his first bull, the second of the afternoon, Emilio took the animal to the horse by elegant *chicuelinas*; managed to get a good series of left-handed *naturales* out of it, followed by chest passes and *estatuarios*; and killed on the first thrust. The president awarded one ear but the public noisily demanded the other, which was eventually conceded. It was his second opponent, however, the magical fifth of the *corrida*, which brought the house down. When Emilio took it to the horse, fluttering the cape under its muzzle and keeping it low to avoid the evening breeze, it needed no coaxing but charged of its own volition from ten or fifteen metres. The picador was faultless, receiving the charge with the lance in the right place (rather than jabbing it in and gouging *after* impact, which is so often the form); then removing and up-ending it as soon as the bull broke from the encounter. The matador gathered it and brought it back with *chicuelinas* to the horse, which it charged again with the same gusto, despite the previous punishment: whatever the mythology of the past, to take two good *puyazos* and be ready for a third is evidence these days of a noble spirit and good breeding. Emilio then performed a varied *faena*, finely tuned to the animal; the bull stumbled and fell once or twice but its bravery always brought it up from the ground and back to the attack.

When he had exhausted the bull's aesthetic possibilities, Emilio lined it up for the kill . . . but at this point there was a spontaneous outbreak of white handkerchiefs all round the ring, demanding that its life be spared (a very rare event) on account of its fine performance and courage. The president refused to pardon the animal. Emilio prepared to kill amid whistles, hisses and catcalls. But instead of plunging forward over the horns, knowing its temper he provoked it to charge one last time; it obliged and he killed it *recibiendo*, that is to say employing the little-used and much esteemed method whereby the bull impales itself on the proffered sword. It fell dead at his feet.

The stadium rose to a man, with a roar of approval. First the bull was awarded a circuit of the ring, drawn by the mules with the chief muleteer cracking his whip over their heads. Then Emilio, having been awarded the two ears, made his circuit collecting hats and tossing them back; picking up wine-skins including Rafael's and deftly suckling from them before his assistant threw them back; gathering up little bouquets of flowers and pressing them to his lips. After this he made a second triumphal round to music, demanded by the crowd and granted by the president. Finally, he brought the picador out into the centre of the ring to receive his ovation too. Thus a brave bull was killed honourably and removed with honours. Furthermore, the old hands were gratified by the confirmation yet again of the adage that the fifth bull is frequently the best. Rafael, who leapt into the ring at the end, was one of those who carried Emilio shoulder-high through the principal entrance and out into the street. I saw no more of him that day.

This was a fair with three taurine spectacles: the mounted *corrida de rejones*, from which I had abstained; the *goyesca* we had just witnessed; and a *novillada* which followed on the third day. The *novillos* (which must be under four years old or over five and can include large bulls which have been rejected for formal *corridas*) were provided by Cayetano Muñoz of Zafra in Estremadura for Manuel Caballero of Albacete, Jesulín de Ubrique (the local hero) and Antonio

Borrero 'Chamaco', son of a tough but inelegant matador of the same name.

Again, I sat next to Rafael, still glowing from the triumph of the previous day. Jesulín, a tall lanky lad, who was top of the league table for the season with ninety-nine *novilladas* to his name, was due shortly to take his *alternativa*, promoting him to full matador, in Nîmes. Today he was unlucky or unwise, or both, with a cowardly and vicious bull. Having placed spectacular *banderillas*, he started his *faena* with left-handed *naturales* in the terrain of the bull near the *barrera* without bringing him out into the centre and dominating him first: he was rewarded with a leg wound and then with a dislocated wrist after hitting bone on his first *estocada*; each subsequent thrust was obviously an agony; finally he succeeded and was marched off to the infirmary, from which he did not reappear.

Chamaco is a sturdy little chap with plenty of courage, not unlike his father, who was there hissing advice from the *barrera*. But he has a wooden style and not enough nous to give the bull his space – as Dad was busy pointing out. He did poorly with his first adversary. His second, the last of the afternoon, was *toraco*, a huge beast of nearly 500 kilos, *negro bragao* (black with white pants), at which he chopped and chipped away with short punitive passes of no elegance whatsoever. To liven things up he turned his back on it several times, switching the lure to the other side in the manner of El Cordobés; the *toro* was not impressed, nor was the crowd and not much came of these antics. Yet, despite his short stature – 'He needs the electric light company's ladder,' yelled one spectator. 'Fetch him the ladder!' – he managed to get in over the horns and kill on his first thrust, for which he received an ear, having salvaged his honour. As Rafael said, 'The business of a matador is to kill, and if he can't do that, the rest is worthless.'

The afternoon was made and indeed much adorned by Manuel Caballero with his cool style, long stately passes and various originalities, which were to earn him comparison in the press with the young Ordóñez. In addition to fighting the first and the fourth bulls of the afternoon and earning two ears with the latter, he also fought the fifth in lieu of the injured Jesulín and once more impressed. But his *estocada*, which looked well placed, was not quite sufficient; the bull lurched to the boards but refused to lie down and become officially dead.

'*Saca la espada, hombre!*' admonished the crowd. 'Take out the steel and let in the air. He is dead on his feet!'

Manuel obliged. He leant over the horns and extracted the sword by hand (rather than hoicking it out with the cross-piece of the *descabello* weapon, as was usual); thus he let in the air of death; the bull duly died. On his way out, before his fans lifted him onto their shoulders, he scooped up a handful of sand, raised it to his lips and kissed it in a gesture of gratitude to the old ring where he had been lucky and whose approval would ease his way to fame and fortune in the future.

Such were the two *corridas* I saw in the Ronda fair; both were above average; the bulls had been adequate or better; the stench of decadence had not defiled the arena. Rafael was delighted.

'What did I tell you?' he asked. 'You can't believe everything you read in the papers.'

That evening I gave a supper party for Ana and her family and others who had been crucial to our survival both in Ronda and the *campo* over many years. I chose the Venta Ventura on the outskirts next to the Opel showrooms and near the Campo de Feria, a modest but decent place where I could entertain as many as I wished without worrying too much about the cost. Also, I liked Ventura with his crinkled dough-coloured face and lively patter.

'Here we are, manning the guns as usual,' he would say when I walked in.

'Aren't we all?'

'But some have more powerful cannon than others!' he

would guffaw. 'For example, I see you have many friendships here and lots of people are glad when you return.'

'That's just because I've been around for a long time.
People know my face.'

The typical noises of a Spanish bar overwhelmed some
of our conversation: the till rang, glasses clinked, voices
oscillated between the husky and the strident. Ventura
barked out orders through the hatch to his wife, who was
the cook, or to his sons who were the waiters. Somehow,
before leaving, I had managed to convey to him that I would
turn up with an indefinite number between ten and twenty
for supper that same evening. There was no problem, he
said.

When we assembled we were seventeen, including
children. Our table had been set on the terrace, close to the
road. A lot of cars were manoeuvring for parking space near
the fair. But the food and service, as always at Ventura's,
were very good. By the time we had eaten, the traffic had
quietened down and I exercised my right from the chair to
oblige every adult and adolescent present to tell me what
they thought of Ronda today. Here are some of their
answers.

Juan Alvaro, aged sixteen, hoping to be a teacher, a
devoted friend of my son Jaime: 'In London girls can't go
out on the streets at night because it is too dangerous. Here
they can, but there is still enough going on for us not to get
bored. Ronda is the ideal mix between pueblo and city.'

Joaquinito, his cousin, a dark, handsome, glowering teen-
ager: 'I like Ronda; there are plenty of places to enjoy
ourselves . . . except that our mothers don't allow it.'

Ani, his mother, with semi-cropped shiny black hair
swept behind shell-like ears, delicate face and neat figure:
'You complain! And then when things go wrong and there
is some sort of incident in the street, the problems are all
for the parents! Yes, I like Ronda too. I wouldn't want to
live in a larger city like Málaga. But even here we could do
with less motorbike noise.'

Anti-noise laws? Almost non-existent, everybody agreed. But how could you legislate for that anyway? London was much the same, I said, and filthy to boot. Ah, said Ani, that was a good thing about Ronda; it was very clean. I can confirm that, whatever the criticisms of socialist maladministration, its street cleaning puts the London Borough of Camden to shame.

Ana, sixty-ish matriarch, with jet-black hair, strong and comely face, high bosom, the type of womanhood that has changed very little since the Iberian busts of the Dama de Baza and the Dama de Elche, mother-in-law of Ani, grandmother of Juan Alvaro and Joaquinito, childhood nurse and second mother of our Jaime: 'I like the *Ciudad*. It's still very peaceful. And the best families, the ones you used to know, still live there. Don't I find the *beatas*, the religious spinsters, a bit hypocritical? Perhaps, but they don't bother me. I never go to *misa*, as you know . . . or hardly ever. But anyway, they're much preferable to the *nuevos ricos* who have moved in and are very pretentious and will have nothing to do with the poor, but are not above having big debts in the small local shops. The old families are *más sencillas* . . . more natural and unaffected.'

Mateo, Ana's husband, just turned seventy, is a retired lorry-driver with a craggy face and a determination not to grow old and round-shouldered over dominoes in the cafés. He still fixes somebody's car most days and despises modern drivers who don't know what's under the bonnet; he has a reputation for blunt wisdom, but had little to say about Ronda: 'Ronda? It's all right. I'm an Aragonese but I've spent all my life since the Civil War here. You become accustomed to places.'

He would go no further, so I asked him instead to repeat a story he had told me before, which he did. Driving his lorry up the (then) notoriously dangerous road from San Pedro to Ronda one day back in the fifties, he suddenly lost control; his steering had gone and he plunged nearly seventy metres into a ravine on the left of the road. Miraculously, he emerged unscathed and neither of his passengers was seriously injured. To what did he attribute his salvation? He pulled out his key-ring with a medallion of the black Virgen del Pilar of Zaragoza, patroness of the Civil Guard. She was much more powerful, he said, than any of your prettified Marys of Andalusia. Later, for there were no cranes then, they had winched the lorry back up in three pieces – cabin and steering, axles and differential, and body work – and loaded it onto his employer's only other lorry, on which it was driven to Madrid to be reassembled and put back into service. Mateo himself went north by train to collect it and bring it home. It ran for several years after this episode. There was not so much waste in those days.

It was Arturo's turn next. I have paid tribute to his heroic period earlier in these pages. Now, at sixty, he has come in from the cold and is married to a charming widow, María, with whom he lives in the neatest and daintiest little house imaginable. This may sound almost too good to be true after all his vicissitudes, but so it is.

Arturo: 'Ronda is the healthiest place in the whole world for me – Ronda and its Serranía. My own pueblo, Villar de Ciervo, near Benavente, is also healthy, but not as much as this.'

Mateo: 'Where is that? Is that not in the Basque country?'

Arturo: 'No, in the province of Zamora.'

Mateo: 'The Basques are good people. I have worked with them. I am not saying anything about ETA and all that, but they are a serious people.'

Arturo: 'Why should I doubt it? Did I not marry a Basque and have a house in Bilbao? They are honest and reliable. They will always stop and help you on the road, if you break down . . . or go with you to the very door, if you ask the way. But my marriage didn't work and I went abroad. Did I not work then? *Opé!* Why, I never slept while I was abroad. And then I came here to the *huerta*, next to Ali, and again I worked until I almost dropped.'

Mateo (mischievously): 'You are old before your time.'

Arturo (gravely, without taking offence): '*Hombre*, it is because of the enormous quantity of work I have done in my life.'

Mateo: 'How many thousands of lorryloads of stone and sand have you loaded?'

Arturo: 'Have you ever worked down a mine?'

I left them to it and turned to . . .

María, in her sixties, a childless widow of pleasant appearance and manners, now married to Arturo: 'Well, I am an Arriateña, born and baptised in Arriate. My family leased and worked the Finca de Gallego; then we came to Ronda . . .'

Arturo: 'Where she fell in love with Arturo . . .'

María: 'Get along with you! Do you know what this man did? He came to my door saying he was looking for a house to buy. All he wanted was to enter into relations with me! And so it was. You must know the proverb:

> 'Cuando duermen dos de un colchón
> Se vuelven de la misma opinión.

'I'm sure you've heard that?'

It means that when two share a mattress, they are soon of a like mind. Respectable ladies in Spain can be surprisingly direct about marital intimacies. On the theme of beds, Joaquín, Ana's son and husband of Ani, came up with:

> Si duermen en literas,
> Se caen las tejas.

According to this jingle, if married folk sleep in single beds, the roof falls in. Not to be outdone, Mateo threw in:

> De tal palo,
> Tal astilla.

This, the Spanish version of 'Like father, like son', seemed hardly relevant, and María immediately took us back to Arriate with a fine tribute to its commercial enterprise:

Uno que se fue a la luna
Encontró a un Arriateño vendiendo pescado.

It was, of course, fascinating to hear that 'One who went to the moon met a man from Arriate selling fish there', but I was keen to steer the conversation back to Ronda.

I turned to Juan, a SEAT mechanic married to Ana's daughter Rosi, and father of Juan Alvaro and two others. He like the majority said he was a lover of Ronda, but he had one complaint. It was disgraceful that the municipal band, in which he played the trumpet, had been privatised with an unpaid back wages bill of three million pesetas. They had been paid a pittance before but at least it was a regular retainer, in return for which they had played on every possible occasion – Easter, Corpus Christi, the day of the Patron Saint, bullfights and so on. But were they not still playing? Had I not seen him at the *novillada* only that afternoon? Yes, but they were only paid by performance now and if you were ill, for example, you got nothing. Why, even Arriate had a proper municipal band, and it didn't have a municipal deficit either!

It seemed impossible to get away from Arriate, where Thatcherite enterprise and latter-day Communism had contracted such a successful marriage. María was immediately ready with another proverb:

Ronda, la bolsa monda,
Y la gente de Arriate
Lo gasta todo en chocolate.

Ronda's purse was empty; the people of Arriate spent all their money on chocolate. For a place long despised by Rondeños as the home of bumpkins, it was impressive to see how it was getting its own back.

I turned determinedly to Jaime, aged fourteen, younger son of Juan and Rosi. He wants above all to work with animals. This is considered unusual in a family which has become urbanised and mechanised, but it is not dismissed as something daft he will grow out of. He saves all his pocket money to buy speckled hens, even though he has only a tiny backyard to keep them in and they do not lay well, if at all. What would he like ideally? To breed brave bulls. But that would require an enormous ranch, wouldn't it? He agreed sadly. His second best plan was to run donkey rides for foreigners. But would there be customers for that? Well, it worked on the coast. But mightn't people expect something a bit more rugged and genuine up here . . . at least real horses? Jaime shrugged, the marvellous Spanish shrug which absolves you from ever doing any serious market research into any project. I said I suspected free-range hens and eggs would have a much wider appeal as Spaniards became faddier. Out of politeness he appeared to accept this advice, which I am sure he will not follow.

Rosi spoke next. Married to Juan, she is the mother of Juan Alvaro, Jaime and Anita, a strong-willed, dark-ringleted little girl of six. She was less enthusiastic about Ronda than the others. Her basic complaint was the lack of jobs for women. She was doing a government-sponsored course from nine to twelve every morning in office administration, typing and computing. She hadn't much experience of this sort of thing but she liked it and it stretched her; there was a 37,000 pesetas monthly benefit payment that went with it, otherwise she couldn't have contemplated it. The bad thing was that there was little likelihood of a job at the end of it. She wanted to work in the clinic, as she had already done a nursing course, but those places were almost a monopoly of the people from the Monte and the doctors, who all manoeuvred their wives and relatives in there: the Buendías, the Troyas and all that lot . . . practically every woman of that class over forty had a post there. Rosi's dark eyes flashed angrily under her long lashes. It was quite wrong that the *señoritos* should mop up the jobs which ought to be for the poorer classes who had no *rentier* income.

Did the clinic still belong to the Monte, then? No, she said, now it belonged to the Junta de Andalucía. On paper it was slightly less a question of knowing someone who knew Don Fulano who knew Don Mengano than before. There were now public examinations and you could complain if someone with worse grades than you got the job. But even so, you got fobbed off with every kind of excuse and explanation. The only thing that had changed was that you could raise your voice now, though much good did it do you if nobody listened!

Rosi went on to talk of the difficulty of running a household on one salary. Juan earned very little. The children needed so many books, materials and clothes for school; shoes alone cost a fortune. Though she did not say so, it was she and her mother who kept the pot boiling, as I well knew. Together they ran a sort of co-operative family kitchen where their men and the children ate. Both were geniuses at making nourishing meals out of virtually nothing. Ana's yellow stews of chickpeas and potatoes and a little stock with a hambone or a morsel of meat were Hilly's and Jaime's greatest delight: so bland, so soothing, so satisfying. When Ortega wrote dismissively about the poor fare of the Andalusians and how a workman in a Basque provincial town ate better than a *señorito* in Córdoba, he entirely neglected the climatic differences and missed the exquisite nuances of the lighter Andalusian cuisine. Even Ortega nods.

Mateo too was a dab hand at certain dishes. His mayonnaise was so delicious that you never wanted to see another jar of Hellmann's or Colman's in your life. His *salmorejo* was another minor masterpiece, consisting of floury boiled potatoes, peeled and sliced while still warm, interlayed with rings of raw onion, to which pepper, salt, parsley, oil and a mere suspicion of vinegar were added. It was served cold but not chilled. Some people, myself included, liked to add hard-boiled eggs, but as a purist he did not approve of this: you only had to throw in some tinned peas and it turned into Russian salad, a much coarser thing altogether.

Earlier, for supper Mateo had ordered swordfish without

Harnessing a carriage-horse for the fair

any garnishing. When I pushed Ventura's excellent fried potatoes towards him, he pushed them back.

'Potatoes are poor man's food.'

'But what about that *salmorejo* of yours?'

'That's what I'm saying. Potatoes are for the family, for home consumption. I don't come out to eat spuds.'

Of the adults only Joaquín, brother of Rosi, husband of Ani, father of Joaquinito, had not yet spoken. He loved Ronda, he said: there were good people, you made good friends and there was work for those who wanted it (though he agreed with his sister's complaint about work for women). And did not Rilke's statue in the gardens of the Hotel Victoria bear witness to the beauty of the place? He himself was only an electronics technician, but that side of

368

life was important too. He wouldn't move to Málaga for double the money. I was surprised by his romanticism.

That was the end of my amateur survey. There was an overwhelming agreement that Ronda was a good place to live in. But there were some beginnings of disquiet over 'quality of life' issues (Ani) and lack of opportunity and continuing domination by the *señorito* class (Rosi). It was noticeable that the men had fewer complaints than the women. However, this was not the time or the place for further analysis. The fair beckoned.

I called for the bill. My guests crowded round me to see how much it had all cost. This may seem indelicate to the British, whose restaurant bills are discreetly folded over when presented to them, while guests avert their eyes, but it is perfectly normal in Spain; besides, my friends were eager to ensure that I had got a fair deal, and Arturo's wife María had a special interest in this as Ventura's wife was her niece. At about £100 for fourteen adults and adolescents plus three smaller children it was generally agreed that I had not been overcharged, especially as several had ordered swordfish, which was expensive. I concurred. We left in great good humour for the fair.

For some years now the Ronda funfair has occupied a great new esplanade, the size of several football pitches, below the road on which Ventura's is situated. Over the decades it has moved from the old Campo de Feria by the barracks in the centre of town to the Alameda (where it did too much damage to plants and trees), to this, presumably its final resting place. Thus it no longer takes over the whole pueblo, as it does in tiny villages and even in larger towns like Olvera, where it is impossible not to get caught up in it. It is just a large noisy event on the fringe. But it is packed on the three main days, and it is not hyberbolical to say, particularly on bullfight nights, that 'all Ronda' is there.

Most of the area is devoted to the usual fairground amusements: wheels, dippers, dodgems and, these days, the 'Palacio de las Galaxias' adorned with large models of Superman, Batwoman and ET among others. These share the space with any number of booths, stalls, mountebanks' stands, *chocolaterías, churrerías* (for sizzling batter rings) and other places of refreshment including the 'Chiringuito de Mohammed Ali', self-proclaimed King of the Kebabs. And everywhere are nubile girls with flashing eyes and younger children with made-up cheeks, all licking huge pyramids of candyfloss.

It was not long before I had become separated from my supper companions in the throng, so I pushed on to where social life is concentrated at the far end round the *casetas* or enclosures erected by a wide variety of local bodies: some large enough to accommodate audiences of several hundred for late-night shows; others smaller and more exclusive and accessible only by invitation. This year I counted nineteen in all. Amongst the largest were the 'Caseta Municipal', where entrance is always free; the 'Casa del Pueblo', the tent of the governing party, the PSOE, entrance also free; the 'Grupo Independiente de Rondeños para Ronda', the Ronda nationalists as it were; and the 'Peña de Empleados de la Caja de Ahorros de Ronda', the Monte's well-stocked marquee for its employees.

Other *casetas* tended more towards domesticity and folklore: the 'Peña Hombres de su Casa', 'El Botijo' (the earthenware water jug), 'Las Castañuelas' (the castanets), the 'Peña Flamenca Tobalo', 'La Damajuana' (the gentry's tent, appropriately named after a demijohn), and the 'Silla de Anea' (the rush-bottomed chair, symbol of conversation and gossip, a battered example of which was nailed up over the entrance). I was contemplating this selection of hives buzzing with social life and wondering which would be easiest to gatecrash – some had burly security guards at the door and in one case a security Amazon – when I was hauled into the 'Hombres de su Casa' by Antonio Villalón, the ironmonger and retired secret policeman who had tailed Diana and me when we were under suspicion as spies.

Antonio sat me down in a place of honour with his friends and another half-bottle of sherry was called for – halves are *de rigueur* in *feria*, however many you have; whole bottles are thought to look immoderate. Soon a folklore group was introduced from – guess where – Arriate, no less, as always busy upstaging its big neighbour. The men, wearing cloth caps, red braces and cummerbunds and carrying shepherds' plaids, looked rather like Morris dancers, while the girls wore Sevillian flounces. The two cultures, incidentally, are not as opposed as might be thought, for Morris dancing ('Moresque' in those days) was introduced into England in the wake of the marriage of Edward I to Eleanor of Castile, after whose title Infanta of Castile we get the popular corruption 'Elephant and Castle'. This link was later strengthened by the marriage of John of Gaunt to Constance, daughter of Peter the Cruel, through whom he laid claim to the Castilian crown.

After a decent interval I thanked Antonio for his hospitality and excused myself. I was then picked up by Maribel Clerc de Lasalle, a girl of good family whose mother, one of the queens of Ronda society, is English. Maribel, who lives and works in Marbella, was doing her tribal stuff at fair-time, but she was critical: 'Ronda is no longer small enough to be a real pueblo, but nor does it have the advantages of a city; there is no theatre; there are no concerts.' Of course, everything depends on your viewpoint. For Paco in the *campo*, for example, 'Ronda is no Cortes or Grazalema; Ronda is a capital in its own right.'

However that might be, Maribel drew me into the gentry's tent, the preserve in effect of three or four clans and their collateral branches. They stage no spectacle of song or dance; they are more than adequately entertained by gossip and mutual admiration. Occasionally members take a stroll round the other *casetas*, but that is slumming, and this is where they feel most at home, talking about crops and jobs and marriages and separations and mistresses among their own class. I was greeted by various landowners, doctors, lawyers and entrepreneurs who said they hadn't seen me

371

for a century. Pepito Márquez, a small, fair, ruddy-cheeked and rather un-Spanish-looking landowner (to whom I had once tried to impart a little English on the insistence of his formidable mother) bought me a drink. He was very cheerful.

'We *latifundistas* are better treated by this regime than we were by Franco,' he said with sly amusement. 'There are more subsidies for everything.'

'Imagine!' I said. 'And under a socialist government . . .'

'Ah,' he grinned, 'but Felipe is busy becoming a *latifundista* too – not directly of course but through his friends and relatives.'

He positively twinkled with delight at the corruption of Spanish politics of whatever hue. It was so comforting that liberals, monarchists, Francoists, socialists . . . you name it . . . were all tarred by the same brush. It was evidence of that continuity which made Spanish civil society possible!

Shortly after leaving the 'Damajuana' I was accosted by two men, both bearded; the larger and older addressed me in the sort of Spanish one might expect from an Italian.

'Is it far, Señor, from here to the famous Plaza de Toros?'

'About two kilometres, I should think,' I replied helpfully. 'I'm afraid you're at the wrong end of town.'

'And the no less famous Casa de Mondragón, where Señor Boyd has a bodega or bar, I believe?'

'That closed a long time ago,' I said, wondering how they had heard of it.

'Are you sure, Señor?'

'Sure, why should I not be sure? Am I not' – I was about to reveal my identity, then suddenly thought better of it – 'a friend of his?'

Then it dawned on me from the widening grins on their faces that I was the victim of a hoax. These were familiar faces . . . if stripped of their beards.

'Who the devil are you?'

'Jesús Jiménez . . . and José María at your service.'

They swept me a bow. In a trice the Italianate look melted away and I saw exactly who they were: Jesús, who ran the best *gestoría* or agency in town for solving the multiple problems thrown up by the many-layered bureaucracy, and his cousin José María. Normally one saw Jesús rattling away into the telephone tucked under his chin about the intricacies of some permit or licence, while half a dozen clients vied to attract his attention. But the spirit of the fair (and the beard) had transformed him. Fantasy was in the air . . .

'You damned clowns,' I protested. 'You quite deceived me!'

'But you too deceived us, pretending not to be yourself,' José María accused me.

'Deception is catching,' I answered, I thought rather cleverly.

'Have you heard,' asked Jesús, 'about the great new wonderful plan to turn Ronda into a *Patrimonio de la Humanidad*?'

'Heritage of the Human Race?' I smiled. 'What high-sounding nonsense is that?'

'No, but seriously,' he said, 'a petition is being sent to the government; it is pioneered by Izquierda Unida.'

'You mean the Communists?'

'Yes, they have had to change their name, poor things. But Anguita is everybody's favourite man of the Left. It is supported by all the other political parties.'

'But surely Izquierda Unida haven't a hope of coming to power?'

'No, of course not. That's why he's so popular. Here we have the best of all possible worlds: a small Hard Left bloc, a small Hard Right bloc and a large Soft Centre, which is everything to everyone.'

'Then if the government is in so strong a position, why should it support such a caprice?'

'They are only human, they want to be loved. Oh, I assure you all the political forces are very enthusiastic, including the PSOE. And the European Commission has promised its backing . . . and we are all good Europeans these days. So you see, all the old houses in Ronda which have been brutalised or destroyed will be beautifully and typically rebuilt or restored. And their charming inhabitants will wear period dress, and all traffic will be diverted, and there will only be carriages and horse-cabs in the town, and it will be *goyesca* time throughout the year, and everyone will live happily ever after. It will be an earthly paradise!'

'Well, you'd better get on with it at the rate the *Ciudad* is being pulled down.'

'Don't worry,' he said gaily. 'It will happen. It is written in the stars. The name of the game is 1992 . . .'

'But hasn't your Nobel Laureate, Camilo José Cela, just pronounced that 1992 will be a disaster?'

'Pay no heed to Cela!' they both said. 'He has no aim in life but to draw attention to himself.'

I tried to remember who had said this before. Of course, it was Don Manuel, the sage of El Gastor. I was about to remark on this when I realised that Jesús and José María had vanished. The crowd had swirled around us and swallowed them up. I wanted to probe them further on their absurd theme of Ronda, *Patrimonio de la Humanidad*. Probably it was just a figment of Jesús's imagination, born out of the feverish spirit of the fair. But then it was just the sort of crazy idea the debt-ridden municipality might have dreamed up as a means of attracting funds. I must find out. I plunged in the direction I thought they must have gone but I never caught up with them, never even glimpsed them again.

Eventually I gave up. After all, it didn't really matter. Whether a public or a private fantasy, it would not come to pass. When the lights of the fairground were switched off and the loudspeakers ceased to blare and the attractions trundled away and the *lunes de la resaca* – the additional local bank holiday for the hangover – was behind, then Ronda would simply become Ronda again, the place one knew and loved – warts and all. A lone rocket soared into the flushed night sky. All Ronda's great projects were something like that, I thought, shooting up and unleashing a cascade of silver rain which never reached the earth.

11

CAMPO COLLAGE

After the fair I went to say goodbye for the time being to my neighbours. Rafael Alarcón occupies the opposite end of La Mimbre – the long range of farm buildings like a one-sided street on the hill – from Rafael Valiente. I found him sitting on his doorstep with his feet stretched out naked to catch the slight evening breeze.

'I am doing the milk-round in town all morning,' he said. 'I have a bit of a rest in the afternoon ... at my age it is justifiable. Then there are all the farm chores ... then there is the milking ... and now in the peace of the evening I can relax with *mi niño*.'

This was his only grandchild to date, a little blond boy of two or three who was trotting around on the cobbles and whom he adored.

'I suppose La Mimbre was all one farm originally?' I asked.

'Yes, then it was left to two brothers. Then they split it among four cousins. We are all related, either by blood or marriage. Luis's wife, may she rest in peace, was my wife's sister.'

'How can it sustain four families today?'

'It couldn't if most of us weren't working in *la calle* also. I distribute my own milk because I get eighty pesetas a litre from door to door against only forty pesetas from the *central lechera*. Valiente is always out and about with his tractor, ploughing for others. Then we all have our cattle, which are very expensive to rear and cheap to sell, but they do yield something.'

He did not mention that they were all virtually self-sufficient from their winter pig-killing and their stored melons and other produce; they bought hardly any food other than their bread. That they were not in want was evident when the round formica-topped table which served to house a charcoal brazier in winter was brought out, light as a feather now without its cloth skirts, and speedily laden by his wife with slices of home-cured ham, bread, olives, *chorizo*, bottles of beer and a flagon of Montilla wine.

In conversation there was some mild derision of Arturo for having married a widow older than himself and gone to town, thus inviting old age prematurely. As this was the desired end of most *campo* lives, I wondered if there wasn't a hint of jealousy, but Rafael was adamant.

'I won't leave here,' he said, 'for the pueblo or anywhere else. Here I breathe proper air. No one molests me. My body aches but if it gets bad I just go to bed till it wears off. So here I shall stay until my time is up. We don't know how long we have, or when it will come, or where we shall go . . . but one hopes up there!'

He pointed to the scintillating canopy of stars, which had just been switched on. I said I hoped we could all cling to earth a little longer. Luis, who had strolled over from next door, agreed.

'Yes, at least we know where we are here. Afterwards, God only knows!'

He pointed to the nether regions as a distinct possibility. Rafael remained impassive. Obviously he could not pre-empt the Almighty's choice. But he felt in his bones, I suspect, that he was a good man who had worked hard and would get his just deserts.

Luis's motherless son Luisillo, aged fourteen, a school drop-out with prematurely decaying teeth and huge, dark, inquisitive eyes, dragged me off to see his rabbits. He had them in an outhouse. It was going to be an industry; he would be able to keep his widowed dad in his old age. Luis and Luisillo looked after each other with much mutual concern, tinged sometimes with exasperation. The son would chide the father for his addiction to sweet anis; the father the son for lack of addiction to school. As for the rabbits, they always developed killer diseases in captivity, Luis said; that was the law of rabbits. But it was better for the boy to have some interest than none, and better for the father to be cheerful than depressed. Neither was too hard on the other and thus they got along pretty well together.

At the far end of the terrace Rafael Valiente came striding round the corner from his cowshed. Compared to Luis with his four cows and no machinery, Rafael was prosperous with over twenty cattle and his tractor and other accessories. He hailed me and led me indoors. His large, bleak living room was furnished with nothing but a round brazier table and four or five upright chairs. The empty grate was overhung by a handsome old mantelpiece with many ledges and cornices on which his wife, Maruja, kept her best china. There was no other decoration but a black bull's head (killed by Rafael at a private fight on a ranch without picadors) mounted on a shield-shaped board, flanked by two expensively framed bullfight posters, on which Rafael's name had been inserted between those of famous matadors. I had thought only tourists in Torremolinos fell for this sort of thing, but there could be no doubt of Rafael's seriousness about bulls. We sat down and went over both the *goyesca* and the *novillada*; his eyes danced because my pessimism had been proved wrong. There was still honour and prowess abroad in the land.

Rafael was generous about Arturo. We talked of his legendary energy and the great stone slabs he had brought down from the Cortijo Grande by cart with no tools but an iron bar and his own arms to load them. Nowadays, you wouldn't dream of doing that without earth-moving machinery. Once Rafael said to Arturo, 'If you go on like that, you'll crack up.' At that time Arturo always kept a sixteen-litre *garrafa* of wine in his stable and would walk about with a brown enamelled pint pot of it, from which he would oblige all comers to drink. His answer to Rafael's concern had been simple: *el vino puedo mucho*, wine can do much. Clearly he saw it like oil for a human machine.

Yet Arturo was not merely a physical phenomenon.

'If it wasn't for him, Ali,' Rafael said, 'we would have no electric light or bridges over the river.'

Arturo would go to Seville or wherever was necessary, wearing his suit and his sunglasses and carrying his leather briefcase, and insist and insist with officials until they gave way. But it was not only a question of fighting the bureaucracy, for he also had to persuade sixty-three households that they needed light, for which they would have to pay that part of the installation cost not covered by government subsidy, when half of them were against it anyway. No wonder he sometimes got irritated and lost his temper! Rafael recalled having to restrain him more than once. All in all, between one thing and another he had burnt himself out and was perfectly right to retire to the town where he was comfortable and happy with his widow. Good luck to him!

All this while Maruja had been busying herself in the kitchen, which was a sort of cabin, not unlike Luis's, across a small yard at the back. Yellow with smoke and somewhat gypsyish, it stood in marked contrast to the austere emptiness of the main room, in which twenty couples could have danced comfortably without encountering any impediment from furniture or bric-à-brac. Here there was one improvement Rafael drew my attention to. He had replaced the old irregular poplar beams, common in farmhouses and usually covered with flaking whitewash, with a fine ceiling of natural Flemish pine with exposed boards and trusses, all smoothly planed.

'It was in bad shape before,' he said. 'I did it all with my own hands. You see I have many talents. What do you think?'

'Very nice,' I said genuinely.

Indeed, his handiwork would have earned the approval of the most earnest devotee of stripped pine in Camden Town. At the same time, I was willing to bet that the flat he was making for himself in his town property would be crammed with such essential elements of Spanish bourgeois life as flounced dolls on the counterpanes, mincing figurines of ballerinas on the shelves and mock leather or mock velvet sofas and chairs.

Spaniards are often criticised for their appalling taste and willingness to trade in their time-honoured utensils and furniture for modern trash, but it isn't really quite as simple as that. It all hinges on what is appropriate, embodied in that almost untranslatable phrase, *lo suyo*: that which is proper in a particular set of circumstances. What is right and fitting in one context is not necessarily so in another. Spaniards do not, on the whole, *want* to bring the comforts of the town to the country: the aim is to live in the town and off the country. There will always be a few exceptions like Alarcón, but the majority see the country at best as an industrial exploitation (as the gentry has always done) and at worst as a bondage. In neither case is luxury, or even comfort, appropriate; it is not *lo suyo*, even if resources allow.

Maruja now brought *salchichón* and more ham and olives. Rafael went for a bottle of wine. I protested that I had already eaten and drunk at Alarcón's but I was ignored; the iron laws of hospitality could not be gainsaid. Maruja and her little girl sat with us, the child colouring in the outlines in a drawing book. Maruja is a slender woman with a mischievous face, quick, darting eyes and restless fingers. She asked after my wife and son, pecking away like a bird at the facts. I duly gave a brief account of the health and activities of Hilly and Jaime.

'She was fine and fat when she was here last summer,' Maruja said. 'Perhaps a shade too plump. But it suits her.'

'She has lost weight since then,' I said evenly. 'Personal

remarks', as we call them, are not rude in Spain.

'Then she should not lose too much. Blonde women are like that. They should be ample. *Es lo suyo.*'

I reflected with amusement that blondes normally think of their darker southern sisters as the heavy brigade.

Enquiries followed about Jaime. He was so handsome. Would he marry a Spanish girl? I said he had an English girlfriend, to whom he was devoted. Ah well, perhaps that would change. As he spoke Spanish so well and had been brought up here, a Spanish wife was – what else? – *lo suyo.*

They both pressed me about my relations with Paco over the *huerta.* I confessed there had been difficulties, to the extent that we were thinking of selling up and getting something smaller near or in a pueblo; that had been the reason behind my recent journeys. Rafael was careful not to be disloyal to Paco, who was *buena persona* but with too much on his hands to attend properly to my place. He had someone ideal in mind: Vicente from La Granja. I would know him; he had worked frequently on the dam and on the track and was younger and lived nearer.

'The one who replaced Paco Vallejo who died?'

'He himself. He would transform the place.'

I made a mental note of this. On one thing Rafael was emphatic. We would be most ill-advised to give up our *huerta;* it was good land and I had many friends around. I would simply get bored in a chalet with a lawn and a swimming pool after all that space. Besides, if I moved, how on earth would we go to bullfights together? Next year we had to go to the *feria* of Antequera, where they always had excellent *carteles* at very reasonable prices. We would take Arturo and make a day of it.

'Till when?' he asked as I took my leave.

'Till Christmas.'

'Well, remember that this house is your own, for whatever you require of it.

It remained to say goodbye to Paco. The next day we sat on

Paco's Antonio with the *yunta*

my terrace looking out over the *huerta*. One large patch of
his maize had failed; it was sown too late and the insects
had moved in and eaten the foliage; there would not be
enough cobs to make it worth picking and storing them.
Would I mind therefore if he brought his cows into the
chirrascal, the strip along the river? He could then scythe
the maize and feed it to them there. Otherwise he would
have thrown away good money for nothing.

I pondered this. I had not obliged him to sow maize at a
loss, but it was obviously a bit of a disaster. I wouldn't

mind, I said warily, provided they didn't come tramping and chomping up to the house and onto the terrace, eating my few ornamental bamboos and oleanders and the new vine shoots we had planted last winter. The stake and wire fence round the domestic compound was half down and there was virtually nothing to stop them. Couldn't his Antonio mend it while he was minding the cows?

Paco frowned. Antonio couldn't be there all the time, because he had many other things to do. Besides, the animals would not stray from their fodder. That was all very well, I said, but supposing they got bored with maize half consumed by maggots and wanted a change of diet? At least he must undertake to mend the fence. Paco rubbed his nose. Well . . . if I insisted . . . and there really wasn't all that much needing to be done . . . just another strand and two or three new stakes. The existing ones, I pointed out, were mostly rotten at the tips. They would hold up nonetheless, he promised: sheep and goats were more persistent but if a cow came up against a single strand of wire, it would turn back. I could rest assured: not a cane of my bamboos nor a single vine shoot would be harmed.

With the second glass Paco became more assertive. I had to understand that he did this out of friendship, out of respect for me. The older he got, the more he put friendship above money. If people knew he had some maize sown here, however poor the crop, they would have a certain respect for the place. Otherwise, every goatherd in the district would be in here, and then where would my precious bamboos and vines be? Why, only the other day he had had to warn off Rafael de las Monjas, who was about to cross the river with all of his flock . . . He wouldn't try that one again!

Over the third glass Paco became confidential. Had I seen anything that really pleased me on my travels? Personally, he was willing to bet I could never improve on this for the money, and with all the friends I had I would be mad to exchange it for unknown territory and unproved neighbours. I replied that I hadn't made up my mind. I had seen all sorts of interesting places and properties, but of course I had to consult my family. In the meantime, I hoped it was clear that if I required the land back . . .

He gave me a pained look. If there was one thing I could be certain of in this world, it was that as long as he was around the place would be respected – and if and when I wanted to sell, he would be more than happy to leave. If he had anything standing on the ground, I could sell that too . . .

'Oh,' I said primly, 'I would compensate you for any standing crops, of course. That would only be fair.'

Then I looked at the maize and regretted this. He grinned.

'As I have told you before, Ali, many times, there need never be any problems between us. We are friends. That is all that matters. Now, until you make up your mind, shall we go on as we are?'

'You mean you want to sow again this autumn?'

'Why not?'

I could not say that Rafael Valiente had proposed Vicente, with whom I had not spoken. Nor was I sure I wanted to enter into a new relationship, particularly if we were going to sell. But the worst of all possible worlds was for the place to become a vacuum. Paco knew this very well.

'All right,' I said, 'but remember it may be the last year.'

He downed his wine.

'Whatever you say, Ali,' he said.

The last port of call, when bound for England, was always *la tienda* to pay the bill. Without this village shop and the adjacent school the straggle of one-storey houses along the old drovers' track which made up the hamlet of La Indiana would have been even more centreless – in fact probably not viable at all. Paco el Bueno and his wife Pepi are an exemplary couple whose modest establishment provides more services than its outward appearance would suggest. First, it relieves the housewives of La Indiana of the need to go to Ronda to shop; Paco's is a bit more expensive, true, but you don't need to wait for the bus or have to hang around in town all day while your husband delivers the milk; you just walk up the track with a neighbour and get all the local gossip thrown in. Next, Paco's is the bar where the men get their supplies of *tinto* or drink at the shop counter, and a *venta* where labourers doing heavy work on the roads or in the fields can get a good meal. And then there is the public telephone, usually monopolised by the young ringing up their *novios* or *novias*, but there all the same for emergencies.

The only threat to the harmonious provision of these basic services was posed by the Legion. There was much heated argument in Ronda as to whether the notorious, and now redundant, Foreign Legion should be invited to take over the empty army camp, which had been occupied for many years by officer cadets on summer training programmes, an altogether more desirable lot. The Right was in favour; the Left was against; the Right carried the day. The supposed benefits for commerce in the town never materialised. The Legionnaires were rowdy and had little money in their pockets except for drink and sex. In the countryside, previously innocent farmhouses blossomed with red lights to supplement the town brothels. Some decent girls, unwise enough to fall for the Legion's macho self-image, were made pregnant – without the consolation that the father was a well-bred officer cadet.

Paco's proximity to the camp put him in a difficult position. If he banned the Legionnaires, he would deprive himself of an obvious source of income which other *ventas* would take advantage of; if he did not, he would lose his bourgeois weekend customers. The locals would stick to him whatever happened, though there might be the odd fight. For a year or so it looked as if the shop might be swamped by braggarts and louts. Then, mercifully, half the Legion was posted elsewhere and the new recruits they had made way for never materialised. The weekend bourgeoisie drifted back. Harmony was restored. Throughout this awkward period Paco's unfailing good humour, coupled with a firm no-nonsense line whenever behaviour began to get out of hand, enhanced his reputation as 'El Bueno'. There was in fact no candidate for the title of 'El Malo', but there were a number of Pacos in the vicinity, so it was a handy way of identifying him, as well as being patently accurate both of himself and his helpmeet.

Paco's pleasant, regular, clean-shaven features habitually wore a slight smile, which broadened into a friendly greeting when I entered the shop. I said I had come to settle up and he responded exactly as always:

'Are you abandoning us for good?'

'No, I plan to be back for Christmas.'

'Then why not leave it till then? There is no hurry.'

I found it strangely tempting to leave this little loose end, not for financial reasons but as a token of continuity, a guarantee as it were both to myself and others that I would be back. But there was always the faint possibility that something would go wrong, preventing my return, and that it would remain flapping around and never get settled.

'I think on the whole I'd better settle up. You never know . . .'

'Indeed, you never know,' he said gravely as he took the money. 'But I have not the slightest doubt we shall be seeing you again before long . . . God willing of course.'

Over Christmas it was unseasonably warm. The sharp crystalline days I remembered in the past refused to repeat themselves. I supped with Ana and her family on Christmas Eve: it was almost the same gathering that I had entertained during the fair, all crammed into Ana's small, cave-like sitting room. The meal consisted of lots of little delicacies, a feast of *tapas* rather than a large bird to be ritually devoured. I then went with the women – the other men ostentatiously abstaining – to the *misa del gallo*, the midnight Mass in the Iglesia Mayor. The residents of the *Ciudad* were there in force, including the best families, whose children pattered about on the great chessboard of black and white marble slabs under the soaring composite columns with their giant Corinthian capitals. Restraint on them was minimal, but no one complained; the great thing was that the right people were there. We all shook hands afterwards – rich and poor, foreigner and native – with mutual satisfaction at each other's presence in a community of the spirit, however temporary and transient.

Back in the *campo* frustration grew. New Year's Day passed and it was still too warm for the *matanza*, when most families killed, salted, cured and turned into a variety of pork products the number of pigs required to provide them with their main protein intake throughout the year. This was still one of the cornerstones of the peasant economy. Only Rafael Valiente had taken advantage of a short cold snap in November to kill four pigs. His neighbours were all still waiting. It was a long time since I had witnessed a *matanza* and several of them had invited me to join them when the happy day arrived. But would it do so before I had to return to England?

Rather than kick my heels, I went in search of Pepe Villalba, who was a fount of old stories. He was a bachelor who had lodged for years with an old lady and her widowed daughter and children; the family had kept a few cows and Pepe had laid out his palliasse every night in their straw loft. Some years ago they had thrown him out for drunkenness. He did not take this amiss, even though he had enjoyed a corner by their fireside for so long. He went to live alone in a cottage just outside the military camp, not far from La Indiana railway station, where I had been told he reared rabbits and cultivated a small kitchen garden sufficient for his needs. I was not exactly sure of the location, so I went first to the Venta de Santiago, an inn right by the station, which had become very fashionable with the bourgeoisie before it (like Paco's) had been stricken with Legionnaires' blight. It seemed not to have recovered.

A number of men in the valley have gold teeth. Rafael Alarcón has a prominent one. I rather think Carrasco, the *cabero*, may have one or two glowing in his cavern of decay. But Santiago has several. His mouth is a rising sun. Also he is an Ordoñista. The walls of his bar are covered with photographs of Antonio Ordóñez in all sorts of classical passes; on his knees with his elbow on the bull's muzzle and hand to his own ear, the act of daring known as 'the telephone'; profiling and killing; being carried out of the ring shoulder high; and above all with Santiago – other Ronda dignitaries such as Don Juan de la Rosa and Don Paco de la Rosa and Don Fulano de Mengano are there, but the important thing is that Santiago, quite prominently, is there too.

Santiago was not much interested in the whereabouts of Pepe Villalba. Yes, he knew where he lived; he came in sometimes but hadn't been in today; if I cared to wait, he might drop by later. So I had a drink and we talked about the last *goyesca*. In Santiago's view the glory was departed. Yes, it was true that Antonio was now the impresario. Should he not then stimulate new talent, run a school, put on plenty of *novilladas*? That would be very nice, very pretty, said Santiago, but who was going to pay the bills? In his opinion Antonio had done an enormous amount for Ronda. Why should he bankrupt himself in retirement to promote nonentities?

'What about Pepe Luis Martín?' I asked. 'Doesn't he deserve a hand on the way up? Why didn't Antonio include him in the *goyesca*?'

'Because he wasn't up to it,' Santiago growled. 'Isn't that reason enough?'

Still no Pepe, so I obtained directions and set off on foot on the path that runs alongside the railway track. After a few hundred metres I came to a single-storey house, barely more than a hut, with a small corral. I knocked and was greeted by Pepe's gnarled and gnome-like face. He immediately fetched a jar of Montilla and filled us both a glass.

'Aren't you lonely?' I asked, observing the bleak little kitchen with a single pot on a paraffin stove.

'No, why should I be? With this' – he raised his glass – 'and tobacco and the radio what more can one want? Compared to some periods of my life this is bliss . . . this is luxury.'

He went on to talk about the Civil War. He had been called up for his national service in 1934. The outbreak of war had caught him in a Republican zone, so his battalion of cavalry naturally formed part of the army loyal to the government. He had on his own account been blessed with seven lives (Spanish cats do not aspire to nine). On patrol from Málaga to test the positions of the encircling troops of the Duke of Seville, his horse was shot from under him and he fled under the fruit-heavy trees of a lemon grove with the enemy cleaning up ruthlessly and efficiently behind him. Somehow he managed to avoid capture, dragging and crawling his way back to the beleaguered city.

Málaga surrendered, and Pepe was sent back to his home town, Ronda. When the trainload of demoralised troops and militia arrived, some were immediately taken away to be shot. He believed his own last hour had come but, as he belonged to no party and had no political antecedents, his life was spared. The Nationalists needed cannon fodder. He was sent to Algeciras, whence he was posted north. In some ways it was a relief to find himself a soldier in Franco's army. His own brother had from conviction begun the war on Franco's side.

'It was a very strange war,' Pepe said. 'If it had been between England and Spain or Spain and Russia, you would have known at least that you were not shooting your own relations.'

When the front lines were very close together, pehaps a mere sixty or seventy metres apart, a curious sort of fraternisation took place in the lulls between the major actions. One trench would shout to the other, asking where its occupants came from, and it would often turn out there were people from the same town or region facing one another. Then they would break the rules of war and crawl into no-man's land to exchange newspapers, tobacco or cigarette paper. But sometimes someone would crawl out under false colours, intending not to create a fragile island of civilisation in the heaving ocean of civil war but to grasp his opposite number and drag him back, a prisoner, to his own trenches. Then the victim's cries would set off the shooting again and one, or both, or more might die.

Pepe's unit, the Algerian Fifteenth, later renamed the Toledan Sixth, was considered a crack assault force and was always given tough assignments. It was switched from one front to another, and Pepe served with it in such famous actions as those of Avila, Segovia, Los Altos de León, La Cuesta de las Perdices, and in the fierce fighting in the University City of Madrid. He also survived the terrible battle of Brunete in July 1937. This was a short-lived Pyrrhic victory for the Republic, which gained a corridor a few miles long and as many wide to the west of Madrid at terrible cost, only to see it speedily retaken. But Pepe's battalion was thrown in early against the crest of the Republican wave and only thirty-six out of over a thousand emerged alive.

'I was four days,' he said, 'lying on a mound of dead and trying not to move in case they came and drove a bayonet through my back. Then I crawled off with one companion into some scrub and we managed to rejoin what was left of the unit. God knows how we survived. When the war was over, there was no barracks for us to go to in Madrid, so we were sent to the Four Winds Lunatic Asylum. The Republic had let all the inmates out. I wasn't demobilised till 1942. So that was eight years of service between one side and the other. All of us in the battalion who were still alive were awarded campaign medals and for Brunete we were supposed to get the Star of Military Merit. There was much advantage in those medals because, if you wore them, you could go up to a municipal policeman in any town and instruct him to find you lodgings; and many things were cheaper for you, like the cinema and public transport. But – would you believe it – when the medals arrived at the Ronda town hall we were told we had to pay for them! I think the Military Merit was 340 pesetas and another was 225 and the lesser ones were forty to sixty. That was a fortune in those days when a man earned two pesetas a day if he was lucky. Of course it wasn't the army's fault. It was those bloodsuckers in the town hall, the municipal functionaries: they sold them to those who could pay, the majors and captains and warrant officers, and no doubt said that I and the likes of me were dead. So I never got my medals.'

Pepe refilled our glasses and held out his packet of cigarettes.

'Everything that is bad for us,' he said with an elaborate wink. 'But then, what else are we to do . . .'

'. . . in the four days we are allowed on earth!' I chimed in, this being the ritual response. I liked to be on the ball over these things. Four is the joker of Spanish numbers, used whenever we British say two or three or a few. It also has a slightly disparaging ring, an additional adjective such as 'wretched' or 'miserable' being implicit.

'Four days?' Pepe echoed indignantly, though he understood me perfectly. 'What are you talking about? We are not here for one minute when you think about it properly. If you live to be ninety, it is only a moment, a fraction of a second of time. A century is nothing . . .'

His eyes glittered. He was on the brink of vast truths that neither he nor I nor anyone else would ever quite fathom. That was the spice of life.

'So what else are we to do?' he repeated, raising his glass.

Before we parted, he expertly killed, cleaned and gutted a rabbit, which he insisted on giving me.

'Will there be another explosion in Spain?' I asked on my way out.

'No,' he said. 'We are more civilised now.'

◆

The weather was still warm, too warm for killing pigs. The men tended to drop in rather frequently at *la tienda*; I did the same. One day I found a corporal of the Legion with steel-rimmed spectacles, sitting on the counter swinging his heels. This was not allowed by Paco, who ordered him down. Sighing, he obeyed. Obviously he fancied himself as a bit of an intellectual.

'I have become an *oficinista*,' he complained. 'I am no longer a *guerrillero*. The major has asked me to do the same document at least five hundred times . . . and each time he wants to change it a little, so finally I said to him, "My Major," I said, "you can fucking well do it yourself," and I walked out to come and seek solace with my friend Paco, because we're living in a democracy, aren't we? I don't know what's in that man's veins, but it's not blood, probably quinine or iodine . . . the arsehole! The captain's OK, but the major! I tell you, the first thing I shall do if we ever go to war with another country will be to shoot my officers.' He paused and took a swig of gin and tonic. 'But before that I shall carry out a *golpe de estado*, a coup d'état, single-handed. First I shall shoot all the politicians and monks and nuns, and then I shall go and grab the first goatherd I can find and make him president – because we are living in a democracy, aren't we? We don't want a dictatorship, do we? We just want a government with clean hands – like a goatherd's, which are only soiled with animal shit!'

He laughed in appreciation of his own wit.

'The present government seems pretty popular,' I ventured.

'Bah, they are simply feathering their own nests, and that is ugly in socialists. And they are afraid. They are afraid above all of malefactors and delinquents, whom they treat as popular heroes and to whom they give all the rights!'

'Well,' I said, 'I look forward to reading about your *golpe* in the press. There hasn't been one since Tejero's in 1981, and that is a long time in Spanish politics.'

'Tejero! Don't talk to me of Tejero! I shan't shoot at the

ceiling, spoiling the *patrimonio artístico*! I shall shoot at the head. You'll see. What we have now is a disgrace. It can't go on.'

He leaned over the counter to pinch Paco's thirteen-year-old daughter on the cheek, winked at his own audacity, downed his drink, gave me a mock salute and left.

Rafael Valiente's elder brother, Eduardo, had been standing quietly with a beer throughout this performance.

'The trouble with the Legion,' I said, 'is that it is bored out of its mind. It has nothing to do.'

'There will always be people who chatter too much,' said Eduardo.

He then asked me if I would drop him at the turning for his farm, Las Caballerías. Apparently he had walked down from town after doing some business at the notary's. I said I would be happy to take him the whole way.

Once in the car, he was careful to explain why he was on foot.

'Whenever I have some business in an office, I go up with my son in the Land-Rover when he takes the milk to the *central lechera*. Then I send him home to get on with the job and make my own way down later. These office folk have only one object in life, which is to take as long as possible over everything and waste one's time and then charge heavily for it. It was ever thus. Democracy or no democracy, that hasn't changed.'

'But in general life is much better, isn't it?'

Eduardo pondered.

'Up to a point, yes. There is *abundancia*. The bars are full. The shops are crowded. There is nothing like the *miseria* of the forties and fifties. But the countryside is badly rewarded. Everything is expensive to buy and cheap to sell. Labour costs are so high that you can't employ anyone. I am lucky enough still to have two unmarried sons.'

By now we were approaching Eduardo's land. Relatively he is a rich man, richer probably than Rafael. Over the years he has patiently and painstakingly accumulated and joined bits of land to form an estate of two hundred *fanegas* or something over three hundred acres, including a small but celebrated vineyard. Las Caballerías is also famous for its cheeses, preserved in oil in great vats.

'But when your sons do marry, will they stay on the farm?'

Eduardo placed a sly finger against the bridge of his Roman nose, a feature he shares with his brother. That finger is the sign of knowledge which sees through mere apearances; it wards off evil and shows awareness of where one's true interests lie.

'They won't leave. They don't need to. Two families can make a good living off my land with all the machinery that goes with it, which is of the best.'

He now pointed to some unpromising-looking hummocky slopes of stubble running down to the river.

'I will sell that. It is the only piece I have now which is separated from the rest. Why don't you find me a foreign buyer and I will make you a handsome present?'

'That is very rough *tierra de labor*,' I said. 'No foreigner will buy that. They want a house and water and some trees.'

'There is plenty of water there, if you drill for it, and space for a house and trees.'

No Andalusian has the capacity to recognise that what he is selling you is not quite what you want.

At last there was a slight frost, and word came that Luis was going to kill two pigs the next day; he couldn't wait any longer. I went up to La Mimbre to check this with Luis himself. When I got out of the car, he emerged from his kitchen, which is a square cabin facing his front door across the cobbles. He led me into his front room, calling for Luisillo to bring coals from the kitchen fire from the brazier under the table. Meanwhile he produced a box of *mantecados*, crumbly cinnamon-flavoured cookies in twists of paper, together with half a bottle of sweet anis and two tiny glasses like thimbles on short stems.

'I can't take the dry stuff,' he said. 'It blows your head off. But this . . .'

His face was like a relief map with crevasses and ravines sculpted by the elements, by grief, by resignation and by a wry determination to accept all these things; humour round the eyes redeemed the harsher incisions round the mouth.

'You haven't put out a glass for me,' said Luisillo.

'You should have no need for this stuff, lad.'

'Nor should you,' came the cheeky answer.

'Now then, keep a civil tongue in your head, son, or I'll have to clip you.'

He made a gesture as if to remove his leather belt, but obviously neither of them took this seriously.

Luisillo helped himself to a swig from the tinfoil screwtop of the bottle and then stalked off to tend his rabbits.

Now Paca came in – Luis's sister, Rafael Alarcón's wife.

'Christmas is boring these days in Spain, don't you think?' she asked me.

I said I had been to a fine family party on Christmas Eve and then to the *misa del gallo*, which was packed.

'No, I mean the *comparsas*, which used to sing and play in the streets and in the courtyards of the great houses,' she said. 'You don't see them any more.'

I had almost forgotten the carol-singers dressed as shepherds and shepherdesses with their tambourines and *zambombas* (that marvellously basic instrument consisting of an earthenware jar covered with a parchment-like membrane pierced by a hollow reed, which you rub with dampened fingers to produce the sound). There was a famous *comparsa* led by 'Antonio el Sillero', a chair-mender hardly larger than a dwarf, whose team was made up entirely of his own numerous progeny. They had played for many years in the Renaissance patio of the Casa de Mondragón.

'He died,' said Paca. 'Now people won't take the trouble.'

Even so, I refused to let her deflate my pleasure in a Christmastide which still seemed to me to attend to the fundamentals of the feast and avoid most of the hectic commercialism of our version of it. Christmas trees were not in evidence at all, and very few cards, in any of the houses I had visited. There was no post-Christmas blight extending like the shade of a upas tree over all activities for at least a fortnight. When New Year's Eve and the Epiphany came round, they received their due but no more, and life went swiftly back to normal.

Next, Paca's grown sons came in to discuss the *matanza* next day. There had only been one frost, and not a sharp one: if you killed before time, the *chorizos* and *salchichones* would go green. But Valiente had killed already when it was not all that cold, said Luis, and he himself couldn't hang on any longer. Other tasks were pressing. The sowing had been delayed by the rains. He wanted to get the *matanza* behind him and get on with that. It was left that they would go ahead in the morning if the weather remained reasonably fresh.

Jack Frost obliged again that night. But *matanzas* do not get off to an early start. The helpers have to arrive and breakfast has to be served. When I came at ten o'clock the big copper was heating on Luis's fire, which was smoking abominably. Otherwise, nothing much was happening. Carrasquito, son of Carrasco the *cabero* of our water system, who was to do the butchering, had not turned up. Then he came on foot up the hill, a young man of twenty or so with a soft face, slight stammer and military moustache. His father's old Land-Rover had refused to start, so some other vehicle would have to go down to bring up the *tablero*, which was an essential part of the equipment. He and others including Luisillo went off in the Alarcón tractor to fetch it.

At about eleven they were back with a zinc-topped table two metres long and slightly sloping towards a funnel at the lower end. This they set up in the kitchen with the funnel overhanging the cauldron on the hearth. Then all the males proceeded to the sty to get the first pig, which they pushed, hauled and dragged screaming up a short flight of steps to the *estancia*, as the long cobbled terrace was called. Here a small square metallic table had been put out in the sun. On this the animal's head was held down by several pairs of hands. Antoñito Alarcón, one of Paca's sons, appraised the victim and thumbed the knife to the accompaniment of cries of: 'Come on! Are you going to take all day to kill it?'

He wielded the blade decisively; the stroke was clean; his mother Paca caught the blood (the essence of *morcilla*, the black pudding) in a well-scoured bucket, chucking some odds and bits of veins to the dogs. When the animal was well and truly dead it was lugged onto the zinc *tablero* in the kitchen. The cast now consisted of Luis, the master of ceremonies, Rafael Valiente, three young men – two of Paca's sons and Carrasquito – and Luisillo. This was men's work. The older men ladled scalding water onto the carcass, while the younger generation shaved the pig with firm, expert strokes of their knives, as nicely judged as if they were shaving their own faces. The used water ran back from the tilted *tablero* into the cauldron and was thus not wasted. Luisillo stoked the fire, which continued to smoke horribly, turning the whole scene into a lachrymose version of Vulcan's cave. The only woman in evidence at this stage was Paca, who was washing containers outside.

After its close shave, the animal's front legs were pierced and slung from a wooden yoke; it was then heaved out – all two hundred pounds or so of it – in order to be hung on a hook in the outside wall. The men who had done the deed and shaved the corpse so exquisitely had difficulty in reaching the hook and it took some cursing and swearing before the great bulk was secured. Then Carrasquito advanced to draw and quarter the beast, so that it swung open like the two wings of a diptych or some anatomical illustration in an encyclopedia. No further butchery was done at this stage, other than the removal of lungs, liver, kidneys and heart, which were all drawn out together, followed by the intestines. Carrasquito had previously

Luis, master of the *matanza*

squeezed, with delicate finger and thumb, the remaining excrement from the gut. We all now crowded round the displayed carcass with something like reverence, in order to perform the naming of names and the numbering of parts.

'These,' said Luis solemnly, 'are the two *solomillos* (loins), and those are the two *cintas de lomo*, the strips hanging down from the neck. That of course is the *espina dorsal*, which cannot be eaten but is the basis for *caldo*, a fine broth. The head also serves for that purpose. The *costillas*? No, we do not just eat the ribs as chops or cutlets like

397

in the town. They will form part of the *chorizos* or they will be cut into small sections and fried and conserved in lard.'

'As an animal,' said Rafael Alarcón, who was dressed in his Ronda clothes and thus standing back, 'the pig is a very complete beast. Everything is used other than the skin and hoofs. Nothing is wasted. The trotters themselves are eaten; also the liver, the lights, the brain, the tripe and even the ears.

'In this country,' Luis added, 'there is no remedy but to live off the pig and its products. In the pueblo you can nip out at any minute and buy a scrap of meat or anything else that takes your fancy, but here pork and *chorizo* in particular are fundamental.'

In a curious way the slaughtered pig managed to symbolise not only Spanish frugality – two of them would keep Luis and Luisillo going for the whole year – but also festivity and hospitality, for slices of ham and *lomo*, the main delicacies, would always be brought out on visits and special occasions. Rafael's allusion to completeness was doubly apt.

The same operation was repeated on the second pig, and that brought the first day's proceedings to an end. The animals would now hang for twenty-four hours.

Next day the women came into their own. Several relatives appeared who had not been at the actual killing. The scene moved to the attic loft that ran above Luis's and Alarcón's houses. This had not been partitioned, but each family enjoyed the use of exactly one half. In his part Alarcón still had six good hams from the previous year slung from the main beam, while *morcillas*, *chorizos* and *salchichones* dangled from thinner poles; there were also jars of quince preserve, a pile of walnuts, two cowboy saddles and various implements and tools; this was the store of a man of some substance.

In Luis's zone the two pigs, which had hung overnight, were spreadeagled on the floor. Carrasquito was again present to wield his delicate knife: excising and trimming the hams and *paletillas* (the front legs) to give them the right shape to please the eye when hanging; carving out the *solomillos* and the ribs; then paring all the remnants of meat off the inch-thick layer of *tocino* or fat, which when salted and preserved would be a vital ingredient in every stew throughout the year. Finally, the *tocino* was separated from the skin.

As each part was detached by Carrasquito's blade, it was handed to the three women who were working round the metal-topped table. They too plied their knives with unerring precision, splitting meat from fat and putting each morsel into the correct bowl according to its eventual destination.

'What are you going to do with the ribs?' the chief woman shouted to Luis. 'Will you use them for *chorizo*?'

'No,' he called back. 'We have *chorizo* from last year still. We'll chop the meat and fry it and keep it in *manteca*.'

'Right,' said the woman, getting to work on the ribs and yelling at Luisillo to get out of her way and go and help his father, who was just going down to scour some pails.

'I shit in the milk of the mother who bore a black cat!' she spat out after the disappearing lad.

This trio of Amazons with their strong arms, nimble fingers, intent faces and shrill voices were an impressive sight. As a widower, Luis was particularly dependent on them. They, for their part, were free to say what they liked about Luisillo and no offence taken: they had no spoils of office but to speak their minds freely.

All in all, by the end of his *matanza*, when the last ham was salted away and the last sausage stuffed into its stocking of gut, Luis would have had active help from four men and four women, mostly but not all kinsfolk. When Carrasco killed and Valiente killed and Rafael Alarcón killed, he would likewise go to their assistance.

'Why, in other years,' he said, 'when the weather has been normal and my brother-in-law has killed six or seven and Valiente four or five and I myself two or three and Carrasco several as well, we have been tied up most of the month of January with the *matanza*, which is the proper time after the olive harvest and before the sowing, but these days the weather is *loco* and you don't know where you are.'

Matanza mornings start with coffee and *churros* followed by thimbles of anis. The anis bottle is always to hand but by the second day sizzling snippets from the pigs themselves begin to appear on the table with bread and Montilla wine. A *matanza* is not an orgy because it is rooted in work and has strict proprieties and protocol; but it has elements of celebration which may cause the head to swim a little. On the second evening I sought relief from Luis's smoke-filled kitchen by walking out onto the *estancia* with its fine views to the south and east, incorporating the clifftop along which Ronda spreads. As I stood there, Rafael Valiente joined me. Dusk was falling. A battery of harsh yellow lights sprang to life across the valley, suggesting some industrial installation wired and patrolled by guard dogs.

'The Hotel Victoria,' Rafael said. 'Ronda is beautiful, isn't it?'

'Will you move up there when you finish your flat?'

'It would be good to put our youngest to a better school than La Indiana. For that we should have to move up to town. Our older girl already works there and has to lodge with relatives. Her *novio* is pressing her to marry but she won't for some years. She wants to accumulate a nest-egg of her own before settling into marriage and children. So we would be able to give her a proper roof. Altogether there is much to be said for it.'

'But how could you run a farm from there? Supposing a cow gave birth at night?'

'Certainly it would mean getting up early and getting home late. But if a cow is going to give birth you know in advance and spend the night. In the summer we could all be here. Yes, it could work . . .'

I had little doubt that Rafael and Maruja would follow in

Arturo's footsteps if and when they could; and that would be Luis's dream too, with Luisillo fixed up somewhere, even if it was only washing cars or mending punctures; Rafael Alarcón's professed intention on clement nights to stay put until carried out feet first would, if adhered to, be the exception that proved the rule; the cynosure of most *campo* eyes was the fair city.

Yet this did not necessarily mean the end of the *campo*. Self-employment on the land was still more honourable than work as a wage-slave, more prestigious than labouring on the roads or on a building site, less demeaning than being buried down a mine. Also, there was always the chance of accumulating wealth through judicious purchase or marriage. The *campo* should not be written off. Choosing a rural livelihood, however, did not mean that one should not aspire to sleep in a house in a proper street and acquire respect, even deference, at a favourite café table – as the gentry had always done. After all, was this not *la democracia*?

Before I left for England Paco came to see me. I could tell from the way his face was bunched up that it was about to burst into some revelation. But he maintained his composure until he was seated and I had poured him a glass of wine.

'Ali,' he said, in a tone of someone breaking bad news, 'I'm afraid to say I am going to have to leave your land.'

I had spent so long weaving nightmares such as Paco going to law to establish an acquired right and wondering on what terms I could sever relations with him amicably before this happened that I was completely taken aback.

'But why, Paco?'

'My Antonio has been called up to do his *mili*. We thought he would be exempted from military service as the only remaining son working with his father, but he was not. He has to go. Mark you, I think it will be good for him, as it was for me. But without him I can't handle my place and yours and my bit of arable and the *olivar* I have up on the hill. Something has to give.'

My family had never been much taken with Antonio, who used to hang about gawping and eating mulberries and taking potshots at birds. My own relief was tinged with some guilt that a nasty bubble of mistrust in my own mind had proved groundless, though of course I was delighted it had been pricked so painlessly. Such was my corresponding feeling of magnanimity that I at once absolved Paco from ploughing in the ugly maize stubble that still remained from his failed crop.

My mood next day was one of deep satisfaction that the place was totally unencumbered and all options were open to us. But it was not long before new pressures asserted themselves. Within twenty-four hours Esteban, a handsome goatherd from La Indiana, one of the few young men in a fraternity which was in decline, arrived to ask if I would rent him the pasture.

My feelings about goats were decidedly mixed. They were so much a feature of the tawny Mediterranean uplands, forming such a link with the ancient world, their inscrutable yellow eyes with narrow black pupils hinting at antique rituals and sacrifices, that their elimination would be almost as mortal a blow to the identity of Spain as the abolition of the bullfight – perhaps more so, as they were still more numerous and evident in the Spanish landscape than the fighting bulls. When the goats went, the Homeric world would finally be dead.

To such an extent had numbers declined that the European Commission was now offering a subsidy for the preservation of the species. Hereabouts public grazing rights had been much reduced. Julián de Zulueta had told me recently of the outrage of the goatherds of Tolox, when their traditional rights of pasture in the Sierra de las Nieves were severely cut back in the interests of reafforestation. 'They have stolen the *monte* from us,' they complained bitterly. 'They have stolen our *monte*.' The result was that the remaining goatherds were not over-scrupulous, living as they did on the fringe of the agricultural community, seizing every opportunity afforded by a broken fence or absent owner to invade their neighbour's land. At least Esteban had come openly with a proposal for a deal. Also, he put me in mind of Rilke's marvellous lines on a shepherd tending his flock on a hillside:

> Let me feel stony, and let
> the shepherd's daily task seem possible to me,
> as he moves about and tans and with measuring stone-throw
> mends the hem of his flock where it grows ragged.
> His slow but laborious walk, his pensive body,
> his glorious standing still! Even today a god
> might secretly enter that form and not be diminished.

Yet, the 'nimby' factor (not in my backyard) was stronger even than Rilke. A flock of goats in the *huerta* was anathema to me and all my family. It would put an end to any attempt to preserve a few ornamental plants and shade trees round the house. I immediately invented a prior commitment to someone else. The options I had been dallying with were ephemeral, for if the place lay empty the goats would come in – if not Esteban's then another's – rent or no rent, with or without permission. I lost no time in driving up to see Rafael Valiente.

'In my judgement,' he said, 'Vicente is your man. He is in his mid-forties, very hard-working and reliable. He will do all the things Paco didn't do for you, like keeping the brambles down and scything the grass.

'But isn't he a full-time employee on the *granja* of Miguel?'

'Yes, but he has time off to attend to his own animals . . . and every other weekend. And he has two boys. The eldest is old enough to work.'

That evening Vicente came round with his children. He had a square head, long flattish nose, wide mouth, strong shoulders, big hands: altogether rather a Basque look. Of course, I realised at once that I knew him a little from casual encounters at *la tienda*. The eldest son of fifteen also looked strong and willing; he had left school and didn't want to work in the town. The younger larked around attractively with his little sister.

We talked terms. I said we might be selling and any arrangement would have to be provisional and reviewed after a year. There would be no rent; I paid the taxes; he would only have to pay for the annual remaking of the dam and cleaning the ditches. In return I wanted the fences repaired, the brambles kept down, access to the house kept clear and goats kept out. I impressed on him particularly that we were a family of tree-lovers, that my sister was a dedicated bird-watcher and that no tree was to be felled without my permission. The mulberry tree by the entrance and the bamboos were especially sacred . . .

Vicente appraised the land through narrowed eyes. Why did I want those old quinces? They were practically dead and difficult to plough round. They provided useful cover, I said, for us and for birds; they must stay. And those clumps of canes, which were also an impediment? They must stay too, I insisted. Ah, so they were a *capricho*? Precisely, I said, a *capricho*. He would have to respect our *caprichos*. In return, he could sow and harvest what crops he pleased.

Vicente nodded. Very well, he said, so be it: it was a deal. Juani his eldest boy would help. I wouldn't know the place when I came out next. It would look like a gentleman's estate. And whether I sold or stayed, its value would be greatly enhanced.

When I reported what I had done to Ana and Mateo in town, they received the news with caution bordering on disapproval. With Paco, who had been proposed by them in the first place, they had felt on firmer ground, despite his shortcomings. Now with this Vicente . . .

'Paco was not a bad man,' said Ana. 'He always sowed that vegetable patch for you. It was just that he took on more than he could manage.'

She was very friendly with Paco's wife Encarna, from whom she got her country eggs.

'I know Vicente,' said Mateo. 'He was with us when we were building the Cartajima road. He is a good worker. Then I think he went to Switzerland. But whether he will do any better than Paco, who knows? He may be worse. In the end everybody is out for himself.'

Ana pursed her lips.

'We shall have to see if he fulfils his promises,' she said. 'Only time will tell.'

Exit Paco. Enter Vicente. The beginning of a new era? That was hardly likely, I recognised. But the old dream of the *campo*, keeping it going somehow, even from a distance, continued to exert a potent influence. Was there still a chance of reconciling British romanticism and Spanish realism? I felt it was worth another try.

12

RITES OF SPRING

Not long into the new year I received an agitated telephone call from Ana. Did I know what Vicente was up to? I had to confess I had no idea; I supposed he was simply doing what we had agreed. Well then, I had better think again, for no sooner was my back turned than he had pulled out several quince trees, burned down much of the boundary hedge on the right, burned the old willows round the threshing floor (threatening the house with flying sparks in the process) and, perhaps worst of all, burned down the long range of canes topping the ridge that protected the *huerta* from floods. The whole place now looked as bare as an aerodrome. Rosi had taken some pictures which she was sending me.

Mateo now came on the line. He had tackled Vicente about all this, telling him roundly that it was in breach of the verbal contract I had made with him. Vicente had said slyly that it was his boys who had burned the canes and willows one afternoon while he was up in Ronda. Wasn't he even in control of his own children, then? Yes, of course, but they must have misunderstood what he told them. Misunderstood? That was nonsense, snorted Mateo. The real reason was that he wanted everything out of the way that would impede a tractor or would keep the ground in shadow once the crop was sown. There was no misunderstanding there – that was deliberate! Anyway, what did I want to do about it? I said there was nothing I could do in person before

Easter, but I would send a letter in strong terms to Vicente, telling him I would wind up the agreement as soon as I got out there, unless he mended his ways and guaranteed to abide by the conditions I had set. Would Mateo deliver it to him and see that he read it? Otherwise it might lie around for days in *la tienda*, which was where all the valley mail was left. Very well, Mateo said reluctantly, but he doubted it would do much good. There had been none of this sort of trouble in Paco's day.

After this conversation I reflected wryly that we seemed to have lurched from Paco who did too little to Vicente who did too much. In a curious way I was reminded of Arturo's first arrival in the valley like an avenging angel: in a few weeks he had burned almost every stick of wood, alive or dead, on his land, inveighing all the while against maggots, grubs, bugs, insects, vermin, mice and rats and bringing fire and the sword to the lot of them. It was a sort of fundamentalism, a puritanism, a determination to smoke or dig out every rotten thing that crept and crawled or grew without permission and subject the earth – thus cleansed – to the discipline of the plough and the excoriation of the sun.

'*Quita, quita!*' Arturo would chant as he performed this holy mission. 'What do we want with all this filth, all this rubbish, all this rottenness? *Fuera, fuera* . . . out, out!'

None of this was going to be of much help to me at my next family council. Arturo had not attempted to apply his doctrine to our land; Vicente by all accounts had. Jaime was the most indignant.

'You can't allow yourself to be pushed around like that, Dad. Whose land is it anyway? When it's mine, I shall put my foot down.'

I handed him a draft of the letter I proposed to send Vicente.

My sister said, 'I never liked Paco much but at least he left the brambles. Can't Vicente understand that birds need cover?'

'He is not interested in birds – except to shoot.'

'Well, even for him to do that,' she said reproachfully, 'they need a habitat.'

Having studied the letter, Jaime returned it to me.

'That good, Dad,' he said. 'That's cool. Send it.'

The wisest comment came, as usual, from Hilly.

'Nature's pretty rampant out there. Sometimes I used to feel it was swamping me. If you don't chop a few things down to size, you feel they're going to eat you alive. There's a lot of stuff out there that could do with a huge cutting back and most of it will come up stronger than before. Wait till the spring . . .'

Hilly was right. When I arrived in April, a green crop flowed almost from the house down to the poplars at the bottom. Vicente had sown crab grass between the *estancia* and the fence; something like a rough lawn was coming up. Along the right-hand boundary much of the bramble-festooned quince hedge had been burned to the roots, so that an ugly, half-finished concrete cow-shed built by Arturo's successor loomed uncomfortably close. But it wouldn't be long before the brambles reasserted themselves, if given half a chance. On the other side, I had a greater sense of exposure. The burning of two hundred metres or so of high canes seemed to bring the *huerta* of José on the other bank much closer. Always a prickly neighbour, it would be much easier for him to watch out for me and bawl at me across the river as he loved to do. But new shoots were sprouting and there would eventually be a fresher palisade, unencumbered by so much old and desiccated growth as before . . . provided of course that Vicente got the message.

When he came over, we looked at each other first in silence. I tried not to relax my features. At the very least a stern demeanour was demanded by his breach of covenant. He was looking at me steadily. A faint smile hovered at the corners of his lips; he was not going to apologise.

'I almost had a family revolution on my hands when they

heard of this,' I said, gesturing at the *huerta*. 'You got my letter?'

He did not answer this directly.

'But it looks better, doesn't it . . . now that you can see for yourself?'

'That depends on whether you want José from over the river observing your every move,' I replied. 'And I certainly didn't want the view on the other side opened up to reveal that hideous shed. This for us is a *finca de recreo*; it is for cultivation, of course, but it is also for repose, so it needs shelter. I never said you could burn the canes. In fact, I remember saying expressly they were not to be touched.'

'It was the boys. They didn't understand. They thought it was for the best.'

I looked him in the eye. I knew – and he knew I knew – that he wanted the canes and hedges out of the way for ease of ploughing and to keep their shade off the soil. Any hint he had let drop to that effect would have been leapt on by his boys as an excuse for a glorious conflagration.

'Well, if they don't understand their own father,' I said, 'who or what can they understand? Besides, there was a danger of setting fire to the house. It narrowly escaped a fire once before when Rafael de las Monjas was burning stubble and the sparks jumped across the water. But to have it threatened by your kids making a bonfire within a few metres of it . . .'

'Nothing happened,' said Vicente stubbornly. 'And the canes will grow again. Look, they are sprouting already. They grow very fast.'

'Yes,' I said. 'And this time they will be left. Apart from anything else they reinforce the bank. And you will have only yourself – or your boys – to thank if you lose everything you have sown in the next flood.'

The confrontation ran out of steam. I had said my piece. People to whom anger does not come readily sometimes have to simulate it and I hoped my performance had been reasonably effective. He would give no ground on the surface but I had some hopes it had sunk in. In other respects, it was true the place looked better farmed and in better shape, and the fences had been repaired; also Vicente had sown a small kitchen garden near the house, no doubt as a propitiatory act.

Easter week was almost upon us. It was a long time since I had been out at this time of the year and I wanted to discover how Ronda's *Semana Santa* was surviving; I also wanted to take in some of the village processions.

In town I went first to see Delgado, owner of the main stationers' where the programmes were sold. I knew he had been a leading figure in one of the *cofradías*, or brotherhoods. He said he did not go out as a penitent any more but was still involved with the administration: membership of the *cofradías* and *hermandades* (the words are virtually interchangeable) still ran very much in the family; fathers brought in their sons and so on. But did the *cofradías* help the poor at all, or were they just a sanctimonious bourgeois display? Certainly, he said, they had acted as charitable bodies in the past and still did to some extent, but the problem of poverty had increasingly become the province of the state and its social security system. Relative to this, the contribution of charity was necessarily very small. Besides, the processions were now very expensive to put on and absorbed most of the funds. Was *Semana Santa* in decline then? Not at all, it was growing. As I could see from the programme (which was indeed large and glossy and cost 175 pesetas), Ronda was bringing out more processions than ten years ago. But the best person to talk to was Emilio Martín, who was still very active in all this.

Emilio has a leathergoods shop almost opposite Delgado. He has a shopkeeper's pasty face, but it is a very mobile one, and his brown eyes, sometimes fixed in contemplation, can also move rapidly. He is the *hermano mayor* of the most celebrated of Ronda's brotherhoods, 'La Antigua y Venerable Hermandad de Nuestro Padre Jesús Nazareno y Nuestra

Señora de los Dolores', known as 'Padre Jesús' for short. Its procession is particularly impressive, for it brings its images out of a low-lying church near the Roman bridge and then carries them with no music but a slow drumbeat up very steep cobbled streets before reaching the town centre; it is thus the most demanding on its members and the most popular with the public.

'The brotherhood is three hundred years old,' said Emilio. ' "La Paz" and "El Santo Entierro" are even older. Since the war four or five new brotherhoods have been founded and all have survived, except that of the gypsies which didn't get off the ground because its main promoter died: a determined leading spirit is necessary for a new brotherhood to prosper.'

'I have always understood that the *hermandades* spring up from the *pueblo*, the people, and the Church is not much involved; that you just pay the priest to bless your procession and walk in it. Is that true?'

'Not exactly,' said Emilio. 'Historically the first *hermandades* were promoted in the sixteenth century by the religious orders, notably the Dominicans. So there has always been a strong bond with the Church. The bishops these days take an enormous interest in these expressions of popular faith. Vatican '65 opened the whole thing up to secular initiative, it is true, but the priesthood is still very much accustomed to command.'

'How many members have you?' I asked next. 'And are the young still joining?'

'Certainly. Allowing for deaths, we have made a net gain over the last year of about fifty, and our total number now stands at 1067.'

'How do you cover your costs? By subscription . . . lotteries . . . charity bullfights?'

'The latter always make a loss. No, by subscriptions mainly. Our *cuota* is six hundred pesetas a year with another two hundred for charitable purposes. The bishops have laid down a minimum of 10 per cent for charity, but we do better.'

411

'What does the money mainly go on?'

He ticked the items off on his fingers.

'Two hundred thousand pesetas for the band; 300,000 for the carnations; then there are the Virgin's robe and train, and the tunics. Those are the main things.'

Nearly two thousand pounds on carnations for two floats! That was a hefty sum. He nodded. It might seem so, but it was traditional. You couldn't take a float out undressed! Then he became intense.

'But of course there is the other side of the coin. If it concentrates only on externals, a *cofradía* will die. The images are only symbols and the decoration an adornment. There has to be a strong spiritual commitment as well to keep the *cofradía* alive. The proof is that those founded on folklore and exhibitionism – and there have been not a few – always die. Fetishistic devotion is not enough.'

I pondered this.

'You say the spiritual element is important. Does it spill over into the daily lives of your members?'

Emilio smiled. Though capable of passion, he is not a solemn man.

'With some more than others, naturally. We have ideal precepts: for instance we should all go to Mass daily in our own church to confirm our devotion, but many don't because it is inconveniently placed. So they nip in anywhere – to the Socorro for example, which is very central. Our priest complains that most of us only turn up for the novena of the Virgin and on important feast days. I am an enthusiast and I live near, so I do go every day. But it is more difficult for others. Isn't it better to go to church somewhere rather than not at all? We have to live in the real world.'

'Talking of the real world, how does the Church survive these days in the socialist secular state? Isn't there some voluntary method of contribution through the tax system? How does that work?'

'Yes,' he said. 'There's a box on your tax form and you can put a cross for the Protestants, the Catholics, the Jews and so forth. The total allocation for this is 1 per cent of the tax take. If you leave your box blank, then your share goes to general social improvements.'

'As a Catholic, do you resent this pluralism?'

'How could I? Have we not passed from a political dictatorship to a democracy? Why should it be different in the religious sphere? With faith the Catholic Church will survive.'

'How do the Catholics fare? Do they get many crosses?'

'Not enough, I'm afraid, to cover the whole cost of the state's subvention to the Church.'

'So the atheist socialist state underwrites the Established Church?'

'Nobody said the socialist state was necessarily atheist.'

'But I thought there was a move towards disestablishment.'

Emilio laughed.

'Yes, there is, and I'm afraid it comes mainly from our side. Saint Paul said the man of the altar must live from the altar. That's fine in theory, but there's an awful lot of competition these days. However much the purists may want to go it alone, there is frankly a strong interest in maintaining the state contribution.'

'But isn't it surprising that voluntary tax contributions are not rolling in in a Catholic country, especially as they are not *additional* to the general level of taxation?'

'Perhaps,' he shrugged. 'But as I have said there is much competition. Also, you have to take the positive step of actually filling in the box.'

'Most of us think of Spain as the bastion of Catholicism, prime mover of the Counter-Reformation, missionary to the New World and so on. I think the bottom would drop out of *my* universe if Spain ceased to be officially Catholic, with other cults and religions – though tolerated of course – still on the fringe.'

'Spain,' said Emilio, '*is* innately Catholic. But *sui generis*.'

◆

Palm Sunday in Ronda was certainly *sui generis*. There was little or no sense of the beginning of a dramatic cycle of religious events. In the Calle de la Bola I passed Don José Aguilera, a retired inspector of police.

'I know you even in your beret!' he called out.

'The good policeman always sees through a disguise,' I conceded genially.

He had been involved in the episode when I was suspected of being a spy, but had always taken it with a pinch of salt as a neurosis of the special branch. He gave me a cheery wave and passed on.

There was a procession somewhere with Christ entering Jerusalem on a donkey accompanied by children but I did not manage to find it. The main road over the bridge and through the town was monopolised by the final lap of the provincial cycle race. All traffic was held up until the leaders had streaked through followed by their team cars and the television crews.

As soon as one could move, I went down to the Barrio, where I found the regular Sunday market in full swing. In the *cafelillo* I met a jolly fellow who had for years sold fish to the remoter farms by horse. He had given this up some time before but kept his fine mare for old times' sake. She was a strawberry roan, with eight years in the mouth and in foal to boot; he was asking 250,000 pesetas. I whistled but he still seemed confident of getting 180,000 (over a thousand pounds) from a gentleman in La Línea, who wanted her badly for his daughter. It appeared that 'fancy' horses were still affected by the equine fever quarantine, but there had been no outbreak in the mountains, where no one imported polo ponies from Africa on the certificate of bent vets, so he was confident of being able to move his animal. Ah, the purity of the mountains in contrast to the corruption of the coasts and plains! What a privilege, we both agreed, to live in Ronda, capital of the Serranía, envied of all the world!

In the doorway of the *cafelillo* a man with a folded

umbrella contemplated the rain that had just come on. He was watching the Sunday stall-holders scurrying to cover up or bundle away their wares.

'It looks as if the saints will get a wetting this Holy Week,' I said.

'Then let them stay in their churches!' he replied with indifference. 'There they won't catch cold.'

I had planned to visit several of the villages but rain and swirling mists made the roads treacherous. When I managed to get out to Cartajima I was confined there for several hours by a blanket of damp mountain fog with a visibility of about ten feet. But everyone was sure the weather would clear for Easter Sunday, which I must be sure not to miss.

In an attempt to break out of the climatic conditions of the sierras I decided to make a dash down to Medina Sidonia and Alcalá de los Gazules. At Medina the procession came out of the church of La Coronada while it was still daylight. No fewer than three floats were manoeuvred onto a special platform built out over the church steps; then they were slowly negotiated down a ramp to street level, to the applause of the onlookers. Christ at the Column came first, followed by Christ Crucified, followed by the mourning Virgin under her canopy. There was clapping at every stage successfully accomplished. In particular a group of girls high in the belfry, right under the great bells, clapped and clapped the swaying progress of the Virgin, whose float was the heaviest, as it was born step by precarious step down into the plaza. When the procession set off, there must have been some two hundred Nazarenes all told in the robes of their various *cofradías*. The crowd was not large as yet, but I was assured the Plaza Major and the processional route through the centre would be packed.

I left in order to get to Alcalá on time. The arrangements there were more rustic. There was no *palio* or canopy to cover the Virgin. Watching from the doorway of his bar, I remarked on this to Paco Pizarro, who smiled in a superior way.

'Alcalá's saints are tougher than Medina's, less spoilt. If it rains, very well – they will get wet, but they won't scuttle back to their temples like those of Medina.'

There was no rain to put this to the test. The *costaleros* carrying the floats were strong youths in ordinary dress, who lit up cigarettes at every halt. An elderly man, accompanying the Virgin with obvious devotion though without any formal role in the procession, chain-smoked the whole way while attempting to march properly and keep in step with the band.

When the procession stopped for one of its rests in the main street, a figure that had come to rest near me removed its *capirote* (the Nazarene's conical hat with a mask over the eyes) to reveal . . . an ethereally beautiful blonde maiden of sixteen or seventeen. I remembered my conversation with Don Diego Romero about the infiltration of the *cofradías* by women. Though he had cautiously welcomed it, he had been rather ambivalent about the break-up of the male monopoly. As I contemplated this magical vision, I thought it was wholly to be applauded.

When I got back to the hills, the weather had improved greatly. I therefore decided to brave Igualeja'a dreadful defile in the hope of coinciding with some part of the Passion Play, which I knew from my earlier conversation with its producer took place over the Thursday and Friday of Holy Week.

Having parked, I walked down to the bar which is almost in front of the church. Jesus and the disciples – they were lads of eighteen to twenty, he a little older – were coming up the main street in their school-play robes. The public stood back against the walls; some peered down from windows; all knew that these young men were not what they claimed to be, yet there was an expectant hush. One of the disciples knocked on the door of the church. Immediately a character representing Simon opened up. There was a short exchange whose words I could not catch; but it was clearly agreed that the last supper should be held in Simon's house (for which the church did duty) and the doors were then thrown open wide.

Christ and the apostles went in first. The villagers flowed in and occupied the pews. A camera crew was already installed. The scene passed to the high altar, which was laid as a table. While this was happening, Mary Magdalene, a dark, smouldering beauty came up the aisle. About halfway to the altar she stopped and began casting off her finery and her jewels with contempt onto the floor; then, having loosened her long tresses, freed of their pearls, she advanced slowly and seductively towards the supper table, where she washed Christ's feet with her tears.

This bit was very effective. Every young and youngish male in the congregation was stirred by the Magdalene's sexuality and then by her prostration at the feet of him who was to die. The Christ himself was not bad, but all the rest were fairly wooden. Judas, leaving the altar and the church to betray Jesus, looked far too nice and fresh a lad, and was clearly embarrassed by his role. All the same, the spectacle seemed to me to express rather well the tussle between animality (represented by the Magdalene) and spirituality (represented by Christ) in Igualeja, a pueblo famed in the world outside for its violence and ruthlessness.

Afterwards in the plaza I ran into Alvaro, the producer. I wanted him to know that I had been as good as my word and had come; also to congratulate him. But he was too busy to pay much attention. He was surrounded by other Ronda intellectuals. They were all complaining about what blockheads the local actors were, how hard it was to get them to say their lines as if they had any meaning. I said I thought it quite an achievement to get a dozen youths to come forward to suffer the gibes of their producer, and the derision of their mates, for no tangible reward at all: that their awkwardness was probably just as effective as any greater theatrical skill; also that the Christ was by no means bad . . .

'That took years,' they moaned.

'. . . and the Magdalene was marvellous,' I added.

'Ah, the Magdalene!' they sighed. 'But alas she is getting married.'

I said I was not surprised.

'God knows what we shall do next year. The Christ, yes, he is OK now, though he took a lot of work. But without the Magdalene . . .'

I had a feeling that out of Igualeja, with its strange dualism, another Magdalene would arise.

Compared to the smaller pueblos, and even to Medina and Alcalá, Ronda undoubtedly has a serious heavyweight Holy Week, with no less than ten processions all told. To pay for these and bring them out onto the streets, several thousand people must be actively involved; and there are many more passive spectators on whom something may be supposed to rub off. The Virgen de la Paz, patroness of the city, does not appear during this week, because she has her own special day. Like Olvera's she has been pontifically crowned: a distinction that requires evidence of a strong and not merely parochial or local cult over a substantial period of time. All this gives some colour to Ronda's claim to be a 'Marian' city. It can also probably by interpreted as the conscience-money of a town of shopkeepers, attempting to serve both God and Mammon. But Ronda's Holy Week cannot be applauded or denigrated in such simple terms: it is much more diverse.

There are two star turns on Thursday night. The first has the modern setting of the bus-station square, surrounded by high-rise blocks of flats whose balconies are crammed with spectators: their bleak exteriors are for once humanised by tier upon tier of people, like passengers on the decks of some great ship. Below, between thronged pavements, the symbolic act of union between two floats takes place: Christ presented to the people, *Ecce Homo*, and Nuestra Señora del Buen Amor, his downcast but divinely pretty mother.

As the floats pass each other in opposite directions, each effects a little swaying dance by way of salutation. This is done first on one side of the square and then repeated on the other, so that none shall miss it, and to great applause throughout.

But now comes a stranger encounter, for a third float advances from a lateral street. This is El Cristo de la Buena Muerte, Christ of the Good Death, a recumbent figure on the Cross borne by Foreign Legionnaires in their green berets – whose patron he is. The mercenaries without a mission nowadays – other than deflowering local lasses and patronising the oldest profession – are nonetheless still pledged to death. Their motto is: *Legionarios a luchar, Legionarios a morir!* – a sentiment out of the same stable as General Millán Astray's famous Civil War battle cry, *Viva la Muerte!* They come on at the jog, raising their dead god to the height of their shirtsleeved arms and then lowering him to shoulder level before raising him aloft again; this triumphalist gesture is repeated several times in quick succession as they advance rapidly to meet the other images. How is one to interpret this? Fascist revival? Vainglorious militarism? Reversion to type? Or is it just a whiff from a more violent past which makes the bourgeois spine tingle a little without any other consequences? Probably the latter, for the large crowd witnessing this religio-military spectacle has long since abjured fascism and is likely to be pretty solidly *Felipista*.

Next follows a homily over the loudspeaker system. This evening the electronics were faulty and I was unable to follow much of it, though one theme did come through loud and clear: 'People of Ronda, do you want to reach the end of your days with the guarantee of an open gate to the Kingdom of Heaven? There you see Christ of the Good Death with his arms flung open wide. Live like him and you will learn to die well!' From where I stood I could not see whether it was a priest who was delivering this oration or not. *Pace* Emilio, there was without doubt some tension between the *cofradías* and the Church. Popular religion was fine but it could get a little out of hand. That was the fear of the bishops. And it was given some substance, it seemed to me, by the words of the *hermano mayor* of the Good Death, whose attitude was made quite plain in the glossy programme: 'And this year, as we have always done, whether the presence of a priest is authorised or not by the ecclesiastical authority, we shall use this platform to shout our message to the people of Ronda.' So, if the broadcast voice was a priest's, it was presumably that of a populist evangelist rather than an orthodox cleric.

The bishops are, of course, in a cleft stick. If they give the *cofradías* their heads, all sorts of strange practices and variants may emerge – of which the death cult implicit in El Cristo de la Buena Muerte is one example. Also, there are the links of some *cofradías* with more secular *peñas* like those supporting a bullfighter, which put on flamenco and more risqué entertainments in their club tents during the fair. But if the bishops stamp too hard on this popular religiosity, they risk losing their flock and becoming shepherds without sheep.

The second great event of Thursday night is the *salida*, the bringing out, of Padre Jesús and Nuestra Señora de los Dolores from the church of Santa Cecilia. This is the procession masterminded by Emilio, and it should give the bishops fewer headaches. The setting could not be more different. The church is right down at the lowest point of the *Ciudad*; in front of it stands the public water-trough of Los Ocho Caños with its eight waterspouts emerging from gargoyle faces. Here mules still drink and women fill their pitchers when the main supply fails to deliver through their taps. Along the flank of the church runs Calle Real, the first post-Reconquest overspill from the fortified city: in the sixteenth century it was the high street leading out towards Granada. Today it is a run-down area with a few grand doorways concealing a warren of tenements.

The art of the *salida*, as always, consists in getting the great floats, carried by sixty or seventy men, out of the confines of the church onto a specially erected wooden ramp and thus down into the street without any mishap such as scraping the Virgin's canopy against the portico or failing on the first attempt to make the tight right-angle turn out of the building onto the narrow platform of boards. This accomplished, the procession sets off up the steep cobbled gradient towards the centre, resting every fifty metres or so. Nazarenes with tall poles like boathooks lift up the hanging loops of electric cable which festoon so many Spanish streets wherever they threaten to enmesh the Virgin in their black coils. The streetlights cast the silhouettes of the Christ figure carrying his cross and of his mother in her sorrowing splendour onto a stretch of windowless white convent wall; their images are etched there for some minutes and it is almost a surprise that the imprint does not remain there when they move on. As if propelled by the drumbeats of the slow march, the solemn cortège creeps ever higher, drawing behind it its long tail of hooded penitents. But the bars are open, and the one facing the Ocho Caños was doing a roaring trade. Entering, I found myself standing next to Ana's son, Joaquín.

'There used to be three days of official abstinence,' he said, 'but the rich always got round it by buying *bulas* or ecclesiastical dispensations. As for the poor, they weren't much affected because they had little money to spend and there wasn't much to spend it on. I can remember when there was nothing to buy in the bars in Holy Week but potato salad and dried cod.'

It was not so now, with everything from giant prawns to quails' eggs on offer. Spain knows to perfection how to domesticate the divine, how to mix the sacred and profane. This is not to say that spiritual, even supernatural experiences do not take place. For example, Ana Mari Segura is the very type of the liberated Spanish woman, but she is also much devoted to the cult of the simple Capuchin monk

Fray Leopoldo de Alpandeire, whose aid she once invoked to find her a peaceful home. Sitting one afternoon in the Plaza del Campillo in the *Ciudad*, she asked a passing woman, 'Do you know of any house to let around here?' Yes, came the answer, a flat had fallen vacant that very morning in a house with a beautiful view over the mountains. Ana Mari obtained the lease and the peace she sought, with the added bonus of the view: when she moved in she discovered from the owner that the house had been placed under the special protection of Fray Leopoldo de Alpandeire.

It was in relation to the Virgin, however, that Ana Mari's most interesting experience took place. She asked the Virgen de la Paz, to whom she prayed regularly, a favour concerning her health. When the Virgin's procession passed by, she gazed up at her hoping for a sign. None was given. Yet, as she watched the image recede, an admirer gave her a red carnation which he had plucked from the float. She took the flower home and put it in water; within a short time the condition that had been troubling her for months disappeared.

On Good Friday the bishops got their way in one respect at least: they succeeded in banning music from the processions on the day of Christ's death. The municipal band, which had performed the previous year, was not required, much to the disgruntlement of Juan and the other bandsmen, who would lose a day's pay. In the event the main brotherhood concerned brought the dead Christ down the Calle de la Bola ringing hand-bells, which apparently didn't count. A single drum was also permitted with each float, without which the bearers would have been unable to march in step. Jesus of Nazareth, angular and gaunt in an ornate glass coffin, with the agony of death still upon his features, was thus carried through the town as the bishops wished.

Easter Sunday was a day of glory in every dimension. The sky was flawless, without even the early cloud cover, later to be dissolved by the sun, common in April. Along the valley men were ploughing the land, an activity which seemed in perfect keeping with the morning of the Resurrection.

I went to Cartajima. The church, which is on the highest peak of the pueblo, was dressed for a wedding with carnations and pink ribbons adorning the pews: a couple was to be married after the procession. The simple building is charming with its ceiling of plain unpainted wood with perforated tie-beams in the *artesonado* tradition. There is unfortunately a large and glutinously macabre painting by Miguel Martín, the celebrated Ronda painter-photographer, dedicated *a Cartajima, mi pueblo natal* in 1947. The damned are burning limply in hell; an angel leans down to pat a tormented old man on the back as he raises his arms in supplication, but the eyes of the Virgin up in the clouds, cuddling her sweetly pretty child, are turned upwards and fixed on other things in complete neglect of her job of intercession. Underneath, two elderly women sat gossiping in a pew, quite unaffected by this grievous scene. Then the priest, who served several pueblos, arrived. Things could begin.

A few minutes later Cartajima's modest float of the Virgin was brought out, carried on the shoulders of four men, each with a type of crook in one hand, on which the shafts were cradled when they rested. The bar of the *ancianos* just below the church steps was packed with people of all ages. Some of the young men were drinking tall glasses of *cuba libre*. A lad with a smattering of coastal English and a skinful of gin and Coke was grasping a sheaf of rockets which – he said, gripping my shoulder with sentimental camaraderie – he would set off up my arse. We exchanged further pleasantries of a like nature to the great enjoyment of our audience. As the Virgin came down the slope, everyone turned out into the street. She stopped right in front of us. Her bearers and escort were all in Sunday suits. There were no tunics or uniforms, though the *hermano mayor* was distinguished by a ribbon and staff of office. Most of us formed up behind with the exception of a few determined atheists who ostentatiously sat it out in chairs they had dragged from the bar onto the pavement. There was no music at all, not even a drum, but occasionally a firework fizzled up into the sky. I kept a wary eye out for my drunken pyrotechnical friend but he seemed to have succumbed to his libations.

When we reached the wide main street of the village it had a gala air. It was lined with lopped-off branches of every type of local tree and shrub – olive, pine, cistus, chestnut, oleander, even the fiercely protected *pinsapo* – all stuck like Christmas trees into special holes in the pavement. All the young women seemed to be wearing something new. The accent was on square shoulders and short skirts of very shiny material, sometimes with an incongruous flounce at the back like a fishy fin. One attractive lass sported a sailor-suit, such as used to be worn by boys making their first communion. A youth standing near me was so overcome by this that he let out a long whistle, followed by: 'Oh my daughter, what beauty! *Que belleza!*'

At the lower end of the rustic esplanade was a bower of greenery, sheltering another image which I could not identify from a distance. The bearers of the Virgin quickened their pace almost to a run; her crown trembled perilously. The figure from the bower, likewise carried by four men in suits, now began to advance; it turned out to be a chubby young Jesus, perhaps five or six years old, holding out the orb of the world in one hand and in the other raising a standard on which were embroidered the words: *Cristo ha resucitado, Aleluya!* In Cartajima it was not Christ the Man who was resurrected but Christ the Child.

The two floats now moved towards one another, their bearers breaking into a trot. When they met face to face, each swayed and bobbed three times to the other. This sequence, I learned, was called *La Cortesía*, the curtsy. It was almost marred by the desire of the Virgin's bearers to enliven the encounter, for such was their vigour that her crown very nearly came off. But they grounded their float just in time to avoid this grave misfortune and a man with a box of tools (who had no doubt been discreetly following) emerged from the crowd and screwed it firmly back into place.

From this point Mother and Son joined forces and were carried back together towards the church. But there was a further ritual to be performed on the way. Hanging from a pole was a crude dummy, a bit like a scarecrow, stuffed with straw and secured with a rope round its neck. When this was reached, the whole procession stopped and everyone stood back. Then a young man in a winged collar, bow tie and dinner jacket (the bridegroom who was later to be married) stepped forward, ran towards the dummy and set light to it. It was presumably impregnated with petrol, for it smouldered, caught fire and then started disconcertingly to discharge rockets in all directions: some zoomed like guided missiles into adjacent balconies or doorways; one soared up into the bright sky, which it stained with a faint smear of smoke. Who, I wondered, was this rocket-spitting Guy? The *hermano mayor* was not far off and I addressed the question to him.

'Who is it?' he asked pityingly. 'Who else but Judas who sold the Lord?'

Though it was obvious as soon as he had said it, I had always thought of Judas as a slinking figure, not as one who spat fire.

'Are you a Catholic?' he asked.

'No, Anglican,' I said, making the form-filling C of E response.

'What is that? Is it like the evangelists?'

'Not really, though we have a new archbishop who is said to have evangelical leanings.'

'The evangelists trick our people with false promises.'

I strove to distance myself from such disgraceful conduct but my efforts soon ceased to interest him.

'*Es igual, hombre.* We're all much the same, when you boil us down.'

Suddenly an unexploded firework burst out of the smoking remains of Judas, snaking horizontally down the street. I leapt back against a wall. The *hermano mayor* took my arm soothingly.

'There is no need to be afraid of Judas.'

He raised his staff and the procession carried on.

My timing that day was perfect. I drove back into Ronda just as the procession of the Risen Christ was winding down from the *Ciudad* to the Barrio, which is its home. The Christ figure – a modern image with rays of glory sprouting from its head and right arm raised – is much less affecting than Cartajima's joyful child. But he was carried by a cheerful troop of stocky young men, who roared out whenever they stopped: *Viva el Cristo Resucitado!* To which the crowd responded respectfully: *Viva . . . viva!*

It was the Virgin's float, however, which was the popular one. It was borne – I had never seen this before – by buxom, nubile girls in white tunics with blue sashes. There are no dunces' hats or masks on Easter Sunday and their hair flowed free; all were flushed with exertion; some wore glasses, others not; nearly all chewed gum; the general impression they gave was of a troop of jolly Amazons – or perhaps a hockey team. Whenever they rested, they called out lustily: *Viva la niña!* – to which the crowd's enthusiastic response was: *Guapa . . . guapa . . . guapa!* The girls were more lively than the boys and more inventive in the management of their float, as they jigged and danced and swayed with it. Beads of sweat were on all their foreheads and the child who carried the water to slake their thirst – no archaic pitcher but a plastic bottle from the supermarket – was much in demand.

Here too there was an *encuentro*, a symbolic meeting, in the delightful setting provided by the Plaza de San Francisco, cleared today of its market stalls but very much alive with several hundred people sauntering and sunning themselves in anticipation of the show; most of them sporting

Guapa . . . guapa . . . guapa!

bright new clothes. The floats duly took up position face to
face, perhaps a hundred metres apart. On the signal of the
majordomo's bell they advanced towards each other, picking
up speed until it turned into something like a charge, to
which the girls imparted a curious serpentine rhythm. The

two teams now looked positively menacing, like rivals equipped with battering rams in some Greek myth. My heart was in my mouth; they were bound to crash. But as they met and touched, they stopped abruptly in their tracks. Then came the *tour de force*: at the identical moment both teams lifted their hefty floats (much heavier than the Legionnaires') up off their shoulders to the full stretch of their raised arms . . . and held their gods triumphantly aloft for fully half a minute. The girls didn't weaken an instant earlier than the boys. When the floats were lowered again, the applause was tumultuous.

'Those girls are as strong as the lads, if not stronger!' said a bystander in a tone of awe.

Indeed, to contemplate the advance of the Spanish female into many areas of life previously the unchallenged province of the male is an awesome thing. It also contributes to a sense of renewal, of something fresh and exciting in the air. I do not mean by this that rampant feminism is on the march. The tendency in southern Spain is of another order: it is one in which women are permeating more and more institutions without wishing to destroy them, and participating more and more in the life of *la calle* rather than remaining confined to *la casa* (to use our learned anthropologists' distinctions). There is thus an enrichment of community life.

This brings me to the slippery word 'community' which we use so glibly in such phrases as 'the international community . . . The European Community . . . the business community . . . the local community . . . care in the community . . .' and so on, where we presume a community of interests to exist. We are often disappointed by the performance of such communities, and criticise their bureaucrats or find the very concept empty of meaning. But Spain in general and Andalusia in particular teaches us that you can have no real communal life unless you have focal and celebratory events throughout the year, in which the large majority of people in that community participate. That is because the only true basis of community is not supposedly enlightened self-interest but actual shared experience. This is much assisted by the preservation of pre-industrial feasts and saints' days and by a due attention to the rhythms of the seasons.

Of course, we in Britain still have some vestiges of this older world: we have holidays at Christmas and Easter; we have a well-defined sporting calendar with such high points as the Grand National, the Derby, Wimbledon, Lord's, the FA Cup Final. What we do not have are: peace at Christmas, positive and public renewal in Holy Week, summer and autumn fairs in which all ages and classes mingle, bullfights symbolic of our nature halfway between god and beast, tenacious pueblo life surviving against heavy odds, or the *paseo* and a thriving café society throughout the year. These are the things that glue Spaniards together, despite their intrinsic individualism. This is the compost in which their egos grow. This is how egoism is reconciled with *convivencia*. Naturally there are good cultural, historical and climatic reasons why we do not have these things, but it is what is lacking in their own societies that all travellers seek. And that is precisely why I shall continue to hover moth-like round the Spanish candle's flame until either I collapse with wings singed and life spent . . . or it burns out. I have no doubt which will happen first.

EPILOGUE

News of the motorway came to me shortly after Holy Week. Suddenly it was on everyone's lips.

Roque said, 'It will be an *autovía*. They have already started at the Algeciras end. It is due for completion in 1996.'

An *autovía* means four lanes. He thought it would come on our side of the river and that land values would double because we should be able to get a link road over the railway track instead of our unguarded crossing.

Rafael Alarcón seemed sceptical at first.

'The new road? Look, there was a plan fifty years ago when I was a boy for one that would run over the hillside just above this farm, and it still isn't there. Anyway, they say it will be on the other side of the valley; it won't affect us.'

I could not agree with him there; if it ran on the other side of the valley, it would bring us nothing but disadvantage from increased traffic and noise without any improvement of access to compensate.

'But on past experience you think it will come to nothing?' I asked hopefully.

'Oh, they'll do it this time, all right,' he said. 'It is traced from Algeciras to Ecija where it will join the national route from Cádiz via Córdoba to Madrid.'

'But why cut through some pretty rough country when

430

there is already a perfectly good road from Algeciras to Ronda and so to Córdoba?'

'Ah,' said Rafael importantly, 'because it is required for military purposes.'

I raised my eyebrows.

'Yes, with the European Common Market and all that, there will have to be joint manoeuvres with Britain and other countries and a fast road is needed down to the Straits.'

'But there is no European *army*,' I said, 'only NATO. There is some overlap but the Community has no army of its own; it has no joint high command . . .'

He shrugged.

'Well, logically, with the United States of Europe there will be one.'

I left him, reflecting how far the valley was from the realities of European diplomacy, only to open a paper the same evening and read that a new NATO rapid strike force under British command would incorporate Spanish units with special responsibility for the 'southern flank' including the Straits of Gibraltar.

Whatever sort of geopolitical sense this might make, it hardly seemed to require a four-lane highway. Why should flying columns of armoured cars need something the width of an airstrip? What about planes and helicopters? And where would the mules, beloved of Spanish generals, pass if not on the old bridle paths?

I went off to see other interested parties. For Paco Sánchez, who was to lose something over an acre, it was all a question of whether the compensation price was right. But was it really necessary at all, this motorway? Paco shrugged. He had heard it was connected with the tunnel that was to be dug under the Straits linking Spain to North Africa. I was slightly incredulous, and said so. Well, hadn't the British just done precisely that with France? Yes, but Spain linked to *Africa*? After all those centuries spent expelling Islam? Ah, he couldn't say. It was just a rumour. When I mentioned the tunnel to Paco el Bueno he smiled and dismissed it as childish talk; there was not the slightest likelihood of it. But as far as he was concerned anything that improved communications between one pueblo and another was good; besides, he sometimes needed to go to Algeciras and it would save him an hour each way.

Others were more dubious. An old *huerta* across the river has been split into three or four *fincas de recreo*. The cashier of the Banco Hispano Americano and his wife have an acre plot; the rough local grass has been painstakingly turned into a fine lawn pleasantly shaded by old fruit trees. The house is a three-bedroomed chalet where they planned to retire. The large garage is a den of DIY wizardry.

How would the *autovía* affect them? Well, they said bravely, it would be at least a hundred metres away from their door; it wouldn't touch their land. But the wife was clearly less than happy. The real threat was the noise. Their Ronda flat was very noisy and as soon as she got down here she could feel the relaxation seeping through her. But with the *autovía* . . . she did indeed wonder if it would be quite the same. Perhaps the speed of the traffic would produce no more than a faint swish, I suggested soothingly. That might be so if it were used mainly by *turismos*, said her husband, but he feared the main traffic would be heavy freight, in particular the great refrigerated lorries that thundered through the night to get fresh fish and seafood onto the Madrid fishmongers' slabs and into the restaurants early in the morning. The pair of them looked at one another with almost identical wistful smiles.

'Ah well,' they sighed almost in unison, 'if it is for the good of humanity . . .'

There was a hint of irony in the man's voice, but it was muted: the idea of some universal advance was, I suspected, what made the motorway just tolerable to them. Their sense of duty, a Spanish equivalent of the stiff upper lip, was touching. Sadly, Spanish suburban sensibility has not yet developed sufficient muscle or self-confidence to fight off such powerful interests as the Ministry of Public Works, the army and the automobile industry, whose combined might seems to possess some of the awesome inevitability of the great religious orthodoxies of the past to which all other views must bow or be crushed.

The last person I went to see was the retired restaurateur. Civilised and a little world-weary, he had been the pioneer of bourgeois penetration of the valley. He had a copy of the plans for the *autovía*. We sat under his old trees beside his not too shriekingly blue swimming pool – he is a man of taste – and he showed me who would be shaved here and who would be spared by a whisker there and who would find himself caught between the two ribbons of the highway. He himself was on the fringe. Yes, it would be a great nuisance. Yes, he too had heard about the tunnel. Threat from the east? He smiled craftily. Had I not observed how arabophile Spanish foreign policy had recently been, with no more than symbolic assistance in the Gulf War? I nodded. I had. But, nearer home, wouldn't a motorway go completely against the Junta's policy of promoting rural tourism? The railway was one thing: it followed the natural contours; it was obliged to work its way up to the head of the valley and describe a great hairpin bend before reaching the town; the landscape was its master, not vice-versa; furthermore, it had many little halts to let people on and off. The motorway would do none of this: it would slide slickly over the natural features; access to the locality would be limited to major sliproads every twenty or thirty kilometres and neither local farmers nor rural tourists would benefit one jot. How did any of this square with the Junta's attempt to attract people from the coasts into the interior? Not at all well, he agreed. But I had to realise that, apart from the additional layers of bureaucracy, the 'autonomy' of Andalusia was largely a fiction. The interests of the national economy and the demands of 'progress' overrode all that.

So there we were, back with progress – but *whose* progress

was uncertain. The progress of refrigerated lorries to satisfy Madrid's penchant for fish? (How absurd to build a capital in the centre of arid Spain, without so much as a proper river, and expect gleaming fresh fish every morning!) The progress of British marine commandos rushing south on some make-believe exercise? The progress of migrant Moroccans flooding north with overloaded old cars and over-numerous families in search of scarce work in northern Europe? Or simply the march of Progress with a capital P in aid of the Good of Humanity, also with capitals? All of these perhaps. But not the progress of the Serranía, whose natural beauty was to be scarred by an impersonal conveyor belt taking people and goods to more important places. Not the progress of the valley, which required, if anything, better tracks to the farms and a piped domestic water supply to replace unreliable old wells. And certainly not my progress or that of my family and friends.

Where then did hope lie? With the geologists revising their assays of the soil and predicting landslides? With rival bureaucrats gaining acceptance for an alternative blueprint up someone else's valley? With the environment department of the Junta de Andalucía plucking up its courage and flexing its muscles against central government? Or with the Mother of God, no less, whose *tierras de María Santísima* were being disembowelled under her eyes? Might she not descend and admonish the planners and engineers and leave them dumbfounded? In such a way did my thoughts smoulder and splutter impotently.

More immediate concerns soon imposed themselves. After the incident of the fire which had got out of hand, Vicente had sown a good crop of oats on our land. When cut and raked and baled there were over seven hundred bales to be collected by people to whom he had sold them verbally. A couple of hundred were removed by one buyer. On the eve of Corpus Christi – we are in June now – it rained suddenly and heavily. This was not good for the oats, but it did not last long and if no more came they would dry out.

The day of Corpus Christi dawned cloudy and damp, but the rain held off. The main street of Ronda was strewn with palm leaves. The procession came out of the Iglesia Mayor. All the bigwigs, the heads of *hermandades* and *cofradías* were there in suits and ties with silver staffs of office; and many other local worthies to say nothing of plenty of solemn rascals walked ahead of the floral float with its sacred monstrance containing the Host, which through transubstantiation becomes the body of Christ and is known therefore as 'El Señor'.

The Alameda had been prepared with the traditional carpet of yellow and coloured sands with thousands of decapitated carnations forming swirling Baroque patterns; this stretched for two hundred metres or more to an open-air altar, where seven priests performed; nearby the municipal band (including my bandsman friend Juan, always glad to earn an additional small wage) struck up with drums and cymbals as the chief priest presented the golden monstrance with the Host to the people. The more devout citizens toed the edge of the sand carpet; others loitered more casually behind the front line. When the Host was raised, many sank to their knees and crossed themselves; even the most ribald inclined their heads. Then the procession with its long tail returned to the Iglesia Mayor, followed immediately, as if they formed an integral part of it, by bustling sweepers making much of their zeal and efficiency in removing the palm fronds that had been laid only an hour or so before. In Spain the minor parts are also important, and usually add a touch of comic relief – like the bullring servants, the *monosabios*, who help the picador up when he has been floored, haul up his capsized nag and scamper out with the bull when it is being dragged by the mule-team from the ring.

All this time it was fine. The Lord looks after his own. But when I got back to the *campo* the heavens opened again and the remaining five hundred or so of Vicente's bales were virtually ruined. If only he had got them off the ground a few days earlier and ploughed and sowed his maize, how divine this rain would have been. In the event it was an unmitigated disaster, to which Spanish stoicism was the only answer. Thoughts of the motorway receded. Fretting about a road some years off and with no absolute certainty of completion suddenly seemed an indulgence compared to this sharp and immediate blow to an individual's economy. On such occasions the shrug assumes heroic proportions.

Nonetheless, the motorway was there on the drawing board; it was a seed that threatened to grow into something rather monstrous on our horizon. Threats have a vibrant life of their own, even if they never come to fruition. My perception of the valley had altered slightly but irreversibly. It would never be quite the same again: whether as threat or as future reality, the motorway already existed. What does an old, frayed romantic do in such circumstances? My answer was to go and buy five straggling Spanish rose plants with thick stems and talon-like thorns, the toughest flowers in creation, and dig them in just below our terrace facing the projected route of the motorway, as a gesture of defiance.

Should you drive along the motorway from Algeciras to the north in a few years' time and look down on your left three or four kilometres short of Ronda, you will see a patch of a few acres cradled in an elbow-shaped bend of the river, whose course is clearly marked by willows and tall swaying poplars. That is the *campo*, more formally the Huerta del Rincón. If the game of life, in the parlance of the landlady of the little hotel in Arcos, is *buscar rincones*, to seek out quiet corners, this was once one of the quietest and most secluded, hard for newcomers to find at all. But now it will be exposed to your gaze like a toy farm, only more untidy, with the foursquare little house set back against the rising fold of the bigger hill farms and the cliff of the table-mountain.

If you have sharp eyes, you may see Hilly hanging out the washing on the terrace or Jaime casually getting out of

436

his Suzuki jeep or me bowed with my adze over an irrigation ditch. Or you may see Vicente and his son turning over bales of barley to expose them to the sun after a wetting. Or you may see none of these things, because the hard shoulders of a motorway do not invite stops except in emergencies and the next lay-by may be miles off. Or we may not be there at all. And the *huerta* in its present form may not be there either: Miguel de la Granja may have bought us out to extend his battery-farming empire, in which case all you will see (out of the corner of your eye as you whizz by) will be long gleaming aluminium-roofed sheds, punctuated by circular silver turrets whose function is to release the feedstock down to the unfortunate beasts penned in beneath.

If that is what meets your eye, we shall clearly have departed: whether to Alpandeire or Benalauría or Cortes de la Frontera or Alcalá de los Gazules or Setenil or El Burgo I cannot say. But I do not think we shall have thrown in our hand, whatever the aggravation. These days no country is an island. Air routes and motorways spread their universal culture around the world. But there are pockets where the island effect is partly preserved. They are not pockets of resistance in the conscious sense, because everyone accepts the main features of the mass culture, notably automobiles and television. Yet, intuitively, such places are still strongly attached to their old roots; in them the concept of the pueblo as Utopia remains deeply embedded and is likely to survive.

Thus, though the state has forcibly shifted the feast of Corpus Christi from the Thursday after Trinity Sunday to the Sunday itself to cut down on the number of religious holidays, the people (having protested vociferously) will still lay their palm leaves on the streets and bring out the Host in its golden vitrine. Thus, Cartajima will celebrate its strange little encounter between the Christ child and his mother with her wobbly crown. Thus, buxom lasses will come swinging down the slope from the *Ciudad* to the Barrio, chanting *Guapa . . . guapa . . . guapa!* in praise of the gorgeous Astarte with her bulbous gilded crown and the mass of lilies at her feet, whom they bear aloft with such *élan*. Thus, the hill farmers will continue to kill their pigs for home consumption at their annual *matanzas*. Thus, civilisation will continue to take the form of the *paseo* in the town. Thus, Ronda's intellectuals will continue their *causeries* in the bookseller's tiny den. All these things will still be found for many a year to come in the sierras of the south.

Of course, they are 'at risk' from such developments as the motorway and other aspects of the mass culture. Yet that is a condition which applies to deep-rooted practices and observances everywhere. The motorway is a metaphor for change, as is the valley for stability, and these are in constant tension. For me this brings an added sharpness and a fresh poignancy to the people and places I have tried to evoke in this book. One intelligent countrywoman refused to believe that a man had been landed on the moon; it was a TV trick. The ground is shifting under them, as it is under us all.

Finally, Arcadia has always been to a large extent a country of the mind. Those of us who thought we had glimpsed it here on earth and have tried to pin it down will always find ourselves in some conflict with the Arcadians themselves, who have their eyes on other horizons. But that is no reason why we should not follow our dream over the mountain and into the next valley, taking a chance that another motorway or another battery farm will not creep up behind us. Who knows, in time the Arcadians may change their minds about these aspects of progress. And even in the worst scenario the hard core of the region will remain inviolate: the people are stubbornly attached to their pueblos and their festivities; the mountains cannot be pulled down or the sunsets plucked out of the sky. Somewhere in the sierras there will always be a refuge for the likes of me and mine, and possibly of you and yours. But anyone wanting a soft option must look elsewhere.

GLOSSARY

Aburrimiento – boredom, a condition much prized among the regulars of cafés and bars; the expression *aburrido* may convey satisfaction; the yawn is a sign of freedom

Acebuche – wild olive

Acequia – irrigation channel

Acoso (y derribo) – testing of brave bull calves in open country; a calf is cut out from the herd, ridden down and overturned with a blunt lance; the test is whether it turns at bay or continues running

Adobe – mud brick, sun-dried, unfired

Aguantando – the method of killing a brave bull when it charges unprovoked, cf. *recibiendo*

Aguardiente – an aniseed-flavoured liqueur, frequently unbranded, raw and strong

Alameda – literally a poplar grove; usually tree-lined walk or gardens in a town, e.g. Alameda de Hércules in Seville

Alberca – irrigation tank

Alcornoque – cork-oak, stripped every nine years, the main tree in the vast *alcornocales* stretching over many thousands of hectares

Alegría – joy, jollity; *me alegro*, I'm delighted

Alforja – pair of saddlebags, usually of cloth, sometimes of leather, hung from the cantle of the saddle

Alternativa – ceremony in which apprentice matador or *novillero* graduates to the rank of full *matador de toros*; on such occasions the senior matador cedes his first bull to the neophyte, who kills it. The new matador then plays the second bull and hands it back to his sponsor for the kill. The normal order is then resumed, the

439

initiate killing the sixth and final bull.

Anciano(s) – old man, pl. the elders; there is often a bar or café known popularly as *de los ancianos*

Andaluz – Andalusian

Arriero – muleteer, member of a famous fraternity of the road and bridle path, now almost extinct except in the cork harvest, cf. *corchero*

Artesonado – wooden ceiling in hall or church, shaped like an upside-down *artesa* or bread trough, but often diversified with coffered panels, carved tie-beams etc.; can be either very simple or very grand

Autonomía(s) – the short term to describe the eighteen regional governments of Spain set up by the Constitution of 1978

Azada – the main digging implement, shaped like an army entrenching tool; much commoner than our fork or spade

Azulejo – ceramic wall tile, usually non-figurative, often employing Moorish designs

Banderilla(s) – paper-decorated wooden dart, 70 cm long, with harpoon point placed in the withers of the bull in the second act of the bullfight

Banderillero – matador's assistant who places the *banderillas*; also known as *peón*; *banderilleros* sometimes become avuncular trainers and mentors of aspirant bullfighters

Barranco – gully, ravine

Barrera – red and yellow painted fence round the sanded area of the bullring; the front row of seats in most rings are also called *barreras*, though they are separated from the fence by the passage called the *callejón* (q.v.)

Barrio – district, ward or *quartier* of a town or city

Barro – mud, clay

Beato(a) – beatified, blessed, a grade on the way to sanctity; *beatas*, excessively devout spinsters

Belleza – beauty

Bocadillo – classic Spanish snack, consisting of an elliptical roll or small loaf with a variety of fillings, e.g. *jamón, salchichón,* tuna etc.

Bombona – orange butane gas cylinder; the staple energy source of country kitchens

Boquerón – fresh anchovy, often grilled as a *tapa*

Bravo – see *toro bravo*

Buscar – to seek; *buscar rincones*, to seek (quiet) corners

Caballero – gentleman, knight of an order of chivalry

Caballerosidad – chivalry, generosity

Cabero – overseer of an irrigation system

Caciquismo – system of patronage by local political bosses

Cafelillo – affectionate diminutive to denote main café and meeting place of a small town or village

Caja de Ahorros – savings bank; see *Monte de Piedad*

Calle – street; *la calle*, outdoors, province of the male, as opposed to *la casa*, province of the female

Callejón – alley, dead-end

Campiña – agricultural plain, especially the basin of the Guadalquivir

Campo – country, countryside, field; used esp. in this book to indicate our smallholding, which Jaime as a child always called '*mi campo*'

Canalla – *canaille*, trash, rabble, cf. *gentuza*

Cante – song, folksong; *cante flamenco*, popular Andalusian gypsy style of singing, accompanied by guitar, including *bulerías*, *fandangos*, *malagueñas*, *petaneras*, *seguidillas*, *soleares* and *sevillanas*; *cante jondo*, unaccompanied variety, frequently a lament

Cañada (real) – drovers' road or track for transhumant flocks; these criss-crossed the whole country and had their own police force in the middle ages

Capataz – overseer, foreman, steward

Capirote – headgear worn in the Easter processions, consisting of conical cap covered with a cloth mask

Capricho – caprice, whim, fancy

Cartel – poster, particularly for bullfights; also the quality of the programme, e.g. *buen cartel*, *mal cartel*, and the reputation of a matador: *tiene mucho cartel*

Casa – house, home

Casco antiguo – old quarter of a town or city, sometimes seen on road signs, conveying the same message as *conjunto histórico*

441

Caseta – tent or enclosure of a club or other body erected temporarily during a fair

Casino – club, political or social; in villages the main bar is sometimes called the *casino* and may have an area reserved for members

Cazador – hunter of game birds and animals, a cut above *tirador* or Sunday shooter who takes potshots at anything that moves. The word *montero* is sometimes used of those who go on *monterías*, which are big shoots, with beaters, of larger animals such as wild boar and deer.

Central lechera – Spanish equivalent of milk marketing board

Centro ciudad – city centre, but not necessarily the monumental zone, to which *casco antiguo* or *conjunto histórico* are the pointers

Chico, chiquillo – lad, chap, fellow; affectionate form of address among men

Chicuelina – cape pass invented by 'Chicuelo'; the matador makes a pirouette in the opposite direction to the bull's charge, wrapping the cape round himself

Chiringuito – shanty bar, often on a beach

Chirrascal – stony ground with willows, oleander, fennel etc., bordering a river bed

Chopo – black poplar common along river banks; also found in irrigated plantations

Chorizo – pork sausage seasoned with red pepper, hung in strings in farmhouse attics; may be eaten hot or cold; requires a strong stomach

Churros – hot deep-fried batter rings; *churrería*, a *churro* stall

Ciudad – city; used esp. in this book to indicate the Old City of Ronda (a municipal district). Madrid is curiously not a city but a *villa*

Clausura – regime to which enclosed orders of nuns are subject

Cocina – kitchen, cuisine

Cofradía – lay brotherhood devoted to the cult of the Virgin or other saint; it is the *cofradías* who organise the Holy Week and other processions, c.f. *hermandad*

Comedor – dining room

Conjunto histórico – monumental zone of a town or city, cf. *casco antiguo*

Conocedor de toros – person in charge of rearing and selecting brave bulls for *corridas*; almost synonymous with *mayoral*

Convivencia – good fellowship, neighbourliness, community spirit; some Spaniards say it is dying and lament its loss

Copa – wine glass, glass of wine

Copla – popular rhyme, song, jingle

Corchero – cork-cutter, cork-stripper

Cordobés – in conjunction with *sombrero*, a flat-crowned hat with circular brim, worn by cowboys, herdsmen, *rejoneadores, corredores* and those connected with bulls and horses in general; the Sevillian version is very similar; only experts can tell the difference

Cornadura – spread of a bull's horns; the wider the spread the more formidable and the greater the likelihood of a *cornada* or horn-wound

Corredor – broker, middleman, livestock dealer; denizen of *la calle* and its bars and cafés; once he has an office and a telephone he becomes an *agente*, which is different

Correría – raid or foray into enemy territory or in pursuit of bandits

Corrida – the Spanish bullfight; also the string of bulls, normally six, selected for a particular bullfight

Cortesía – courtesy; also used to describe the curious bobbing of one image to another in an Easter procession, which I would like to call a curtsy, but the dictionary word for that is *reverencia*

Costalero – one of the bearers of an Easter float, a role theoretically restricted to members of the brotherhood concerned, though in Seville stevedores from the docks used to be hired, and a foulmouthed, rumbustious lot they were

Costumbrismo – a literary *genre*, celebrating local life and customs, kicked into life by the European Romantic movement; the leading Spanish exponents were Fernán Caballero and Pardo Bazán (both women) and Gabriel y Galán, a bucolic poet

Coto de caza – reserved hunting or shooting ground; private 'shoot'; many pueblos now have a *coto social* to which the local inhabitants can subscribe

Cuadrilla – patrol, gang, squad; also the matador's team

Cuba libre – the Spanish version of this long, cool, heady drink is gin and Coke, *not* rum; it is becoming a favourite with the youth of the pueblos in their *discos* and *pubs*, knocking out traditional wines and beers

Cuota – monthly or annual subscription to a *casino, cofradía* etc.

Dehesa – pastureland, meadow; also rougher grazing on foothills, sometimes used of a bull-breeding ranch, cf. *hacienda, monte*

Derecha – right, right-hand; *La Derecha, Las Derechas*, political parties of the Right

Derechazo – right-handed pass in bullfighting

Descabello – stab in the neck which severs spinal cord of a brave bull and should kill instantly; may be used after the first failed *estocada*, but the bull's head must be sufficiently low; the weapon employed, known as *el verduguillo*, the little executioner, is a sword with a cross-piece six inches from the point, which has been called 'a dagger with a long handle'. After a brilliant *faena* a matador may get away with one or a maximum of two *descabellos* if his original sword-thrust was honourable, but after that his credit drains away into the sand.

Don – form of address to which all Spaniards are entitled in correspondence with the state (fem. *Doña*); used verbally by lower classes when referring to or addressing professional and upper classes; also used, both respectfully but also to bring him down to earth, of the monarch, e.g. Don Alfonso XIII . . . el Rey Don Juan Carlos etc.

Ecologista – ecologist, member of 'Green' movement

Encuentro – encounter, meeting, match (football etc.); also the ceremonial meeting and symbolic greeting of two images during an Easter procession

Escuela taurina – bullfighting school, where aspirant *toreros* learn the art; also describes a style, e.g. 'Escuela de Ronda' (classical), 'Escuela de Sevilla' (flamboyant) etc.

Estancia – outdoor sitting area, veranda, vine-covered terrace (Andalusia); in Latin America the meaning is cattle ranch, country estate

Estatuario – a high pass with the *muleta* pricked out by the sword, in which the stationary matador incites the bull from a distance and does not budge as it thunders towards him; one of the specialities of Miguel Baez 'Litri', senior

Estocada – the thrust made with the *estoque* in order to kill the bull; the weapon is curved downwards at the tip to ease passage between vertebrae, ribs etc.; it should be placed between the bull's shoulderblades when the animal's front legs are together (if they are apart they will narrow this aperture). A *media estocada*, which only goes in halfway, may be sufficient if properly placed. The thrust is called a *pinchazo* if the sword hits bone and bounces out.

Faena – literally task, job, labour; in tauromachy the whole of the matador's work with the bull, using the *muleta* (*not* the cape), from the moment he takes it over after the withdrawal of the picadors until he lines it up for the kill. The *faena* is the core of the bullfight today. But the kill is crucial: it either crowns or ruins a good *faena*.

Fandango – one of the modes of *cante flamenco* and the accompanying dance, especially associated with the port and province of Huelva

Fanega – measure of grain required to sow a certain area of land; hence a measure of land, usually in Spain approx 1.6 acres but there are regional variations. Countryfolk tend to talk in *fanegas* rather than *hectáreas*.

Felipista – supporter of Felipe González

Feria – fair, applied to the whole gala period in a town or village; also to the fairground where the attractions are

Festival taurino – a *novillada* without picadors, fought in country dress, cf. *traje corto*; major matadors sometimes appear in *festivales* for charity or just to keep their hand in off-season

Fiesta – party or entertainment to celebrate an engagement, a wedding etc.; religious feast-day or civil bank holiday; *fiesta brava*, *fiesta nacional*, the bullfight, whose semi-mystical claim to be the highest expression of national identity has not yet been toppled by football, golf, or any other sporting activity

Finca – any property in land or buildings from an urban flat to a large country estate; the main sub-categories are *finca rustica* and *finca urbana*

Fino – a pale dry wine which has been through the *solera* process, usually sherry or a relation of sherry such as Manzanilla or Montilla; if you ask for *vino blanco* in a bar in the south, you will often be given *fino* unless you specify *blanco de mesa*

Fonda – the lowest-ranking lodging house with no frills but usually very clean, with plain decent meals; recommended for low-budget travellers; the old jibe about 'rancid olive oil' no longer sticks, but without a faint whiff of that divine substance one would feel defrauded and most *fondas* provide it

Gallo – cock; *misa del gallo*, midnight mass on Christmas Eve; *pelea de gallos*, cockfight, cf. *reñidero*

Ganadería – both the breed of brave bull produced by a particular rancher and the estate on which it is raised

Ganadero – stockbreeder, rancher; in Andalusia the word applies especially to the breeder of brave bulls

Garbanzo – the humble chickpea, staple of stews, delicious with tripe; despite its association with third-world economies, e.g. Pakistan, Spaniards show no sign of abandoning it in their new affluence; they are guided perhaps by nineteenth-century intellectuals who celebrated it as a symbol of wholesome peasant life

Garrafa – basket-sheathed wine flagon; giant *carafe*; largest size contains 16 litres

Gentuza – scum, trash, rabble, riff-raff, cf. *canalla*

Golpe de estado – *coup d'état*, palace revolution

Granja – farm, originally applied particularly to dairy and poultry farming; thus it had a daintier ring than *cortijo* and was used in the Marie Antoinette sense in the name of the royal palace of La Granja; today it is more likely than not to indicate a factory farm where nothing remotely graceful remains

Guapo(a) – handsome, elegant, smart (males); beautiful, pretty (females)

Hacienda – large farm, estate, ranch; it has a Latin American ring and is not found often in Andalusia, where it sounds a shade pretentious

Hermandad – brotherhood, usually of lay people for religious purposes. cf. *cofradía*

Hermano(a) – brother, sister; *hermano mayor*, chief executive of a brotherhood

Hidalgo – literally son of something, thus member of the small gentry, possessed of a modest patrimony; the dictionary is wrong to translate as 'nobleman'; no title of nobility is required to authenticate a claim to *hidalguía*; Don Quixote was a *hidalgo*. The correct plural, incidentally, is *hijosdalgo*, not *hidalgos*.

Higo – fig; *higo chumbo*, prickly pear, fruit of the cactus

Honradez – honesty, probity; not to be confused with *honor*, honour, fame

Hortelano – owner of a *huerta*, market gardener

Hostal – modern lodging house, usually well-plumbed with a high proportion of individual bathrooms; often without a restaurant

Huerta – market garden, orchard; frequently a bit of both; average size in the area covered by this book, about six or seven acres

Huerto – kitchen garden; may form part of a *huerta* or be cultivated on any farm or in any forest clearing where there is water; usual size one to two acres

Inquietud – anxiety, worry, restlessness; pl. *inquietudes* denotes a querying and questing sort of mind

Instituto – institute, but especially a state secondary school at which the *bachillerato* is studied

Izquierda – left, left-hand; *La Izquierda*, the political Left; *Izquierda Unida*, a grouping embracing the parties of the Left

Jerez – pre-prandial wine, made by the *solera* system, from the region of Jerez de la Frontera, from which the English word sherry is derived via Sherris Sack (*Jerez Seco*)

Larga – a pass to draw the bull towards and then send him away from the man, made with the cape fully extended and held at the extremity by one hand (Hemingway); *larga cambiada*, flashy pass done on the knees, usually when the bull first bursts into the ring from the *toril*, in which the cape is pulled away and whirled over one shoulder as he plunges by

Latifundio – large estate, often poorly cultivated and in recent times subject to expropriation by the state on such grounds; *latifundismo*, reactionary landlordism

Levante – Levant, east; wind from the east

Limpieza – cleanliness; *limpieza de sangre*, pure blood, an important concept in the heyday of the Inquisition, linked to the status of Old Christians as opposed to Jewish and Moorish converts of doubtful authenticity

Loco – mad, crazy, wild: covers a whole range of conditions from 'wild with joy' to clinical insanity

Lote – share, portion, job-lot; in tauromachy the two bulls drawn by each matador out of the six which make up a *corrida*

Lunes – Monday; *lunes de la resaca*, local bank holiday to allow for recovery from the *resaca* or hangover after a major feast-day

Madalena – light spongy moulded cakelet; *magdalena* in the dictionary but there is no trace of a 'g' in the south

Madroño – the arbutus, the emblem of Madrid (with a bear stretching up for the fruit)

Maestrante – member of one of the five *Reales Maestranzas de Caballería* of Spain

Maestranza – equestrian body limited to the aristocracy and those of gentle birth

Maletilla – itinerant would-be *torero*; *maletilla* is a small suitcase

Manoletina – right-handed pass with the *muleta*, in which the matador pivots in the opposite direction to the bull's charge; popularised by Manolete but purely an *adorno*, which has since suffered in popular esteem from being overdone

Manzanilla – (1) camomile tea, usually served in tea-bags (2) a dry sherry-style wine with a tang of the sea from Sanlúcar de Barrameda, delicious with seafood (3) a certain type of olive. Ask for *una copa* to get the wine and *una infusión*, if you want the tea.

Matanza – domestic pig-killing, carried out in winter; a two- or three-day event which includes the whole process of preparing the hams and other products for unrefrigerated storage which may last over a year

Mayoral – foreman on a ranch in charge of rearing and selecting brave bulls for *corridas*; cf. *conocedor*

Media Verónica – a *recorte* or cutting off of the bull's charge, used to wind up the initial series of cape passes called *verónicas*

Mercado de Bestias – livestock market; for domestic marketplace see *Plaza de Abastos*

Merendero – picnic site; place for an al fresco *merienda*, which is the stopgap between lunch and supper

Mierda – excrement, filth, shit

Mili – popular term for military service; *está haciendo la mili*, he is doing his national service

Misa – Mass; *misa del gallo*, midnight Mass

Miseria – abject poverty, destitution

Monte – mountain, wild country; *monte alto*, forest populated with game; *monte bajo*, scrubland, suitable for grazing bulls, pigs, but rougher than a *dehesa*

Monte de Piedad – originally a pawnshop, later a non-profit-making bank with the obligation to make loans to poor farmers at less than usurious rates of interest

Montería – a big hunt of driven game on foot with perhaps sixty or seventy 'guns', packs of hounds and beaters; the quarry are mainly wild boar and deer

Morillo – the hump of neck muscle of a fighting bull; this is where the *picador* should place his lance and the *banderilleros* their shafts

Morisco(s) – nominally converted Moors who remained in Spain from the recapture of Granada in 1492 till their final expulsion in 1609–14 under Philip III

Mudéjar(es) – Muslims authorised to live in territory reconquered by the Christians; they were famous for their building skills and artefacts; such communities flourished throughout the middle ages; the term also describes a pseudo-Moorish style popular in Spain ever since the Reconquest

Muleta – scarlet cloth doubled over a wooden stick, with which the matador performs his *faena*; much smaller than the cape

Municipal(es) – municipal police, butts of ridicule, which turned to salacious comment when women were first admitted to the force

Natural – the natural pass made with the *muleta* held low in the left hand; the fundamental pass of bullfighting and the most dangerous; the touchstone of the *torero*'s courage and art

Negro bragao – the colouring of a fighting bull which is black with white pants or stockings

Nieve – snow; also the term used for ice in small pueblo bars and taverns, cf. *pozo*

Novillada – bullfight with bulls judged unsuitable for a *corrida*; the animals should be under four years old or over five; ticket prices are usually half those for a *corrida* and in many small towns a *novillada* is the principal taurine event

Novillero – matador of *novillos-toros*; the *novillada* is the springboard to the big time and the leading practitioners may fight up to a hundred times in a season before ascending to the rank of full matador via the *alternativa*

Novillo – bull fought in a *novillada*

Novio(a) – fiancé(e), sweetheart; pl. courting couple, bride and groom

Olla – cooking pot; *la olla*, stew whose main ingredients are usually potatoes, *garbanzos* and *tocino* with a little stringy meat; this may sound like a poor man's diet but it is extremely nutritious and keeps gnarled old folk going into their dotage

Paguita – little payment; *la paguita*, social security benefit or pension for the elderly or disabled; see also *vejez*

Palio – canopy, something like that of a four-poster bed, stretched over the Virgin's float when she is carried in procession

Paro – stoppage, unemployment; *el paro*, unemployment register and benefit.

Parroquia – parish and by extension the parish church

Pase de pecho – culminating pass of a series of *naturales*, in which the *torero*, rather than winding the bull round him in a circular fashion, turns and brings the bull past his chest with a backhanded sweep of the *muleta* over the horns

Paseo – the great public promenade which takes place on Sundays and feast-days and every evening in summer; also the entry of the *toreros* into the bullring and their march across it to salute the president

Pasodoble – musical march played when the *toreros* make their entry and also during the *faena* when the performance merits it; often the public will demand *música* of a niggardly president

Patrimonio – heritage, inheritance

Patrona – patron saint, usually the Virgin in one of her many avatars

Pelea – fight; cockfight, cf. *gallo, pollo, reñidero*

Peón (peones) – day labourer; also applied to the *banderilleros* who assist the matador

Peste equina – fatal horse disease (though there is a vaccine); said to have been imported from North Africa through inadequate veterinary controls and much resented for the ruin it has brought on breeders and the threat posed to the 1992 Olympics

Peto – mattress covering chest, right flank and belly of picador's horse; introduced in the 1920s at the behest of Queen Victoria Eugénie of Spain, a granddaughter of Queen Victoria

Pica – *picador's* lance consisting of the pole (*vara, garrocha*) about eight feet long and the steel *pica* or *puya* with a circular metal guard to prevent excessive penetration

Picadero – riding ring used for training, breaking, practising *haute école* etc.; sometimes attached to the bullring, like the *Picadero de La Maestranza* in Ronda

Picador – man who pics bulls on horseback under orders of the matador (Hemingway)

Pilastra – stone parapet with columns supporting the roof of Ronda's bullring; seats on this are the nearest you can get to the action; they are not found in other rings where the front row, though called the *barrera*, is further back

Pinchazo – matador's sword thrust that has not gone in far enough or has hit bone; in the latter case, if well placed, it is not to his discredit and the situation can be retrieved by a successful *estocada* on the next attempt; but if one *pinchazo* is followed by another and another in a cowardly effort to kill the bull by degrees, this will be received with contempt

Pinsapar(es) – territory of the *pinsapo*, subject to fierce preservation orders

Pinsapo – Spanish fir (*Abies pinsapo Boiss*); found only in the Sierra de las Nieves, Sierra de Grazalema and Sierra Bermeja above the 1000m line; the foliage is tight and sharp and is linked like a chain of caterpillars

Piscina – swimming pool; all self-respecting mountain pueblos have built one at municipal expense

Playa – beach, plage

Plaza – public square; *la plaza*, the main or only square in a small pueblo; *plaza de toros*, bullring; *plaza de abastos*, food market. (In this book the town square is not italicised in the text; *plaza*

indicates the marketplace.)

Pollo – chicken; *los pollos*, the chicks, popular term for fighting cocks

Poquilla – a very little

Posada – old-fashioned inn with stabling for animals, now virtually extinct

Pozo – well; *pozo de nieve*, pit in which packed snow was stored on the mountainside and sold in lieu of ice in days before the refrigerator

Pueblo – small town, village; but also 'the people', e.g. *'el pueblo español'*; one of the commonest and most emotive words in the Spanish language both in its macro- and its micro-sense

Puya – see *pica* above

Puyazo – the act of inserting the pic in the bull

Qué – exclamation and query; *Qué va, hombre!* What on earth are you talking about? Don't be so ridiculous!

Quejigo – gall-oak; gnarled and lichenous forest tree worthy of a pantomime set; the subject – like the *alcornoque* and the *pinsapo* – of a fierce preservation order

Quincalla – ironmongery, trinket; used by Ortega y Gasset to denote the flashy side of Andalusian life, e.g. folklore cynically exploited for the tourist

Quincena – fortnight

Quitar – to get rid of; *quita . . . quita!* was frequently used by Arturo to express disgust at anything rotten, impure, or dishonourable

Recibiendo – method of killing the bull by provoking his charge, so that he impales himself on the sword. 'Most difficult, dangerous and emotional way to kill bulls; rarely seen in modern times. I have seen it executed completely three times in almost three hundred bullfights.' (Hemingway)

Recreo – amusement, recreation; *finca de recreo*, nearest thing in Spain to a weekend cottage

Rejón (rejones) – main weapon of the *rejoneador*; a stick, dart or harpoon some five feet in length with a leaf-shaped six-inch blade; the *rejoneador* also places *banderillas*

Rejoneador – *torero* who fights all the stages of the bullfight on horseback, using *rejones* and *banderillas*. He is socially a cut above the matador, has notionally amateur status and prefixes 'Don' to his name, unlike his pedestrian counterpart. He is the vestigial survival of the sixteenth- and seventeenth-century *caballeros en plaza*, who fought their bulls on horseback with lances, assisted by *peones* on foot; the latter gradually rose to dominate the *fiesta*, as the *caballeros* declined in skill and courage. The superbly schooled horses (any resemblance to the *picador*'s nag is purely accidental!) are the real heroes of the act today. But it nearly always ends in anticlimax with the *caballero* having to dismount and kill on the ground like any old matador but less expertly. A whole *corrida de rejones* can be very tedious and this form is best as an appetiser to the serious business of a true *corrida*.

Reñidero – cockpit; licensed ring in which cockfights take place

Ribera – shore, river bank; also the string of small farms on an irrigation loop fed with water taken from the river by means of a primitive dam

Romería – local pilgrimage to country shrine on a feast-day; has boisterous and licentious elements and is perhaps the nearest thing in Spanish life to an orgy

Salchichón – a hard spicy sausage, resembling salami

Salida – exit; also the act of negotiating a heavy float with an image of the Virgin out of its church

Semental – sire, stud animal, seed-bull

Señorío – regime of overlordship; Spanish version of the feudal system

Señoritismo – derogatory term applied to the supercilious behaviour of *señoritos*; those of recently bourgeois origin may fall short of the ideals of *hidalguía* and *caballerosidad*

Señorito – young master, young gent, rich kid, usually applied to the sons of landowning families; sometimes used by old retainers in addressing the current owner of an estate; *los señoritos* denotes the class from which such people come

Serrano – mountain dweller; *serranos*, people of the sierras; *serranía* is a mountainous region with a complex of ranges, e.g. Serranía de Ronda

Sevillana – flamenco dance and tune from Seville

Sierra – mountain range, e.g. Sierra Bermeja, Sierra de las Nieves
Solera – system of making sherry and similar wines in tiers of barrels, through which the newer wine passes down and blends with older vintages; it is designed to produce a constant quality
Solomillo – sirloin
Sopa – soup; *las sopas*, broth with bread pellets eaten by the *corcheros* in their morning break; taken from the same stock as *la olla*, the heavier lunch-time stew
Suyo – possessive adjective and pronoun: his, her(s); their(s); *lo suyo*, that which is fitting or appropriate, a very important concept in southern Spain with a big influence on behaviour, fashion etc.
Tajo – cleft or gorge, inland cliff; El Tajo de Ronda combines both these features
Tapa(s) – appetisers served at the bar counter with sherry, wine or beer (but not with spirits or coffee, which would not be *lo suyo*). Originally thrown in free with the drink (the less exotic still were when I first came to Andalusia), they are now charged separately and some, especially seafood and mountain-cured ham, are expensive. *Tapas de cocina* are hot delicacies, e.g. fried fish or squid, tripe and chickpeas etc. The name derives from the verb *tapar*, to cover: according to Hemingway *tapas* were originally placed on top of the glass and eaten with the fingers, rather than as now with a little fork from an oval saucer. Larger portions, which can be treated as a dish for one person or shared among several, are called *raciones* or *medias raciones*. In their variety and inventiveness *tapas* have become an art form and are much the best feature of the Andalusian cuisine.
Tendido – the rows of seats in a bullring which rise from the *barrera* to the beginning of the higher *gradas*; equivalent to the stalls in a theatre; the *tendidos de sombra* are the most expensive seats in the ring, other than the *barreras*
Tertulia – a group or circle of friends who gather regularly in the café-bar or club; applied especially to literary ·causeries
Tienda – shop, especially a small corner food-store; grander establishments are *comercios*
Tienta – testing of female calves in a ring on the ranch to determine their suitability or otherwise for mothering brave bulls; the

male calves are tested nowadays in open country by the method called *acoso y derribo*

Tierra – earth, world, land; *tierra de labor*, cultivable land; *mi tierra*, my homeland, place of birth

Tinto – died or stained, as in Río Tinto, copper-coloured river; but most commonly red wine; *tinto de verano*, a summer drink in a tall glass consisting of *tinto*, soda or pop, ice and lemon

Típico – word perverted by the Romantic movement to mean any of the following: quaint, picturesque, folkloric, traditional, regional; *tipismo* (not admitted by the Spanish Royal Academy of the Language), the sum of all these things and their exploitation commercially

Tirador(es) – Sunday shooter of small birds etc.; much despised by the *cazadores*, the mighty hunters who kill game in the *cotos de caza* and on *monterías*

Tocino – fat of the pig, separated from the flesh during the *matanza*, salted and stored and used as an essential ingredient in all stews; when sliced it resembles a very fatty, streaky bacon

Torear – to play a bull with a lure; Roy Campbell invented the verb 'to torry' but it has not gained wider currency, perhaps because so few of us (unlike him) go 'torrying'

Torero – the correct word for a bullfighter of whatever grade, matador, *banderillero* or *picador* and used collectively of them as in *los toreros*; but it also applies especially to the matador as a mark of approval, e.g. *muy torero*, very much a bullfighter. (*Toreador* now belongs only to opera and is used disparagingly by Spaniards, says Hemingway, to refer to French bullfighters.)

Toril – bull-pen, from which the bulls are released into the ring

Toro – bull; *toro bravo*, fighting bull specially bred for the purpose from strains descending via *Bos Taurus Africanus* from *Bos Primigenius*, the primordial bull or giant auroch of antiquity

Tortilla – Spanish omelette made with potatoes and onions; it may be an inch thick and is best served cold; it is the classic fare of picnics and long train journeys; also the staple of a worker's packed lunch

Trago – swig, gulp, mainly of wine; taken in a jet from a wineskin raised above the head, the amount that can be swallowed before you start spluttering

Traje – dress, suit; *traje de luces*, the 'suit of lights' of the *toreros* in a *corrida* or *novillada*; *traje corto*, bolero jacket, cummerbund and striped trousers worn in a *novillada sin picadores* or *festival*; *traje de gitana*, the spotted, flounced and frilled gypsy dress worn by flamenco performers and by flocks of young women and girls at fair-time

Trapío – fine appearance and presence of bull of good caste in prime condition

Tremendista – a writer out to shock; a matador who gains his following from stunts and tricks, inducing nervous agitation in his audience; he may be brave but is also a bit barbaric; classicism and repose go out of the window

Tresillo – originally an upright sofa for three, now a three-piece suite; also a game played by three with a pack of forty cards, very popular in the seventeenth and eighteenth centuries as 'ombre' and still popular in the pueblos

Tu – thou; familiar second person singular form of address used to both sexes; pl. *vosotros, vosotras*

Turismo – tourism, divided by the planners into three categories: *internacional*, from abroad; *nacional*, native holidaymakers and sightseers; and *rural* which is the great white hope of Junta de Andalucía for the interior. The latter is really a development of the earlier backpacking *excursionismo*, pioneered by the Catalans in the nineteenth century. *Un turismo* is a family saloon car.

Turista – tourist, who should require no gloss; but his original purpose of travelling with pleasure has largely given way to confinement in resorts controlled by the tourist industry; beating the system is always hard but it can still be done in the sierras of the south by all bold spirits not obsessed with where the next bed or meal is coming from

Usted – you, polite and formal mode of address, where *tu* is not appropriate; it is a contraction of *Vuestra Merced*, Your Honour; the pl. is *Ustedes*, usually abbreviated in writing to *Vd, Vds*

Vara – pole, rod, wand of office; in tauromachy one of the many elegant variations for the *picador*'s lance; *suerte de varas*, the *picador*'s act

Vega – fertile plain, e.g. Vega de Granada, Vega de Málaga; also pastureland and one of the names used for a bull ranch, e.g. Vega Blanquilla

Vejez – old age; *la vejez*, the old age pension

Venga – Come! Come here! *Venga, vamos!* come on, let's be going

Venta – wayside inn, where drinks and simple food are served; some act as shops; also frequent in the names of large glittering roadhouses on the outskirts of towns and cities in an attempt to preserve some of the flavour of a rural hostelry

Verónica – the classic cape pass in bullfighting; almost mandatory when the bull first enters the ring and is perfectly fresh; often repeated in the centre of the ring when he has been slowed down by the *picador*; the *verónica* is to the cape what the *natural* is to the *muleta*

Vida – life, but it also means much more than the difference between breathing and not breathing; it means also bustle, business activity and above all employment. A semi-dilapidated pueblo will lament, *aquí no hay vida*; most people will affirm that roads and tourism bring *mucha vida*.

Villa – country or suburban house; also – the most important sense in Spanish – a small town, usually a dependency of a seigneurial stronghold in medieval times; Madrid is still (and proudly) a *villa*, not a *ciudad*, and its town hall is called the *casa de la villa*

Vino – wine needs no comment except to warn that in the south a request in a bar for *vino blanco* may produce *vino fino*, which will be a member of the sherry family; this can be avoided by specifying *blanco de mesa*; red wine is *tinto*; *tinto de verano* is a long drink with soda or pop, ice and lemon; *tinto con casera* is a less sophisticated version of this. *Tinto corriente* is a perfectly adequate base for mixtures but if you are going to drink *tinto* straight, it is best to ask for *Rioja* or *Valdepeñas*.

Voltereta – the somersault of a young bull overturned by a horseman with a *garrocha* during the testing in open country called *acoso y derribo*

Yegua – mare

Yeguada – a stud of mares

Yunta – a pair of mules or oxen yoked together for ploughing

Zaguán – cobbled porch, often with mounting block and drinking trough, found in old town mansions (*caserones*); from the *zaguán* the front door usually opens into a patio and there may be a stable door as well

BIBLIOGRAPHY

Alfonso X, 'the Learned', King of Castile and León, *Cantigas de Santa María*, Real Academia Española, 1889

Aguayo de Hoyos, Pedro et al, *Estudios de Ronda y su Serranía, No 1*, Universidad de Granada, 1988

Alberti, Rafael, *Poesía (1924–1967)*, Aguilar, Madrid, 1972

Anon, *Spanish Pictures Drawn with Pen and Pencil*, The Religious Tract Society, London, c. 1870

Bernal, A. M., *La Andalucía Contemporánea (1868–1981)*, Vol. VIII of *La Historia de Andalucía*, Barcelona, 1981
La propiedad de la tierra y las luchas agrarias andaluzas, Barcelona, 1974

Borrow, George, *The Bible in Spain*, John Murray, London, 1843

Boyd, Alastair, *The Road from Ronda*, Collins, London, 1969

Brenan, Gerald, *The Spanish Labyrinth*, Cambridge UP, 1943
South from Granada, Hamish Hamilton, London, 1957

Caballero, Fernán, *Un Verano en Bornos*, Brockhaus, Leipzig, 1873

Castro, Américo tr. King, E. L., *The Structure of Spanish History*, Princeton, 1954

Cervantes Saavedra, Miguel de, *El Ingenioso Hidalgo Don Quixote de la Mancha*, Madrid, 1798

Chaves Nogales, Manuel tr. Charteris, Leslie, *Juan Belmonte, Killer of Bulls*, Heinemann, London, 1937

Chetwode, Penelope, *Two Middle-Aged Ladies in Andalusia*, John Murray, London, 1963

Corbin, John, 'Insurrections in Spain: Casas Viejas 1933 and Madrid 1981', in *The Anthropology of Violence*, ed. Riches,

David, Blackwell, Oxford, 1986

Corbin, J. R. and M.P., *Compromising Relations*, Gower, Aldershot, 1984

Urbane Thought: Culture and Class in an Andalusian City, Gower, Aldershot, 1987

Domínguez Ortiz, Antonio y Vincent, Bernard, *Historia de los moriscos, vida y tragedia de una minoría*, Revista de Occidente, Madrid, 1978

Epton, Nina, *Andalusia*, Weidenfeld and Nicolson, London, 1968

Fernández García, Joaquina y Palma Silgado, Manuel Jesús, *El Gastor*, Diputación de Cádiz, 1988

Ford, Richard, *Handbook for Travellers in Spain*, John Murray, London, 2nd ed. 1855

Gatherings from Spain, John Murray, London, 1846

Gamboa, Antonio, *Olimpiada del Espíritu para Jovenes Inquietos*, Servicio de Ediciones FAC, Almería, 1986

García Mercadal, J., ed., *Viajes de Extranjeros por España y Portugal*, Aguilar, Madrid, 1972

Gautier, Théophile, *Voyage en Espagne*, Charpentier, Paris, 1845

Hemingway, Ernest, *Death in the Afternoon*, Jonathan Cape, London, 1932

For Whom the Bell Tolls, Jonathan Cape, London, 1941

Hernández, Miguel, *Obras Completas*, Losada, Buenos Aires, 1960

Hurtado de Mendoza, Diego, tr. Shuttleworth, Martin, *The War in Granada*, The Folio Society, London, 1982

Irving, Washington, *Tales of the Alhambra*, Richard Bentley, London, 1835

Chronicle of the Conquest of Granada, John Murray, London, 1829

Jiménez Sánchez, Francisco et al, *Recuerdos de Ronda . . . y sus gentes*, Colectivo Cultural 'Giner de los Rios', Ronda, 1989

Juderías, Julián, *La Leyenda Negra y la Verdad Histórica*, Madrid, 1914

Lea, Henry Charles, *The Moriscos of Spain: Their Conversion and Expulsion*, Bernard Quaritch, London, 1901

Luard, Nicholas, *Andalucía: A Portrait of Southern Spain*, Century, London, 1984

Macaulay, Rose, *Fabled Shore*, Hamish Hamilton, London, 1949

McCormick, John and Sevilla Macareñas, Mario, *The Complete Aficionado*, The World Publishing Company, Cleveland, Ohio, 1967

Machado, Antonio, *Obras, Poesía y Prosa*, Losada, Buenos Aires, 1964

MacNab, Angus, *The Bulls of Iberia*, Heinemann, London, 1957

Mármol Carvajal, Luis de, *Historia del Rebelión y Castigo de los Moriscos*, 2nd impression, Madrid, 1797

Marvin, Garry, 'Honour, Integrity and the Problem of Violence in the Spanish Bullfight', in *The Anthropology of Violence*, Blackwell, Oxford, 1986

Moreti, Juan José, *Historia de la Ciudad de Ronda*, Ronda, 1867

Morris, Jan, *Spain*, Faber, London, 1970

Ortega y Gasset, José, *Teoría de Andalucía y otros ensayos*, Revista de Occidente, Madrid, 1944

Pitt-Rivers, J. A., *The People of the Sierra*, Weidenfeld & Nicolson, London, 1954

Pritchett, V. S., *The Spanish Temper*, Chatto and Windus, London, 1954

. *Marching Spain*, Chatto and Windus, London, 1928

Rilke, Rainer Maria, *Selected Works, Vol 2: Poetry*, The Hogarth Press, London, 1954

Sackville-West, V., *The Eagle and the Dove*, Michael Joseph, London, 1943

Simo, Manuel, *Arcos*, Diputación de Cádiz, 1989

Starkie, Walter, *Don Gypsy*, John Murray, London, 1936

Tynan, Kenneth, *Bull Fever*, Longmans, London, 1966

Valera, Juan, 'Concepto de España', in *Obras Completas, Tomo XXXVII*, Madrid, 1913

Veblen, Thorstein, *The Theory of the Leisure Class*, George Allen & Unwin, London, 1945

Viçens Vives, Jaime, ed. and tr. Ullman, J. C., *Approaches to the History of Spain*, University of California Press, Berkeley and LA, 1967

. tr. López-Morillas, Frances, *An Economic History of Spain*, Princeton, NJ, 1969

461

Warner, Marina, *Alone of All Her Sex: The Myth and Cult of the Virgin Mary*, Knopf, New York, 1976

Watson, Major J. N. P., 'View from the Sierras', in *Household Brigade Magazine*, 1966

Wright, Alison, *The Spanish Economy 1959–1976*, Macmillan, London, 1977

INDEX

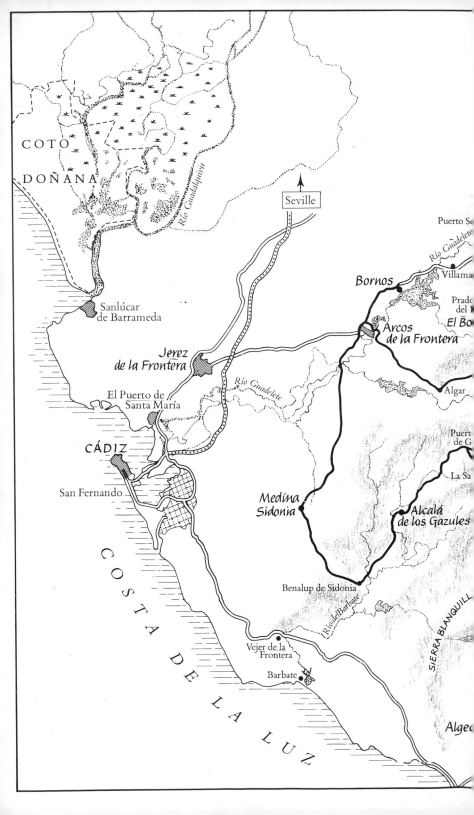